Close Calls

Narrow Escapes
Living on the Road

By

Bryce E. Yarborough

This book is a work of non-fiction. Names and places have been changed to protect the privacy of all individuals. The events and situations are true.

ISBN: 1-4107-7322-1 (e-book)
ISBN: 1-4107-6881-3 (Paperback)
ISBN: 1-4107-6880-5 (Dust Jacket)

Library of Congress Control Number: 2003094488

This book is printed on acid free paper.

Printed in the United States of America
Bloomington, IN

1stBooks – rev. 10/08/03

Acknowledgments

As every author and artist knows, he or she receives assistance from many people during their creations. Undoubtedly, I'll miss someone in this acknowledgment, but the following people are those dear to my heart.

First and foremost, I want to thank Lidia, my beautiful and creative wife. She's my friend, lover, editor and critic. Her presence in my life makes for a wonderful and joyful journey, not to mention better books.

I greatly appreciate my long-lasting friendship with composer, songwriter and English professor Brad Lycan, whom I've known for more than 25 years. His ideas and editing suggestions were most valuable.

I also want to thank my good friends, writer and musician Janey Kenyon and her unflappable husband, composer, songwriter and music engineer/producer Tupelo Kenyon. I appreciate their input on this book as well as their uplifting and inspiring music.

And then there are my stepdaughters, Kelly and AJ. Thanks for your support and understanding regarding the solitude I need to write books. You both are beautiful, and it's wonderful to have you in my life, despite the fact I rarely express it.

Of course, I want to thank my parents for putting up with me for so many years, and for accepting my unconventional path. Yes, I am a rebel, and I caused my parents far too much worry during my hitchhiking days, but I certainly gave them something to talk about with relatives.

To my brother, sister, sister-in-law and brother-in-law, thanks for the joy you brought mom and dad by giving them the grandchildren for which I never had the time, maturity nor responsibility. And thanks for giving me a place to rest between my journeys.

I also want to thank the universal spirit that flows through each of us, as well as all the wonderful librarians. It's no accident I mentioned those two in the same sentence. Librarians are a godsend for all writers, even though they are underpaid and overworked. In fact, when one librarian asked me what I was writing about, and I told her "the close calls I experience while living on the road," she said that would be a great title for the book. I had to ask her what she meant. She replied, "close calls."

And last but not least, I want to thank you, the readers. May all your aspirations come to fruition. Cheers!

Bryce Yarborough

CONTENTS

Author's Note

These stories are a result of encouragement by family and friends to document my most intense encounters during my travels from 1976 through 1989. The names of those involved have been changed, and the dialogue has been reconstructed as accurately as possible. Although I kept journals during these excursions, two years of writing material vanished when someone stole my backpack in Hawaii in 1978.

By some standards you could say I've traveled a lot, but by a world traveler's standards I've just begun. My journeys include treks through every state in the United States, the Yukon and all of Canada's provinces, all the countries of Western Europe, parts of North Africa, Central America and South America, the West Indies and much of Mexico.

All but one of the close calls in this book came about while hitchhiking in the United States. People outside America may use this fact to confirm their allegations that the U.S. is the most dangerous country in the world, but please note that I accepted a ride from everyone who stopped. The close call outside the U.S. occurred in Morocco.

Readers may find some of the stories difficult to believe. All I can say is that the cliché "truth is stranger than fiction" had to be coined by a world traveler.

For those interested in why I began traveling, it was a combination of personal problems and several interview articles with Ray Bradbury in the 1970s. In the articles, Bradbury talks about beginning writers and offers hints and advice on writing. "So, what you have to do is be a kind of hysterical, emotional, vibrant creature who lives at the top of his lungs for a lifetime," Bradbury said in an interview for *Writer's Digest*.

As for the personal problems preceding my travels, it was a failed marriage and drug overdose at age 22 that made me perceive life as rather meaningless. With nothing to lose, I decided to live out a dream: to hit the road and live in the moment.

With few material possessions, little money and the desire to stay present each moment, my journey began. Oh yes, a few members of the music group the Ozark Mountain Daredevils graduated from my high school. A line from one of their songs said you had to "raise a little hell if you want get to heaven." I was ready to be that "hysterical, emotional, vibrant creature" prepared to "raise a little hell" if necessary. I wanted any experience that would move me closer to discovering who I was, why I was here, and the truth about the life force that runs through us all.

After graduating from the University of Missouri with a general studies degree, I drove away from Columbia, Missouri, in a faded turquoise Dodge

Polara loaded with a box of books, a typewriter, guitar, backpack and tent. When the gas money ran out, I left my car in Oregon and hit the road with my guitar and backpack. That too was a dream of mine. I had done some hitchhiking between the larger cities in Missouri, but never farther than 200 miles. After reading Jack Kerouac's *On The Road* and James Michener's *The Drifters*, I had great expectations and romantic visions of life on the road.

Most certainly there is excitement traveling the world's highways and byways, and the unknown risks are a part of that excitement, but there are also days of loneliness and destitution. I have been more than 3,500 miles away from friends and family with just the clothes on my back: no money, no passport, no identification—nothing! It's a strange and scary feeling, but once you've been there, your outlook and perception on life drastically changes. You realize the fleeting allure of the physical possessions desperately sought by most people, as well as the ephemeral nature of the human body.

I would like to add that while some of these stories involve drug use, I vehemently discourage the use of all drugs, including alcohol, caffeine and nicotine. I have been drug free for nearly 20 years with one exception—I smoked hashish (a concentrated form of the drug that's found in marijuana) while in Morocco. I smoked it not because I wanted to, but because failure to do so might have resulted in my death. You'll find that story at the end of this book.

Today, more than ever, I see how important it is to stay in the moment. We miss far too much life either lamenting over the past or fearful of the future. We are most alive when fully conscious of our bodies, aware of our thoughts and feelings, and cognizant of the fact that the choices we make determine the life we live. And what's even more wonderful is that at any moment we can make a new choice and thus influence the world around us.

Happy travels to all of you, whether it's in your imagination or upon the roads of life, or in the skies of this world and beyond.

Bryce E. Yarborough
September 2003

Prologue

At first it was more of a curious wonderment when the tingling, prickling sensation began. It was similar to the feeling you get in your arm or leg when it falls asleep, except the sensation covered my entire body. I jumped around to keep my blood circulating.

It was unusually bright for midnight in the middle of Missouri. The falling snow pummeled my hooded coat at a 45-degree angle. As the flakes reached the ground, the wind grabbed them and whipped them into miniature white tornadoes that scooted across the road and faded into the snowy surface and falling veil of white. A two to three-foot snowdrift in the ditch beside me resembled a breaking ocean wave.

Then the pain started. The tingling turned into stinging pricks—like someone poking me with pine needles, and poking me hard. I began jumping even more vigorously.

"Jesus!" I screamed.

Suddenly, a violent blast exploded inside my head. It felt like someone had thrust a knife into the base of my neck. My head snapped back while my body spasmodically jerked as if a jolt of electricity had shot through it. Pain rushed throughout my body. Ripples of burning waves reverberated through my brain. An uncontrollable shiver ran down my spine. Then it struck me again. This time, as the pain hit, my consciousness rose 15 feet above the road. There was a moment of bewilderment while viewing myself hopping up and down on the road below. Then I was back in my body.

"God," I whispered reluctantly, "what the hell was that?"

Again a sharp stab of pain pierced the bottom of my skull and charged through my body, and once more I was outside myself looking down, except this time I was probably 30 to 40 feet above the road. It felt like it took longer to return to my body than the first time.

"I'm freezing to death," I said aloud, staring into the windswept snow falling around me.

I looked down the road. About 75 yards away, I could barely see the gas pumps beside the store I had passed earlier. It had been closed since I arrived. A voice spoke inside my head.

"Go down and break into that store," it said. "Call the police and tell them you broke in because you were freezing."

The sharp pain returned with a jolt. My consciousness rose to the bird's eye perspective. This is weird, I thought. That's me down there. But how can that be? As soon as I realized I was thinking while outside my body, I was back in it. This time, without hesitation, I picked up my backpack and walked toward the store. My body was numb. I felt nothing except heaviness, as if the snow beneath my feet was sucking me into the frozen earth. The falling flakes danced before my eyes mesmerizing me with its beauty.

I'm not going to make it, I thought. There was no malice or disappointment in my realization. In fact, the idea of death seemed like a relief, and even funny. My journey had brought me back to my home state. It seemed quite ironic yet fitting to die hitchhiking between the two cities I considered home.

CB Squabble

With the morning sun shining on my face, I raised my thumb high into the air at each passing vehicle. Despite the early hour, the humidity and warm temperature caused my forehead, chest and armpits to sweat. The sparse Sunday traffic on the outskirts of Tulsa, Oklahoma's Interstate 44 dampened my hopes for catching a ride quickly. After about 40 minutes, a guy in a late-modeled white Plymouth station wagon pulled over to pick me up.

"I really appreciate the ride," I said, opening the backdoor of the car. Rags littered the floorboard and clothes draped the backseat.

"Don't worry about the clothes. Just throw your stuff on top of them."

As I did so, I looked in the back of the station wagon. I saw a worn flat tire, a tool box, two playboy magazines with the cover of one magazine partially ripped from its binding, and lots of greasy, dirty tools scattered around.

"My name's Bryce," I said, as I climbed in the front seat. I reached out my hand.

"Glad to meet you. I'm Jack." He had a firm grip.

A red faded ball cap that said "Keep on truckin'" fit snugly on Jack's head. Embroidered beside the words stood a guy leaning backwards with his hands on his belt and his big foot protruding forward as if he were going to walk right over you. Jack's curly, short brown hair stuck out haphazardly from beneath his cap. He wore a soiled white tank top, frayed and faded blue jeans, scuffed and dirty suede cowboy boots, and a wide leather belt with a huge silver buckle showing a cowboy riding a bucking bronco.

A tattoo larger than a tennis ball decorated Jack's right bicep. The tattoo showed a woman sitting at a slight angle with her head turned so her eyes were looking at you. She had long dark hair, large sensuous lips partially parted as if she were about to kiss you, and a small mole just below the left corner of her

1

mouth. Her thin transparent dress revealed most of her voluptuous breasts, and her nipples appeared firm and swollen beneath the hint of translucent fabric. A beautiful woman, but at the same time she appeared to have an aggressive quality. I could easily imagine her climbing on top of me.

Initially, I had an uncomfortable feeling about Jack, probably because he looked like a typical hard-nosed redneck. But with Jack's sparkling blues eyes and bright friendly smile focusing on me, I quickly felt at ease.

"How long have you been on the road?" He rolled down his window as we eased up to the Oklahoma Will Rogers Turnpike tollbooth. He lowered the volume of his crackling CB radio mounted to the dash. It seemed out of place in the station wagon.

"This time, only about a month and a half."

He took an entrance ticket and thanked the lady as he stuffed it above the sun visor. Even though Jack struck me as a ladies' man, the side view of his face was rather homely. His long nose had a slight bend to it—probably caused by someone's fist. His chin protruded out past his nose, making him look like one of those African carved wooden figures you see in gift shops. If you slightly exaggerated his profile, he would have made a great cartoon character.

Jack picked up his CB mouthpiece. "Breaker one two, breaker one two, this is the White Elephant leaving the Tulsa ticket gates northeast bound on 44 for Springfield. Can I fly, or has anyone spotted some roadblocks? Over."

I had never been exposed to a CB radio before. As I tried to crack Jack's code, he adjusted the volume.

"I got a line on you White Elephant," a voice said through the hissing sound. "This is the Thunderbolt on a streak. I've been running hard ever since Springfield. It's been clear sailing all the way. Over."

"Roger Thunderbolt, thanks for the weather report. You got a clear shot to Oklahoma City. Just follow your streak of lightning. Over and out."

The other guy laughed over the CB.

"Did you hear that Lightning?" he asked.

A new voice now joined the conversation.

"Roger. I can see the gates ahead. Where are you White Elephant? Over."

Jack looked at the trucks passing us on the other side of the turnpike going in the opposite direction.

"I'm in the white four-wheel buggy. I'm picking up my eighteen-wheeler in St. Louis. Over."

"Just passed you," the voice said. "I got you in my rearview mirror."

Jack glanced in his rearview mirror and then turned and looked over his shoulder. I looked too. There were three trucks in a line.

"Are you the humper? Over." On the back of the truck closest to us it said, "Humpin' to please."

"No, I'm the one in front of it. Over."

"Got ya. Enjoy a smooth ride, over and out."

"We can make some time now." Jack hung the mouthpiece beside his CB. He pressed on the gas pedal and turned down the CB's volume. A faint but distinct static resonated. "Why are you out here?"

"What do you mean?" I asked.

Jack looked straight ahead, and then glanced down at his speedometer as he spoke again. "I mean why do you do this? Why don't you get a job and settle down?"

He turned his head toward me, grinning as if he already knew the answer. His smirk seemed to condemn me to a life on the road, yet he appeared to know it was a sentence I wanted and needed.

"I don't know. I guess it's the excitement of the moment."

"Breaker one two for a northeast bounder. Over."

Jack picked up the mouthpiece and held down the bar.

"You got a live one. Talk to me. Over."

Jack increased the volume on the CB.

"This is the Rough Rider bound for OC. How's it look down that way. Over."

"Kick in your spurs and skedaddle. The trail is clear. Over."

"Sounds good. What's your twenty? Over."

"Uhhhh, marker 102. Over."

"Roger. We must have just passed each other. You got a clear shot to Joplin. Had reports of a bull between Joplin and Springfield, but I never saw him. Rough Rider out."

Jack turned down the CB and looked at me.

"You got a sweetheart somewhere?"

"I got'em everywhere," I lied. "That's the fun of traveling."

Jack laughed. "Could be."

"You got a wife and kids?" I asked.

"I had a wife, but I got into a little trouble a few years back, so she left me."

I assumed he got caught cheating. I waited for him to explain what happened, but he didn't. He looked in his rearview mirror and then checked his side mirror.

"What happened?" I finally asked.

"I got locked up for a couple of years."

"In jail?"

"The state pen."

"For what?"

"I got into a little ruckus with a guy in a bar," Jack said slowly but without any emotion. "The guy was getting the best of me, so I had to use my knife."

I glanced at his belt. I didn't see a knife sheath, but knew he had seen mine.

"Did you kill him?" My tone shocked me. It sounded cold and uncaring, almost as if I wished he had.

"No, but almost. I'd been drinking quite a bit and went crazy on him."

"Did you know the guy?"

"No, but he was being rude to the waitress, so I told him to go stick his dick in a dog because that was the only bitch that could stomach the likes of him." Jack laughed. "That put some fire in his eyes."

I laughed too. "Was it worth it?"

Jack looked at me, the grin fading from his broken, weathered face, his eyes cold and hard. A sick feeling churned in my stomach. Jack turned his head back to the road ahead of us.

"The state pen is another name for hell." The way he said it sent a chill down my spine. "On my fifth day in prison, four guys pinned me to the ground while a fifth guy pulled my pants down. When he couldn't get inside me, he held a long jagged rusty pipe in front of my nose. 'You gotta a choice pretty boy,' he said. 'Me or this. What's it gonna be?'"

"Woooo..." came over the CB, "...it's a bull, it's a bull...he's got me!" Jack automatically hit his brake, and we both lunged forward. "I'm cooked," the voice said. "I'm at marker one ten." That put him five miles ahead of us. Jack pressed on the gas pedal and slowly increased his speed again.

"It's a fuckin' cat and mouse game," Jack said, sounding as if he were pissed.

I wondered if he meant the highway patrol, prison, or me and him. Thinking about what it must have been like for him during the rest of his prison term made me nauseous. Neither Jack nor I said anything for several minutes. At mile marker 109 Jack slowed down.

"There he is," Jack said as we approached a truck on the side of the road with a highway patrol car behind it. We both glanced at the two men sitting in the patrol car as we passed. Jack looked in his rearview mirror as he slowly mashed down on the gas pedal. He picked up his CB mouthpiece and pushed on the breaker bar.

"Breaker one two, breaker one two. This is the White Elephant northeast bound on 44. We just passed a bull sticking it to an eighteener. They're at marker 110, so watch your tails. Anyone coming out of Springfield? Over."

"Yeah breaker, you got the Road Hog here," a voice said over the CB. "You got a clean shot. Join the stampede. Over and out."

Jack pushed down the bar. "Thank you Road Hog. White Elephant signing off."

Jack hung the mouthpiece beside the CB and picked up a pack of unfiltered Lucky Strikes on the dash in front of the steering wheel. He jerked the pack toward his mouth twice before a cigarette popped out about an inch. He pulled the cigarette out with his lips and offered the pack to me.

"No thanks. I don't smoke."

He tossed the pack onto the dash and picked up the lighter on the seat between us.

4

"Good for you," he said as he flipped his wrist, sending the lighter lid back on its hinges. He fired up the cigarette and took a big drag, holding the smoke in momentarily as he flicked the lighter's lid over the burning flame and dropped it back onto the seat. He blew the smoke out the corner of his mouth toward the open window.

"Have you ever smoked?"

"No, not really. When I was seven, a friend and I found a pack of cigarettes under the front porch. The cigarettes were so old that the paper turned yellow. We smoked the whole pack, and I got sicker than a dog." We both laughed.

"When did you start smoking?"

"At ten, but I didn't really get into it until I hit twelve or thirteen." He blew more smoke toward the window. "By the time I turned fifteen, I smoked a pack a day or more. I made it to three packs a day last year, but I'm down to about a pack a day now—maybe a little more."

"You trying to quit?"

"Naaaaw, just cutting back some. I like it too much to quit."

I asked Jack about life as a trucker. He told me he owned his own truck before going to the pen. He'd been out for two years and wanted to buy another truck. He lived in Oklahoma City. He planned to leave his station wagon in St. Louis and drive a truck to Florida, and then make runs up and down the East Coast for several weeks before returning. Jack always had one ear on the CB, and on several occasions he started to pick up the mouthpiece for a breaker, but someone beat him to it. We had probably been talking 15 minutes when we were interrupted.

"Breaker one two, breaker one two. Anyone got a southwest weather report out there? Over."

Jack picked up the mouthpiece. "You got a taker breaker. This is the White Elephant stampeding northeast. We passed a bull that penned an eighteen-wheeler at marker one ten. Keep your ears on. Over."

"Roger, White Elephant. Saw a bull working just south of Springfield, otherwise she's all clear. This is the Chrome Wheeler over and out."

Jack pushed on the mouthpiece bar again.

"Come back Chrome Wheeler, over."

"You got me listening, over."

"Are you the Chrome Wheeler from Atlanta? Over."

After several seconds of silence, the voice came back on.

"Might be. Who's wanting to know? Over."

"The Sidewinder Lounge in Houston. Ring any bells?"

This time laughter filled the CB before the voice spoke again.

"I know the place. Who is this?"

"Cowpoke John—you no good scoundrel. How's Diane and Cindy?"

"Well I'll be damned," the voice said sounding excited, "I heard about your trouble, but never heard the outcome. How the hell are you?"

"Still alive and kicking. What's your twenty?"

"Marker one thirty-nine."

"We just passed you. I might be at the Sidewinder in a month or two. How about you? Over."

"I'll be there on my return run this trip. I'll leave a message for you. Over"

"Roger. Are the girls still there? Over."

"Diane is, but Cindy got married. Diane asks about you every time I see her. Over."

"Oh? And how often is that? Over."

All of a sudden the CB blasted with music. The blaring country song lasted at least five seconds.

"Who's the asshole?" Jack blurted into his mouthpiece.

Again loud singing came on over the CB, but this time for 15 to 20 seconds. As soon as the music stopped, Jack's friend spoke.

"I'll leave a message at the Sidewinder. Whoever the jerk is, screw you. Over and out."

Jack picked up his mouthpiece and pushed down on the bar.

"Who's the smart ass, and what's your problem? Over."

Only a static hiss came through the CB.

"Whoever you are," Jack continued, "your mama sucks a big one and must have done it with a moron before shitting you out. Over and out." Jack hung up the mouthpiece. "That cocksucker."

After a few seconds of silence, a voice spoke over the CB. "You got a big mouth buddy. Stuff it or back it up."

Jack quickly picked up the mouthpiece and pressed down the bar.

"Are you the radio asshole?" Jack released his bar.

"You needed stuffing," the man said.

Jack pushed down the bar again and spoke.

"Why don't we finish this discussion man to man. I just passed marker 146. I'll be waiting for you at 147, unless of course your papa was a rooster, and your mama a hen—making you a chicken shit. Over and out."

Several seconds passed before the guy answered.

"I'll be there in five minutes, over and out."

Jack slowed down. I could see marker 147 in the distance.

"Hey," I said, "the guy's not worth fighting. He's a jerk."

"Yeah, well somebody's got to teach him a lesson."

We pulled onto the shoulder and stopped beside the marker. Jack turned off the engine, and then reached under his seat and pulled out a small handgun. He sucked his stomach in and pulled out his jeans, slipping the barrel and half the gun down his pants. He pulled his t-shirt over it. I sat there stunned.

"What are you doing?"

"You don't think the guy's gonna get out of his truck without a tire jack do you?" A truck went by on the other side, and Jack looked at it.

"You can't just shoot the guy."

"Huh," Jack grunted and looked at me. "That's his tough luck for being an asshole."

"It's not worth it!" Jack glared at me as if I excused the trucker's actions. "Let's forget it and keep going."

Jack put his hands on the steering wheel and looked straight ahead. A truck approached. Maybe I imagined it, but the truck seemed to be slowing down. Jack watched the truck. The situation seemed ludicrous. In minutes a man could be dead beside the interstate for putting his CB mouthpiece up to a blaring radio. I thought about the trucker and thought to myself, if you have any sense mister, don't stop. Then I realized I would be a witness to the shooting and probably the only person who could positively identify Jack.

Jack reminded me of Mike, a hitchhiker I picked up while returning from Kansas City to the University shortly before my divorce papers were signed. He too had a quick temper. He climbed into my car with only a small rucksack. He also had recently broken up with his wife after she left him for someone else. When I told Mike about my situation, he called Melanie a fucking bitch and said I was lucky to be rid of her. For some reason, his words made me feel better. Although it had been several months since she moved in with her boyfriend, I told Mike I had gotten over it and intended to stop by and see her the next day.

"I want to return a pair of Melanie's earrings that I found in my glove box," I said.

I lived in an apartment complex several blocks from the small house Melanie and her boyfriend were renting. A friend told me where they lived. On several occasions, I thought about stopping by their home. After finding Melanie's earrings in my glove box, I had a great excuse to visit. I planned to drop off the earrings, wish them well and let Melanie know I felt fine, even though that was a big lie. I hoped to find Melanie sorry she had left me, and her boyfriend mistreating her.

"You should smash the earrings first and then give them to her," Mike said.

We arrived in Columbia after 10 p.m., so I offered Mike my couch to crash on. He accepted. The next day, with the sun shining, the temperature reached 50 degrees by noon.

"It's a good day to hitchhike," I finally said to Mike, expecting him to take the hint to leave.

"Are you going to see your wife today?"

It sounded strange to hear him call Melanie my wife.

"I thought I would."

"Can I come along?"

"Why?" I asked, thinking his request odd.

"Oh, just to keep you company."

"Suit yourself." I glanced at my watch. "Might as well go now. It's almost one o'clock."

I went to my room and took Melanie's earrings out of my top dresser drawer. They were my last physical link to Melanie. I had burned all of her pictures during one of my drunken stupors. As Mike and I approached Melanie's house, grave doubts about this visit surfaced. Despite the air's cool temperature, I felt extremely warm, my hands clammy. A knot twisted in my stomach. My breaths became shore and erratic. If alone, I would have gone back to my apartment, but Mike walked briskly and determinedly, so I kept pace with him.

When we climbed the steps to the front porch, I could feel my heart pounding. Other than talking over the phone a few times, Melanie and I had not seen each other since she moved into the house with her boyfriend. Her boyfriend's blue Chevy Nova Super Sport sat by the curb. I rapped on the storm door and looked back toward the street, hoping they were out for a walk.

No one answered the door. "I don't think they're home."

"I thought I heard something," Mike said. He opened the storm door and knocked on the inside window, then let the aluminum door shut. "Here comes someone."

I turned around to see Melanie opening the door. My heart leaped in my chest. "Bryce," she said reluctantly from the other side of the storm door. "How are you?"

"Fine," I replied, half dazed from seeing her. I felt awkward and embarrassed. "I just wanted to stop by and say hello."

She hesitated a brief moment, and then pushed open the storm door. "Come on in."

"This is a friend of mine," I said, gesturing toward Mike as we entered the hallway. "Mike, this is Melanie."

Melanie said hello, and Mike nodded his head.

"Is your boyfriend here?" Hearing myself ask that question made me realize what a bizarre visit this was. I had just asked my wife about her boyfriend.

"No. He walked to the store."

Melanie turned and entered their small living room. "Have a seat if you'd like. I can only talk a few minutes. I have to go to the hospital to finish up some things I didn't get to last week." She sat down on the couch and looked at me. "You're looking good."

"So are you," I responded, sitting beside her. Mike sat in a chair across from us. "Is everything going okay?"

8

"Yeah," she said, "it's going fine. We've had some trouble with Dan's car, but other than that, things are good."

Dan. It was the first time I had heard his name. He had just become more real. I felt sad about the way she casually used his name with the pronoun "we."

"You've got a nice little cozy home," Mike said sarcastically as he stood up. "Yes, a nice cozy nest. What's this?" He abruptly strutted over to the wall and looked at a large sword in a sheath hanging horizontally between two nails. "Is it real?"

Melanie looked toward the kitchen, and then looked at me. "Yes, it's real," she responded in a flat voice. I could feel her apprehension and nervousness.

Mike reached up and took the sword down. He withdrew the sword from its sheath.

"Mike," I said, "I think you should put the sword back where it was."

He dropped the sheath on the carpet.

"I'm not going to break it. I just want to check it out." He felt the blade. "It's even sharp."

He grasped the sword handle with both hands and pointed it toward the wall. Then he turned slowly until the sword's tip pointed straight at Melanie. Her breathing became shallow and erratic. Her eyes opened wide. She glanced toward the kitchen. I assumed she saw it as a possible escape route. Then she looked at me.

I stood up. "Mike, please put the sword back."

Mike smiled and took several steps back. He raised the sword as if blocking another sword being swung at him. He then twirled once with the sword held close to his body. When he stopped, he quickly thrust the sword forward as he bent his knees slightly and screamed, "Ya!" The tip of the blade stopped three feet from Melanie's head. She looked at me, her eyes imploring me to stop this crazy man. After a slight pause, Mike's malicious stare changed to a satisfied grin.

"This thing's pretty heavy," he said, lowering the blade as he looked at it. "I wonder if it's ever been used to kill someone. That's why they make swords, you know."

He stared at Melanie as he slowly stooped down and picked up the sheath off the floor and slipped the sword into it. He hung it back on the nails sticking out of the wall, but now it hung crooked.

Melanie stood up. "Bryce, I really need to get ready for work. Maybe you can come back some other time."

"Yeah," I said, rising and moving toward the hallway. "I should have called before stopping by." I entered the hallway, walked to the front door and opened it. Melanie stood behind me, but Mike hadn't entered the hall yet. "Mike?"

A moment later, Mike quickly walked past both of us and pushed the storm door open, holding it for me.

I looked at Melanie. "See ya."

"You take care, Bryce."

Mike and I walked across the yard to the street.

"Shit," I said. "I forgot to give Melanie her earrings."

I spun around and ran across the brown lawn and leaped over the three steps to the porch. I knocked on the storm door hard, and then turned around to see if Mike had followed me. He stood on the lawn near the street. I heard the inside door open and turned around just in time to see a long-haired man throw open the storm door and lunge at me. His hands hit my chest and knocked me backward, causing me to spin and jump off the porch. I landed on my feet before falling down to my hands and knees. I stood up and turned around to see him still coming at me. He was several inches taller than me.

"What the hell do you think you're doing!" he said as he shoved me again. I stumbled backward several steps. "You come into my home acting like an ass and scaring Melanie. Who the hell do you think you are?"

He pushed me another time, and I floundered backward once more. His charge caught me by surprise.

"I happen to be the man who's married to the woman in that house."

"I don't give a shit." His hands slammed into my chest again as I backpedaled to keep my balance. "You have no right to come on my property. So get out of here before I kick your ass!"

Mike, who had been waiting by the street when I went to the door, suddenly moved swiftly past me and smashed his open hands into Melanie's boyfriend's chest, causing him to stumble backward.

"Come on you big mother fucker!" Mike screamed at the top of his lungs. "I'm on your property. What the hell you going to do about it?" Mike shoved him again. "You want to fight? I'll give you a fight you fucking bastard."

It was really weird seeing Mike, who was at least four or five inches shorter than Melanie's boyfriend, aggressively pushing the guy across his yard. The whole thing happened so fast I just stood there and watched.

Mike lunged into him again as he yelled loud enough for the whole neighborhood to hear. "Come on you mother fucker! Take your best shot, because I'm going to kill you, you fucking asshole! You hear me? I'm going to kill you!"

I had no doubt that Mike meant it. You could hear it in his voice. Whatever hostilities he held during his own breakup were emerging full force. Melanie's boyfriend must have realized he faced a lunatic. Stunned, he showed no aggressive behavior toward Mike. If he had, I'm sure Mike would have unleashed all of his rage. I rushed over and got between them.

"Mike," I said, putting my hands on his shoulders. "Take it easy."

"What do you mean take it easy," Mike yelled, keeping his eyes on Melanie's boyfriend as I back-pedaled to keep him from getting past me. "This son of a bitch doesn't deserve to live, so I'm going to kill the mother fucker! You hear me?" he screamed once again, looking at Melanie's boyfriend. "I'm going to kill you!"

"No one's going to kill anybody," I said, putting my arms around Mike and moving him off to one side. "Please go back to the apartment." Mike's eyes were glaring at Melanie's boyfriend. "Please, go on back, okay?"

"But what about this fucking bastard?" Mike bellowed loudly.

I guided Mike across the yard toward my apartment. He kept his eyes on Melanie's boyfriend. I tightened my grip on Mike and continued walking. I glanced back to see Melanie standing beside her boyfriend, their house behind them. Sorrow wrenched my gut. That should have been me standing there.

"Please go," I said to Mike. "I'll be along in a few minutes, okay?"

Mike nodded, and I released my grip on him. He walked to the street, and then stopped to look back. He pointed his index finger at Melanie and her boyfriend; then raised his thumb to simulate a gun. His hand lifted twice as if he had fired two shots. He gave a sneering grin before turning around and heading down the street.

I turned and walked to Melanie and her boyfriend.

"I'm sorry. I didn't mean for this to turn out as it did. I really didn't."

Melanie looked at me. "Bryce, who is that?"

"He's a hitchhiker I picked up on my way back from Kansas City. He crashed on my couch last night."

I forced my hand toward Melanie's boyfriend. "I didn't come here to cause trouble. I guess we've never really been introduced."

"Dan," he said as he took my hand and shook it.

We heard the squeal of car wheels and looked up to see two police cars speeding toward us. The cars stopped as close to us as they could without driving on the lawn. Both officers got out of their cars.

"Is everything okay here?" one officer asked as both walked toward us.

"Everything's fine officer," I spoke up. "The person who got upset is gone."

"Who?" asked the second officer.

"A friend of mine. We had him calmed down before he left."

"What's his name?" the first officer asked.

"Mike."

"Mike who?"

"Mike Caldwell."

"Where did he go?"

"Back to my apartment. He's visiting me."

"Which way did he go?"

I pointed toward the side street. "Down that road."

11

"And where do you live?"

"In the Greensboro apartment complex."

The officer doing most of the talking looked at Melanie. "Is everything all right?"

"We're fine officer. Thanks for stopping."

Her reply made me wonder if she had called the police. The officer nodded his head. He stared at us as he walked to the squad car.

"You folks enjoy the rest of the day," he said.

The officers got in their cars and sped down the side street in the direction Mike took.

"Looks like they're going to pay your friend a visit," Dan said with a tinge of sarcasm and satisfaction in his voice.

It's lucky for you, I thought, that I didn't let him break your neck. I reached into my pocket.

"Here, Melanie. This is why I came over in the first place." I handed her the earrings. "They were in my glove compartment. I'm truly sorry," I said again, looking at both of them. "If I had know this was going to happen, I would never have come by."

Between the cops and my apology, Dan had calmed down considerably.

"Look," Melanie said, "why don't you come in for a little while. I really do have to go to work soon, but we can visit for a few minutes."

We went inside and sat in the living room. The sword still hung crooked on the wall. Dan and Melanie sat on the couch. I sat in an armchair across from them. Dan moved slightly as if he were going to put his arm around Melanie, but then changed his mind. The scene seemed surreal and downright weird. Here I sat in the house of my wife's boyfriend, when months earlier this woman and I were sleeping together in our apartment. And just 18 months before, we walked down the aisle—she in her long white gown and me in my tux—and we vowed to honor and cherish one another for a lifetime.

Melanie spoke first. "You should be careful about who you let stay at your apartment, Bryce. That guy's crazy."

"I didn't plan on him coming with me, but he insisted on tagging along."

"Just the same, picking up hitchhikers can be dangerous. You never know."

Her concern for my well-being seemed ironic considering her lack of concern over my distraught emotional state during the past several months.

"So you're a painter, Dan?" I asked, looking at the paintings on the wall and wanting to change the topic.

"I'm learning," he said with an embarrassed smile. "I have a studio upstairs, but it's hard to find time to paint much."

One painting exhibited a landscape with mountains and a lake, while the other a nude portrait. Both were a bit blurry for my taste, and the colors far too dark. I felt impelled to say something.

"It'll work out," I said at last, trying to muster up some enthusiasm in my voice. "Just keep at it."

"Thanks." After a lengthy pause, he finally said, "Look, I didn't plan any of this. It just sort of happened."

Of course, I knew what he meant, but just the same I asked, "What's that?"

"You know. Melanie and me."

I could feel my body heating up and my anger rising. I recalled Melanie telling me that during their first few conversations he had told her about his past girlfriends and the problems they experienced. It seemed to me a rather intimate thing to be telling another man's wife.

"Why did you lay all that shit on Melanie about your past girlfriends?"

Dan looked at Melanie. He obviously expected those conversations to remain private. Melanie curled her lips inside her mouth and slightly shrugged her shoulders.

I stood up, unsure I could contain my anger. "I need to go."

They both got up as I headed toward the door. I opened the front door and turned to face them. "Bye Melanie." I pushed open the storm door, my stomach queasy.

"Take care of yourself," Melanie said.

I turned my head and looked at her. "I will. So long."

Jack kept his eyes focused on the approaching truck. Two cars zoomed by in the lanes beside us. I looked away from the approaching truck to the flatlands of Oklahoma on my right and silently prayed. "God, don't let the guy stop." I closed my eyes momentarily, and then turned my head and glanced over at the truck passing on the other side of the highway. Jack still had his hands on the wheel, but he too glared at the truck driver. The driver looked at us, and then turned his head forward. Jack followed the truck with his eyes.

A truck and several more cars whizzed by us on our side of the road before it hit me. What if the trucker is going our way? He might pull in behind us any second. I glanced through the rear window, but saw no trucks in sight.

After sitting in silence for two or three minutes, I finally said, "Whoever the jerk is, he's not going stop. People like that are tough over the radio, but when it comes down to it, they're cowards."

After a long pause, Jack replied, "You're probably right." He leaned back, pulled the gun from his pants and slipped it back under the seat. He started the station wagon's engine and put it in gear. As Jack eased out onto the turnpike, he spoke again in a monotone voice.

"The guy's probably laughing at us for stopping." Jack reached down to the CB and clicked it off. As the car gained speed, he looked over at me with a big grin—the twinkle returning to his eyes. "I bet you've never experienced something like that, huh?"

I let out a breath. "It's a first, that's for sure."

Jack laughed. "You can relax. It's over."

He gave a light slap to my arm. Jack—a Dr. Jekyll and Mr. Hyde—one moment ready to kill, the next moment happy and carefree.

"I need to control my temper," he said. "Sometimes it gets the best of me, or maybe I should say the worst of me."

"Would you have shot the guy?"

Jack curled up his lower lip and raised his eyebrows before he turned and looked at me. His jaw dropped. The lines on his forehead stood out. "Probably," he said, shrugging nonchalantly. He turned to face the road ahead of him. "I don't feel like shooting the guy right now, but I did then. He still needs to have his balls kicked in. Hey, are you hungry?"

A billboard sign announced gas and food at the next turn. Before I could answer, Jack spoke again.

"Hamburger, fries and a shake—my treat. What do you say?"

"Sounds great."

After our meal, Jack dropped me off at Interstate 44 and Bypass 65 where we wished each other well. I walked the remaining three miles to my brother's home. No one answered when I knocked on the door, so I headed around to the secluded backyard bordering a golf course. I set my gear down next to his pool, and then pulled off my hiking boots and socks to let my feet rest on the refreshingly cool tile. Within seconds, I ripped off the sweaty white t-shirt and soiled blue jeans and dove into the swimming pool's placid water. The cool wetness tingled as it flowed over my skin.

Breaking through the pool's surface, I squirted water out my mouth and looked up at the huge oak limbs hanging above the pool. How fast things can change, I thought, as I floated on my back. One minute I'm a hot, sweaty, stinking bearded vagabond lugging a heavy backpack and toting a guitar, and the next minute I'm buck naked floating in a clear, cool, chlorinated swimming pool in an affluent and secluded neighborhood. I thought back to the previous year when my journey began from Columbia, Missouri.

Breaking Point

A mountain of yellow and orange that descended into blackness stood before my eyes. Although it seemed strange, a pleasant peacefulness surrounded it. Suddenly, something touched my cheek. I flinched and raised my head to realize my face lay in the folds of my yellow and orange bedspread. I rolled over on my back still wearing my soiled clothes. My bladder felt ready to burst, my mouth dry.

Then I recalled the night before. The smoking. The drinking. The drugs. Surprisingly, I felt rested and alert. That alone intrigued me. I looked at my alarm clock. The dial showed a little after three o'clock. That meant I slept nearly 15 hours. I climbed out of bed feeling light headed and slightly dizzy. Something had changed inside of me, but what? I felt lighter or unfettered, as if my lungs had been congested and now were wide open—freely and eagerly accepting the oxygen.

In addition to sensing a physical change, I also felt a corresponding emotional change. Exhilaration might be a bit strong, but certainly upbeat and hopeful. Compared to my severe depression hours before, it meant a 300 percent improvement.

After using the bathroom, I headed toward the refrigerator. On my way to the kitchen, I flipped on the stereo. The rock band Fleetwood Mac sang, "Don't stop thinking about tomorrow, don't stop, it'll soon be here. Yesterday's gone, yesterday's gone..."

"Anyone here?" I yelled. Both Barry and John were gone. I glanced out the window. With the sun shining, I figured they were enjoying the day with their girlfriends. What a shock it was to find the apartment clean. The bottles and cans were in plastic bags, and all the ashtrays had been emptied. I opened the refrigerator door to see 15 to 20 beer bottles neatly placed in rows at the back of the refrigerator. I closed the door and opened the freezer. Fortunately, it held a can of concentrated orange juice. As I squeezed the frozen juice into a plastic pitcher, the disc jockey came on the radio as Fleetwood Mac faded in the background. "Yes, and if tomorrow's as beautiful as today, it won't be so hard to take those Monday morning blues."

Today's Saturday, you idiot, I thought.

"And if you're out for a Sunday drive," he continued, "there's live music in Peace Park until five o'clock today." The sound of a cash register opening with a thumping bass guitar came over the speakers. "Right now, let's move on with a cut from Pink Floyd's album *Dark Side of the Moon.*"

I looked at the calendar on the kitchen wall. "This can't be Sunday," I said aloud. I called time and temperature. It was Sunday, which meant I had slept nearly 40 hours!

I discovered later that my roommates had left late Saturday morning. Barry spent all day Saturday and Saturday night at his girlfriend's apartment, and John drove to Kansas City to see his hometown girlfriend. As I sat drinking the juice, I realized I could have—and probably should have—died from an overdose.

My roommates planned a Friday night party at our duplex. That same night, I had been invited to another friend's party on campus, so I chose to go there first and end up at home. I arrived at my friend's party a little after nine o'clock. I downed several beers and smoked lots of pot. By 10:30 I was smashed. Just before leaving, I popped two soapers (depressants) a buddy gave me. Somehow, I drove nearly 10 miles to our duplex.

By then, at least 20 cars were parked up and down the street. Several people stood in the front yard. I remember stumbling and nearly falling before making it to the front porch. The people in the front yard turned and looked at me. I didn't recognize any of them, but waved and said "hey." A couple of them waved back.

Once inside, John saw me from across the room and immediately headed into the kitchen. A few seconds later he handed me a beer.

"How are you doing?" he asked.

"Fine," I lied. Although I didn't know John well, I liked him. I moved in with John and Barry about two months before. "Where's Barry?" I asked slightly stuttering, my mouth and brain having trouble synchronizing.

"He and a few other people just went into his room."

"Think I'll join'em." I raised my beer bottle. "Thanks."

"You're welcome."

A dim lava lamp bubbled languidly in Barry's room. The county rock group Ozark Mountain Daredevils played on his stereo. Eight or nine people sat on the floor knee to knee in two small groups passing joints around. When I

16

entered, Barry stood up and walked to me as he pulled a joint from his shirt pocket. "You doing okay?" he asked.

"Still breathing," I said, shutting the door behind me.

"That's a good sign." Barry fired up the joint and took a big hit.

Thanks to Barry, I moved into his duplex's third bedroom during the second week after I discovered Melanie had met someone else. Barry stopped by our apartment late one morning after hearing what had happened between Melanie and me. I greeted him drunk and in tears when he arrived.

"You can't go on like this, Bryce," Barry said after we had talked for 10 or 15 minutes. "Have you looked in the mirror lately? You look like hell."

He looked at his watch. "It's not even noon and you're drunk. I know you've got classes today. Have you been to any classes this week?"

I looked down and shook my head.

"This is a bunch of shit. Sorry, I like Melanie, but she's fucking you over. Come on." He stood up. "You're moving in with us. We've got a spare bedroom." He looked around the apartment. "Between our two cars, we should be able to get your clothes—and probably most of your stuff—in one trip. We can strap your bed to the top of your car. What do you say?"

The thought of Melanie returning home that night to a half-empty apartment gave me some satisfaction. The next day I called married student housing and told them we were giving up the apartment at the end of the month.

Both groups on the floor in Barry's room were engrossed in conversations of their own. Barry handed me the lit joint, and I took a long, slow hit before handing it back to Barry. Jerad, a closer friend to Barry than me, stood up and joined us.

"How are you doin', Bryce?" Before I could answer, he continued. "Barry told me what's been happenin' between you and Melanie."

Jerad glanced at the groups on the floor, and then slipped a piece of foil into my hand. I looked at him.

"It's a little something to help out," he whispered. "Valium. It'll help cut some of the pain."

I blew out the smoke in my lungs. "Thanks." I slipped the foil into my jean pocket. "I gotta use the john."

Once in the bathroom, I opened the foil to find seven pills. I threw them in my mouth and washed them down with one gulp of beer. I returned to Barry's room where I drank another beer and smoked more pot. When I realized everyone else in the room had a date, the sadness and sorrow became overwhelming, and I got up and went to the bathroom again. I sat on the toilet seat and cried.

My whole life is falling apart, I thought, and here I sit on the can. I looked around the bathroom. Between my watering eyes and what I could see, I knew one thing for sure. I wanted more than living with two guys and going from party to party, bar to bar. I had done enough of that before I got married.

Someone lightly rapped on the door. I figured the person heard me crying. I used the bathroom countertop to keep my balance and reached for the doorknob.

"Hi Bryce," said Kevin, an old fraternity friend who had recently gone through a breakup. He now dated his former girlfriend's best friend.

A tear dripped off my chin. I knew I looked a wreck. I made an effort to wipe away the tears with the back of my hand only to hit myself in the eye.

"I got something for you buddy," he said as he entered the bathroom and shut the door behind him. He reached in his shirt pocket and pulled out two capsules. "A couple of ludes."

I reached out, and he put the Quaaludes in my hand. I looked around and saw my beer sitting on the back of the toilet. Kevin grabbed the beer and handed it to me. I washed the capsules down my throat. Kevin had no idea I had taken several soapers, seven hits of Valium and drank more than a six pack of beer. I looked at him, smiled and nodded my head.

"You're welcome," he said. "If you need more, just let me know."

It's the last thing I remember about the evening. I assume that's when I went to my bedroom, shut the door and flopped down on the bedspread. My roommates later said neither of them helped me to my room, so I must have made it there on my own.

Thinking about my 40-hour snooze, however, caused me to reevaluate my life. A change had to be made and soon. Columbia and the University of Missouri campus, which had given me so many good times and joyful experiences, now reminded me of the pain, sorrow and hurt that churned in my gut. In addition, the thought of starting a 9-to-5 job filled me with fear—a fear of responsibility and loss of freedom. What do you want? I asked myself. The answer came immediately. I want to see the world: to be carefree and flow with the wind; to answer to no one except myself; to see places I've read about such as Paris, Rome and Athens; to visit places in the United States like California, Alaska and Hawaii. The thoughts of those faraway places filled me with hope.

Then, I considered my situation—broke and in debt with school loans. What good is a person who is dead to the world, I thought. Besides, the 3 percent loans would not start accruing interest until nine months after graduation. The contemplation of hitting the road felt right. It offered a chance for a new life filled with excitement, challenges and changing experiences.

My thoughts that morning paved my path for the next 10 years. School textbooks remained on the bookshelf as travel books took their place next to my reading chair. Dreams of adventure blossomed in my imagination like wild mountain flowers irresistibly stretching toward the radiant sun. For the first time in months, I felt in control.

With no idea how long my journey might last, I decided to divorce Melanie. Months earlier, when I asked Melanie if she wanted a divorce, she said she didn't care if we got one or not. Her response gave me hope that we might get back together. My 40-hour snooze, however, shed new light on my situation. I realized things could get more complicated. What if Melanie got pregnant by another man? I called the courthouse and told them I had no money, but wanted a divorce. They suggested calling the law school for counsel. The school assigned me a student lawyer. I told her what happened during the past few months.

"You have grounds not only for divorce," she said, "but for payments from your wife to help with your education. I'm fairly confident a judge will agree to..."

"Thanks, but no thanks," I said, interrupting her. "All I want is out of the marriage."

Several months later, I called Melanie and told her I wanted to see her one last time before starting my travels. She and her boyfriend had moved into an apartment on the west side of town, so we arranged to meet in an adjacent parking lot. When I arrived at Melanie's apartment, she stood beneath a huge oak tree. She looked beautiful. I got out of the car and walked to her. We embraced in a long hug.

"I had to come over and say good-bye. I'm not sure if I'll ever see you again."

I put my hands on her shoulder and moved her slightly back to look at her. Surprised to see her crying, my heart melted.

"Bryce," she said, her lips trembling and her voice cracking, "I never meant to hurt you."

"I know you didn't. Don't worry about me. I'll be fine. Besides, I wouldn't be heading out on this journey if we were still together, and this is something I've always wanted to do."

Melanie smiled meekly as tears flowed down her cheeks and dripped off her chin. For the first time in a long time, I felt free and empowered. I leaned against my car, now packed with all my belongings. Columbia, where I had spent nearly five years, would be behind me within minutes. Although I felt excited about my future, Melanie's slumped shoulders, trembling lips and red eyes made her appear the way I had felt for months—weak, confused and insecure.

I experienced a weird combination of feelings. While I felt a huge amount of love and compassion for this woman I had once planned my life with, it seemed ironic that now, with my renewed state of being, she had become the vulnerable one. For a moment, I saw her from a detached and unemotional perspective. It seemed like the process had come full circle, and that she got what she deserved. At the same time, I knew Melanie's betrayal reflected my own unfaithfulness. In fact, the bigger betrayal had really come from me. I was the one who never shared my deepest feelings: my feelings of fear and mistrust, my feelings of jealousy and anger. I was the one too afraid to tell her about a dream I had where she left me for another man. I was the one too busy to give her the attention she wanted and needed. I was the one who, on more than one occasion, let the phone ring when I knew it was her calling me. I was the one not there for her. I was the one who repeated the wedding vows, but who never really committed.

"Are you okay?" I asked.

"I guess."

I waited a few seconds for her to speak, but she didn't. Love, compassion and sorrow filled my heart. I took her in my arms again and held her close. She shook as she cried.

"Come on, please don't cry." I wiped away some of her tears.

"I can't help it, Bryce. Please be careful out there. You trust people too much. Promise me you'll be careful."

I pulled her to me again. "I'll be careful, I promise."

After holding her close for a short time, I stepped back and looked at her red, swollen eyes and wet cheeks. I wanted to kiss her, but I couldn't bring myself to do it. "Good-bye, Melanie."

I wanted to tell her that I loved her, but the words stayed stuffed inside. I wanted to tell her that I was sorry for not being there for her. I wanted to tell her that she was a beautiful person, and I'd never forget her. There was so much I wanted to say. Instead, I turned and walked to my car. Melanie watched me open the door and climb in. We waved to each other as I drove away. In my rearview mirror, I saw her standing motionless, her eyes fixed on my car until I could no longer see her. In my heart, I wished her well and kissed her good-bye.

Once on the interstate, I took a deep breath and exhaled. I looked at my watch. Ironically, my watch had stopped at 12:37 p.m., about the time I drove away from my apartment. I took off my watch and tossed it onto the floorboard. I already knew the time. It was time to leave. Time to enter a world with no deadlines, no tests to take, and no classes to attend. Time to return to the present moment and start the rest of my life. I felt ecstatic, and now knew with every part of my being that I had made the right choice. In fact, any other decision would have been suicide.

I mashed down on the gas pedal, shooting the speedometer up to 75. The outskirts of Columbia, still in my rearview mirror, were slowly fading into the gentle slopes and fields of Missouri's farmland. I thought of a quote I had read: "Horace Greeley said, 'Go west, young man.' I say, go any place."

Busted

I drove away from the University of Missouri at Columbia in my faded Dodge Polara and a trunk filled with camping gear, a backpack, a box of canned foods and a guitar. I had attended schools for 17 years, and now—as a 22-year-old divorcee—I looked forward to a future of boundless experiences. I saw my journey as a test of survival and faith, a chance to remain totally in the moment and see places I had read about in books and magazines. I had no time restraints. It would take as long as the urge remained to travel. My first destination? A place to reconnect with nature.

Halfway across Nebraska, I stopped at a rest stop. As I looked at a huge map of Nebraska on the wall, a short, bald, bearded man walked up and stood beside me.

"Where you headin'?" he asked.

"Over to Wyoming and then up through Montana to Glacier National Park."

"Really? I picked up a hitchhiker who's going to Glacier."

"Are you serious?"

"Yeah. He's in the restroom right now."

"If he wants a straight shot to Glacier, he's welcome to ride with me."

A tall, lanky kid came out of the bathroom.

"Hey," the bearded man said to the kid, "this guy's on his way to Glacier National Park."

Pimples dotted the kid's cheeks and forehead. Although he looked thin, he appeared healthy and strong. Long ringlets of thick dark brown hair hung to his shoulders. "No shit?"

"That's where I'm going," I said. "You got a straight shot if you want it."

"Wow, what luck. Only two rides and I'm home free. No one's going to believe this." He held out his hand. "I'm Brent."

Brent's siblings were Kansas farmers. His brothers took over their parents' farm. His dad now helped manage a farm equipment retail store. Brent, the baby of the family, worked for nearly two years helping his brothers on the farm after he finished high school. He appeared to be good-natured and laid back.

"Do you smoke?" he asked me, after we had talked for nearly an hour.

"Not cigarettes," I said, and laughed.

Brent turned around and leaned over the seat to dig into his pack. "I've got some hash I think you'll like."

That night we pulled off the road just inside the Wyoming border and threw our sleeping bags on the ground. We sat on the car and smoked more hashish. There were a few clouds in the western sky, but other than that, we enjoyed a clear and cool evening. It felt good being away from the city lights and viewing the swath of distant stars. The twinkling lights were strewn across the darkened sky like a black-jaded bracelet studded with tiny diamonds reflecting its power, brilliance, freedom and excitement.

"You know what?" I said to Brent, as we lay on our sleeping bags. "You can't beat this. Sometimes we get so caught up in the world that we forget what it's all about. What we're looking at right now doesn't exist for people in the city. The city lights and smog block it out. I'm sure there are people our age who have never seen so many stars in the sky."

"Never thought about that," Brent said. "Growing up on a farm, this is how it is all the time."

I took a deep breath. "Do you ever wonder where you were before you came here?"

"What do you mean?"

"I mean, before coming to Earth. Look at all those stars. We had to be out there somewhere."

After a slight pause Brent replied, "Yeah, I guess."

Several minutes later, Brent's long and slow breaths told me he'd drifted off to sleep. I stared at the stars for a long time before finally slumbering.

We awoke before sunrise, tossed our sleeping bags in the car and headed out. Being in no hurry and wanting to save on gas, I drove 60 mph or slower. I never knew about the great plains of eastern and southern Wyoming. It felt terrific seeing unfamiliar territory. With the Laramie Mountains to our west, I enjoyed the names on road signs and on the map—Bighorn, Buffalo, Greybull and Antelope Butte. We spent the evening at a campground in the Bighorn National Forest.

The next day, a few miles before Bozeman, Montana, we stopped and picked up another hitchhiker. Mark, who looked to be around 30 years old, stood close to six feet tall with blond hair that covered his ears and a curly, thick beard. He held a sign that said Seattle, but when we told him we were going to Glacier National Park, he asked if he could ride along.

"I've never been there," he said, "and I hear it's beautiful."

Mark framed houses in Ohio for a living. He saved up some money and decided to hitchhike around the west for a few months visiting friends. He said he had done a lot of hitchhiking in the late sixties and that it felt good to be back on the road. When I told him I planned to hitchhike when my gas money ran out, he took the role of a hitchhiking tutor.

"There's a code of ethics when it comes to hitchhiking," he said. "For instance, if you come to a turnoff or on-ramp where there's another hitchhiker, it's not cool to get in front of him. It's understood that you walk past any hitchhikers to give them first shot at a passing car."

When we stopped in Missoula for gas, Mark immediately got out, grabbed the squeegee and a paper towel, then proceeded to give the windows a scrubbing. He even checked the oil. As we drove away from the gas station, I thanked him.

"It's the least I can do," he said.

That evening, we stopped at a campground beside Flathead Lake just north of Missoula. We got there before sunset and took a dip in the ice-cold water. We felt great once we were dry and had on clean clothes. Some clouds rolled in as we sat around a campfire. At one point it sprinkled for a few minutes, and then quit. As we prepared to bed down, Brent asked if he could stay in my car. I chose to sleep on the ground where I could stretch out. In case of rain, I threw my poncho over a picnic table and climbed under it with my sleeping bag. Mark put out a thin foam pad on the ground and laid his sleeping bag on top of it.

It sprinkled some more late that night, but it never rained hard. At daybreak, the sound of a car woke me up. After hearing a car door slam shut, I peered out from beneath the picnic table to see a police car speeding away from the picnic area. I rolled over and fell back asleep. I probably slept another hour before getting up. Mark remained asleep, and Brent lay curled up in his sleeping bag next to the picnic table. He stirred as I walked past him, and then he mumbled that a guy kicked him out of my car.

"What are you talking about?" I asked.

Brent raised up slightly. "The guy that's in your car made me get out so he could sleep there."

I turned toward my car to see someone sitting in the front seat. "Who is he?"

Brent put his head back down. "I don't know, but he's big."

I walked over to the car to see a huge Native American slumped over in my front seat, the top half of his shirt splattered with vomit. Thick drool covered his lower lip and chin to make a slimy bridge of slobber down to his black and red flannel shirt. He wore tattered blue jeans covered with dirt and grease stains. His long stringy black hair streaked with strands of gray hair hung around his face. His nose, crooked and pointing to one side, needed wiping. I looked for vomit in my car, but saw none. I opened the door. The smell of vomit and BO caused me to turn my head for some fresh air.

"Hey," I said. "Wake up and get out of my car."

He sat motionless, his stomach rising and falling slowly.

"Did you hear me?" I said louder. "Get out of my car."

He didn't stir. He looked too big to grab and shake. I glanced over at Brent and Mark. Both were sleeping. I slammed the car door shut to see if that might awaken him. He still didn't budge. I decided to find a secluded spot to calm down and meditate. Maybe the guy would wake up and get out of my car on his own. When I returned to the campsite about 45 minutes later, Mark and Brent sat at the picnic table.

"Looks like you got a buddy in your car," Mark said as he took a bite out of an apple.

"Is he awake?" I asked.

"Not yet."

"What happened, Brent?"

"A cop dropped him off here. He came over to the car, opened the door and climbed in. I was in the back seat and asked him what he was doing. He told me to get out of the car so he could sleep there."

"So you just got out?" I asked, feeling a bit disgusted.

"You better believe it. The guy's a monster. And with that nose of his, you can tell he's been in a few fights."

I walked over to the car and looked in again. He looked the same as when I'd been there before. I opened the door, and as before, the stench reeked.

"Excuse me," I said. "This is my car, and we're ready to leave."

He didn't move.

This time I shook his arm. "Excuse me. Excuse me!"

He mumbled, but his eyes remained shut.

"Hey!" I touted louder, gently rocking him. "You need to wake up. Come on, open your eyes."

He moaned, and his lips opened just enough to let some more slobber slide down to his chin. This time I left the door ajar to air out my car.

I opened the trunk and got out a Frisbee; then walked back to the picnic table.

"How's the chief?" Mark asked.

"He's out of it." I felt pissed and helpless. I didn't know what to do. "Why don't we toss the Frisbee around until he wakes up?"

After playing Frisbee for nearly an hour, we went back to the car to check on "the chief" as Mark kept referring to him. At least he had wiped his mouth and chin. He also had on my old sunglasses. I recognized them right away because the arm going to the right ear had been broken off during a basketball game. It meant "the chief" had rummaged through my glove box.

"Hey," I said more demandingly as Mark and Brent stood beside me, "are you awake?"

He mumbled, but still sat slumped over with his head down.

I shook him forcefully as I spoke. "You got to get up and get out of the car. We're ready to leave now."

"Uuh, uuh," he mumbled, indicating no.

"What do you mean 'uuh, uuh.' We need to go. Come on, get out of the car. And, what are you doing with my sunglasses on?"

"These are my sunglasses," he mumbled.

"No they're not. You got them out of my glove box." He now became a liar and a thief.

"They're mine. Drive me to town," he demanded.

"We don't have room."

"Drive me to Missoula," he said.

"Like I said, we don't have room. Besides, we're going the other way."

"Then drive me to the next town," he commanded.

I looked at Mark and Brent, thinking that the three of us might have to drag him out of the car.

"There's not much going on around here," Mark said. "We can all squeeze in until the next town."

Brent got in the back seat with the two backpacks, and Mark slid into the front, leaving 'the chief' in the middle. We rolled all the windows down to circulate the air. I perceived a noticeable difference in weight as we moved up the hill out of the campground. The "chief" must have weighed close to 300 pounds. We drove about 15 minutes before we came to a small town. I pulled over and Mark hopped out.

"We're here," I said. "Time to get out."

The "chief," with my sunglasses cockeyed on his nose, raised his head and slowly looked around. "Not here," he said. "Drive me to the next town."

"You asked for a ride to the next town," I said, "and this is it."

"Drive me to the next town," he demanded.

I looked at Mark, who shrugged his shoulders and got back in. We took off driving once more. No one spoke. I'm sure Mark and Brent wondered whether the "chief" would get out at the next stop. About 15 minutes later, we hit another town. I pulled over next to a park and once again Mark jumped out.

"We're here," I said.

The man once again raised his head and looked around. "Not here," he said. "Drive me to Kalispell."

"Hey mister," I said. "This town is as good as any."

"Drive me to Kalispell," he repeated robustly, irritated by my remark.

25

"Hey chief," Mark said, reaching into his back pocket and taking out his wallet. He stepped back away from the car and pulled out a five-dollar bill. "There's a nice park here for a nap. Here's five bucks so you can buy yourself a drink."

He stared at the $5 bill. After a slight hesitation, he scooted toward Mark. He took hold of the door for support and pushed on the car seat to lift his huge frame. Once standing, he took the $5 and sauntered toward the park still wearing my broken sunglasses. He was finally gone. Mark slid back in and pulled the door shut.

"Thanks," I said as I drove away from the curb.

"It was the only way I could think of to get the jerk out," Mark said. He looked over his shoulder at the Native American now sitting on a park bench. "He's got major problems."

"Yeah, but we screwed over the Indians," Brent said from the back seat.

Mark turned around and looked at Brent. "What do you mean, we?"

"White men."

"That's true only to a point," Mark said. "I don't know about you, but I haven't screwed over any Indians or black people. I really get tired of people that think society owes them something. It's bullshit. Sure, there are people screwing over other people daily. It's not right, and it's not good for anyone. But if I screw with you, does that make it okay for you to screw with Bryce? Or, if your grandfather beat up my grandfather, does that give me the right to beat you up? That's the kind of logic those people are using. It's a crock of shit, and they know it. Let's face it; they're jerks. They want something for nothing. That Indian happened to be a jerk, a drunk and a jerk. He didn't see us as people; just something he could use to get what he wanted. You said he told you to get out of the car because he wanted to sleep there, right? He didn't ask, he took."

Mark didn't wait for Brent to answer, but kept on talking.

"He certainly didn't ask Bryce for a ride. He told Bryce to drive him to the next town. He's a big asshole and figures his size gives him the right to get what he wants. No wonder he's had his nose rearranged a few times. Some people won't put up with that shit, but his behavior doesn't give us the right to give shit to the next Indian we see, does it?"

Mark paused a few seconds as he glanced out the window.

"It all comes down to a one-on-one thing. People react to the way we act. Take the Indian, for instance. He got what he wanted, but in a negative way. If he would have talked to us like people, and treated us with some respect, he probably would be riding to Kalispell with us. Now that I think about it, I screwed up by giving him five bucks. That only reinforced his asshole behavior."

"Look," screamed Brent from the back seat.

We all saw them at the same time. A black bear and her two cubs were several hundred yards in front of us beside the road. I slowed down.

"Better honk your horn," Mark said.

I beeped the horn twice, and all three bears turned and headed back into the ditch. I stopped the car, and we watched them gallop across a ravine and disappear into the woods.

"That's the first bear I've seen out in the wild," Brent exclaimed.

"Bears with cubs are really dangerous," Mark said, "even black bears. And where you guys will be hiking, it's grizzly bear country. In fact, we're in grizzly bear country now."

I could see Brent looking at Mark through the rearview mirror. "Have you ever seen a grizzly in the wild?" he asked.

"In Alaska. They're all over the place up there."

Mark stressed the importance of hanging food away from the tent. "And, if you've been standing around a fire while cooking food, hang your clothes with your food," Mark added. "Bears have a great nose, and if your clothes smell like fish or something good to eat, count on them taking a bite to see how it tastes."

That night we made it to the Apgar campground in Glacier National Park. The next day, Brent and I decided to spend another night at Apgar before beginning a four-day backpacking journey. Mark wanted to continue on to Seattle, so we drove him to West Glacier.

"It's been real," Mark said as he shook both of our hands while we stood beside my car. "Thanks for the lift, Bryce, and if you end up hitchhiking, maybe I'll be the one driving next time."

Brent and I climbed back in my car.

"And by the way," Mark yelled. I turned to see him pull something out of his backpack. "Always carry a good book with you. Once you finish it, I guarantee you'll find another hitchhiker willing to trade."

"What book are you reading?" I asked while starting the car.

"*Be Here Now* by Ram Dass. Now is the only place to be, right?"

"Right on," Brent shouted. "It's the only place we can be."

I honked as I watched my first hitchhiking mentor wave in the rearview mirror. Brent flashed the peace sign out the window. Hitchhiking means no gas or car bills, I thought.

Brent and I stopped at the Park's headquarters where we picked up a topographical map and spoke to a ranger about the backcountry hike Brent wanted to take. The ranger said the trails were beautiful but quite rugged. He also talked about the danger of grizzly bears.

Later that morning, we drove to a trailhead near Logan's Pass and completed a four-hour day hike. Brent, being several inches taller than me and sporting longer legs, kept us going at a quick pace the whole trek. When we got back to the campsite, I felt exhausted and ended up sleeping nearly two hours in my eight-by-ten tent. I awoke at sunset in time to see beautiful long finger shadows stretching across Lake McDonald as shafts of golden light reflected off the mountain peaks in the distance.

Two girls sat at a campsite's picnic table next to us. Before the sun went down, two guys on bicycles with saddlebags rode into the campsite across the road. A bearded man in a pickup with a camper shell took a site on the other side of our campsite. I got out my guitar and improvised some words to a Rolling Stones' tune.

It is the evening of the day,
I sit and watch the sunlight play,
Smiling shadows I can see
as the sun slowly slips away
I sit and watch the sunlight play...

When I stopped playing, the two girls clapped as they walked toward me.

"That sounded good," the taller blonde-haired girl said.

"Thanks," I replied. "Have a seat if you'd like." The girls sat next to me on the picnic table bench. "Where are you from?"

"We're from Ohio," responded the blonde.

"Really," I said. "We picked up a hitchhiker from Ohio. Mark Houlder. Do you know him?"

"No," the blonde responded and grinned. "Ohio has a lot of people."

I laughed. "True, but you never know."

Just then, Brent came strolling into the campsite.

"Where have you been?" I asked.

"Taking a walk along the lake," he said, eyeing the girls sitting next to me.

"Brent, let me introduce you to..." I stopped, realizing I didn't know their names.

"Brenda," the blonde next to me said.

"I'm Janet," the other girl replied.

"They're from Ohio," I added.

As it turned out, they had two other girlfriends with them who were out hiking. About 30 minutes later, they too joined us along with the bicycle riders and the bearded man with the camper. We sat around the campfire as I played the guitar.

"Hey," said Butch, the bearded man, "it's only nine o'clock. Why don't we go to the bar in West Glacier for a few beers?"

The bicyclers said they needed to get their rest, and the two girls who were hiking earlier said they were tired too. So Brenda, Janet, Brent and me climbed into the front seat of the bearded man's truck with the camper on the back. I sat closest to the door with Brenda on my lap. She thought she might be too heavy to sit on me, but I found her warm smooth skin and sweet fragrance wonderful. It had been a long time since a woman pressed so close. Feeling my loins shift slightly, I looked out the window and forced myself to focus on the trees and bushes whizzing past us.

We arrived at the small bar in West Glacier to find it packed. After being there for only 20 minutes, the music stopped and everyone sang happy birthday to one of the barmaids. Just before the singing ended, the jukebox blasted out the Beatles' song *Birthday*. Everybody went nuts. People jumped on the chairs and tables and danced. The windows and door had been opened to let in more fresh air, which of course let the music out. Due to the crowded bar, 15 to 20 people went outside to dance. Janet and I stood by the window. We danced too. People outside climbed on top of cars to twist and shout. It was crazy. I thought this only happened in the movies.

We all got smashed that night. At 1 a.m. the bar shut down. With slurred speech, Butch suggested Janet and I ride in his camper so there would be more room up front.

"Butch, you're bloody slurring your words mate," I said, dramatically slurring my words with a terrible Aussie accent. Everybody laughed. "Why don't you let me drive, mate?"

Butch became defensive. "I've been a lot drunker than this and driven a lot farther than we gotta go tonight," he bellowed, stuttering slightly and continuing to slur his words. He opened the door to the camper. "I can handle it. Just climb on in there and leave the rest to me."

Reluctantly, I climbed in and Janet followed me.

"The light's burned out," he said, "but there's a flashlight under the mattress." Butch shut the door to the camper and locked it.

I twisted the handle. "Hey, you don't need to lock us in."

"I don't want you guys falling out," he screamed, and then laughed.

I felt under the mattress and found the flashlight. We sat on the bed, but not too close together, at least not close enough for me. We heard them climb into the cab and the doors shut. I flipped on the flashlight.

"This would be a good way to travel," I said, shining the light around the camper. It contained a single bed, sink and cabinets with pots, pans and other items hanging on nails.

Tires spun on the gravel before we finally moved out of the parking lot onto the paved highway. Although we were only two or three miles from our campsite, the road had several sharp curves with steep ravines on both sides. We rode less than a minute when the truck careened around the first corner. Janet and I were pushed closer together. I put one hand down on the bed and the other on her shoulder to keep from falling on top of her.

As the truck straightened out, Janet said, "I think Butch is too drunk to drive."

"Yeah," I agreed. "Lucky we don't have far to go."

A moment after saying that, the truck rocked back and forth. At first, Janet and I were knocking into each other as we tried to brace ourselves. Pans rattled on the walls. Then the jerking motion became longer and more drawn out, throwing us from one side of the camper to the other. Butch had to be turning the steering wheel from side to side.

"What the hell are you doing?" I yelled as we slammed against the wall.

Pots and pans fell to the floor while cooking utensils, spices and canned foods hurled out of the cabinets as their doors opened and banged shut with each swerve. I dodged flying debris and at the same time tried to help Janet. Between one swerve, I pushed off the wall toward the bed and grabbed the pillow.

"Use this to cushion yourself," I said, handing it to Janet as we were thrown together on one side of the truck.

When she took the pillow, the truck straightened out.

"What the hell's going on up there?" I yelled as loud as I could. "Get on the bed," I said to Janet, guiding her toward it. "Lean against the wall and put the pillow behind your head."

She did what I asked. I pushed up against her and planted my feet into the other wall to keep us braced in the corner.

"Stop the truck!" I yelled.

"Let us out of herrrrre!" Janet screamed at a pitch that nearly broke my eardrums.

The truck swerved back and forth more violently than before. More canned foods and utensils flew out of the cabinets as the remaining pots fell off the walls.

"Hold on!" I said to Janet.

The truck careened around another curve. We were pushed hard into the wall as the tires screeched. Janet, who had been holding the pillow around her head, now clung to me. In my mind, I could see the truck toppling over the guard rail and rolling down a thousand-foot incline. To my surprise, the truck made it around the curve and slowed down. I thought we were going to stop, but instead we stayed at a slow steady speed. Although we remained braced for the short, quick swerves, they never came. A few minutes later we turned off the road and gravel pecked at the bottom of the truck before we came to a stop. We heard the truck doors slam, and then a key unlocked the back door. Janet and I were sitting on the edge of the bed when the door opened.

Butch's huge grin turned somber as he looked at the floor of his camper. "What the hell did you guys do in here?"

Pots, pans, canned goods and one tennis shoe blanketed the floor. We couldn't walk out without tripping over the clutter.

"What did we do?" I asked incredulously, my face beginning to burn. "Somebody swerved their fucking truck all over the damn road, which threw us around like rats in a cage. We're lucky we didn't get hurt with all this shit flying out of the cabinets and falling off the walls."

Janet got up and shuffled out of the camper to keep from stepping on anything. Butch moved items out of her way.

"I wasn't swerving that much," he said.

"You hop in here and let me drive down the highway a ways," I said, scooting out of the camper. "Then you can see for yourself what it was like."

"Shit, what a mess," he said.

"You got no one to blame but yourself," I added.

We all stood there looking at his ransacked truck in silence. Then Brent spoke up.

"I'm starving. Anyone else hungry?"

"I am," I said. "How about pancakes? I got some pancake mix and honey."

"We've got some eggs and potatoes," Brenda said, "and I think some syrup."

As Butch picked up pots and pans from the floor of his truck, we went to our campsites. Everybody returned with a contribution for the communal meal. Brent tried to get a fire started under a steel grate that covered our campfire ring. He finally gave up and built the fire next to the ring. The girls cut up the potatoes, and I prepared the pancake mix. I put cooking oil in the pan and began spreading out the fiery red coals when a ranger pulled up in his truck. It had to be after 1:30 a.m.

"What are you doing?" he asked as he shut his truck door.

"Making breakfast," I said. "Would you like to join us?"

"You can't have a fire outside the fire ring," he said, ignoring my invitation.

"We couldn't get the fire going inside the ring," I said. "As soon as we've finished cooking, we'll push it back under the grate."

"Do it now," he said.

"But the coals are ready for cooking," I blurted. "If we push them under the grate, there won't be enough heat to..."

"Just do it," the ranger commanded.

"But..."

"Go on," he ordered. "Put it where you should have put it in the first place."

Butch kicked the coals and wood under the grate with his boot. The ranger stood there with his arms crossed until Butch had all the burning embers inside the ring. Some of the final kicks scattered dirt atop the coals.

"Fuckin' asshole," Butch muffled as the ranger drove away.

"Maybe it's hot enough to cook the pancakes," I said.

I put the skillet on the grate and dipped out two good-sized pancakes. After several minutes, it became obvious we'd have to build up the fire.

"I'm going to bed," Brent said, and left the group.

"Me too," Janet added, turning and walking toward her campsite.

I looked at Butch. "I'm out of here. We can clean this mess up tomorrow."

I climbed in the tent and plopped down on my sleeping bag. The next thing I knew, someone tapped on the tent. I heard it, but I didn't feel like moving. There were several more taps followed by a man's voice.

"Excuse me. This is the ranger. I want to speak to you please."

Although I heard the man, I figured Butch had decided to play a joke on us.

"Sure," I said, rolling over and closing my eyes.

The tapping came again. "Would you please come out here. Bears have been at your campsite."

Brent unzipped a corner of the tent door and peeked out. "It is a ranger," he whispered to me.

"Really?" I sat up to a throbbing ache at the base of my skull. "I'll be right out." I looked at Brent. "What time you got?"

"A little after seven."

I pulled on my jeans and a t-shirt and unzipped the tent door. The ranger stood by the picnic table. The honey and syrup bottles were unbroken, but lay on the ground. The pan on the grate the night before was upside down beside the fire ring. The pancake batter, which had been in a plastic bowl, lay smeared all over the picnic table. My crushed Styrofoam cooler had several half-chewed oranges strewn around it.

The ranger gave me a stern look. "Did you read the camping rules posted on the board over there?"

"No."

"Well you should have, and I suggest you do so after I leave. Under no circumstances are you to leave food out on a picnic table unattended. As you can see, several bears paid your site a visit last night."

The ranger proceeded to lecture me on what they had to do to bears that kept returning to campsites for food. Ultimately, it could mean death for them. I asked him if he was the ranger who visited us the night before. He said no. I briefly explained what happened and ended by saying that had we eaten, we would have cleaned up after ourselves. He showed no sympathy. After cleaning up the site, I went back to bed for several more hours. The Ohio girls and the bicyclers were gone by the time I got up. Although Butch's truck remained parked at his site, we never saw him again.

Brent and I broke camp about noon. We drove over Logan Pass and through the Continental Divide, and then took Highway 17 to a trailhead near the Canadian border. After loading our backpacks for the four-day trip, we began our journey. We hiked several miles before setting up camp. Later that night it rained, and it kept raining through the next morning. We decided to stay put until it stopped, but it rained all day. We created a lean-to out of our ponchos so we could sit outside our cramped tents without getting soaked. We smoked hash and pot most of the day while I played my guitar. The bottom of my tent became drenched because I failed to dig a trench around it.

That evening, just before the sun went down, the clouds broke and we could see sunlight on the far mountains. We looked forward to a sunny day so we could dry everything out. To protect my guitar, I wrapped it in a plastic trash bag and kept it inside its case. I also put a bag around the case. It stayed in my two-man tent with me. Brent had his own pup tent. Later that night it rained some more. By the next morning, the rain slowed to a light mist with no indication of ending.

"I think we should break camp and hike," Brent said.

I looked at Brent. "But everything's wet. It will be twice as heavy to carry."

We each were packing close to 50 pounds under dry conditions.

"It might be nice on the other side of Stony Indian Pass," he said. "It's not that far a hike. Just a few miles."

After eating some food and smoking more hash, Brent talked me into leaving. As soon as we had our tents down and ready to pack up, it poured. Water and mud were rolled inside our tents. By the time we had our packs on we were completely soaked. Muddy and slick paths made the hiking miserable. At first I avoided the mud puddles, but within the hour I walked right through them. My feet sloshed inside my boots.

When the handle pulled out of my guitar case's soggy cardboard shell, I wrapped both arms around the case and carried it like a baby. It got colder the higher we climbed toward Stony Indian Pass. Each exhalation sent out vapor clouds before our eyes. Brent said we might run into snow. Although I wore a pair of cotton gloves, they were sopping, making my cold fingers wrinkle like an old man's.

Brent encouraged me to see the positive side. I guess he felt guilty about getting me out there.

"Look at it this way," Brent said, "it's an experience you won't forget, and it'll make your next backpacking trip seem like heaven."

I must have given him a rather sour look, because he added, "I've got a feeling that on the other side of the pass it's going to be sunny. We can hang all our stuff out to dry and bask in the warm mountain sunshine."

I could easily imagine what he described, but the rain pummeling my head, backpack and guitar case diminished any true hope of relief. I watched for a large pine tree that might harbor a dry spot to stop. The cold weather and altitude were getting to me. I slowed down, which meant Brent got farther ahead. Occasionally, I would hear Brent make a loud yodeling sound as if to say, "Come on, you're almost there." Only a few small trees were near the top of the pass. Brent was probably 30 minutes ahead of me when the rain became mixed with sleet. I had never been so physically miserable in my life.

To help me cope with my discomfort in this shitty weather, I thought about Melanie and the first year of our marriage. I remembered Melanie's kind and compassionate heart. One evening we were walking down Main Street and saw a blind man begging. Melanie clutched my arm as we walked by the corner where he stood. After we were a few steps past him, she stopped.

"Wait a minute," she said. She opened her purse and took out a dollar. She went back and put it in the man's cup. "I've always been told that people like that are faking it," she said, as we walked on. "I don't believe it anymore." I put my arms around her and looked into her eyes. They were so pure, innocent and loving.

Then we were back in our warm cozy apartment lying on pillows in the living room wrapped in each other's arms. Melanie looked at me.

"If you could be anyone in the world, who would you want to be?"

"Me," I had said without hesitation, "and right here with you."

I stumbled over a rock and nearly fell down, which brought me back from my pleasant reverie to the rain, sleet and freezing cold. Pangs of jealousy and rejection shot through me as I thought of the guy living with Melanie. I recalled the first night she failed to come home.

After Melanie told me about meeting another man and her doubts as to whether she still loved me, we decided to remain together, but lead separate lives. It meant behaving like roommates. Actually, that was Melanie's idea, and I went along with it. From that point on, Melanie consistently returned home from work late in the evening. When Melanie did get home, usually around 8:30 or 9 p.m., she turned on television and got a beer from the refrigerator. We stopped eating meals together. We always shared supper before, but now we rarely spoke to one another. If I asked her a question that concerned our relationship, she'd say she didn't want to talk about it and would either take a walk or go to bed early. Although we slept in the same bed, we never touched. I initially went through the motions of going to school, but I couldn't concentrate. Finals were less than two months away, and I had no motivation to do my daily homework much less prepare for exams.

About the fifth or sixth night living together and leading separate lives, Melanie didn't come home. By 10 p.m. I imagined her stranded or hurt. By 11 p.m. my concern turned to anger. And finally, by the time midnight arrived, the images in my head drove me crazy. I knew what must be happening, if it hadn't happened already. I wept profusely. I screamed. I yelled. I cursed myself. I cursed Melanie, and I cursed her fucking, bastard boyfriend. I finally took off my clothes, climbed into bed and cried myself to sleep. I awoke early the next morning as Melanie came through the door. She entered the bedroom without saying a word and began to undress.

"Where the hell were you last night?"

Angry, I wanted a confrontation. She didn't answer. She already had her dress off and was putting on another one.

"Huh?" I yelled.

She still refused to answer.

"What's the matter? Did fucking all night give you laryngitis?"

That did it.

"I don't have to listen to this," she screamed. "We said we were going to live separate lives."

She left the bedroom and went into the bathroom. Naked, I climbed out of bed. I walked to the door of the bathroom. Somehow I thought that if she saw me nude, things would fall back together naturally. I couldn't imagine her not being attracted to me. She stood in front of the mirror putting on makeup.

"I think we should talk."

"We'll have to talk later. I have to get to work."

She snapped a small powder case shut and walked toward me. She didn't slow down. I moved out of her way and she continued on into the bedroom. I followed her.

"Call in sick. You haven't missed a day of work yet...or have you?"

"I'm not going to call in sick. I'm not sick and have responsibilities. Someday you'll understand."

She picked up her purse.

"Don't you think our marriage is as important as your job?"

She didn't reply. As she walked past me, I grabbed her by the arm.

"Let go of me," she screeched, shaking her arm free. "I've got to get to work."

As she reached for the door handle, I grabbed her and spun her around, then pinned her arms up against the door so she was facing me. I'd never done anything like that before. The fear in her eyes surprised me. I let go and gave her a push.

"Get out of here you fucking whore!"

She left quickly, slamming the door. I felt ashamed and sick to my stomach and collapsed onto the floor sobbing. I stayed in the apartment all day feeling sorry for myself and praying we'd get back together.

Sleet pummeled my cheeks as I forced myself to put one foot in front of the other along the mountain trail. If I had a gun in my backpack, my emotional anguish and physical agony would have ended there and then on the mountain pass.

As I walked around a switchback, I spotted a small stubby tree that looked more like an evergreen bush. I lifted a branch and pushed my guitar under the tree, then slipped off my pack and climbed under it, dragging the pack behind me. The tree only provided partial protection from the sleet and rain, but it felt good to sit. About 10 minutes later, a man approached on the path. My green poncho must have provided good camouflage because he walked right by me. I felt tempted to say something, but didn't. A minute later, a girl came around the switchback.

"Hello there," I said.

The girl stopped, glanced backward, and then looked at the path ahead of her.

"How are you?" I asked, enjoying her puzzlement about the mysterious voice.

With a hooded poncho surrounding her head, she couldn't tell where the utterances came from. She looked around quickly. "Is someone there?"

Her perplexed look made me hesitate before replying, "I'm over here."

She pulled the hood off her head. "Where?"

"Here. Under the bush."

She walked over to the bush and bent over. "Are you okay?"

"Yeah. I'm just resting and trying to keep warm."

Her breath condensed to form a misty burst of fog in front of her mouth.

"How long have you been under there?"

"Fifteen minutes or so."

"Hypothermia is a real threat," she said. "You need to keep moving."

"What's hypothermia?"

"It's when your body loses too much heat, and it happens most often when someone's wet and cold." She straightened up. "People die from hypothermia. You'll stay warmer if you keep walking. Which way are you going?"

"Up," I replied. "I got a buddy that's probably over the pass by now."

She took a step back from the bush. "Come on. If you want, we can walk together."

"That's all right. I'll start walking in a few minutes."

"Are you sure?"

"Yeah."

"Okay, but really, don't stay here much longer."

"I won't."

"Good." She began moving up the path. "Take it easy."

"I will, and thanks."

Five minutes after she left, I forced myself to get out from under the tree and continue upward on the trail. Trying to mentally block out the wet and cold, I focused on one step at a time. In a trance, I walked about 30 minutes when Brent's voice startled me.

"How are you doing?"

Brent walked toward me without his pack.

I smiled weakly, glad to see him. "Tired, wet and cold. How about you?"

He laughed. "The same, but I have good news. I found a huge pine tree to keep us dry, and I've got a big fire burning."

"Yeah, sure."

"I mean it," he said. "Here, let me take your guitar."

"Trees around here aren't tall enough to get under," I said, looking to my left and right as he took my guitar case.

"A hundred yards from here we go over Stony Indian Pass," Brent said. "The tree is about a mile down the other side—and it's a huge tree."

Brent took off walking and I followed him. "I ran into two hikers," he said half turning toward me. "The girl said she saw you under a bush shivering."

"Yeah, I stopped to rest for a little while."

We barely talked for the next mile. To my surprise, Brent did have a big fire burning beneath a huge pine tree. We ended up drying our clothes, heating up some beans and smoking two bowls of hash to celebrate our newly invigorated state. After being there for two hours, Brent wanted to move on. I protested. I wanted to wait until the rain stopped. It made me sick to think about getting wet and cold again.

"The couple that passed us on the trail told me there's a huge pavilion and fireplace about three or four miles down the trail," Brent said. "It's where a ferry brings tourists so they can picnic and go on short day hikes."

He pulled out his map and looked at it. "Here it is," he said, pointing to the spot and showing me the map. "We can spend the night at the pavilion, and then catch a ferry across the lake in the morning." Brent pulled the map closer to him. "From there, it looks like a short hitchhike back to your car."

When it's cold and rainy, there's little to do but eat, so we were nearly out of food. Realizing this, I finally agreed to move on. Within an hour we were completely soaked again. To keep me hiking, Brent kept reminding me of the pavilion and a hot fire. When we got there, three other hikers were sitting around the fireplace. They were glad to see my guitar. That evening, with our clothes hung out to dry, we sat around the hearth. One of the other hikers also played guitar, so we took turns singing songs. Later that night, after everyone had fallen asleep, I awoke. Something scrambled across the pavilion's timber beams above us. I flipped on my flashlight to see wood rats as big as cats climbing on the rafters. I turned off the light and zipped myself inside my bag, too tired to care.

The next morning we caught the ferry across Waterton Lake and entered Canada. While on the ferry, a married couple from New York struck up a conversation with me. They were in their 30s. They wanted to know what it was like hiking in the backcountry. When I told them we planned to hitchhike back to the border for my car and then drive farther north into Canada to hike other wilderness areas, they offered us a ride to the border.

When we got to the border, we joined the line of cars slowly proceeding through customs. I had never been through a border check before and neither had Brent. When we pulled up to the station, an officer bent over and looked through the driver's window.

"Hello," he said. "Are any of you Canadian citizens?"

He must have seen the New York license plate on the car.

"No," said the driver.

"Where did you go in Canada?" he asked.

"We drove over this morning to catch the ferry across Waterton Lake. It's a beautiful tour. Have you done it?"

"Sure have. Come back and see us again."

"Thanks," the driver said. We pulled on through and drove several hundred feet to the U.S. border patrol. Again, we waited in line for several minutes before pulling up to the station.

"How are you folks today?" asked the officer.

"Fine," said the driver.

"Are you from the United States?"

"Yes," the driver said. "These guys are hitchhikers we picked up," pointing his thumb toward us, "but they're from the States too."

The officer looked in our direction. "I see. You guys need to get your gear out of the car and go over to the other station."

The driver got out of his car and opened the trunk. As we retrieved our packs, the officer pointed toward the station where cars were lined up two rows to our right.

"Go over there and put your things on that table," he said. "The officer will be with you shortly."

We could see one officer rummaging under the seat of a yellow Volkswagen beetle parked next to the table. Both car doors were open. A longhaired man stood talking to another officer beside a table where stacks of stuff from the car were piled. As we neared the area, the longhaired man emptied the contents of his pockets out onto the table. Suddenly, I felt sick. My pockets held a small bag of pot and a pipe. I knew Brent had his hash and pipe in his pocket as well.

"Shit," I said soft enough for only Brent to hear.

Brent understood my concern, but it was too late to do anything. We set our packs on the table. I looked for a place to get rid of my pot. There were two possibilities, but both were risky. I could drop the pot and pipe into the back seat of the Volkswagen, or toss them under the car. Either way, it would be difficult to do without being seen, not to mention a devastating sham on the Volkswagen driver. Oh well, I thought, as my heart pounded against my chest, you've smoked pot since you were 17 and never got busted. It looks like your time has come.

The officer finished searching the Volkswagen and walked to the table.

"I'll be right with you," he said, looking at us. He reached for the Volkswagen driver's backpack.

"I'll get that," said the other officer who had just inspected the items the longhaired man had put on the table. "You take care of these guys." He nodded in our direction.

The officer first rummaged through Brent's pack. Satisfied Brent had nothing illegal in it, he pushed it aside and dug through mine. As he looked into one of my side pouches, his hand darted in and pulled out a vile wrapped in foil.

"Aha! What have we here?" he exclaimed loudly.

The other officer and longhaired man turned and looked at him. Even people at the next station spun their heads in our direction. The officer tore off the foil and held the small vile up to let the sun's rays shine through the thick yellow substance.

"What is this?" he asked, looking at me.

"It's soap," I said.

The longhaired man driving the Volkswagen broke out laughing first, and then we joined him.

"I was afraid the container might leak," I said, "so I wrapped it in foil."

The embarrassed officer pushed the vile toward me.

"Here," he said, "you guys can go."

Without saying a word, I took the soap, slipped my arm through one of the straps, grabbed my guitar and briskly walked away. My heart raced as my ears remained keenly aware of the conversation behind me.

"How long did you say you were in Canada?" I heard the officer ask the man driving the Volkswagen.

"Like I said, three weeks," he replied.

I moved so fast that Brent, even with his much longer legs, had to hustle to catch up to me.

"Keep walking fast and don't look back," I said softly without looking at him. "I don't want them to change their minds."

Once we reached my car, parked about a quarter of a mile away from the U.S. border checkpoint and hidden behind some evergreen trees, my heart still rapidly pounded against my chest.

"We were lucky," I said, leaning my pack and guitar against my Dodge Polara. "It freaked me out when they made that guy empty his pockets."

"You and me both," Brent said, smiling and shaking off his pack. "Put it there."

He held his hand up, and I gave him a high five.

"Hey," we heard someone yell. We both turned around to see one of the guys we spent the night with at the pavilion. "What was going on back there?"

We told him how close we came to getting busted.

"This calls for a celebration," he said. "I've got a pint of Jack Daniel's in my car."

He retrieved the bottle, and we passed it around. Brent pulled out his pipe and filled it with hash. We each took a hit of smoke and then washed it down with a shot of whisky. When we told our mountain friend we planned to visit wilderness areas farther north in Canada, he advised us to be careful going back across the border.

"Don't worry," I said, "they're not going to find our stash."

Fifteen minutes later we were packed and ready to cross the border. Neither of us had taken a shower or bath for more than a week. Our clothes were filthy, our hair long and dirty, and we both had scraggly beards—if you could call them beards. In addition, our breath smelled like liquor, and our clothes probably reeked of marijuana. Still, we expected to drive past the border officials without complications.

First, we pulled up to the U.S. border station. Basically, it's a formality check when you're leaving a country. The officer asked us if we were U.S. citizens and where we were going. After we told him, he wished us a good time. The Canadian border patrol handled things a bit differently than when we left the country less than an hour before. We were in a line of about 10 cars. An officer talked to the driver of each car and then let them pass through. When the car in front of us proceeded into Canada, my heart began pounding once more as we pulled up to the Canadian officer.

"How are you gentlemen today?" he asked.

"Great," I said.

"Where are you going?"

"Were going up to Banff and Jasper to do some hiking."

"Those are nice areas. How long do you think you'll be in Canada?"

"Two, maybe three weeks."

"Is this your car?"

"Yes."

"I need to look at your car registration and driver's license."

I grabbed the car registration from the glove box and handed it to him. Then I took my license out of my wallet.

"I need to see your driver's license too," he added, looking at Brent.

He examined my registration and license. "Is this your current address?" he asked.

"Yes," I said. It was my Columbia, Missouri, address.

He handed the registration and license back to me and took Brent's license.

"It's my current address," Brent said before the officer asked.

The officer looked at it briefly before handing it to me to give back to Brent.

"I'd like for you to pull your car over to that parking area on the other side of the station," he said, pointing to the general location. "Someone will be with you in just a minute."

"Sure," I said, confident that everything would be fine, but still feeling uncomfortable. "Is something wrong?"

"No. It's just a custom spot check."

We sat in the parking area for several minutes before a guy about my age came over to us. He wore a brown uniform and had short red hair.

"I need to have you get out of your car for a few minutes," he said.

We got out, and he hopped into the front seat. He first opened the glove box and looked inside, shuffling through several maps. Then he reached under the dash with his other hand. He moved from the glove box over to the steering column. Finally, he looked and felt under the seat. Within a few seconds, he raised up.

"Whose pipes are these?" he asked, holding a pipe and a beer tap in front of him.

He held Mark's (the hitchhiker from Ohio) pipe and a beer tap I had under the seat. Mark had set his pipe under the seat and forgot it. The beer tap would have made a great pipe, but I hadn't thought of converting it into one.

"That's not a pipe," I said, "it's a beer tap, and that's a hitchhiker's pipe."

"Please wait here," he said.

He turned and walked to the station.

"Shit," I said, "I can't believe Mark left his pipe in my car. We're screwed."

"Maybe not," Brent said. "They haven't found anything but paraphernalia. I don't think they can do anything if that's all they've got."

The young officer returned with another officer about 40 years old.

"Stand back gentlemen," the older officer said. "We'll be a few minutes."

The officers jumped in my car and thoroughly searched it. They even took out the back seat, and then asked me to open the trunk. They looked through my guitar case, typewriter case, our backpacks, and even flipped through all of my books. They found several pipe screens at the bottom of one box.

"What are these?" the older officer asked me, holding the screens in the palm of his hand.

"Faucet screens," I replied without hesitation.

In fact, they were. I bought all my pipe screens at a hardware store because they were cheaper. The officers found no other evidence in the car.

"Well," said the older officer, "since we found some pipes under your seat, we'll have to conduct a personal search."

"What does that mean?" I asked apprehensively.

"It means you must come inside for a few minutes. Please follow us."

I looked at Brent. My heart knocked hard against my chest. When we got inside, they asked for identification. When the older officer had our driver's licenses, he asked Brent to have a seat and then directed me down a hallway to a room. Inside the room there were three chairs against a wall. Five feet in front of the chairs sat a desk and another chair. The older officer parked himself in the chair behind the desk as the younger officer shut the door and stood beside me.

"Mr. Yarborough," the older officer said, "because we found these two pipes in your car, we are conducting a personal search." He put the pipe and

41

beer tap on the desk. "That means you will have to empty your pockets and remove your clothes. I will be writing everything down that you have. Officer Johnson will serve as a witness. All items will be returned to you as long as they are legal. Could you please start by emptying your pockets? Please put the items on the desk."

I reached in my right pocket and removed my car keys, dropping them on the desk.

"One set of keys," Johnson said as the officer at the desk wrote on a piece of paper.

In my left pocket I had 67 cents, lip balm and a Swiss Army pocket knife. In my back pockets were a comb, handkerchief and $14—a ten and four ones. My flannel shirt pockets had one harmonica and three strips of folded toilet paper.

"You never know when you might have to go," I said as Johnson unfolded the strips of toilet paper to make sure nothing hid inside them.

"Please remove your shirt and give it to Officer Johnson."

Once I had done so, he asked me to take off my boots. As I sat to remove them, I could feel the pipe and pot in my crotch. Johnson took my boots and turned them upside down, then reached inside them.

"You can take off your socks now."

I had two pair of socks on—a pair of wool socks covering my cotton socks. I handed them to Johnson.

"Now your t-shirt, please."

I removed the t-shirt, but remained sitting as I handed it to Johnson.

"Your jeans."

I stood up, unsnapped my jeans and slowly pushed them down. I sat on the edge of the chair to take them the rest of the way off. Somehow the pot and pipe remained inside my underwear. After handing the jeans to Johnson, I decided to play it out to the end, hoping they would return my pants and tell me to put them back on.

"Okay, stand up, turn around and drop your shorts."

I stood up, turned around facing away from them, and dropped my shorts. The pot and pipe fell out onto the floor, the pipe bouncing once before it lay flat next to the half-filled ziplock sandwich bag. Still partly drunk and stoned, I picked them up and turned around smiling, holding out the pipe and pot toward Johnson.

"Damn," I said, "you caught me with my pants down."

They couldn't restrain themselves and broke out laughing.

When Johnson reached to take my pot and pipe, I looked him in the eyes and said, "That's the best pot I've ever smoked."

I could see and feel it in his eyes that he smoked pot. He took my stash and looked at the older officer.

"Go weigh it on our scales," the older officer said. "You can put your clothes back on, Mr. Yarborough."

What hypocrites, I thought. They're busting me and they probably both get high. Before I had all of my clothes on, Johnson came back through the door.

"It doesn't register on our scale," he said.

The older officer nodded. "Well Mr. Yarborough, if that's all you've got, you might even get your pipes back."

"That's not my pipe," I said, pointing to the pipe that got us into this situation. "You can keep it."

They led me back to the front room and asked Brent to follow them. I gave Brent a reassuring nod. Brent's strip search, however, seemed to take longer. When they came out, I could tell something had changed. I stood up and walked to them.

"What's the matter?"

"We found more than just pot," the older officer said.

"It's just concentrated pot," I interjected. "My pot's better than that stuff."

"Hashish changes things," the officer added. "We have to call in the authorities from Waterton.

"What does that mean?"

"It means they take over from here. Please have a seat."

I looked at the young officer, Johnson. He gave a slight shrug of his shoulders and raised his eyebrows, indicating there was nothing he could do.

We sat there for about 30 minutes before a police officer arrived. He talked several minutes to the older officer who then motioned his head toward us. The policeman looked in our direction. The older officer then gave the policeman a large envelope and several papers. The policeman walked over to me.

"Mr. Yarborough?"

"Yes."

"I'm Officer Holstein. You are the owner of the car outside?"

"Yes."

"We need to go to the Waterton Police Department." He looked at Brent. "Are you Mr. Shields?"

"Yes," Brent replied.

"I would like for you to ride with me. I have your license, Mr. Yarborough. I want you to follow me. Is that understood?"

"Yes."

The whole thing seemed so idiotic. What was the big deal about smoking a dried plant, or smoking some crusted sediments made from a plant? Why should anyone care? It wasn't hurting anyone else. The more I thought about it, the madder it made me. On the other hand, I thought about what my parents would say when they heard I got busted. Also, how would getting busted affect the rest of my life? I decided that whatever happened, I wouldn't call my parents for help—even if it meant going to jail.

Once we got to the Waterton Police Department, we were taken inside. Another officer, who appeared to be in his 30s, sat at a desk that faced the door.

"So these are the two?" he asked.

"Yes," the officer with us said.

"Have a seat over here, gentlemen." There were two chairs beside his desk. The officer continued talking. "It's going to cost $300 a piece for bail. Otherwise, you'll have to go to jail."

There was a moment of silence before I spoke.

"I don't have the money," I said. "Is it okay if I bring a few books and my guitar into the cell so I have something to do?"

Before either officer could speak, Brent asked, "I'm broke too. Do you guys have hot showers?"

The officers looked at each other dumbfounded. Although they said nothing right away, the look on the face of the officer closest to me was saying, "Hell, these guys are moving in." Obviously, this had never happened before. They didn't know what to do. After a long pause, the officer sitting at the desk finally spoke.

"How much money do you have?"

"I've got $100," I said.

"I think I've got that much," Brent said.

We later discovered that before you can enter Canada, you must have at least $300. No one asked us about money. If Canadian authorities had known we had less than $300 between us, we would have been sent back to the United States.

There was another long pause before the officer at the desk spoke again. "I'll tell you what we'll do. We'll charge one of you with possession of everything, and then set bond at $200. How's that sound?"

"Who's going to get busted?" I asked.

"You guys will have to decide that."

Brent reached into his pocket and pulled out a quarter. "Heads or tails?"

He flipped the coin into the air and caught it between his palms.

"Tails."

He took one hand off the other. It was heads.

"I guess that's justice at its best," I said, frustrated and upset at the outcome. "Now what do we do?"

"We have to fingerprint you."

"Wait a second," I added. "This doesn't seem fair. I only had a small amount of pot."

"If you guys want to talk things over," the officer said, "you can go in there." He pointed to a room next to the jail.

"Thanks," I said.

We entered the room, and I shut the door.

"Look," I said to Brent, "I don't think I should get busted. Your hash got us here. If all we had was my pot, they would have let us go at the border."

"I know," Brent said, "but I've already been busted in Kansas for pot. It's really going to look bad if I get busted here too. You'll still have a clean record in the States. That's all that really counts."

I took a deep breath and exhaled. After a few moments of silence, Brent spoke again.

"Please. It could make a big difference for me. I don't know what my parents will do if I get busted again."

"Okay," I said, still feeling lousy about the deal.

We joined the officers in the other room.

"Where do you fingerprint me?" I asked.

"Officer Holstein will take care of you over there." He pointed to a counter in front of their desks. Holstein took an ink pad and paper from a drawer.

"Is everything accurate on your license?" the other officer asked me as I approached the counter.

"Yes," I said.

Although I no longer lived in Columbia, Missouri, it was as good an address as any. Holstein took my right hand.

"Just relax your hand and let me do everything," he said.

He took my hand as I let it go limp. He pushed my thumb onto the ink pad.

"Tell me something," I asked, "who will know about this?"

"It will go on record here in Alberta, and a copy will be sent to the FBI since it happened at the border." He rolled my thumb onto the piece of paper, leaving a long flat print. "Other than that, nobody will know."

The officer at the desk spoke up. "Why did you try to bring it across the border? You could have just got some here."

"Really?" I said sarcastically. "Who's your connection?"

He gave me a stern look before he returned his attention to filling out the form on his desk.

Once Holstein finished fingerprinting me, he pointed toward the jail cell. "You can wash your hands in there," he said. "Try not to get ink all over the sink."

As I washed my hands, the water rose higher and higher in the washbasin. I returned to the front room holding my hands together to keep them from dripping.

"Your sink's stopped up," I said. "The water's going to run over if I finish washing my hands."

45

Holstein, who had taken a seat at a desk, got up and followed me into the cell. He looked at the sink. "Hmmm," he said, "your hands are already dirty. See if you can unplug it."

I pushed my first and second finger down into the drain, and then quickly yanked them out and held them in front of me. For a second nothing happened, and then blood spurt from my fingers and ran down into my hand.

"Damn! It's broken glass in there."

"Hang on a second," Holstein said.

He left the room. I assumed he went for a first-aid kit. My fingers throbbed. I covered them with my thumb to help stop the bleeding. Holstein returned with a coat hanger. "Here, try this."

His insensitivity to my bleeding fingers pissed me off. "Do it yourself," I said, raising my voice. "I ain't your damn plumber!"

I stormed out of the cell into the other room. The second officer, still sitting at his desk, heard the commotion. He looked at the door as I came through it. When he saw my bloody hand, he jumped out of his seat and unsnapped his holster.

"What the hell's going on?" he bellowed.

Holstein, who knew I left furious, came running into the room after the other officer screamed. The fact that both of them thought the other one might be in trouble seemed humorous to me. I couldn't help but grunt a laugh.

"Nothing's going on," I said. "Just a small case of police brutality."

I meant it jokingly, but they took it seriously. The comment brought a flurry of action. Both officers checked out my hand as Holstein applied medication and two band-aids. It's amazing what a few words can do.

"Now what?" I asked, once they had finished.

"We need to have you sign a few papers and pay the $200 for bail. Your court date has been set for the day after tomorrow in Pincher Creek."

Pincher Creek was a small town about 40 miles north of Waterton. The papers I signed forbid me from seeking employment in Canada and barred me from returning to the province of Alberta. It also stated that immediately following my court case, I must return to the United States via the nearest route.

After paying our bail money and getting booted out of jail, we camped along Waterton Lake that evening. Concerned about my appearance for the hearing, we decided it would be best to get a hotel and clean up. Nearly broke, we stopped at one of the cheapest looking hotels we could find in Pincher Creek. An old woman, whom I assumed owned the place, wanted $25 for the night. I told her we were low on funds, and asked what she would charge if we slept on the floor in our sleeping bags and used only the shower. She dropped the price to $15. I got her down to $10 by saying we would use our own towels and be gone before 9 a.m.—the time I had to be in court. I shaved the scraggly long whiskers on my face that evening, but kept my hair that hung down my shoulders.

The next morning, I put on my best pair of blue jeans and the only sweater I had. We arrived at the courthouse just before 9. After telling the woman at the reception area why I had come, she directed me to the cashier's window. The cashier attendant asked to see my driver's license, had me sign a waiver of some sort, and then gave me the $200 we put down for bond. I slipped it in my pocket, and we entered the courtroom. Several people were already there. We sat in back. A few minutes later, someone announced the judge's arrival and asked us to rise. We stood as a man entered dressed in a long black robe. Carrying a folder of papers with him, he climbed the steps to the bench and sat down, putting the folder in front of him.

"You may be seated," said the bailiff, who stood beside a long table at the side of the courtroom.

The judge slipped on a pair of glasses and glanced over the papers.

"Is there anyone here in a hurry and would like their case to be first?"

No one said anything. I wanted to get a sense of the judge before my hearing. The judge pulled out a slip of paper and called a man up for a traffic violation. He stood in front of the judge, who sat behind a bench elevated four or five feet. The bailiff read off the charges. The man pleaded guilty and the judge fined him. The judge then called a 17-year-old kid who sauntered to the front of the bench with his head down. As the bailiff read off the charges, the kid looked at the floor. His feet nervously twisted and turned his old work boots. He had hair to the top of his shoulders, and wore a pair of dirty blue jeans and a red plaid flannel shirt that hung below his soiled denim jacket. His charges included disorderly conduct, contributing liquor to minors (two 14-year-old girls) and driving under the influence of alcohol.

"I can't believe what I'm hearing," the judge said. "Do you have any idea the seriousness of your actions?"

The kid jammed his hands into his pockets and continued to keep his head down.

"Young man?" the judge said. The kid shuffled his feet. "Look at me, young man."

The kid glanced up briefly before staring back at the ground.

"I said look at me," the judge demanded in a slow, emphatic voice.

He finally looked up as the judge leaned forward and glared into his face. Standing eight to 10 feet away from the judge, the kid now seemed unable to disengage eye contact.

"You were not only endangering your own life," the judge bellowed as he spoke slowly and distinctly, "but contributing to the delinquency of two young girls and putting them in a perilous situation. And, that's not even considering the potential for destruction and mayhem you could have brought to innocent people who might have been driving along that highway."

The kid, who had been standing perfectly still and gaping at the judge, swayed slightly as his body trembled.

"Are you listening to what I am saying, young man?" the judge asked in a severe and threatening tone.

The kid's tremors turned into uncontrollable shaking. He took a step back to keep from falling.

"Yes, sir."

In one swift motion the kid's left hand brought a cigarette from his pocket to his mouth as his right hand snapped into life a burning flame from a lighter. The kid moved so quickly that he had taken in his first huge inhalation of smoke before the judge could react.

"What do you think your doing?" the judge screamed as he stood up. "You don't smoke in my courtroom."

The kid blew out the smoke in his lungs. He rapidly moved the cigarette from his left hand to his right and raised the front of his boot as he prepared to drop the cigarette and squash it out on the floor.

"Don't you dare drop that cigarette on the floor!" the judge screamed in a hurried flow of syllables. "Somebody get him an ashtray. Who is representing this young man?"

A gentleman about 30 years old and dressed in a suit sat at a table near the bailiff with his hand on his forehead. He slowly pushed his chair back and stood up. A police officer approached the young man with an ashtray.

"Please remove your client from this courtroom until you receive further word from me," the judge said.

The kid snuffed the cigarette in the ashtray as the police officer took him by the arm and guided him toward the back of the room. The kid's body and lips trembled as he walked past us. The lawyer met him in the back of the room, and the officer held a swinging door open to let them out. The judge sat down, still visibly upset as he shook his head back and forth. He shuffled through the papers and then stopped.

"Will Bryce Yarborough please come forward."

A sick feeling churned in the pit of my stomach. I regretted not going first. Brent and I sat in the next to the last row. I stood up, walked to the bench and looked up at the judge who appeared ominous and powerful as he peered down at me. The bailiff read off the charges.

"Bryce Edward Yarborough, a United States citizen from the city of Columbia in the state of Missouri," barked the bailiff, reading from a piece of paper, "is charged with the transportation of contraband materials across the international border separating the United States of America and the province of Alberta, Canada. The materials found, either in the vehicle owned by the subject here named, or found on the person here named, includes narcotic paraphernalia, eight grams of hashish and a quantity of marijuana weighing not more than one ounce."

After a slight pause, the judge spoke. "Mr. Yarborough, how do you plead?"

"What he said may be true," I began, "but the charges sound a lot worse..."

"Mr. Yarborough," the judge interrupted me, "for a number of years we've had U.S. citizens transporting narcotics across the border and selling them to Canadians. It has contributed to the disruption and corruption of our towns and cities. Unfortunately, it does not appear to be getting any better. Do you have anything to say for yourself?"

"Well, yes," I said. "From the amount of hash and pot we had, it should be apparent we barely had enough for our own use. All we wanted to do was go to Banff and Jasper and hike back into the wilderness to get away from it all. We had no intentions of socializing with Canadians, much less selling them drugs."

"If I understand correctly," the judge spoke up before I could go on, "some states in the United States have become more lenient on the use of marijuana and its related substances, but Missouri is not one of those states, is it?"

The way he pronounced the state made it sound like "misery."

"No, it's not," I said, "but I'm on my way to Oregon where..."

"Under these circumstances," the judge interrupted me again, "I think a two hundred dollar fine is appropriate. Do you have two hundred dollars, Mr. Yarborough?"

His question made me mad. He knew bond had been posted at $200.

"What happens if I don't have the money?"

"What do you mean what happens if you don't have the money?" he responded in an incredulous tone, the bridge of his nose and forehead wrinkling up like the end of a large white raisin.

"Well, what will happen?"

"You'll be under my custody," he replied sternly, glaring at me.

"What would you do?"

"What do you mean what would I do?" he asked, raising his voice again and squinting as he tilted his head slightly.

"What would you do to me?"

"I'd throw you in jail," he said pointedly, leaning back in his chair and crossing his arms.

I turned around toward Brent in the back of the room. "Do you think I should..." I started to say to Brent before the judge interrupted.

"If you don't have the money, Mr. Yarborough," the judge blurted out, which caused me to turn around and look at him, "you'll stay in jail until you get the money."

The judge sat up straight and put his forearms on the bench in front of him. I couldn't believe what he said. That meant if I had no money, I would be in jail for the rest of my life. The look on my face must have asked the question that I thought.

"If you don't have the money," the judge continued, speaking slower and in a lower voice, "you'll just have to wire for the money."

"Who am I suppose to wire?" I asked, "the president of the United States?"

The judge's face flushed as he leaned forward. He appeared ready to hit me. I reached into my pocket and withdrew the $200. I walked to the bench and held it up to him.

"Here's your two hundred dollars," I said.

"You don't pay me!" the judge exclaimed. "You pay the cashier. And you're not leaving until you pay. Is that clear?"

"Where do I pay?" I asked in a softer and more submissive tone.

"Right through that door," he said with restraint in his voice as he pointed to an exit behind the bailiff.

As I walked through the door, I saw Brent get up and head out the back of the courtroom. Once the cashier had my money, she gave me a copy of the papers I signed at the police station the day before.

"You will need to give these documents to the officer at the border upon your departure," she said. "According to these papers, you must leave the country immediately from the nearest departure point, which is at the border crossing near Waterton Lakes. Is that clear?"

I nodded. She had me sign two more forms. Once outside the courthouse, I felt much better.

"You had a lot of nerve," Brent said as we got in the car. "I thought the judge was going to throw something at you. What were you trying to do?"

"I figured we might be able to get our money back if I spent a few days in jail, but I don't think the judge and I were on the same wavelength."

After looking at my Atlas road map, I decided to leave Canada through a different exit than written on the exit papers. In relation to Oregon, I would be going the wrong direction via Waterton, and without the extra $100 for gas, I needed to conserve every dollar. Brent questioned my decision.

"If you don't feel comfortable continuing with me," I said, "I understand. And if you're going to Kansas, it might be shorter for you to return the way we came. But I'm on my way to Oregon by the shortest route possible. Whatever exit I choose, they're not going to send me back to the one written on this piece of paper."

Brent stuck with me. As we camped that night in Canada, I felt like a fugitive. Sitting beside the campfire, I imagined the life of an outlaw—leery of everyone and careful not to stand out in a crowd. They had no photo of me, however, only fingerprints. So unless they arrested me on a different violation and matched up fingerprints, I was just another U.S. citizen among some 300 million. The next day, I drove a few miles under the speed limit and paid close attention to my driving. I didn't want to get stopped for a traffic violation that could worsen an already bad situation. We crossed the border on Highway 95 at Kingsgate. After handing the officer the papers, I explained to him that this exit was closer to where I wanted to go. He had me enter the station where I signed a release paper of some sort. It basically stated that I had left the country.

That evening Brent and I drank a few beers in Spokane, Washington, as a farewell gesture. Brent asked if he could keep my carbon copy of the bust and exit papers.

"Why?"

"As a souvenir," he said.

I smiled. "Sure."

I had no use for the papers, and in fact they could become a liability if I were stopped and another officer found them. When I dropped Brent off beside a highway the next day, it crossed my mind that he could use the papers to blackmail me. The thought made me laugh. I might have cared if I were someone with something to lose.

The Perfect Farm

I spent three weeks in Portland, Oregon, with Hank, a long-time friend who also served as best man at my wedding. We hadn't seen each other since that day. After fishing with him every weekend and looking for a job during the week, I felt it necessary to either start paying rent or move on. With a little more than $100 in my pocket, I asked Hank if I could leave my car in front of his house. I gave him the keys and told him to use the car as he wished.

"If I'm not back by this time next year," I said, "the car is yours."

During our last weekend together, we drove along the Columbia River to Astoria. We reminisced about a hunting incident that happened five years earlier. We were both 18 and bow hunting for deer in southern Missouri. We crossed a field, came over a hill and saw an enormous steer with large horns glaring at us. The huge bull held his head high, sniffing the air. He took a few steps toward us and stopped.

"What should we do?" Hank asked me out of the corner of his mouth.

I looked around. About 40 yards to our right ran a barbed-wire fence.

"Let's move slowly toward the fence," I whispered, motioning my head in that direction.

As we crept cautiously, not taking our eyes off the beast, the steer took a few menacing steps toward us and shook his head as he snorted.

"I don't know about you," Hank whispered, "but I'm running for it."

"No!" I commanded softly, but too late. Hank dashed away from me as fast as he could run.

I glanced at the steer as I too darted toward the fence behind Hank. The beast charged after us.

"He's coming!" I yelled to Hank. Hank's bow flew in the air above him as he dove head first over the fence. I could hear hooves pounding the earth behind me. I too threw my bow over the fence and dove, curling as I hit the ground and rolled onto my back to end up in a seated position. The rickety old fence certainly lacked the strength to stop the steer if he chose to go through it. Fortunately, he stopped, snorted, and then turned around and trotted back into the field with his head and horns held high. Safe behind the fence, we burst out laughing. We laughed again recalling the hunting excursion. It felt like it happened yesterday.

About midafternoon just south of Seaside, Hank let me out on Highway 101. I planned to visit San Francisco, southern California and then return to Missouri, about a 2,600-mile hitchhiking excursion. Standing beside the road with my backpack, guitar and leather wine flask, I watched Hank drive away. He honked his horn and waved out the window. As his car disappeared down the road, a strange sense of freedom overcame me. It brought a mixture of exhilaration and fear. Until that point in my life, I had lived surrounded by either family, friends, school, a home or an apartment. After leaving Columbia, my car—which I had owned for five years—became my major anchor. I now had no car. My security blankets were gone.

I stood there quite a while before taking out a harmonica and blowing a blues rift to keep me company. Eventually, an elderly man stopped and gave me my first ride. He wasn't very talkative, so I looked out the window and enjoyed the scenery.

The old man let me out in Tillamook where I finally caught a ride to Newport by a businessman driving a sports car and wearing a suit. He dropped me off at the southern end of Newport next to a small grocery store. I bought a box of vanilla wafers and a quart of milk for dinner. I sat outside the store and savored my treat. Sunset was about an hour away.

"Hello," someone said. "I looked up to see a guy about my age carrying a backpack with a sleeping bag strapped to it. His sandy-brown hair barely covered his ears. "Where are you going?" he asked with a distinct British accent.

"San Francisco," I replied. "How about you?"

He sat on the step beside me and slipped his arms out of his pack. "San Francisco. Are you traveling alone?"

"Yeah. Where are you from?"

"Leeds, Yorkshire." He paused slightly. "It's in England."

"That's cool," I said. "How long have you been in the United States?"

"This is my second day."

"Well welcome. My name's Bryce." I held out my hand.

Karl had flown to Montreal, Canada, a month earlier. He crossed Canada by train to Vancouver, British Columbia, where he visited relatives. He spent one night in a Seattle youth hostel before leaving early that morning for California. I shared my vanilla wafers with him as we talked.

"Are you going to camp tonight?" He asked as he tossed a vanilla wafer into his mouth.

"You bet. Hotel's are too expensive for me. I've got a good sleeping bag. How about you?"

"Camping sounds good. Are you going to camp around here?"

"No," I said. "There's still time to catch another ride."

"Would you like to travel together?"

"Sure," I said, "if you want to."

I figured if we had trouble catching a ride we could split up later.

"These are good," he said, tossing another wafer into his mouth. "Thank you."

Within ten minutes two men in a pickup stopped. We jumped into the empty truck bed and got settled. After we had been traveling for a while, I smelled marijuana burning. The two men were sharing a joint. The driver saw me look at them and smiled. Several minutes later he knocked on the cab window. We turned around.

"You guys want to finish this off?" he yelled.

I nodded my head, and he held the remainder of the joint out the window. I grabbed it and took a big hit, then handed it to Karl. A pickup with a camper top approached us from the rear. By the time I had taken my second hit and handed the joint back to Karl, the camper shortened its distance to three car lengths away. The blonde-haired girl driving smiled as she bounced up and down to music. We waved, and she waved back. The driver knocked on the cab window again.

"This is my turnoff," he yelled as he began to slow down.

There were eight or 10 hitchhikers standing in a row at the intersection. I turned back to the girl behind us and motioned that we were getting out, then gave the hitchhiking sign and pointed at her. She nodded affirmatively.

"Cool," I said to Karl. "I think we've got us a ride."

We pulled over and she pulled in behind us. The other hitchhikers saw us get out of one truck and climb into the camper.

"Jesus," said one hitchhiker about 20 feet away, "someone must be looking out for you guys."

Bonnie, an Arizona schoolteacher on vacation, picked us up because she saw us smoking the joint. She was disappointed when neither Karl nor I had any pot. She also picked up a guy and a girl at that same intersection and let them ride in the back of her camper. When Bonnie told us it was her 26th birthday, we stopped and purchased wine to celebrate. That evening, while camping near the Oregon Dunes National Recreation Area, we drank wine and ate hot canned beef stew. Karl also played guitar, so between us, we filled the night with songs.

Eager to get to San Francisco, Karl and I declined Bonnie's invitation to visit Crater Lake National Park with her. She gave us a ride to Highway 5. By late that afternoon, we arrived in San Francisco.

Awestruck and captured by San Francisco's grandeur, I told Karl I had to walk the Golden Gate Bridge before it got dark. He wanted to join me. We checked into the Embarcadero YMCA for the night and left our backpacks. We made it to the bridge in time to catch the sunset.

"I've heard on the news that people have jumped off this bridge," I said. We both looked down. It had to be about a 1000 feet to the bay's surface.

"Did any of them survive?" Karl asked.

"I guess one guy did. I wonder what he thought on his way down."

"Life is short," Karl said. "It seems foolish to throw it away."

"I agree," I said, thinking about the times I nearly threw my life away during my marriage breakup.

The first time I almost ended my life was the day after Melanie told me she had met someone else. She quickly left for work early that morning to avoid a confrontation. Not having slept all night, I pretended to be asleep when she awoke. I feared losing her, and at the same time felt devastated, hurt and angry.

How could Melanie do this to me? How could she even consider another man? She was my friend, my lover, and the woman who said she wanted to bear my children. The woman I planned to grow old with. The woman who knew me better than anyone else in the world. My wife, for better or worse, "till death do us part."

I could not leave our apartment and attend classes that day. Crying, I kept asking myself over and over, "Why me, God?" I wanted God to end my life and the suffering.

By late afternoon, I stumbled out of the apartment drunk and stoned. With tears streaming down my face, I descended the back stairway toward the driveway leading to a four-lane thoroughfare called Providence Road. It must have been close to 5 p.m. because all four lanes were filled with cars. With glazed eyes, I entered the driveway. I planned to cross Providence Road, traffic or no traffic. My rage and intoxicated mind told me to clear the path by kicking the massive tons of polluting steel off the road. I knew I would lose, but I welcomed defeat.

As I approached the thoroughfare, a man ran toward me from the other side of the road. He hopped out into the middle of the first two lanes of traffic and literally dodged cars before making his way to the center of the street. I stopped walking and watched him. That guy must be crazy, I thought. He edged out to the middle of the second two lanes and—after a car zoomed by— darted across the last lane and headed straight toward me. I recognized him. It was Sten, a college classmate.

Sten and I took the same philosophy course the previous year. On the last day of class, after our final, we discussed the purpose of life. I hadn't seen Sten since our conversation that day. I faked a cough into my hands and wiped away my tears as discreetly as possible.

"Hey, how are you doing?" he said, genuinely happy to see me. "Long time no see." He slapped me on the shoulder, and then slid his hand to my upper arm and gave it a gentle shake. Anyone viewing the greeting would have thought we'd known each other for years. It even felt that way.

I smiled and mumbled I was fine.

"I live just down the street," he said. "Since I saw you last, I got married. Come on." He guided me by the arm toward a long grassy embankment. "Let's grab some tea at my place and talk. It's just down the hill."

Sten made cinnamon-spice tea, and we talked about our classes. I kept asking him questions so he would do most of the talking. I never mentioned Melanie, and Sten didn't ask about her. If he sensed problems, he didn't show it. I turned my cup up and swallowed the last gulp of tea.

"Would you like another cup?"

"No thanks. I really need to get going," I lied.

"Now you know where I live," Sten said, taking the cup from my hands. "Come down and visit when Michelle's here. I know she'd love to meet you." Sten set the cups on the kitchen counter, then reached out and firmly shook my hand. "You're always welcome here."

"Thanks," I said. "We're neighbors now. I'm sure we'll see each other around."

It was the last time I saw Sten. He never knew that he probably saved my life.

"Are you okay?" Karl asked, as cars whizzed along behind us on the Golden Gate Bridge's multiple lanes.

"Yeah, I was just spacing out a little."

The next day, Friday, Karl and I visited several art galleries before venturing into San Francisco's Golden Gate Park. The 1,000-acre park impressed us both. After walking through two museums, viewing the aquarium and attending a planetarium presentation, we sat in the park playing my guitar and singing songs. Within a few minutes, a guy and a girl stopped and stood beside us. After Karl finished a song, they both clapped.

"Can we listen?" the girl asked.

Karl handed me the guitar. "Sure," I said. "I'm Bryce and this is Karl."

"I'm Jean and this is Ray," the girl said as they sat down.

I played a song by the Ozark Mountain Daredevils. They clapped at the end of the song and asked us where we were from. After we talked for several minutes, they told us they lived in a house with a bunch of writers and musicians who came from all over the world. Although neither of them played music, they said they were poets.

"Would you guys like to come over and have dinner with us?" Jean asked.

I looked at Karl. "Sure. It sounds like you guys are a lot like us. When?"

"How about tonight? Some other people are already coming over."

"That sounds great," Karl said, looking at me. "We have no plans."

Jean took out a piece of paper and wrote down the address and telephone number before telling us how to get there. "We'll expect you around 6:30," she said as they both stood up. "See you then."

Karl and I spent more time in the park before returning to the YMCA. After taking showers, we walked to the address Jean gave us. A girl about our age answered the door. When I asked for Jean and Ray, she invited us in. People filled the hallway, a front room and the dining room. It was a large, two-story house. Most people already had a plate of food and stood around eating and visiting.

"Hi," Jean said, emerging from the living room area. Ray followed behind her. "Did you have trouble finding the house?"

I smiled. "No. You gave good directions."

"Come on. Let's get something to eat. Are you hungry?"

"Sure. That sounds great."

Jean led us to a room off the kitchen where we filled our plates with salad, a rice and bean dish, and rolls. We moved to a corner in the living room and ate.

"How many people live here?" Karl asked.

"Eleven people. We have a few guests from the farm."

"What farm's that?" I asked.

"It's a retreat center," she said. "We call it the Perfect Farm. We're going to show some slides of it a little later. But tell me, how long have you guys been traveling together?"

Jean proceeded to ask us about ourselves and why we were traveling. Ray remained fairly quiet, but he always seemed interested in the conversation. About 8 o'clock, a man announced that a slide show would begin in five minutes. Everyone crowded into the living room.

The presentation began with a distant view of mountain foothills.

"In these mountains a few hours north of here," the man making the presentation said, "we have a beautiful, peaceful mountain retreat."

As the man spoke, the slides progressed from an overview to more specific shots of people swimming in a small pond, picking fruit in an orchard and working in a large garden. The people, who all appeared to be between 20 and 30 years old, were often leaning on each other with big smiles on their faces. The man talked about the camaraderie and how the "Perfect Farm" was self-sufficient. The slideshow took about 15 minutes and ended with a distant shot of the farm and the hills around it.

"If you want to visit the farm, we would like to invite all of you out for the weekend," the moderator said as someone turned on the light. "It's about two hours north of here. We have a bus that will be leaving around nine-thirty this evening. All you need is clothing, a few personal items and a sleeping bag. We'll bring you back at the end of the day Sunday. How many of you are interested in going?"

More than half the group raised their hands. I looked at Karl.

"What do you think?" he asked.

"It sounds really cool, but we've already paid at the YMCA. Besides, I wouldn't want to leave my things there."

"Are you traveling with backpacks?" Jean asked.

We nodded.

"And my guitar," I added.

"Maybe we can pick up your things in the mini-bus," Jean said. "I think they're planning to take it to the farm this weekend. If so, we could probably all ride up together."

"You guys are planning to go to the farm too?" I asked Jean.

"Ray and I usually go there for the weekend."

Karl looked at me. "Do you want to go?"

"It sounds like a great time."

Jean got up. "Let me find out if we can get the mini-bus," she said.

"It's a neat place," Ray said after Jean left. "And the food's fresh too. It's all grown right there on the farm. You guys will really like it. You'll meet other writers and musicians from all over the world."

The more Ray talked, the better it sounded. Jean returned and said we could get the mini-bus, but not until 10 o'clock. By 10:30 we were back at the YMCA to pick up our things. At 11 p.m. we drove out of San Francisco. The mini-bus, basically an elongated van, held 12 people comfortably. There were 10 of us all together. Two guys sat in front to drive. They drove to Highway 101 and turned north.

For the first hour on the road, we sang songs by the Beatles and the Eagles, and sang in three parts "Row Your Boat." By 12:30 everyone curled up in their seat with their sleeping bag. I sat in the back of the van too wired to sleep. We got off the freeway and took a two-lane highway. The stars were brilliant. Their sparkling lights looked as if they were dipping in and out of the hills as the van swayed around each curve.

"Are you sleepy?" I heard the man in the front seat ask the driver.

"No. These curves keep you awake."

We rode a long way in silence before I finally felt the van slow down and make a turn. We stopped in front of a 12 to 15-foot-high fence with a large gate. My heart leaped. It looked like a prison gate. The front-seat passenger got out and unlocked it. I looked at Karl next to me. He was asleep. In fact, everyone was asleep except the driver, his copilot and me. After we drove into the compound, I looked through the back window and watched the copilot close and lock the gate, and then saunter back to the van. I thought we might have just entered a work camp and was horrified. We drove about half-a-mile before we stopped again.

"This is it," the driver announced. "Rise and shine."

Everybody raised their heads and stared out the window. The parking area held several cars, a large white bus and the mini-bus.

"We have to walk from here. It's not far, maybe a hundred yards."

It seemed unwise to say anything to Karl about the fence until we were alone. If this turned out to be some kind of slave-labor camp, acknowledgment of my suspicions might cause problems.

"Be sure to get everything out of the mini-bus," the driver said. "We'll be taking it back to San Francisco early tomorrow. Also, once we get to our sleeping quarters, the girls will sleep in the building to the left and the guys will be on the right. Bathrooms are in the center. Be as quiet as possible. Those who came earlier are already asleep."

We passed two trailers before arriving at our destination. After using the restrooms, we entered our sleeping quarters, which turned out to be cleaned chicken coups with old wood floors. A group of guys were already asleep in sleeping bags on one side of the room. Ray had the only flashlight and guided us to a spot to spread out our bags. Once we were settled, he whispered good night.

With Ray sleeping beside us, I had no chance to say anything to Karl. At the break of dawn, after a sleepless night, I slipped out of my sleeping bag and quietly left the building. I hiked to the top of a hill overlooking the grounds. It all looked and felt very peaceful. As the sun rose, people slowly came out of the buildings to use the restrooms. From the hilltop, I could see two valleys. A crew of 20 to 25 people walked along a road leading to the valley farthest from our sleeping quarters. They were singing and carrying tools that appeared to be shovels and hoes. They eventually disappeared around the hillside.

Near the two dormitory chicken coups directly below me, a man encouraged people to join him in exercising. Although I could hear his voice, I couldn't make out the words he said. People lined up and followed his direction. He rotated his arms one way, then the other way. He did torso twists to the right eight or 10 times, then reversed and twisted to the left. Everything seemed tranquil and serene. My fear and paranoia from the previous night faded. Even if my fears were true—that this place turned out to be a work camp of some sort—it would be easy to hike out if necessary.

I closed my eyes and took in a deep breath. A breeze rolled through the trees and gently ruffled my hair. From the valley below came the muffled sounds of the man directing more exercises. With my back relaxed against a huge bolder, my attention calmly settled onto the wind that periodically wafted through the trees and over the rocks around me. The short meditative reprieve on the hillside provided a welcome rejuvenation after the sleepless night.

Upon my descent to the camping area, I slipped and fell, cutting my right hand. It wasn't a serious cut, but it hurt nonetheless. I no longer believed in accidents, so it made me wonder about the significance of the incident. During my last two years at the university, I had become interested in dream analysis. In my study of dream symbols, hands represented purpose, while blood stood for life force. What's my purpose for being here, I wondered, and how does it relate to the life force within me? Upon nearing the chicken coup, a hand on my shoulder startled me.

"Bryce, I was worried about you this morning."

I turned to find Ray beside me.

"Is everything okay?"

"It's fine," I said. "I took a morning hike to get some exercise. Unfortunately, I slipped and cut myself."

I looked at my hand. Ray took a step closer to see it.

"That's a nasty cut," he said. "There's a first-aid kit in the trailer. Let's put something on it."

Ray moved toward a path leading to the trailers as I followed him. "You really shouldn't be hiking in the mountains around here, especially by yourself. It can be dangerous."

His comment amused me. The thought of the hills being dangerous struck me as funny. After applying some hydrogen peroxide and a band-aid to the cut, we joined the others for breakfast. We ate granola mixed with sliced apples and raisins. Everyone stood outside visiting. Later, we were directed to one of the larger buildings, which served as a lecture and entertainment hall. There were a lot of us, maybe 80 to 100, sitting in rows on benches. A male moderator, who appeared to be 28 to 30 years old, stood up and gave us an oral agenda.

"You will be joining a group of about twelve or thirteen people, and that will be your team for the weekend," he said. "There will be three meals a day, and lights go out at eleven. We'll wake you up at seven sharp each morning for some exercises. Men and women will continue to use separate sleeping quarters, and drugs are strictly prohibited. During the day, your team will be involved in discussions, and to get a little exercise, teams will play each other in some easy and fun games. We'll all regroup for meals and lectures. We know it's a big farm, but don't worry about getting lost. A person will be assigned to each of you to answer any questions and help you find your way around. Now, I'd like to introduce you to our first group lecturer, Noah."

Noah gave a 20 to 30-minute talk about the disintegration of the world and its movement toward greater and greater chaos. It reminded me of a church sermon, except Noah wore blue jeans and a Polo shirt. He ended his talk by discussing truth and the power of love. Everybody applauded when he finished.

Ray became my partner, and Jean hooked up with Karl. They led us outside to a large tree where we met with eight other people. The leader of our group, an attractive young woman, appeared very confident, genuine and full of energy. We all sat in a circle beneath a huge Eucalyptus tree.

"Welcome everyone," she said. "We're going to have lots of fun for the next two days, and at the same time receive important information that can radically change your life for the better. The first thing I would like for us to do is to get to know one another a little. We'll go around the circle and let everyone say a few words. Start by giving your name and where you're from, and then talk a little about yourself: like schools you've attended, jobs you've held, what you're doing now, what's important to you in life, and anything else you would like to share."

Once everyone spoke, we discussed what was said in the lecture concerning the state of the world. My fears of a work camp subsided quickly. The people in my group, at least the ones who had come for the weekend, were like me. They were searching for life's purpose and their roles in it.

After eating lunch, we joined the other groups in a large open area where we played each other in dodge ball. Each group had a slogan or saying they used for inspiration, such as "God is love" and "The truth shall set you free." Everyone chanted their slogan as one team threw the ball to hit and eliminate members of the team inside the circle. The games stimulated a lot of energy and enthusiasm.

Later that afternoon, we had another lecture followed by discussion within our small groups. Our group leader told us that the evening program would host a talent show for those who wanted to participate. We were encouraged to put on a skit, recite a poem or sing a song. Karl and I said we'd each play the guitar and sing a song.

Before the evening lecture, a rock band played some music, and we sang popular songs, but altered the words slightly. For instance, we sang "Blowing In The Wind" by Bob Dylan, except instead of singing "the answer is blowing in the wind," we sang "the answer is in the hearts of men." After the lecture, the talent show took place around a campfire. There were some very talented people in the group. Although the bulk of the show consisted of people playing guitars and singing, there were also a few skits and poems recited. After each presentation, whether good or not, we all vigorously applauded. I felt nervous when I sang my song. In fact, I forgot the third verse, so I repeated the first verse.

After the show, one of the leaders asked people to stand up and say what they thought about the "Perfect Farm." Everyone who spoke said how wonderful it was to be around such high-energy people who were interested in the true nature of man and God. Although I didn't stand up, I felt the same way. Everyone was friendly and smiled a lot. Ray and Jean were perfect hosts. They always served drinks and food to Karl and me first before helping themselves. Ray's constant presence did bother me a little. He only left my side when one of us had to use the bathroom.

To sum up the themes of the lectures and discussion, it would be love—Christ's main message to the world—and serving God through exercising our divine nature. I viewed the group as a strong Christian commune with strict morals. For the most part, these were the same values and beliefs I grew up with. But here on this "Perfect Farm," people were trying to live their religion every day instead of one day a week.

The next morning a guy playing his guitar and singing, "You Are My Sunshine," awakened us. Ray and a few others chanted, "Rise and shine everyone. It's another beautiful California day." After breakfast, Ray and Jean asked Karl and me to go for a short walk. "What do you guys think of the farm?" Jean asked while walking along a path leading to a grove of trees.

"Seems cool to me," I replied. "There's a lot of positive energy here."

"I agree," Karl said. "I've never experienced anything quite like this."

"You guys are both very creative," Jean said. "You fit in here. I loved the songs you played last night." She looked at Ray.

"Yes," Ray said. "It sounded great. We're really glad you came."

"Thanks for inviting us," I said.

"Would you guys like to stay longer?" Jean asked.

I looked at Karl.

"We'd like to invite you to stay for the week," she continued. "We have some guest lecturers coming in that I think you'll really enjoy." She looked at me, and then Karl.

"What do you think?" Karl asked me.

"It's been cool so far, and we've met a lot of nice people."

"We'll be doing a lot of the same things we've already been doing," Jean added, "but for a couple of hours each day we'll all pitch in and either work some in the fields or the orchard. That's how we keep food on the table. Actually, the work is fun because we do it as a group. It's a chance to sing songs and tell stories."

"I've got no problem with helping out," I said.

Karl looked at me. "I think I'd like to stay."

"Me too."

Jean smiled. "Great. The only stipulation is that you stay for the full week. We want you to hear all the lectures and not just stay a few days and then leave. Is that okay?"

"Sure," Karl said.

"I'm on no time schedule," I added.

"You'll be glad you stayed," Jean said. "We have a lot more to share with you. We have a sign-up sheet for those who decide to stay. It just states that you've agreed to stay the full week."

Later that afternoon, about a third of the people returned to San Francisco. During the evening discussion, the leader announced that there would be new groups for the week. Karl and I were separated, but retained our same personal hosts—Jean and Ray. There were fewer participants than before, so the groups were smaller—eight to nine people per group. The routine remained the same as during the weekend, except for a few hours a day we would either help prepare a meal, wash dishes, pick up around the compound, or work hoeing the fields. While working, we'd talk about lecture topics, discuss personal relationships or problems, and sing songs. Jean was right. It turned out to be fun. In addition, group leaders rotated. We had one group leader for a day or two, and then a different leader took over. Ray's constant presence at my side, however, continued.

Once, when Ray had to use the bathroom, I took a short hike to relax and enjoy some solitude. After returning an hour later, Ray found me. He asked me to refrain from wandering off. I laughed and told him not to worry about it, and that even if we got separated, we'd surely run into each other eventually. He agreed, but asked me not to do it again.

Because the size of the whole group had decreased, we all ate together in a doublewide trailer where we took off our shoes and sat on the floor. Occasionally, during an evening lecture, visitors would join us. Two new girls with huge smiles and sparkling eyes came to one of the lectures. They looked high on drugs to me. After that night, I never saw them again. Also, several Germans visited the second day of the week. They looked scared and paranoid. I figured they saw the tall fence at the farm's entrance. I asked Ray about it. He said they installed it to keep unwelcome people out.

"There are some people who don't agree with what we're doing here at the Perfect Farm," Ray said. "When you are doing God's work, there is always an evil element that tries to suppress your efforts. It just makes us stronger."

The lectures and discussion groups were much the same as during the weekend, but in more detail. On several occasions the speakers said they believed in the second coming of Christ, and added that they thought the time was at hand for his return. In one group discussion following a lecture, our leader asked us what we thought of the second coming of Christ. I told the group I thought the second coming would be a reawakening of a higher consciousness within each of us. Although the leader said she believed that too, she also thought Christ would return in the flesh.

Within three to four days, I felt ready to leave the farm. I had nothing against their teachings, but their beliefs seemed limited to me. For instance, in one of our discussions, I asked about higher planes of existence and out-of-body experiences.

"There is heaven and there is Earth," our leader said. "As above, so below, which means they are directly connected. Satan has many forms, and one of them is to create the illusion of separateness."

"Have you ever had an out-of-body experience?" I asked the leader.

"I have not, and I'm glad. It's the work of the devil."

"I've had one, and I don't think it's evil. I think it's a natural progression of one's spiritual growth."

"That's an interesting thought," she said. "Why don't we talk about it later, maybe during lunch. We have quite a bit to cover today, and I'm afraid we won't get through it all if we divert to unrelated topics too frequently."

We never got back to the topic. Later in the week, the group sat around a campfire one night, and once again we were asked to stand up and say what we thought of the farm. As before, every statement came out enthusiastically positive.

One guy, a talented musician and singer, stood up and said, "When I first came here, I thought this place was a religious cult I'd read about. Now I see that they are seekers like me—people looking for the truth and wanting to make the world a better place."

When he mentioned "religious cult," I noticed two leaders exchange a peculiar glance between one another.

After the campfire gathering that evening, Ray had to use the bathroom. Once again I took the opportunity to explore on my own. Although it was around 10 p.m., a full moon made it easy to follow a path leading into the hills. After walking about half-a-mile, I got a strange feeling that someone was either following me or watching me from a distance. I walked under a huge tree to hide within its shadow. I scanned the area looking for whoever it might be, listening closely for any sounds. The wind gently blew through the trees. The longer I stood there, the more I felt the presence of something.

"Is someone there?" I called out.

No one replied. Instead, an eerie silence remained. Fear grew inside me.

"I know you're there. Do you want to talk to me?"

I looked to the left behind me, and then to the right. I sat down and surveyed the area in front of me for any movement while listening closely for crackling twigs or jostling rocks. I scrutinized every log and shadow for any kind of change or shift. Silence seemed to be my best protection. After what seemed a long time, I concluded that someone wanted to scare me. They had succeeded, and it made me mad.

"Okay, come on out," I said loudly, standing up.

Again, only silence. I walked out from under the tree into the moonlight.

"I'm right here. If you want to mess with me, come on."

No response. I got even madder.

"What are you afraid of?" I yelled.

I stood there waiting, prepared to challenge who or whatever lurked in the shadows. Strangely enough, the intense fear I felt moments earlier transformed into feelings of strength and sureness. Confronting whatever it was caused it to leave. From the distant hills came the sound of a dog barking. I wondered if the dog sensed a passing presence. Upon returning to the lodging area, I saw Ray talking to one of the group leaders.

"There you are, Ray," I said, walking up to him and gently slapping his back. His concerned look made me laugh. "You keep running off every time I go to the bathroom. What am I going to do with you?"

My comment made Ray smile and shake his head.

"Where'd you go this time?" he asked.

"Up into the hills to meditate a while."

I told them about my experience.

"That's the reason we don't like people wandering off by themselves," the group leader said. "There are beings who don't want us to succeed here."

"You think it could have been an evil spirit?" I asked.

"Yes. Satan works in many ways. He'll do whatever he can to disrupt what we have going. If you want to go for a walk in the hills, go with someone. Ray would be glad to go with you."

"Anytime," Ray said. "Just let me know."

I nodded. "Sounds good."

On Friday, more people came in from San Francisco for the weekend. During the week, we had been told about a special guest lecturer that might speak Saturday evening. A man in his 40s gave the lecture. He talked about service to God and your neighbor while having complete faith in the Heavenly Father. He seemed to say that if you are a Christian, live a Christian life every day and adhere to such things as the Golden Rule. He also performed by dancing to a classical piece of music. Although he appeared 30 pounds overweight, he danced quite gracefully.

The next day, Ray and one of the group leaders—a girl who led our small group for several days—said they'd like to talk to me. We walked away from the main lodge and sat beneath a tree.

"Everyone here really likes you, Bryce," she said. "You're very energetic and enthusiastic, which are wonderful qualities. In addition, you have...well I guess you could call it a calmness or gentleness. You seem to really welcome life, and that's good. We've enjoyed your participation and willingness to share with us. Now tell me, what do you think of the farm?"

"Everyone I've met has been great. You've got a neat place here. I think your teachings help people learn about brotherly love, and that's really needed in the world today. It's the same message Christ came to give."

"That's exactly what we're trying to do," she said, "but in a week's time you can only cover so many things. We have a lot more we'd like to share with you. We want to invite you to stay longer and attend our three-week program. The program gives you an opportunity to explore in greater depth some of the divine principles we have to offer. It also gives you a chance to learn about the divine love you spoke about, and to serve God. The only thing we ask is that you stay the whole three weeks, and not leave after a week or two. For the most part, you'll be following a similar routine that you've been doing for the past week. There will be lectures and discussions, some cleaning or work around the farm, and then recreational time. What do you think?"

She put her hand on my knee and gently shook it like a sister. A part of me wanted to stay. In addition to receiving three meals a day at the Perfect Farm, people were positive, cheerful, full of love and committed to making the world a better place. Yet, another part of me felt the need to leave. After all, my journey had begun only three months earlier. I still had much to see and learn. Also, their talks about Satan and the evils of the world disturbed me. It reminded me of religious scare tactics discussed during a world religion course I took at the university. Another important part of my life revolved around music. During the past week, my guitar sat idle most of the time. Something inside me felt left behind and unexpressed.

"You're really nice," I said to the leader, "and Ray's been a perfect host. In fact, everyone I've met here has been super, but I think it's time for me to go. I really appreciate all you've done for me and the sharing of Christian love."

For several moments, no one said anything.

"You know, if you leave, it won't be the same out there as it was before you came here," she said. "At the farm, you've had a taste of what the world can be. Unfortunately, it's not like that out on the streets. Some of the things we teach can help protect you. Three weeks is not a very long time when you look at the benefits."

Her words made sense. What's three weeks out of a lifetime? Yet, a strong inner voice moved me to speak.

"You might be right, and maybe I'll regret my decision later, but I really feel it's time to go."

"Come on," she said, getting up. "You don't have to decide right now. Think about it. Lunch should be ready soon. Enjoy a good meal first, and then let me know what you've decided. Why don't you and Ray go on over to the dining hall. I'll catch up with you."

During lunch, Ray spoke about what he had learned since he first attended a Perfect Farm seminar some 10 months earlier. Ray was a soft-spoken, gentle person. As he talked, I looked over the group and the grounds.

The Perfect Farm was ideal if you didn't like children or old people. It contained a utopia of 18 to 35-year-olds: a positive and high-energy place for physical, emotional and spiritual stimulation. My study of other religions and metaphysics made the Perfect Farm less than fulfilling for me. My promise to stay a full week became the major reason I remained for seven days. Otherwise, I would have left after three or four.

Once we had eaten, Sara, a different group leader, approached Ray and me.

"Hi Bryce. Hello Ray." She put her hand on my shoulder. "Are you staying for the three-week group session?" she asked.

I liked Sara. Besides being attractive and intelligent, she had lots of enthusiasm and energy. Although she never led my group, we spoke to each other several times.

"I think I'm going to move on."

She looked into my eyes. "Is that what you really want to do? You seem to fit in here."

Her large and soft brown eyes seemed to reach out and hug me.

"There are a lot of places I still want to see," I said slowly, "and I've had no time to work on my music since I've been here."

"Come on," she said, taking my hand. "We'll be back in a little while, Ray." She pulled me toward a path leading to one of the white trailers on the hillside. "Your decision to stay or leave will make a huge difference in the rest of your life," she said. "Before you make your final choice, I'd like you to talk to a few people."

Sara knocked on the door of a small white trailer.

"Hi Sara," John said after opening the door. John, one of the lecturers, had spoken several times during the past week. "Come on in."

"John, this is Bryce," she said, as we entered the trailer.

"Sure. Hi Bryce," he said, shaking my hand. "We haven't actually been introduced, but I've seen you around."

"Bryce is not sure whether he wants to stay for the next group session," Sara said, as we slipped off our shoes. Typically, we removed our shoes before entering any of the buildings except the bathroom. Ray told me it was for cleanliness.

Three other people were in the room: a female group leader, along with a girl and a guy who helped as event coordinators at the farm. The man, named Thomas, frequently introduced speakers at the lectures. They joined John to form a semicircle around me.

"Bryce, why don't you begin by telling us why you want to leave?" Sara asked.

"I just feel it's time to move on. Everyone's been really nice to me, and I've learned a lot, but I haven't been meditating, and I've hardly touched my guitar since arriving. I believe music is one of my avenues for expressing spirit."

"You do have a talent for music," said the female group leader at the left side of the semicircle. "I've enjoyed the songs you've played." Her words were sincere. "During the next three-week session, you will have more time to work on your music if that's what you want to do. We each have talents that should be developed in order to serve God, and everyone should follow the calling they feel in their heart. You might be interested in working with some of the other musicians here, like the guys in the band. Have you met any of them yet?"

"No, but..."

"You've only been here for a week," interrupted Thomas standing next to her. "That's really not a lot of time to learn all we have to offer. The world is getting more hectic and chaotic every day. According to the Bible, that's the way it will be before the return of our Lord. Out there in the cities, and even in the rural areas, people are hurting each other—backstabbing whenever it will further their own cause, and disregarding the ways of divine love. You haven't been here long enough for us to share everything with you. We have a lot more we want to teach you. We really care what happens to you, Bryce. Have you felt the love from everyone here? Can you see that we're sincere in wanting to serve God and help our fellowman? Is there really anything more important than that?"

"No, it's just..."

"Bryce, you know what it's like out there," said the female coordinator standing beside Thomas. "It's a world filled with hatred. Here we can join forces and become strong with the power of love in our hearts. We have the chance to make a difference by joining together. The support we provide each other gives us strength to carry on. It keeps divine spirit where it belongs—in our hearts and in our minds. Together, with God's love, we can make this world a better place for everyone—just like here at the farm. It's one big beautiful family. Wouldn't you like to see the world treating everyone like we do here? Don't you think that's what it's really all about? Do you really believe you'll find something better out there? Something more important than God's love? Is it really necessary to waste more time before getting down to what's really important? We can be your family. A group of people who really care about you. Brothers and sisters who will help you reach the Kingdom of God. Isn't that what you want?"

"Sure, it's just..."

"If you really want to know truth and serve God," John exclaimed quickly before I could continue, "you've got to be willing to sacrifice. You've got to be willing to commit yourself to knowing all you can about love and goodwill, about giving and taking, about letting go of the ego and working with others to bring about the Kingdom of Heaven here on Earth. After all, that's why the Perfect Farm exists. That's the reason we are here—to develop the qualities of divine love and truth so we can bring about God's divine principle. To do that we must first purify ourselves, and purify the mind that's been filled with greed and lust from those seeking to serve themselves. It's too difficult to do in today's society because of all the negative influences: drugs, war, famine, and fornication. I know, because I've experienced it. You're not going to find a place better than this to develop the power of God within you, to work off your sins through sacrifice and discipline. With one-hundred-and-ten percent commitment we can enter the Kingdom of Heaven here and now."

"Amen," said the female coordinator. The others nodded affirmatively.

"There are too many distractions out there that lead our brothers and sisters astray," John continued. "By developing a foundation among people that love you, you will have the strength to resist the temptations of Satan. You will not only be able to ward off Satan, but also spread the peace and love of God to all brothers and sisters throughout the world. We must work together to build the Kingdom of Heaven on Earth. We must unify."

"Amen," said the female coordinator again.

This time, the others said 'amen' too as they all nodded. John raised his hand in a call for silence. He paused briefly.

"I have no doubt you are sincere about finding truth and expressing love," he continued, now putting his hand on my shoulder, "but alone you are like a lamb among wolves. If you wait and put off the opportunity to live the Kingdom of Heaven, you may never find it. Bryce, what are you really looking for? Do you want to be a part of establishing the Kingdom of God on Earth? We honestly do care about you. Do you care about us? Do you want to try to fight the world on your own? Wouldn't it be better to unite with people that love you? With people that have the same goals as you?"

He paused slightly as my eyes filled with tears. I did want to live with a group of people who loved one another. I wanted to belong. I wanted to unfold my talents and contribute to the world. I wanted to share the goodwill I felt in my heart.

"We love you, Bryce. We want you to join us in establishing God's Kingdom now. Don't you see, Bryce? You can have it all here. You can develop your music and use it to spread the word of God, but first it's important to have a solid foundation, and that's what you'll be getting during the next three weeks—a solid foundation. Together, as one in God's love, we are that foundation."

Tears streamed down my face. My mind was confused and filled with doubt about the decision to leave the farm. It seemed appropriate to respond, yet I didn't know what to say. While taking a breath to speak, John removed his hand from my shoulder. As he did so, my consciousness withdrew from the top of my head, and I found myself outside my body and standing—or maybe the appropriate word is floating—behind the semicircle of people surrounding me. I literally watched myself exhale and take in another breath. It was as if I had a twin brother, and I now stood watching him from the back of the room as he faced the group in front of him.

"We all have our mission for being on this planet," came the words from my lips. Although I knew the person speaking was me, or at least my mouth moving, I had no bodily sensations of talking or breathing. I became an observer no different than the people being addressed, and remained completely detached from my body while something, which I now believe to be a higher aspect of myself, spoke through me.

"For you, the mission lies here on this farm," my voice continued. "It is your desire and choice to join with others and do what you believe is right for you and those with similar goals. The calling that comes from inside you leads to a greater understanding of yourself and the world you create. But the calling of spirit for one person is not always the calling for another in God's universe. There are as many paths to our heavenly father as grains of sand upon the beach.

"Neither judgment nor insolence is intended from these words; only respect for all who seek the ways of love on their journey home to the almighty creator. Love is the key, and we each must give love and serve the world in our own way. Today, your service is here on this farm, for you are making it so. Each person must find his or her own means and vehicle to express the divine love you speak of, and certainly every spot on earth can use more love. As you perceive this farm to be the place for developing love, so it is with the world. It matters not where you are out here," flowed the words as I observed my fingers spread wide and my arms motioned to the area around us, "but where you are in here."

I watched my open hands move to the center of my chest as my right hand covered my left hand over my heart. When my hands touched my chest, I popped back inside my body and stood there looking at them, tears wetting my lips with a tinge of salt. Silence filled the small trailer.

Finally, after a prolonged stillness, Sara spoke. "Bryce, why don't you go into the hills and be by yourself for a while. Think about what's been said here and what you've learned so far, and then make your decision."

Never before had someone on the farm encouraged me to seek solitude.

"That sounds like a great idea. I will do that. Thanks."

I turned and walked to the door.

"We hope you decide to stay with us," John said as I slipped on my hiking boots and tied the laces.

I looked at him, smiled, and then left the trailer. After stopping by my sleeping quarters to get a poncho from my backpack, I hiked the same path I took into the hills the first morning at the farm. Doubts about leaving echoed in my mind.

Were they right? Could I be leaving too early? Were there other things they could share with me that might be new and enlightening? Is this the place I've been looking for? A place to call home and share from my heart with others? Can these people satisfy that yearning inside me? Is the answer found in a group setting, a group consciousness? What about the desire to see the world? Will I be sorry if I leave now? What's three weeks in relation to eternity?

Climbing onto the same bluff as my first morning there, I sat on my poncho, leaned against a rock and closed my eyes. Slowly inhaling and exhaling relaxed my body and turned the torrent of mental questions into images recapping my experience at the farm. When I opened my eyes, I remained no closer to a decision than when I shut them.

"I'm not sure what to do," I said aloud, looking up through the branches of an ancient towering oak tree a short distance away.

"Give it their test," came an inner voice.

On numerous occasions, people at the farm said that the third time provided the true test. They had a reverence for the number three. I looked around, wondering what could serve as a physical test. The trunk of the huge oak tree, which stood some 30 to 35 yards away, had a knot on it the size of a grapefruit.

I will give them the benefit of the doubt, I said to myself. If I can hit the knot, then I'm leaving. If not, I'll stay for three more weeks. The first rock missed the tree trunk completely. The second rock hit the trunk, but missed the knot by several feet. A feeling of panic swept over me. Shit, I thought, am I staying? In one motion, I picked up the third rock and let it fly—hitting the center of the knot.

"That's it," I said, getting up. "It's time to go."

A few hours of sunlight remained, just enough time to hitchhike back to San Francisco.

Moving swiftly down the hillside, I walked to the old chicken coup that served as our sleeping quarters and put my poncho in my pack; then snapped my guitar case shut.

"So you've decided to leave?"

I turned around to see Ray.

"Yeah. I was going to find you and say good-bye first."

I held out my hand and we shook.

"I appreciate your hospitality."

"I wish you would stay longer," he said, "but come back if you change your mind."

"Thanks, Ray. Have you seen Karl?"

"No."

"I'd like to say good-bye."

"I'll help you find him," he said as we walked outside.

"So you're leaving?" It was Thomas, the male coordinator from the trailer.

"Yeah. I still feel a need to travel. Have you seen Karl?"

"Karl?"

"The guy I came here with. He's from England."

"Oh yes, Karl. No, I haven't seen him lately, but he's decided to stay for the next session."

"I'd like to talk to him."

Thomas tilted his head slightly. "Why?"

"Because he's a friend of mine," I added.

"He could be anywhere. It might take you a while to find him."

"That's okay," I said, "I've got more time than money."

"Hey man, are you leaving?" asked a guy I had spoken with several times.

"Yeah, it's time for me to move on."

"You'll be back," he said. "I've left this place three times, and here I am again. Nice people are hard to find. Have you ever seen a place like this before?"

"No, not really."

"Well, you won't," he said. "I've been all over the country."

"You're probably right," I said.

After shaking hands, two other people stopped to say good-bye. As they were walking away, Thomas returned with Karl, Jean and Sara.

"There you are," I said, looking at Karl. "I haven't seen much of you lately."

"Thomas tells me you're leaving," Karl said.

Thomas, Sara and Jean stood beside Karl.

"Yeah. It's something I've got to do. There are too many places I haven't seen yet. So you've decided to stay for the next session?"

"Yes. This place is wonderful, and I'm learning a lot."

"That's cool. What about your visa?"

Karl's U.S. visa would expire in two weeks.

"I'm not going to worry about it. No one will find me here."

"That's true. I just wanted to say good-bye before leaving."

"Good luck to you," he said, as we shook hands.

"Our bus has already left for San Francisco," Thomas said, "but a few people are leaving in a car shortly. I'm sure there's room. We'll take you back to San Francisco if you want?"

"That would be great."

We walked back to the trailer.

"I'll let them know you're waiting out here," Thomas said. "They'll be out in a little while."

While waiting outside the trailer, several people stopped to say good-bye and asked me to reconsider my decision. The guy who had stood up and said he first thought the farm might be run by a cult, stopped to talk to me. He decided to stay. He and I, along with many other people at the farm, were kindred spirits. We were all searching and seeking for the meaning of life, hoping to find something or someone to believe in that would fill the void of loneliness and the longing for love. Although I met these people only days before, it felt like we were long-time friends.

After standing outside the trailer for more than an hour talking to people with whom I had worked, shared meals, discussed the purpose of life, played games and slept beside, it became apparent my ride had been put off. With the sun now behind the hills and darkness quickly approaching, I put on my backpack and picked up my guitar. With each step farther away from the trailers, anger and anxiety boiled inside me. I sensed deception and trickery. Seeing the tall fence in the distance made me feel enclosed and trapped. As I approached the gate, a tall, husky man came out of a small hut beside the entrance.

"Can I help you?" he asked in a low, deep voice.

"I'm leaving," I said, looking him in the eyes.

His hesitation sent a wave of fury through me like I had never experienced before. I wanted out. I had to get out. I became a caged animal that sought freedom either through escape or death. My breathing quickened. Keenly aware of this man's enormous size, I engaged him in a battle of the eyes. It made no difference he outweighed me two to one. Anger and hostility possessed me to the point of madness.

You're going to have to kill me to stop me, I thought, as my body filled with rage and our eyes remained locked upon each other. I set down my guitar in preparation for battle. I glared deeper into his eyes, the fingers of my hands curling into fists. I knew I could shed my backpack within seconds. And if you don't kill me, I thought, I will kill you.

At first he seemed defensive, ready to take me on. Maybe he was trying to bluff me, or see if I would back down. His reaction only increased my rage and hatred toward what he represented—confinement, loss of autonomy and imprisonment.

He cocked his head sideways as suspicion appeared in his eyes. His look turned to wonderment briefly before he took half a step back. He must have realized that I was poised to attack. He turned on his heel and walked to the entrance. Without hesitation or saying a word, he unlocked the chain and pushed the gate wide open.

I picked up my guitar, stared straight ahead, and marched past the towering fence. I heard the gate close behind me, the chain links being bolted together again.

My rage slowly percolated while standing beside the highway waiting for a ride. Chills covered my body as I considered what might have happened had the gatekeeper refused to let me out. A full moon peeked over the hills to the east.

After an unsuccessful attempt to hitchhike for more than an hour, I walked into the woods and lay on my sleeping bag beside a fence bordering the Perfect Farm. Alone and feeling sorry for myself, doubts about my decision to leave the farm resurfaced. It became so strong that I decided to return. I packed up my things and hiked through the woods to the road. From the road, I saw the small town that bordered the farm. Seeing a phone booth outside a local tavern, I got the notion to call home. I walked to the phone booth and called collect.

My mother answered, delighted to hear from me. Dad got on the extension. I told them about the Perfect Farm and my uncertainty about what to do. Both were concerned. My mother suggested waiting until morning before making a decision. It seemed like good advice. As we were saying our good-byes, I could see an older woman and a young waitress in the restaurant across the road that had a bus terminal sign hanging in front of it. I walked to the restaurant and ordered the cheapest thing on the menu—a short stack of pancakes. The older woman turned out to be the cook and manager of the restaurant. When I asked about the farm, they told me that people from the farm appeared to be good neighbors.

"They always have smiles on their faces when they visit town," the cook said. "They even pitch in and pick up trash around the area. But several people who came in here said they had to more or less escape from there."

Her statement validated my decision not to return that evening. I told them about my experiences on the farm, which were very positive except when it came time to leave. After leaving the restaurant, I stopped at the local tavern to see what they knew. I ordered a beer and asked the bartender about their neighbor. Neither he nor two men sitting at the bar knew anything. Finishing my beer, I left the pub. Once outside, I heard a "pssst." I turn to see the young waitress from the restaurant motioning to me from a doorway attached to the back of the tavern. I walked to her.

"Would you like to come in and talk for a while?" she asked.

"Sure," I said as she pushed open the screen door to let me in.

It was a studio apartment with a bed, a small table, refrigerator, stove and a crib in the corner with a sleeping baby in it.

"That's Jake," she said, seeing me look at the crib.

"Is he your child?"

"Yes. His father left about three months ago, and I haven't heard from him since."

Kate wanted to know more about the farm and my travels. She said she felt trapped by her situation. We visited for more than an hour before I got up to go. She offered to put me up for the night, but I declined. It didn't feel right, so I left.

When I got about 75 yards away from the tavern, someone yelled, "Hey you!" I turned to see two guys staggering toward a parked car. "Yeah, you, hippie. We want to talk to you!"

They were obviously drunk. I briskly moved away from them as their car engine roared to a start. I crossed the street and walked about 100 feet into someone's front yard where I hid behind a huge oak tree. The drunks stopped their car beside the yard. Although they couldn't see me, they knew I was there.

"Hey," one of them yelled, "Come on out. We want to talk to you."

A dog barked from inside the fenced backyard of the house less than 20 feet behind me. Although only a shadowy figure in the dark, he looked large.

"Come on," the other drunk yelled. "Get your butt over here. We want to tell you a few things."

I feared the boisterous drunks and barking dog would awaken the people in the house, who would then turn on their front porch light and see me standing beside the tree next to their home. After several more yells, the drunks finally drove off. Although the dog kept barking, I waited a couple of more minutes before walking several blocks and finding a small white church. I spread out my poncho in the church's back yard and unrolled my sleeping bag. It seemed ironic to use the church as a place of refuge considering my disturbing departure from a Christian commune hours earlier. I fell asleep within the church steeple's shadow from the moon.

I awakened the next morning with sunlight peaking through the trees that surrounded the church. I decided that any decision to return to the farm should be put off for at least a week, which would give me time to sort things out. Within minutes after putting out my thumb, two brothers, who were building contractors, stopped. They were on their way to San Francisco.

In an article I read while on the East Coast nearly a year later, I discovered that the Perfect Farm in California was part of a religious group that had been under scrutiny by the press for several years. Surprised, and feeling misled and hoodwinked, I thought about the musician who stood up in our group and said he had first thought the people were members of a particular religious cult. I recalled the peculiar eye contact that passed between two of the group leaders following his comment. I wondered how the musician reacted when he discovered his initial suspicions were true.

City On The Edge

I spent my first night back in San Francisco at the YMCA again. With my money nearly depleted, a second night was out of the question. In order to take a morning and afternoon sightseeing tour without carrying all my gear, I asked the YMCA attendant if they had lockers for storage. He said no, but offered to store my belongings in his office. At 9 a.m., I hit San Francisco's streets unencumbered.

A little before noon, I reached the Golden Gate Bridge. Even though my calves and feet were tired and aching, I jogged across it. On my return, I stopped in the middle of the bridge and looked at the notorious federal penitentiary Alcatraz. Known as "the rock," Alcatraz appeared to be a floating fortress anchored in the bay. My mind pondered possible atrocities that could have taken place within its walls. It had housed some of the toughest criminals in America, such as Al Capone and Machine Gun Kelly.

Then I imagined what it must have been like when San Francisco was isolated from the rest of the bay area—a peninsula with no bridges connecting it to Oakland or Marin County. What was it like when the 1906 earthquake shook the city into an inferno of chaos? And what was the city's ambiance during the 1930s when the bridge beneath my feet was under construction?

"Ahhhhhhhhhhh!" I screamed at the top of my lungs until my throat hurt. I looked down at the murky bay waters to see a tug boat heading out to sea. "Am I any different than the guy standing on that tugboat's deck, or the guy driving by in his Mercedes dressed in an Armani suit?"

I glanced over my shoulder at the passing cars, and then returned my gaze to the bay. Questions ran through my head. Are we all free and searching for the meaning of life? Could I have already come upon the meaning of life and have let it pass me by like an unfamiliar word in a book that I'm too lazy to look up?

After crossing back over the bridge, I walked along the Golden Gate National Recreation Area. A man stood at the end of a pier playing his saxophone. I sat on a park bench listening to him. The smooth and melodious tones flowing in and out of major and minor arpeggios seared my heart with sadness. I recalled the day that became the beginning of the end for my marriage.

Melanie had been working her new job as a hospital public relations specialist for several months. With my summer school classes nearly completed, I had a few more weekends before the fall semester began. For entertainment that Friday, I bought six hits of LSD. My source warned me about its potency, so I suggested to Melanie that she take half-a-hit first, and then take the rest later if she felt she needed it. She planned to take the first half just before leaving work, and then we would meet at our apartment between 5 and 5:30. She knew I planned to fast for the day and take four hits immediately following my last class, which ended at 1:15.

I enjoyed visiting friends while tripping on acid. It gave me a new look at who they were and how they dealt with their lives. Invariably, my altered state of consciousness caused me to initiate topics that involved the nature of the universe and why we were here. My friends seemed to enjoy these philosophical discussions as much as I did. I rarely told my friends I had taken LSD. I feared that if they knew, they might try to pull a trick on me or mess with my head.

Anyway, after taking the acid, I walked down a railroad track near our apartment and sat beside a bridge in the woods. Often acid is heavily laced with speed (amphetamine). I could always tell because the speed would hit first, and then the LSD would strike 10 or 15 minutes later. This acid, however, had no speed in it.

Within 15 minutes, my perception of the world changed. The trees seemed to be reaching up and drawing energy from the fluid fluffy clouds and translucent blue sky. I could feel the blood running through my arteries and veins. My skin tingled as the air molecules danced upon the sheath surrounding my network of muscles, bones and internal organs. I realized that my body was not mine, but a vehicle loaned to me to experience this bizarre and strangely beautiful world of color, shape, sound, smell, taste and touch.

"Why?" I asked, looking to the whirling clouds changing shape upon the canvas of blue as if it were paint at the fingertips of a child. I saw my voice vibrations emanate into the air and surround the trees like heat waves rising on the horizon above a sun-baked desert highway.

A moment later a swirling breeze whipped through the trees causing the branches to sway and bend as the leaves whispered softly and gently, "For you to love and enjoy."

Life seemed so simple. Why did we complicate things? I was immersed in the pure moment of beingness. All thoughts of school, tests, writing papers, finding a job, paying bills, Melanie and a family were put on hold to allow this instant of uninhibited bliss. I could clearly see and feel the answer to life. It was beingness. The moment. The now. I recalled the biblical saying that we must become as little children before we can enter the kingdom of heaven. It made sense. A child lives in the now. Children deal with life from moment to moment without thinking about the past or future.

I felt good. I felt strong. I felt present—living life as it was meant to be. I looked around at my colorful lush surroundings of huge maple and oak trees, tall grass and lilac bushes. The small creek beside the railroad track babbled gently, supplying the chorus background for a cardinal whistling and robins chirping. I breathed deep through my nostrils to smell the wafting scent of lilac. As the warm fragrance filled my lungs, I felt oxygen energizing the blood cells circulating in my lungs and then flowing through my veins and arteries. My whole body gently vibrated to an inner peace found within the enthralling beauty of nature. I could see the bushes, trees, clouds and molecules of the blue sky moving and oscillating within its own frequency. I recalled from chemistry class that everything is in a constant state of motion, even if it appears to be stationary.

Putting my hands on the ground, I dug my fingers into the soft cool dirt mixed with pebbles. I could feel its power, its life force. I looked at the green grass, the wild flowers and the trees—products of the soil beneath me. I laid back and pushed my shoulder blades into the dirt, wriggling down into the dusty earth. I understood why dogs and horses rolled on the ground. It felt good, it felt natural, it was energizing. The trees gently swayed above me as if weaving their way into the blue sky. I saw a myriad of changing faces and shapes in the scattered clouds that appeared to be swirling faster than normal, as if I were watching a time-lapsed film clip on the nature of cloud movement.

I'm not sure how long I laid there, but it must have been an hour or two. Time seemed irrelevant. When I finally got up, I walked on the railroad ties back toward town. Nearing Providence Road, I could hear the cars and see the tall smoke stacks beside the huge coal-burning furnaces that provided the energy to run the university's generators. A queasiness churned in my stomach. The same atoms behind me were now in front of me, but they had been heated, melted, twisted and reshaped to form glass, steel and cement. I felt ashamed, appalled and angry at what we—me and the human race—perceived as progress. Where did we go wrong? I wondered. Can't we see that the world we're building is destroying us? I wanted to scream and cry at the same time. I looked at the dormitory across the street from the generators. On its huge wall

I saw numerical and geometrical patterns dancing within the red bricks. At times, numbers actually appeared, and then it would look like a kaleidoscope of red abstract geometrical designs. I stopped and viewed the wall as if it were a television. How long I stood there, I have no idea. As I walked on toward campus, I kept turning around to see if the changing geometrical figures continued. They did.

I walked beside the engineering building and crossed the campus quadrangle. In the center of the quadrangle stood six huge stone columns—the remains of a university building that burned many years before. The standing joke was that the columns represented the remaining six virgins at the university. A breeze swirled into the quadrangle. The stone pillars swayed gently in unison with the trees. I crossed the street in front of the journalism school and entered the three-story brick apartment. Bouncing up the steps two at a time to the third floor, I rapped on a door with my knuckles. Music played inside the apartment, but I didn't recognize the group.

"Come on in," Michael yelled. I turned the doorknob and pushed the door open. "I'm in the kitchen. Who is it?"

The distinct smell of marijuana permeated the room. An open bag of pot sat beside a water pipe on the coffee table. The apartment looked cleaner than I had ever seen it.

"It's the police," I said in a deep voice. "Is this the Michael Kelly residence?"

I stifled the urge to break out laughing. I heard a pan clang against the stovetop. Michael was washing the dishes. The music kept playing. A second later Michael came through the kitchen door wiping his hands on a towel. As he entered the room, I could tell by the look on his face he had fallen for my prank.

"You son of a bitch," he said as he broke into a smile. "I about shit in my pants."

We clasped hands. Michael had long, light brown curly hair that hung down past his shoulders. His hair, combined with his six-foot-three frame, composed a formidable sight. His gentle nature and pleasant smile made him a popular man on campus.

I laughed. "It's good to see you."

"It's good to see you too," he said. "Since you've gotten married, we hardly ever see you anymore. You and the little lady have pulled a disappearing act on us. Come on; let's sit down and smoke a bowl."

"I didn't mean to interrupt your cleaning," I said as we sat on the couch.

"Hell, I've done enough. Don can finish the dishes."

Don was Michael's roommate.

"Have you ever seen this place look so clean?"

Michael stuffed some pot into the water pipe. It was true. The place usually looked like a child's playpen, except instead of scattered toys you found clothes, books and albums strewn throughout the apartment.

"We're having a party tonight. You and Melanie should come. We're gonna have a keg." Michael handed me the water-pipe tube and struck a match. "You'll like this stuff. It's from Morocco."

We each took a couple of hits before Michael retrieved two beers from the kitchen. The pot and beer added a punch to my acid high. The walls, carpeting and ceiling were gently expanding and contracting as if the building slowly inhaled and exhaled. When I looked closely at an object, I saw it oscillating at a high vibratory rate, making it appear fluid. At times I wondered if I could put my hand through objects and cause their molecules to swirl around like a wisp of smoke.

Michael and I sank into one of our spiritual and philosophical exchanges. We discussed the university and how it related to the universe. We talked about ourselves as sentient beings encased within a shell that protected us from earth's harsh elements. We spoke as if we were from another world, as if we were viewing reality like an alien watching a movie about the human race.

"We're like explorers for the king and queen," I said, inferring that the king and queen represented God. "The royalty has given us the means and tools to venture out into reality and experience this vast playground of sensory stimuli."

I often found myself using words and phrases picked up from my courses and textbooks. The words flowing from my mouth sometimes amazed me. I found myself listening to the words as much as the person in front of me. It was as if something or someone had taken over my mental and physical controls. At first these detached types of experiences confused me, but as I read more metaphysical and spiritual literature, I began to see that these were moments when another part of myself came through. It usually happened when speaking to others about my perceptions and understandings on life.

Michael's roommate interrupted our conversation when he returned to the apartment a little before 5:30. I had lost all track of time. I bid farewell and quickly headed across campus to meet Melanie.

As I approached the brick dormitory near the coal-burning furnaces, I passed a bushy tree that hung low to the ground. Children often passed beneath this tree on their way home from school. The lower branches were at their eyelevel. I had three one-dollar bills in my pocket. I stooped beside the tree and tied them onto the lower branches out of view from a passing adult. I imagined children walking by the tree and finding dollar bills on its branches, and then running home to tell their mothers and fathers that money really did grow on trees. A vibrant surge of energy flooded my body and sent me running gleefully across the dormitory parking lot, down an embankment and between two houses before crossing Providence Road and bounding up the hill to the apartment. As I got to the door, I saw my car in the parking lot, which meant

Melanie was home. A wave of joy and love shot through me as I pushed the apartment door open.

"Hey beautiful? Where are you?"

Melanie came rushing down the hallway from the bedroom, her eyes wide open and tears running down her cheeks. She rushed to me and threw her arms around me.

"Thank God you're okay." She clung to me with all her strength.

"Of course I'm okay," I said, putting my arms around her and holding her tight. "Is something wrong?"

"Not any more," she said, still holding on to me like a frightened child.

"Hey," I said, putting my hands on her arms and prying her away from me, tears still flowing from her glossy eyes. "Tell me what's wrong."

"It's just I'm so high, Bryce, and I only took half a hit. I knew you took four hits, and when you didn't show up by 5:30, I was afraid you were hurt, or in the hospital."

I pulled her to me and wrapped my arms around her. "I'm sorry," I said, "I didn't mean to scare you."

"I love you so much," she said.

"I love you too," I whispered, moving my nose around the side of her cheek to bring our lips together. I could taste the salt from her tears. She raised my t-shirt up to my neck as I lifted my arms up to let her remove my shirt. As I slowly lifted her shirt up over her head, she unsnapped my jeans and pulled the zipper down. We made passionate love on the apartment floor as we'd never done before.

In fact, it felt so different that on several occasions I opened my eyes and looked at Melanie. The first time Melanie had her eyes closed, but for a split second I saw another woman's face that quickly changed back to Melanie's face. I looked at her again when she pulled her feet out from her jeans and panties and wrapped her legs around my waist. I was on the verge of climax. Melanie had her eyes open, but it wasn't Melanie. Not only did she have a different face, which appeared just as beautiful if not more beautiful than Melanie, but also her green eyes exuded power and lust. Her pupils were sparkling with satisfaction and domination from conquering and subduing her prey. Her fingers dug into my scalp as she savagely pulled me to her, furiously kissing me. She bit my upper lip several times while wildly panting and gyrating her hips upward. Her bites were not severe enough to break the skin, but hurt nonetheless. As I pulled away, she kept coming at me. Her aggressive attack repulsed and excited me at the same time. My whole body tingled in a sensation of mixed passion and love. The look in her eyes made me push her shoulders down to the carpet and stare at her.

"Melanie," I half whispered. She started to reach up and bite me again, but then dropped her head back and let it rest on the floor. The other woman's face melted back into Melanie, and the eyes of power and lust became that of compassion, warmth and love. Her legs, still wrapped around my waist, slid down my hips and wrapped around my legs. Her right hand gently caressed the back of my head. She gently swirled her hips up into me as her left hand slid down between us and enveloped my scrotum—gently massaging. This time she slowly pulled my head toward her, parting her lips as they neared mine. I exploded inside her as our lips came together. She gave out a soft soothing moan.

"I love you," she whispered in my ear.

After remaining locked together for several minutes, Melanie firmly pressed her lips to mine and rolled over on top of me. She rose slowly and swirled down, exciting me once more. I watched Melanie, who periodically opened her eyes. One moment it was Melanie, the next moment someone else. Her expressions changed from that of a surprised curious child to a seductive sensuous harlot; from a loving, kind and faithful housewife to a conniving, cheating mistress; from a wise mature woman to a hardened, bitter and lustful old lady. Her sounds and actions matched each change; a crazy eerie laugh, a seductive and sensuous kiss or bite on the neck, an eruption of tears, a glare of hatred, a smile of victory, an agonizing plea for help.

Melanie returned from these bizarre characters about every second or third change. At one point numerous changes took place without Melanie reappearing. I grabbed Melanie's head and pulled her face close to mine.

"Melanie," I said. I looked deep into the eyes of a cunning and shrewd woman of maybe 45 or 50. They were eyes of victory and conquest.

"What's going on?" I asked.

The eyes softened and Melanie spoke.

"I don't know," she said, crying. "Help me, Bryce."

"Come on," I said, rolling Melanie off me to one side and pulling my legs out from the jeans and underwear encircling my knees. I stood up, taking Melanie by the arms and helping her stand. Tears streamed down her face. She looked like a scared, helpless child. Suddenly, both her hands hit me in the chest hard, knocking me back a step.

"What do you think you're doing?" she burst out in rage. "You don't own me."

She now became as a defiant 15 or 16-year-old girl. Although tears still dripped from her chin, the look in her eyes showed no signs of fear or sadness. Her pursed lips and tense jaw made her appear on the verge of grinding her teeth. She turned to walk down the hallway to the bedroom. I leaped to her side and grabbed her right arm with my left hand, spinning her around. As she turned, her left hand swung toward my face. I caught her wrist with my right hand and pulled her arm down.

"Melanie," I screamed.

Her distraught face relaxed as teardrops rolled out from the corners of her eyes. I drew her to me to keep her from falling.

"Bryce," she said as she began sobbing, "what's happening to me?"
Her hands gripped my arms for support.

"It's just a bad trip," I said, "but it's okay. It'll be over soon. We'll be fine. Come on."

I put my arm around her and guided her down the hall to the bathroom. Her head fell against me. Her tears dripped onto my chest and made a cool tingling streak toward my navel. Once in the bathroom, I reached behind the shower curtain and turned on the hot water. The shower nozzle spit and spurt water before a steady stream flowed from its tip. Melanie kept her arms tightly around me as if I were a buoy floating on top of a turbulent bottomless sea. As steam rose from the shower stall, I turned on the cold-water spigot and adjusted the water temperature.

"Come on," I said to Melanie, "a shower will do us both good." I pushed the curtain to one side, and we stepped into the stall. As the water sprayed over us, Melanie released her grip and turned to face the pummeling drops of water. She adjusted the shower nozzle, and then put her face directly beneath the spray and opened her mouth. I could see her neck move as she swallowed some of the water. She took her hands and brushed the water back over her long brown hair. The familiarity and warmth of the shower pumped life and vigor back into Melanie like air filling a balloon. Her body relaxed, and there was a pleasant smile of peace and calm on her face. I picked up the soap and lathered my hands; then massaged Melanie's shoulders and neck. She relaxed even more and leaned back against me. The whole time in the shower, Melanie remained herself. When we got out of the shower and dried off, Melanie once again started changing.

Although Melanie looked the same, unlike when we made love on the floor, her eyes and emotional expressions changed sporadically. It frightened Melanie, and it scared me, but I tried not to show it. I held her tightly in my arms for what seemed like a long time.

Several of Melanie's best friends, who lived together in a house on the other side of campus, were having a party that night. We talked about going to it earlier in the week. I knew the party would be good for Melanie. Like the shower, I hoped the party would be a safe and familiar anchor for her.

"Hey, let's go to Mary and Carole's party," I said enthusiastically, moving her shoulders back and looking into her eyes.

She smiled meekly, tear streaks still wet on her face. "I can't go like this."

"I know," I said, putting my hand on her breast. "You'll have to put some clothes on."

She pulled me to her. "I love you."

"I love you too," I said. Her smile and reaction made me feel much better. It was the Melanie I knew. I lightly smacked her butt.

"Hey," she said, pulling back and looking at me with a gleam in her eye.

"Let's get going," I said. "Do I have to dress you too?" Her smile changed to a serious expression. "Melanie?" I asked, wondering if something was wrong.

She pulled me to her again, and we hugged. "Just stay close to me."

On our way to the party, we stopped at a liquor store and bought two six packs of Miller. We arrived at Mary and Carole's house a little after eight. Mary and Carole had invited their boyfriends and several couples for dinner. They were in the process of cleaning up when we arrived. Music by Bonnie Raitt blasted from the stereo. Several people sat in the living room smoking a joint. Mary and Carole were surprised to see us so early. I could tell they were embarrassed that they hadn't invited us for dinner. They had a lot of food left over. They tried to get us to eat, but we weren't hungry.

Melanie stayed in the kitchen with Carole and Mary while I joined the others in the living room. As I introduced myself to a St. Louis couple I had not met, Carole's boyfriend, Jeff, handed me a lit joint. I sat on the floor and took a big hit. Despite the blaring stereo, I could clearly hear Melanie talking to Mary and Carole in the kitchen. She told them that we had taken acid and that she had freaked out. I looked at the other people in the room. They obviously could not hear the conversation. I shouldn't have been able to hear it either, but I knew it wasn't my imagination. When the joint came back to me, I took another hit and got up.

"Anyone need anything?" I asked, moving toward the kitchen doorway. Everyone was content. Entering the kitchen, I saw Carole washing dishes and Melanie helping Mary take slices of celery, carrots, broccoli, cauliflower and red peppers out of white plastic bags and putting them on a vegetable tray.

"What's going on in here?" I asked.

Melanie looked up and smiled. She appeared to be her normal self.

"How are you feeling?" Mary asked me in a playful manner. "Must be nice where you are."

I smiled. "I feel good." I looked at Melanie. "How are you doing?"

Melanie stood on the other side of Mary. Her smile said it all. She dropped two pieces of celery on the tray and walked around the table to me. We hugged as she said, "I feel wonderful." We pecked each other on the lips with a kiss.

"Mush, mush," Carole said as she dried her hands on a towel and grinned.

Melanie and I looked at each other and smiled. Jeff yelled my name from the living room. I turned my head toward the door and said, "What?" loud enough to be heard above the music. At the same time I yelled, Jeff screamed my name again.

"Bring me another beer, will you?"

Mary, Carole and Melanie looked at me.

"Sure," I said. "Anyone else?" No one spoke.

"How'd you know that?" Carole asked.

"Know what?" I said.

"That Jeff was going to yell to you."

"What do you mean," I said, thinking Carole might be pulling a joke on me. "I have ears."

"You answered him at the same time he yelled," Mary added.

"Right," I said, waiting for them to start laughing, but they didn't. I looked at Melanie. "You heard him yell, didn't you?" I said it more as a statement than a question.

"Not until you shouted to him," she said.

I looked at Carole and Mary. They were doing a good job of fooling me. "That must have been the second time he yelled," I said. "You didn't hear him the first time."

They looked at each other.

"Mother nature's calling," I said, and walked down the hall to the bathroom.

As I stood above the toilet looking into the bowl, the walls started breathing again. It seemed like I was swaying. As the urine splashed into the toilet, the water swirled slowly in the bowl like a time-lapsed weather clip showing a huge hurricane on the evening news. From the bathroom, I could hear everything. Sarah, Jeff's girlfriend, suggested playing cards on the kitchen table. John and Debbie, a couple we all knew, were approaching the front door talking. I heard the door open and greetings take place as they entered. The voices in the living room were clearly audible, even above the blasting music. By focusing on a particular voice, I heard exactly what they were saying. In the past I had similar experiences when smoking really good pot, but it had never been this intense.

After the last few drops of urine spurted out, I flushed the toilet. The swishing sound sucked my attention into the vortex of swirling water. A rush of emotion moved through me as the water gushed down the toilet bowl and began to swell again with clean water. I stood there watching the water until the bowl filled and the water stopped running.

Slowly my gaze shifted to the mirror. I looked into my eyes as my body, and the room around me, melted into a waxy substance. Only my eyes were recognizable. While this took place, I could distinctly hear conversations between my friends. My attention shifted, and suddenly my body and the flowered shower curtain behind me appeared. My arms extended down to the marble countertop. My palms were flat on the marble top with fingers spread wide apart. For some reason, I had to look at my hands, and not just the mirror image of my hands. It took all my willpower to force my head downward. Once my hands were in view, they became my link with the concrete world. I raised them slowly in front of me until both my hands and my face were visible in the mirror. Jeff's knock at the door yanked me back to my senses.

"Ten more seconds," I said. My voice sounded like someone else. I flipped on the cold-water faucet and stuck my hands beneath it. The water felt greasy, as if it were coating my hands with a thin film of oil or paraffin. I turned off the faucet and dried my hands on the pink hand towel. It seemed strange and unnatural in some way—like it was the first time I'd ever done it. I opened the door to find Jeff leaning against the wall next to the door, a beer in his hand.

"Hallelujah," he said and laughed. "You're out before the holocaust. Did everything come out all right?"

I smiled. "There's an upstairs bathroom." My voice sounded funny, like listening to a tape recording of myself.

He brushed past me as he spoke. "I tried, but two girls are using it. I got my beer, thank you," he added sarcastically, but good-naturedly, as he held the bottle up in a salute.

As soon as he said that, I could hear the girls laughing upstairs. I heard them before, but I didn't know they were in the bathroom. As Jeff shut the door, I walked around the corner into the kitchen. Four people sat around the kitchen table, with Sarah at the far end. They were playing hearts. I knew what cards everyone had in their hand and who would take the next trick. I couldn't understand why anyone would play such a stupid game. It seemed senseless and a waste of time.

"Would you like to play?" Sarah asked me.

A rush of sexual energy hit me. Then I heard Sarah's voice, but her lips weren't moving.

"I'd like to take you upstairs to Carole's room," she said. "Melanie's pretty out of it. She'd never know."

I looked at the other people to see if they heard what I heard. They were looking at their cards and seemed oblivious to what Sarah said. I looked back at Sarah. She smiled in a very seductive and sensuous manner. I felt naked. She glanced at her cards. "I know you'd like to," Sarah said again, her lips shut tight.

What's going on, I thought. This is weird. "No thanks," I said, turning to go, "I'm not into cards."

"You sure you don't want to visit Carole's room?" Sarah asked.

I turned and looked at her. "Why?"

Everyone at the table looked at me, then looked at Sarah.

"Why what?" Sarah asked.

"Why did you ask me that?"

"Ask you what?"

"About Carole's room?"

"I didn't ask you anything," she said.

I looked at the others. They looked bewildered.

"Shit, do you know what I'm thinking?" Sarah looked at me, but her mouth stayed shut. She looked embarrassed, curious and excited.

"Sorry," I said as nonchalantly as possible. "I thought you said something. Anyone want a beer?"

I opened the refrigerator door. My question seemed to throw everyone back into their game. No one wanted anything. Sarah kept looking at me. She had a large glass of rum and coke in front of her. As I turned to get a beer from the refrigerator, I heard Sarah say, "I'll have a Miller."

I wasn't sure if she actually said it or not. I pulled out one bottle, shut the door, and then grabbed the towel draped through the refrigerator's door handle and twisted the top off. I looked at Sarah. She looked up from her cards.

"Well?" she said without opening her mouth.

I put the beer to my lips and took a big swallow; then turned to leave the room.

"Shit, that was weird," I heard Sarah say.

I walked into the dining room to find Melanie and Carole talking about one of Carole's journalism classes. The music stopped playing and Mary flipped through the records in the next room. As she did, it sounded to me as if she were reading the titles aloud. When she came to Cat Stevens' *Tea For The Tillerman*, I yelled, "Yeah Mary, put on *Tea For The Tillerman*."

"How'd you know I was looking at that?" she yelled.

"He can do that sometimes," Melanie said.

Melanie and I had experienced telepathic communications on several occasions.

Carole looked at me. "That could be a real advantage," she said to herself.

The only reason I knew she said it to herself was because her mouth didn't move. Things were getting very strange.

"So you did know what I was thinking," Sarah either said or thought while playing cards in the other room.

At that point, a flood of thoughts sounding like the voices of my friends bombarded my mind. Although unsure if people were actually speaking or just thinking the words, I knew which people the thoughts were coming from. It sounded like a room full of people talking. The weaker thoughts were like soft background voices, while those containing more emotion were clear and strong.

"I need another beer, we need dance music on the stereo, some of these people are weird, I'm really high, why am I here, I can drop the queen of spades now, she must be bluffing, I wonder if that nod meant hearts, I'd like to rip her clothes off, I could get him anytime I wanted to…"

I felt sick and walked toward the front door. Cat Stevens stopped singing and Mary replaced the album with the Allman Brothers Band.

"I need some fresh air," I said.

"Are you okay?" Melanie asked.

"Yeah," I lied, turning and looking at her, wondering if she had asked or thought the question.

"Are you sure?"

"Yeah. I just need some air."

Once outside in the darkness, the house became a fiery ball of thoughts spitting out sparks of voices and images that penetrated my mind. It was like hearing voices from a distant crowd, but whenever I focused on a particular voice, the image of the person and their words became distinct and clear.

"You don't love me and you don't love the kids," a woman behind me said between sobs. I spun around to see no one, but heard a man's voice say, "You know that's not true. I have to work, don't I? I'm doing it for you and the kids."

I realized the voices were coming from the house across the street. Then I heard voices from up and down the street. I put my hands over my ears hoping the voices would stop. I walked up the street quickly before breaking into a run. I had to get back to the apartment—a safe place that would protect me from the thoughts of others. As I ran up the street, more voices, cries and moans bombarded my mind: two adults were making passionate love while two others were in a heated argument; children were laughing, playing and throwing temper tantrums; a woman was nursing her child. Their voices and thoughts created vivid pictures in my mind.

Surges of emotions from each situation enveloped me, causing me to run harder. Running faster focused my attention on the sidewalk below me, which weakened the voices, images and emotions. The relief it brought caused me to speed up even more. I entered the edge of campus at a full sprint. Halfway across the quadrangle I slowed down, gasping for air. The sounds, images and feelings diminished into internal pleas to God for help. By the time I reached the apartment, about two miles from the party, my neighbors' voices and emotions pierced my consciousness. At first it was just my next-door neighbors, and then it escalated into hundreds of voices throughout the complex. Entering the apartment quickly, I pulled my clothes off and jumped into bed, covering my head with both pillows. The voices remained.

"God," I said, "please let me go to sleep and wake up normal. Please!"

I repeated the plea over and over. Although I wanted to go to sleep, my mind remained alert and listening to the voices. I could hear the couple upstairs making love; our friends next door were talking and there were voices I didn't recognize laughing. I jumped out of bed and grabbed a screwdriver. I removed the bathroom air vent and covered it with cloth and aluminum foil before screwing it back in place. I went around the apartment tightening screws on every table and hinge I could find. The search for another screw to tighten kept me focused, causing the voices in my head to soften.

After tightening every screw in the apartment, I tried reading a journalism textbook, but it only created an internal voice that seemed to welcome back all the other voices. Again I turned to physical action, scrubbing the bathroom toilet and sink with Ajax, and then vacuuming the rugs. Although the kitchen already had been clean, I wiped everything down and scoured the sink anyway. I then jumped in the shower and wiped down the tile as the hot water pummeled my skin. After drying off, I returned to bed hoping to fall asleep. Lying there with voices still talking in my head, I heard the apartment door open.

"Bryce?" Melanie called. She waited for a moment, and then shut the door. I don't know why I didn't answer her. She went next door searching for me, and then proceeded on to another apartment. I could hear her asking my friends if they had seen me. One friend, whose wife had gone to St. Louis to visit her parents, was sexually aroused by her presence and invited her in. Jealousy surged through my body. Melanie asked him to call her if he heard from me. She then returned to the apartment. When she entered into the bedroom, I pretended to be asleep.

"Bryce!" she yelled, coming over to me and sitting on the bed. "Are you okay?"

I pushed the covers away and looked at Melanie.

"I don't know."

My reply scared her. I had always been the stable one, acid or no acid. Now I was reduced to a scared child pulled from its mother's arms; an innocent boy facing the truth of illusion; a young man pushed into a psychic realm of paranoia and fear by a world of voices and realities that should have remained private.

"Bryce," she said softly as she reached down and took me in her arms. I held on to her tightly.

"I can't get these voices out of my head," I said. "They won't leave me alone. I think I'm going crazy."

"Come on," she said, slightly pulling me up. "I'm driving you to the hospital."

"No," I said, pushing her away from me and looking at her. "They'll just pump my stomach, and there's nothing down there. If I'm still hearing voices tomorrow, I'll go."

Melanie kicked off her shoes and climbed into bed with me, still wearing her clothes.

"What voices?" she asked, holding me as she worked her way under the covers.

"They're thoughts that people are having right now. Like at the party. I knew what everyone was thinking. Their thoughts became voices that I heard. I wasn't sure if people were talking or just thinking. I had to leave the party. I just couldn't take it anymore. I'm sorry I ran off."

Tears rolled down my cheeks.

"It's okay," she said, as she kissed my face and ran her hands over my neck and through my hair. "We're together now. Everything will be fine, you'll see."

I heard her words and desperately hoped they were true, but inside me something changed.

Although by the next day the voices were gone, paranoia and fear still ripped through my mind. I remained in the apartment for four days, too afraid to venture out and face the world. On Monday and Tuesday I skipped classes and called in sick at work. Melanie never knew. She left for work before I went to class and returned home later than me. During these four days, I became suspicious of Melanie seeing someone else. My suspicions were completely unfounded, but the mind has a funny way of finding evidence to support whatever it believes.

After several months of distrust festering inside me, I dreamed of catching Melanie in bed with a friend. I wondered how many of my friends had slept with her. My fear became an obsession that pushed Melanie away. I lacked the courage to talk to her about my thoughts and feelings. To do so would have made me appear weak and vulnerable, and I refused to let down my guard. I viewed silence as protection. Instead, it became a raging infection of paranoid hysteria.

I snapped back to sitting on the park bench. The musician had already put his sax in a cloth case and walked in my direction before I realized he had quit playing. As he passed in front of me, I smiled and thanked him for the music. He smiled back and nodded, but said nothing.

Walking eastward through Golden Gate Park, I came to what's called the Panhandle, an entry way into the park from the Haight-Ashbury district. The Panhandle is lined with Victorian homes hosting exquisite flower-covered balconies, Queen Anne turrets and gables. Once on Ashbury Street, I turned south toward Haight. Two men holding hands caught me by surprise. I never saw an open display of homosexuality in Missouri. As the male couple neared me, they released their hands and put their arms around one another.

"Hello," said the male closest to me.

"Hi," I said, looking away as I passed them. Their show of affection made me feel awkward and uncomfortable.

I walked to the other side of the street and sat on the bus stop bench. I saw five African American men walking up the street toward me. They were passing around two bottles wrapped in paper sacks. As they got closer to me, a bus rounded the corner several blocks away and headed toward us. I wondered if the bus would get to me before the men did. One man looked at me and yelled something as he pushed the bottle up over his head. They were now about 30 feet away. The bus quickly approached. The man with the bottle above his head moved in my direction. Another guy in the group followed him. I could tell they were drunk by the way they swayed and bumped into each other. They appeared to be having a good time, yet nonetheless, I questioned the intentions of the man coming closer.

"Hey," he hollered again, now 10 to 15 feet from me, "would you like a drink?"

He held the bottle out in front of him. The bus, now 25 to 30 yards away, closed in fast. At first I thought the man planned to stay on the back side of the bus stop bench, but at the last minute he changed direction and walked around the bench, possibly to sit beside me. I stood up. At nearly the same time, he either hit the bench seat with his leg or stumbled over his own feet, causing him to fall toward the street. His buddy, walking beside him, saw the bus.

"Look out," he screamed.

With his arm and bottle of wine still stretched out toward me, I lunged forward and grabbed the man's wrist and bottle with my hands. For a split second I saw the bus driver's surprised look as he hit the brakes. We both knew the bus could not stop in time. With a firm grip on the man's wrist, I pulled him toward me with all my might. He made an arching swing toward the street and then slammed hard into the curb at my feet. Wine sloshed out of his bottle onto my t-shirt before it hit the ground and broke inside the paper bag. The front wheel of the bus stopped two or three feet past the man's head, missing him by less than 10 inches.

"Shit," he said, turning his head to stare into the underside of the bus that nearly touched his face.

Within a few seconds, his buddies were dragging him away from the curb.

"You trying to get your ass killed?" I heard one guy say as they dragged him onto the sidewalk. Although dazed, the man appeared to be fine.

Hearing the bus doors open, I turned around to see the driver coming down the steps. He stopped on the last step.

"Is he okay?" the driver asked me.

"He'll be all right," I said, "but it was close."

I walked toward the bus door as the driver went back up the steps to his seat. As the bus drove away from the curb, I looked back to see the men helping their buddy to his feet. My heart raced, and not just because a bus nearly hit a man, but because of my fear of five intoxicated African Americans.

At the YMCA, where I retrieved my gear, the clerk told me to take the BART (Bay Area Rapid Transit)—San Francisco's subway system that sends aluminum trains under the bay at speeds up to 80 mph—for the fasted route to Berkeley. I found the BART terminal and headed toward the University.

The University of California campus at Berkeley lived up to my expectations; clean, spacious, lots of trees and a laid-back atmosphere. I sat at the base of a tree and leaned back against its trunk. While making myself a peanut butter sandwich, two gray squirrels cautiously approached.

"Hey there," I said to them. "I have a feeling you'd like this sandwich."

I broke off a small piece of my sandwich and tossed it toward them. One squirrel scurried to it and picked it up, and then sat on his haunches and ate it two feet away from me. I took another small piece and held it out to the other squirrel.

"Come and get it." He inched closer to me. "That's it. Come on."

To my surprise, he climbed up on my thigh, took it out of my hand, and ate it while sitting on my leg. I had never had a wild animal sit on my leg. I looked up to see two people standing on the sidewalk watching me.

After playing my guitar in the park until dark, I walked along one of the campus sidewalks until I spotted several huge bushes surrounded by trees. Two guys and a couple were in front of me, so I walked past the bushes before returning and discreetly slipping into them unseen. It was a perfect place to camp for the night, but I felt sticky from the day's sweat and spilled wine. I took out my small daypack and filled it with clean underwear, a t-shirt, towel, notebook and my wallet. Then I slipped off my jeans and put on some running shorts. Hiding my larger pack beneath my green poncho, I slipped out from under the bushes, making sure no one saw me. I followed two guys carrying gym bags. Fortunately, no one checked identification as I walked confidently behind the two guys into the locker room.

A long hot shower revived and relaxed me. I went back to my bush and crawled under it without anyone seeing me. I spread out my poncho and put my sleeping bag on top of it. As I lay on my back looking at the bushes above me, I thought about my experience in the Perfect Farm's trailer. It now seemed more like an expanded consciousness than an out-of-body occurrence. It felt different from what I experienced nearly two years before while sleeping with Melanie.

Melanie and I had gone to bed earlier than usual that night. The experience began somewhat like a dream. I found myself hovering near the ceiling looking down at two people in a bed. Then I saw the woman roll over, her face moving into the light shining into the room from a street lamp outside the window. It took several seconds before I recognized Melanie's face. I looked at the other clump covered by a sheet and then zoomed in like a movie camera for a close-up. Shock mixed with panic hit me when I saw myself. My perception immediately switched back to an overview from the ceiling.

My God, I thought, I must be dreaming. But wait, if I'm dreaming, then I'm aware that I'm dreaming. And if I'm aware that I'm dreaming, then I'm no longer dreaming. What's going on here?

Thoughts sped through me. A rush of emotion exploded inside my head. I'm dead, I concluded. I've died in my sleep. If I'm not dead, and this is not a dream, then wake yourself up.

My consciousness moved down to my body and tried to enliven it. Terror overtook me when I realized I couldn't get back inside my skin.

I am dead, I thought.

Suddenly, I popped back inside my body and immediately sat up and looked around. I raised my hands and looked at them.

"Melanie," I said, excitedly shaking her. "Wake up!"

Melanie raised up and looked at me. "What's the matter?"

"I was just outside my body looking at us from the ceiling."

She laid down. "You were dreaming," she mumbled.

"I wasn't dreaming. It really happened. I just now came back and woke myself up."

"Uh huh," she mumbled, before falling back into slow, rhythmic breaths.

I scooted down in bed and looked at the ceiling. I know it was real, I thought. It took a least an hour before I fell asleep again. The next morning when we got up, I told Melanie once more what had happened.

"You were only dreaming," she repeated, and headed to the bathroom.

I talked to numerous friends about the incident. Most friends attributed my experience to either drugs, or a flashback from using drugs.

I became fascinated with replicating the occurrence. One evening, wishing to attempt another out-of-body experience, I managed to get Melanie to join me in an exercise I found in a book. I first talked us both into a very relaxed state; then proceeded with the exercise. I could actually feel myself moving out the top of my head. Then I felt myself hugging Melanie as if on another dimension. It felt like we were uniting above our bodies.

Melanie suddenly jumped up. Her action startled me, causing my body to jerk backward as if I were falling.

"I'm not ready for this," she said.

She remained reluctant to talk about what had happened, and when I pressured her, she finally said, "I'm not interested in talking about this ever again."

During the Perfect Farm incident in the trailer, however, a shift of consciousness better describes my experience. I recalled the group surrounding me and delivering their barrage of evangelical thoughts and perceptions, and then my emotional, mental and verbal faculties breaking down. It left me speechless and totally frustrated. Unable to respond, yet with a great desire to do so, a different part of myself took over. It felt like my personality got kicked out of the way to give a more intuitive and creative part of me its voice.

In many ways it was similar to when I picked up the third rock and hurled it at the tree knot. The frustration, fear and loathing of not following my heart and allowing others to create doubt in myself shocked my body into a state of connection, which helped put me back on course. I fell asleep knowing a higher part of myself had awakened, and whether I listened to it or not depended on me.

The next morning I awoke to the sound of students walking to their classes. Although I lay in my sleeping bag only 30 feet from the sidewalk, no one could see me through the low-hanging tree limbs and thick hedges unless they actually walked into the bushes. I wondered about the huge evergreen thickets I often passed at the University of Missouri, and whether there might have been someone lurking within them.

It felt great lying there and knowing I had the whole day to myself. No classes, no work—nothing but playing my guitar, reading and contemplating life.

I played my guitar for several hours before going to the campus student union late in the afternoon. There were chairs and tables outside, so I took a seat and pulled out a bag of granola from my pack. A guy walked by me with a flute sticking out his backpack and carrying a huge walking stick. He wore blue-jean shorts and a light gray pullover cotton shirt with sleeves that almost reached his wrists. I started to say something to him, but then refrained. A few minutes later he walked by me again.

"How's it going?" I asked.

He stopped and looked at me. "Not bad, but it could be better."

I held the bag of granola toward him. "Like some granola?"

"Sure," he said, moving closer to me while shifting the walking stick to his left hand and reaching into the bag with his right. His wavy brown hair hung down to his shoulders, and he had a curly short beard.

"Where you from?" he asked, tossing a few kernels of granola into his mouth.

"Missouri. Have a seat if you'd like." I pushed a chair away from the table with my foot so he could sit down. He slowly removed his pack. "How long have you been traveling?"

"Almost three years now," he said between chews as he sat down.

"Really?" I pushed the bag of granola toward him again. "Where have you been?"

"This is good," he said, reaching in the bag and taking a handful this time. "I've been all over this country and parts of Mexico. How about you?" He tossed some more granola into his mouth.

"I've been on the road a few months. Made it to Canada and parts of the Northwest. I just came from a commune in Northern California called the Perfect Farm."

"Is that right?" He tossed the rest of the granola into his mouth and dusted the crumbs off his hand.

"Yeah. They also have a house across the bay not far from Golden Gate Park."

"If it's the group I think it is, they have a house in Berkeley too," he said. "I know a girl who's hanging out there. What did you do at the farm?"

I told him what happened. Except for the departure debacle, it was a positive description of the farm.

"I wonder if Linda is still there," he said after hearing my story. "Their Berkeley house is not far from here. It would be nice to talk to her again. Do you want to go?" He stood up.

"Sure," I said, standing up.

"I'm Tim." He held out his hand.

"Bryce." He had a strong handshake.

It took us a while to find the house. Tim knocked hard on the door, and a girl opened it about six to eight inches.

"Can I help you?" she asked.

"Yes," Tim said, "I've come to see Linda Blackwell. Is she here."

"Is she expecting you?"

"No, but we're friends."

"What's that?" she asked, pointing to his large walking stick.

"It's a stick I'm carving on, why?"

The stick, at least three inches thick and six feet tall, had all of its bark stripped off with a ram's head carved on top.

"What do you use it for?"

"It's a walking stick. Could you tell Linda I'm here?"

Tim's voice sounded impatient. She paused and looked at me.

"Haven't I seen you before?" she asked.

I didn't recognize her, but she may have seen me at the farm.

"Possibly," I said. "I spent almost two weeks at the Perfect Farm."

She nodded her head as if she remembered something. She looked at Tim. "What do you want to see Linda about?"

"I'm a friend and want to say hello. Is there a problem with that?"

"I'll go tell her you're here. What's your name?"

"Tim Kellerman."

She shut the door.

"She's acting like we're up to something," I said.

"She's acting like an asshole."

"How well do you know Linda?"

"We traveled together for a while. She's really nice."

The door opened, and there stood the same girl as before.

"I'm sorry, but Linda wanted me to tell you that she's busy and can't see you right now."

"Why can't she tell me that herself?" Tim asked.

"She's busy. Have a nice day," she added while shutting the door.

"Oh well," I said.

"That's not like Linda," Tim said, looking up at the second floor window.

I looked up too, but saw no one. Although the sun had just gone down, no lights were on in the windows.

"Where do you plan to sleep tonight?" Tim asked me as we walked away from the house.

"I slept on campus under a bush last night. Probably do the same tonight."

"Watch out for the campus police. They can get rough. I know a good place not far from here. It's a small park, and I've never seen any cops or been hassled by anyone. You're welcome to join me if you want."

"Thanks. I think I will."

We walked up a winding road through a district of magnificent homes surrounded by beautifully landscaped English gardens and huge trees.

"Look at the bandits," Tim said.

Two raccoons were going up a stairway leading to the back porch of a whitewashed Spanish-style home with a red-tile roof. Tim reached over his shoulder and pulled out his flute. He played seven or eight notes.

Both raccoons simultaneously stopped in their tracks and turned toward us, the black around their eyes making them appear suspicious. Tim raised the flute to his lips again, this time playing a longer phrase of notes. In unison, the raccoons dropped their ears back and sat down as if smiling.

"Wow," I said, "you're talking to them."

Tim laughed as he put the flute back into his pack.

"We caught them," he said, as he walked on. Both raccoons remained seated on the steps. "I'm sure whoever lives there puts food out for them."

Two houses away we saw a whitetail buck peacefully grazing on the grass in an open backyard as if in a wilderness meadow at the base of a mountain.

As we walked up a steep hill, Tim asked, "How long do you plan on traveling?"

"I really don't know. Up to this point, it seems like I've spent my whole life in school. I want to see all the places I've read about. Have you been to Europe yet?"

"No, but I plan to go." After a slight pause, he continued. "Are your parents giving you money to travel?"

"I wish," I said. "I'm still in debt from school loans. I had to leave my car in Oregon because I couldn't afford gas. How have you been financing your travels? Three years is a long time."

"I've done whatever it takes to get by. Right now, I'm pretty much down to broke."

"What are you going to do?"

"I don't know, but I'm going to have to do something soon."

"You could check the classified ads for a temporary job," I said.

He looked at me and gave out a little laugh. "I could."

"I've worked for Manpower during Christmas breaks," I continued. "You go in that day and hang out until an employer calls for help. I've usually gotten jobs the day I went in. Some jobs lasted a couple days, while others for a week or two. The work's usually not that hard. I've put together lockers, and..."

"Look," he said, sounding impatient and disturbed, "I know all that." He gave me an odd glance. "You just be concerned about yourself. I'll take care of my business."

I felt taken back by his abruptness. A long pause ensued before he asked, "How much money did you start out with?"

"Four hundred bucks, but between buying gas and getting busted, I'm down to nearly broke myself."

"You got busted?"

"Yeah, in Canada."

As we continued up the hill, I briefly summed up the Canadian bust fiasco and the incident with the judge. We eventually came to the small park. Although twilight had moved into darkness, I could see a tennis court on the far side of the open field. A short 12-foot fence on one side of the field served as a backdrop to a baseball diamond.

"This is nice," I said.

"Let's go over there," Tim pointed, "and check out the view."

We walked toward one end of the field. From where we stopped, we had a clear view of the Golden Gate and Oakland Bay bridges through an opening between the trees. Tim stood behind me. The bay lights twinkled and reflected off the water as a nice breeze swirled through the trees above us. Peacefulness overcame me. I took a deep breath and released it when a startling and eerie image penetrated my calm.

I envisioned Tim, not more than three or four feet behind me, slowly raising his walking stick, gripping it like a baseball bat, and then bashing me in the head. Fear and anxiety left me breathless. I heard Tim move or shift his weight. My first inclination was to spin around and confront him. Instead, I closed my eyes, deeply inhaled once more, and then slowly exhaled.

Is it my time to go? I questioned within. If it is, God, then let me go quickly. I focused my attention on the bridge of my nose. I took another breath and slowly exhaled. My body relaxed as my shoulders drooped. The anxiety and fear I felt minutes before transformed into tranquility. Small sparkles of light flashed on the dark screens of my eyelids as if dancing to the sound of a soothing musical symphony. I slowly inhaled and exhaled again, releasing any remaining tension in anticipation of being clubbed. A strong breeze blew some hair around my head to lightly tickle my cheek and neck.

Okay, I thought, I'm ready.

I took another breath, filling my lungs, and relaxed even more as I quietly exhaled. I waited, wondering what would come next. Nothing happened other than the shifting of light and darkness upon the screen of my mind's eye. After what felt like a long time, I opened my eyes. The two bridges and their lights glistened off the bay before me. I slowly and cautiously turned around. Tim clutched the stick near his left shoulder with both hands, apparently leaning on the stick as he stared toward the bay. He looked hypnotized. Relief washed through my body and then confusion."Tim?"

He remained motionless; his eyes wide open.

"Tim?" I said again, this time gently touching his arm.

He slowly turned his head, and then his body jerked as his eyelids blinked. I instinctively stepped back from him. He swayed slightly before gripping his walking stick more tightly. He blinked again, and his eyes now focused on me.

"Wow," he said, taking a half-step back himself. "I feel strange."

He sounded dazed, confused, and almost pleading for help. Although I now sensed no hostility, I didn't trust him.

A sudden swishing sound startled us both. Water shot from sprinklers on the field behind us. We turned and looked at the spurts of water that formed long crisscrossing sprays to cover the field. We stood there in silence for several moments. I was grateful for the distraction.

"Are you okay?" I finally asked.

He looked at me, and then looked out over the bay as if embarrassed and annoyed. "I'm fine," he mumbled.

I took a deep breath for the first time, thankful that he seemed to be having second thoughts. A ship's horn blasted through the ethers to break the silence.

"I think we have similar circumstances," I finally said. Tim cocked his head and looked at me as I continued. "It gets harder and harder to stay in the present moment when wondering if there will be food to eat." I paused and looked out at the bay bridges.

"Why did you say that?" Tim asked.

I looked at him and shrugged my shoulders. "I don't know."

"But why did you..." Tim paused and looked back out at the bay. I waited for him to continue, but he said nothing.

"What?" I finally asked.

"It's just that, well, your timing hit right on the mark." He looked at me again. "I needed to hear that. Thanks."

I searched his face to see if he was being sincere. Tim stooped down next to his backpack. He was less than three feet from me. If he pulled a gun or knife from his pack, I felt like I could have my boot in his face before he could do anything.

"One thing I've discovered while on the road," he said as he untied the straps that held his sleeping bag to the top of his pack, "is that a good night's sleep can certainly wake you up to a new perspective."

I found myself wanting to believe him.

"Those," he added, looking at the water sprinklers shooting across the field, "would have soaked my ass last night. I slept right where they're spraying."

He laughed and I smiled.

"They must be set on a timer to operate every other night," he added, as he spread his sleeping bag out on the ground.

The thought of sleeping near Tim worried me. "I feel like playing my guitar," I said, "and I don't really want to bother you. I can go play over there."

I nodded toward a spot nearly halfway around the field that remained untouched by the spraying water.

"I could use some music," Tim said. "It will help me relax."

I hoped it was true. Something inside of me yearned for companionship, and the thought of walking back to campus in the dark and finding a bush to sleep under made me shudder. He sat on his sleeping bag and took off his boots. I spread out my poncho and sleeping bag a little ways from him; then sat down and got my guitar out of its case. Tim stretched out on his back and took several deep breaths.

"The air's good up here," he said, taking in another deep inhalation.

As I tuned my guitar, I glanced over at the other side of the field, wishing I were there. You're just being paranoid, I reassured myself, and strummed a few major and minor chords together. I looked at Tim. He already had his eyes closed.

Trying to distract myself, I locked into a sequence of chords and began improvising lyrics that related to the bridges and the sights before me. Within a few minutes, however, the words came from somewhere other than my mind, like automatic writing, but in this case automatic singing. I became a listener the same as Tim. I wish I had written the words down right after I sang them.

Although I can't recall exactly what I sang, the song spoke about San Francisco and its continual state of flux: about changes in the earth and how they were connected to a world consciousness. It talked about San Francisco's earthquakes and how they were related to the consciousness of the city's inhabitants. It said that certain people were now leaving the bay area and others appearing, making things conducive for another huge quake. It made me wonder if I might be part of the catalyst for a big one. The song also said that while pressures were building for a catastrophic shaking, it could be reversed quickly if the consciousness of the city changed. If a change failed to happen soon, however, then the quake would wreak havoc on the city and alter its inhabitants' awareness.

I wondered if I was really singing about my experience with Tim. If I transformed my fear of him, would I be safe? At the close of the song, Tim opened his eyes.

"That was interesting. Did you just make that up?"

"Yeah. I'm getting chills thinking about it. It was as if something sang through me. Do you think an earthquake is coming?"

"They happen all the time out here," he said casually, "but according to your song, it sounds like a big one's brewing."

"Do you think it means tonight? I get the feeling it's going to happen soon."

"I guess it could," Tim said. "They don't know how to predict quakes. The idea of associating earthquakes with consciousness is intriguing. Have you ever thought of that before? Or read anything like that?"

"No, not that I recall. I'm thinking maybe I should pack my stuff and leave."

Tim laughed. "And go where?"

"I don't know, but at least leave San Francisco."

The thought of the ground shaking with nowhere to go terrified me. I imagined the ground opening up to create huge canyons and tidal waves 100 feet high sweeping over the city. At least in the Midwest, when a tornado strikes, you can seek shelter in a basement or cellar. In regard to earthquakes, unless you're lucky enough to be in an airplane, there's no protection.

"If it's our time to go, then it's our time to go," Tim said.

He's right, I thought. If it's my time to go, I'll die whether I'm with him or not.

After a short pause he added, "Besides, in geological terms, soon—and I'm referring to immediately—could mean as little as 20 to 50 years, or even hundreds to thousands of years. The odds are in our favor that it won't happen tonight."

I took a deep breath to help me relax.

"But tell me something," he continued. "You said it felt as if something was singing through you. What did you mean?"

"I listened to the words the same as you. I had no idea what words would come out next."

"That's how it is when I play my flute," he said. "Have you ever heard of the Rainbow Tribe?"

"No."

"You should go to their next gathering. A lot of musicians will be there doing just what you did in that song."

"And what did I do?"

"You tuned into spirit and let it flow through you. That's what the Rainbow Tribe's all about. Letting spirit flow."

Tim went on to tell me that the Rainbow Tribe is a tribe of all nations and everyone is welcome to attend their annual gathering, which takes place the first week of July. He said their goal is to heal the Earth by listening to spirit and following its guidance.

"Where do they meet?" I asked.

"It changes every year. They're meeting in the Southwest this year."

"Where in the Southwest?"

"I don't really know. If you want to go, just head to the Southwest at the end of June. You'll find it."

Tim's slow and deep breathing told me he had fallen asleep. Once again, I wondered if Tim really considered hitting me over the head and robbing me. Maybe I was just paranoid about him and earthquakes. Either way, I chose to take what money I had left out of my pocket and place it between my sock and my leg. Shortly after putting my guitar away, I fell asleep.

Tim proved right. It's amazing how much better you feel after a good night's sleep. Of course, the spellbinding morning vista helped. We awoke to see the sun rising amidst the fog behind the Golden Gate Bridge, with the bridge's twin towers vaulting above the misty haze.

The Phone Call

As the sun burned off the morning fog, I felt whole, strong, vibrant and in control of my life. Fears of earthquakes and the threat of being clubbed and robbed the night before seemed distant and unreal. I felt refreshed and ready for the joy and challenges the day held.

Even so, a flood of relief washed over me when Tim decided to travel north to Red Bluff and Redding in search of a temporary job. I went south to visit friends in Los Angeles.

I followed the coast along Highway 1 looking for a place to camp, preferably on a beach. A guy and his girlfriend picked me up just south of Santa Cruz. They told me about Big Sur's Andrew Molera Walk-In Campground only 30 miles below Carmel. They dropped me off at the campground's parking lot. According to the sign near the trailhead, you had to hike .6 kilometers to the campground. That kept a lot of people away, especially those unfamiliar with the metric system. Half a kilometer is approximately a quarter of a mile.

At the campground I met a remarkable person. John was a small, slender and gentle man. He had a shaved head and clean-shaven face. He wore baggy white pants, sandals, and a light pastel-blue shirt that hung loosely about him. I introduced myself to John after seeing him practice Tai Chi near his campsite. Although I had heard of Tai Chi, I knew very little about it.

"We need harmony and balance in our lives," John said to me as we sat beside a campfire one night. "This state of peace I'm talking about can be found by being in harmony and balance with what surrounds us outwardly and inwardly." He stood up and said, "Push your hand through the air."

He put his hand on his chest and then extended it outward toward the flames. As I did the same, he asked me what I felt. I described the feeling of air moving over my hand and the warmth of the fire.

"Exactly." Although he spoke softly, an excitement emanated from his voice as if discovering something new while he spoke. "The air that you feel is not empty space. It's a gas consisting of oxygen, nitrogen, carbon dioxide, hydrogen and a few other elements. The space we see in front of us is a substance." He stared straight ahead as if he were looking at something suspended an arm's length in front of him.

"Have you ever studied science?" John turned and looked at me.

I nodded and told him I took chemistry, physics and biology at the university.

"Then you know about matter and its chemical makeup. These floating atoms in the air are also energy."

John swung his hand swiftly through the space in front of him and curled his fingers into a fist as if he'd just caught a fly or mosquito. "What if you could tap that energy? In my hand I now hold thousands, even millions of atoms. The amount of energy found within these atoms is enormous. Take this fire, for instance." He looked directly into the flames rising above the glowing red coals. "Matter is being converted into energy right before our eyes."

He picked up a small stick and held it in front of him.

"The energy contained within this twig is powerful. Although we can easily see and feel the wood's energy from the fire, it's less apparent in this stick, or the living tree behind me. The tree has an energy force, and as a living thing its energy is much stronger than this fire, or this decaying twig."

John gazed into the fire as if hypnotized. Just as the silence started to make me feel uncomfortable, he continued.

"Energy fields are all around us wherever we go, whether we see them or not. Being aware of this energy force is the first step in studying Tai Chi. If you learn how to use that energy—to move with the energy forces—then the chi becomes a tool, a tool that can be used in self-defense when needed. That's a part of what Tai Chi is—working with the energy around us and being in balance with it."

Every morning for the next week I watched John perform his Tai Chi dance. When the right side of John's body moved into motion, a corresponding movement from his left side followed. His movements were slow, graceful and smooth. Sometimes he stood on one foot for 30 seconds or longer as he slowly lifted his other foot high into the air and twisted his torso before returning his foot gently to the ground. He made it appear so natural and peaceful that I wanted to try it.

His power of concentration remained impenetrable. His eyes looked straight ahead. His stare became that of a snake. He seemed to be looking everywhere at once. When I asked him about it later, he told me he was seeing a "total picture." To explain, he had me focus my eyes on him, and then he asked me to simultaneously look at all things that were beside him as well as behind him.

"Try to see if you can bring everything into focus," he said, "as if all the objects you see are one big photograph that extends from one corner of your eye to the other."

It certainly yielded a different way to look at things. As I did what he said, the trees, mountains, clouds and blue sky began to move slowly as if painted on a large canvas gently blown by a silent breeze. The longer I concentrated on the total picture, the more it felt like I had taken an hallucinogenic drug. He laughed when I told him what I experienced.

"Try to see like that all the time," he said. "It will give you greater insight to your surroundings."

John decided to leave the campground at the same time I did. John's destination was Santa Barbara and mine Los Angeles. We stood beside the road hitchhiking together. I stuck out my thumb every time a car drove by, but John would put out his thumb about every third car. He appeared indifferent about catching a ride. After 15 or 20 minutes, it began to rain—not hard, just a light sprinkle. John got out a hooded rain jacket and put it on.

"Don't you have any rain gear?" he asked.

A few days after I arrived at the campground, I met a man whose belongings had been stolen, so I loaned him my poncho for the night thinking he would give it back the next day. When he failed to return it, I didn't have the heart to ask him for it. John heard about the theft, but he hadn't met the guy. When I told John who had my poncho, he slipped off his jacket and handed it to me.

"Here, you take this. I have a poncho I can use."

As I took the jacket, John unzipped a pouch on his backpack with his left hand and pulled out a poncho. I quickly slipped the jacket on. The sprinkle increased to a steady rain, but within a few minutes it turned to drizzle. Fifteen minutes later we still stood in the drizzle beside the road. No cars even slowed down. We were standing on a wide shoulder with plenty of room for cars to safely stop, so we had an excellent hitchhiking spot. I wondered what a driver might think seeing two male hitchhikers, one with a shaved head and the other with hair hanging past his shoulders.

"Maybe it would be better if we split up," I suggested. "It's always harder with two guys. Too bad you're not a girl. We'd have it made."

John laughed. "No doubt about that."

I slipped the jacket off and held it out toward him.

"Keep it, it's yours."

"But it's not really raining now." A light mist fell.

John put his hand on my shoulder and looked into my eyes. "I want you to have it."

"But..." His grip tightened on my shoulder.

I looked at the jacket, admiring it. "Are you sure? This is a nice jacket."

The blue hooded North Face jacket had a zip-tight pouch in the front and an inside pouch for your hands. It looked new.

"I'm sure," he said.

"Gee, thanks."

"You're welcome." He extended his hand and we shook.

The twinkle in John's eyes seemed to reach out and give me a hug. In that moment of contact, we established a bond—not a bond of obligation or debt, but of unconditional friendship. A part of me wanted to savor the moment, but another part of me felt embarrassed by the intimate feelings that passed between us. I looked away.

"I'm glad we met," he said.

I looked back at him. "It's mutual. Good luck."

"Thanks."

I turned and walked down the road to give John first shot at any passing cars. After walking 20 feet or so, I turned and looked at him. As he pushed his poncho into his backpack, I yelled, "Hey!"

He looked up at me smiling.

"Keep that thumb up!" I gave him a thumbs-up sign.

He laughed and pushed his thumb into the air above his head while still bent over his backpack.

I walked to the end of the turnout area and put my guitar down. I started to remove my pack when a girl with long sandy-blonde hair stopped her car beside me. Clothes and books filled her small Peugeot's backseat. She told me to toss my backpack and guitar on top of her clothes. I looked at John. He was grinning and flashing me the thumbs-up sign. I waved good-bye to him and hopped into the front bucket seat, pulling the door shut behind me.

"Thanks for stopping," I said, looking into a face of freckles and an innocent smile as she pulled onto Highway 1.

Nancy was on her way to the University of California at Los Angeles. She had made a trip to Santa Cruz to pick up some things that didn't fit in her car during her first trip to L.A. She returned to Santa Cruz via Highway 101 and decided to take the scenic route back. She sounded nervous and spoke in short breaths. We discussed the weather and scenery before she finally said, "You're the first hitchhiker I've ever picked up."

"Were you afraid to stop?"

"Not really," she said after a slight pause, sounding much more relaxed. "You have an honest face. I also saw your guitar. I figured if you played music, most likely you were the peaceful type."

I laughed. "I don't have a guitar in the case."

A moment of silence passed before she asked the question I expected. "What's in there?"

"Pot. I'm delivering it to some friends in L.A."

Everyone in the area knew that the mountains around Big Sur had a reputation for growing some of the best marijuana in the United States. The look on her face made me laugh again.

"I'm only kidding, but things might not always be what they appear to be."

My joke made her nervous again. She asked me to play a song for her. I told her it would be too hard with the size of her car and the curves, but she insisted. She probably wanted to make sure my case contained the correct contents. I played two songs before putting my guitar away.

About 40 minutes before sunset, Nancy dropped me off in Redondo Beach between A and B avenues. I walked down the sidewalk along the beach looking for a spot to spread out a towel and relax. Beach cottages, each with a patio facing the ocean, bordered the sidewalk. Four guys sat on one patio playing cards and drinking beer. One guy glanced at me, then looked back at his cards as he confidently drew a card out of his hand and tossed it to the center of the table. The card swirled once and landed face up.

I walked a ways down the sidewalk before stepping off the pavement and setting my pack and guitar on the sand. I slipped off my thick leather hiking boots, pulled my socks off and pushed them inside the boots, and then plunged my feet into the sand. It felt cool beneath the surface. Tying my boots together, I rolled up my jeans, slipped on my backpack and then slung my boots over my shoulder, causing one boot to dangle in front of my chest. I picked up my guitar and walked toward the breaking waves.

The cool, wet-packed sand felt good. I walked to the water's edge and stopped. A wave washed over my feet and covered my ankles. I expected the water to be warm, but it was cold. My feet sank below the surface of the sand. The sun, still hanging just above the horizon, radiated through the cloudless sky. I glanced back at the cottages and tall condominiums behind the cottages. This is it, I thought, the big Los Angeles. The place where dreams come true. No telling what could happen, or whom you could meet. The guys you saw on that patio could be movie stars—or become movie stars. Anything can happen out here. In fact, movie stars might be walking along the beach right now. They probably live in the condominiums over there. Hell, I might be living in those condominiums some day.

I tried to lift my right foot out of the wet sand. Another wave flowed over my ankles and came halfway up my calf. As the wave receded back to where it came from, I pulled at my foot again, creating a sucking sound. I pulled harder, stumbling a step backward and nearly falling when my foot popped out of its hold. I laughed, feeling embarrassed, and looked around to see if anyone had seen me. As far as I could tell, no one paid any attention to me, and besides, the few people close to the water's edge were looking the other way.

I strolled along the shoreline for maybe a quarter of a mile, and then moved way from the breaking waves and walked onto the dry sand. Thousands of miniature quartz spheres were being pushed behind me as my toes curled into them. I wondered about the energy in the sandy quartz crystals compared to that of a live tree or the ocean. I put down my gear and pulled a towel from my backpack. Facing the sun, I spread the towel on the ground and plopped down.

"God, this is the life," I said aloud, looking at the beach and the beautiful sunset. The ambiance filled me with awe. The sun, slowly descending toward the ocean, soon would be on the other side of the earth. I imagined somebody halfway around the world watching the sun rise. Out of the billions of people on the planet, I thought, could there ever be a time when nobody is looking at the sun? Even for a split second? The bottom of the persimmon ball touched the distant waves.

There's something mystifying about the sun sinking into a vast horizon of water.

Just a month earlier, while in Oregon, I watched the sun disappear into the ocean for the first time. I wondered if people saw what I saw. Being a kid from the Midwest, the sun merging with the sea represented a mystical and magical moment—a revelation. And, to think that several months before, I questioned the sanctity and value of life. I felt grateful to be alive.

Sitting on the beach, I pondered where I might have gone during my 40-hour nap. Wherever I went, something had been resolved within me. It also made it clear that I had to make some kind of transformation. And here I was, living out my dream of hitting the road and letting adventure take me wherever it willed.

I thought about life and how quickly things change. Less than a year before, I had completely different beliefs about what life held for me—a beautiful wife I loved, eventually a challenging and rewarding job, and of course a family once we could afford it. It's amazing how one or two decisions can radically alter one's life.

As the sun dropped below the horizon leaving a bluish-green hue above the sea, a cool breeze spurred me to dust the sand from my feet and pull on my socks and boots. Scanning the area for a phone booth, I saw what looked like a telephone next to the beach restrooms. Trudging through the sand in my boots made it feel like hiking through snow. Before reaching the sidewalk beside the restrooms, I could see three payphones attached to a large six-foot metal pole.

I went to the phone, set down my guitar and took off my backpack, then pulled my address book from my shirt pocket. Reaching in my jeans' pocket, I pulled out what money I had left, 87 cents. I spent my last two dollar bills when Nancy stopped at a McDonald's for a late lunch. Actually, I had a twenty hidden in my wallet between my social security card and a picture of my nephew, but I had vowed to use the money only in an emergency. I flipped open the address book and found Darrell's name. I held the book with my left hand and tucked the receiver under my chin. After dropping two dimes into the slot, I heard the normal low hum. When I punched the first number, the dial tone remained. I went ahead and dialed the phone number anyway— nothing but a dial tone. I pressed the coin release, and then pushed it again.

"Damn it!"

I hit the phone with my right hand and tried the coin release once more. Nothing. I hit it harder, this time slightly injuring my hand. I stepped back from the phone.

"Take that!" I yelled, kicking the phone as hard as I could.

"Hi," someone said behind me.

I turned around to see a tall, muscular man with short black hair and mustache smiling at me. The guy looked like an undercover cop. I smiled back, somewhat embarrassed, yet still irritated at the phone. "Hello."

"What's the matter?"

"Oh, this damn phone just ate my money, and I'm a little short on cash." I looked at my aching hand and then massaged it with my left hand.

"Where are you from?"

"Missouri." He stepped closer and looked at my hand.

"Are you okay?"

"Yeah," I said half laughing and looking at the phone. "This piece of junk wasn't worth hitting."

"Have you been on the road long?"

"A couple of months."

He jumped up and twisted around to sit on a five-foot wall next to the phones.

"I tried to call some friends of mine," I said as I pulled on the coin release one last time, "but this stupid thing doesn't want to cooperate."

"Is this your first time in L.A.?"

"Yeah."

"Welcome to Los Angeles, the city of angels. See that condo over there?" I looked in the direction he nodded his head. "That's where I live. You can come over and use my phone for free if you want."

"Really?"

"Sure." He hopped off the wall. "Come on. What's your name?" He extended his hand to shake. I told him my name as we shook.

"I'm Rudy."

I slung my pack over my shoulder.

"Here, let me carry your guitar," he said as he stooped and picked it up.

"That's okay, I can carry it."

"Nonsense. You've got enough to carry. Besides, it's not that heavy."

We walked up a set of steps and headed toward his condominium. He asked me what kind of work I did. I told him I had just finished college and wanted to do some traveling before I settled into a full-time job.

"How about yourself?"

"I've been managing a restaurant for the past four years, but I'm getting ready to start a new job."

"Doing what?"

"Selling insurance."

"Oh yeah? My dad sold insurance."

"Really? For who?"

"New York Life."

"That's a good company. I'm going to work for Prudential."

When we entered his condo, I saw insurance books and pamphlets spread out on his coffee table.

"That's the stuff I'm studying," he said as I looked at it. "It's not easy. It's been a while since I've done any studying."

He set my guitar down and shut the thick white door behind him. "Are you thirsty? All I've got is apple juice or water."

"Apple juice sounds great."

"Sit down and relax. I'll get it."

He went to the cabinet, took out two glasses and put them on the counter; then opened the refrigerator door. I sat on the edge of the couch and looked over the insurance booklets on the coffee table.

"What was your major in school?" he asked as he poured apple juice in the glasses.

"Originally, I planned to be a veterinarian, but then I changed to pre-med and biology, then to sociology, then journalism, and I finally graduated with a general studies degree." Rudy handed me a glass of juice and sat on the couch beside me. I took a big drink. "Where's your phone?"

"Over there." He pointed to the wall in the kitchen. "Help yourself."

"Thanks," I said, setting my glass on top of a pamphlet on the coffee table and walking to the phone. I flipped through my address book to Darrell's number. The phone rang twice before Ellen, Darrell's girlfriend, answered. She sounded surprised and pleased to hear my voice.

"How are you?" she asked with genuine enthusiasm.

"Fine," I replied. It felt great to hear someone who sounded sincerely interested in my welfare. Ellen and I had always gotten along great. Although she was a year younger than me, I always viewed her as the older sister I never had.

"Where are you?"

"I'm here in Los Angeles."

"Great!" I could hear her telling Darrell I was on the line. "Here's Darrell."

"Heyyyyyy, how ya doing?" Darrell bellowed over the phone. "Can you stay with us, or have you already got a place to stay?"

"I thought I'd stay with you guys, if it's all right?"

"Of course. You know it's all right. Where are you?"

"Redondo Beach. Do you know where that is?"

"Sure, it's close. Just a couple of miles. You can drive to our place in a few minutes."

I laughed. "I don't have a car anymore. I left it in Oregon. I've been hitchhiking for the past several months."

"Wow, that's cool," Darrell said. "I've always wanted to do that. Where exactly are you, and we'll come and get you. Are you at a phone booth?"

"No, not exactly." I looked at Rudy who sat listening to my conversation. "Hang on a second and I'll get the address."

I lowered the phone.

"What's the address here. They're going to come by and pick me up."

"Where do they live?"

I lifted the receiver to my mouth as I looked at my address book. "Darrell, is this still your address?" I proceeded to read it.

"That's it."

I gave an affirmative nod to Rudy.

"I know right where they live," Rudy said. "It's close to here. I'll run you over there."

"Did you hear that?" I asked Darrell. He had. "I'll see you in a little bit."

"Great. Oh, Ellen wants me to tell you not to eat anything. Dinner's about ready and we've got plenty."

"Sounds good to me. See you soon. Bye."

Looking forward to seeing familiar and friendly faces, I walked to the coffee table and picked up my glass of juice.

"Why don't you sit down for a second longer; then we'll go."

Although I wanted to leave, here was a guy nice enough to let me use his phone and then drive me to my friends' apartment. The least I could do was spend a few minutes. I sat down and took a big gulp of juice.

"Do you think you'll stick around L.A. and find a job?"

"I don't really know. If I do, I doubt I'll stay long."

"Where will you go from here?"

"I want to go down to San Diego and then on to Arizona and New Mexico."

"How long do you think you'll travel?"

"Until I get sick of it I guess."

"How do you pay for it?"

"Hitchhiking doesn't cost anything," I said, "and since I camp out, the only expense I have is food, and I don't mind skimping on that. Give me a jar of peanut butter and some bread, and I can last a long time. I eat a lot of fruit too, and in Oregon and California there are a lot of apples and oranges in the orchards along the road."

"Be careful taking fruit from the orchards. You can get shot doing that."

"I only take fruit that's on the ground. I figure if I don't eat it, the bugs and worms will."

I didn't tell him I was down to my last $20, half a jar of peanut butter, some crackers, an apple, and half a bag of granola. I knew I would have to find work before too long, but viewed it as a test of my faith in living in the moment.

I picked up my glass of juice and finished it in two swallows. "Thanks for the juice." I got up and carried my glass to the kitchen, rinsed the glass out with water and set it in the sink. As I came out of the kitchen, Rudy got up and strode toward me. He walked directly at me, so I stepped to one side, assuming he would do the same. He didn't. We bumped into one another. I knew it wasn't my fault, but I said, "Oh, sorry man."

Rudy set his glass on the kitchen counter and walked to the apartment window. He said nothing. I expected him to shut the shades and head for the door, but he just stood there. He didn't appear to be looking at anything outside. He turned and looked at me, then looked back out the window. Finally, he walked toward me again. He spoke when he got about five or six feet from me.

"Hey man," he curled his hand into a fist and brought it up to his chin as he came closer. He then punched me in the arm—not hard, but not easy either. He hit me the way you might hit your brother if you were a little pissed off at him or wanted to aggravate him. "Do you have a sexual preference?"

For a second I stood there breathless. He stepped closer to me before I answered. "Uh, yes I do." I moved a step away from him. "I think I'd better be going."

I turned around to pick up my backpack and guitar. My heart pounded. I just wanted to pick up my gear and get out of that apartment. As I reached for my things, Rudy grabbed me from behind, pinning my arms to my sides with a tight bear-hug hold. Rudy stood at least four inches taller than me. He weighed 190 pounds or more versus my 5'9" frame and 140 pounds.

As he squeezed me tightly, my heart rapidly thumped against my chest. Everything in the room became exceedingly clear. The gold doorknob and its gold-painted casing stood out like a bright star surrounded by black sky. The condominium door separated me from where I wanted to be. It was my avenue to freedom. Despite being a mere 10 feet from me, the door felt like an impassable barricade. Even the dark curly hair on Rudy's large muscular arms wrapped across my chest became clear and distinct. His huge hands and well-manicured fingernails dug into his forearms as they pressed into my breastbone. My mind raced. I struggled for a breath, totally cognizant of his massive arms constricting my ribs to the point of pain. Unexpectedly, my mind flashed back to a scene at the walk-in campground where I sat next to a campfire with John.

"If a person ever grabs you from behind," John said, "the first thing you do is completely relax. When you do that, whoever's holding you will relax too—always. It's a natural reaction. When you feel the other person relax, you make your move. You can do one of several things. You can throw your feet straight out in front of you so you sit down, slipping out from the person's grasp. You can raise your foot and stomp on the arch of their foot as hard as you can, which will immobilize the person long enough for you to get free. Or, you can give the person a hard elbow jab to the stomach and knock the wind out of him. Your purpose is to get away. Once you're out of their grasp, you can either run or work with the chi to protect yourself."

The enormous arms around me tightened against my chest with a short quick yank, forcing a pocket of air to escape from my lungs. My head snapped back. My vision blurred. I saw a sparkle of light reflect off the gold doorknob. The thought of being raped filled me with terror. As the gold doorknob and white door came back into focus, I once again viewed the surroundings as if it were one big photograph. In addition to the door and its handle, I now saw the couch, the lamp sitting on the end table, the coffee table with pamphlets and books on it, the small kitchen on my left, and Rudy's hands firmly gripping his forearms. I saw the total picture just as John had discussed. Rudy's large arms surrounding my chest tightened and pulled me closer. His hips pressed hard against me. My heart furiously pounded against his hairy forearms. I knew what I had to do.

When I relaxed my body, a strange thing happened. I became a partial observer to the scene, as in a dream where you are watching yourself do something, but at the same time you are actually doing it. Just as John predicted, Rudy's grip loosened. Slipping out from under his hold, however, seemed impossible. I doubted whether I could raise my foot and scrape down his shin to stomp on the arch of his foot, but knew I could give him a hard elbow to his ribs and stomach. I hesitated, and then chose to talk, and talk fast.

"Rudy, I'm not into this at all. If you thought I was leading you on at the beach, I'm sorry. I wasn't. I had no idea this is what you had in mind. I accepted your offer to use the phone because that's what I would have done for someone. I have nothing against you personally; it's just that I'm straight. I've never had an attraction to men. I'm sorry. That's just the way it is. I respect your right to live how you wish. All I ask is that you respect mine."

My calm voice surprised me. Although the words came from my mouth, I still remained a partial observer listening. Rudy released me. I immediately stepped away and turned around to face him. I forgot about running out the door.

"I'm sorry." I looked into his eyes. "I'm just not into this type of thing." I backed up a few steps to put more space between us. "I don't want to fight. I'll just pick up my things and go quietly."

"That's okay," he said. "Let's put your gear in the car and go."

"You don't need to give me a ride," I replied quickly. "I can find my way."

"Look," Rudy said, raising his voice and sounding upset, "I said I'd give you a ride, and I will."

Although no longer wanting a ride from him, I felt afraid to decline for fear it might lead to further conflict. To be in his car on a public street seemed much safer than the seclusion of his apartment.

"Okay," I said, "if you still want to."

He picked up my guitar as I grabbed my pack. I walked outside first, and he slammed the white door behind him. We entered the garage and climbed in his Chevy Malibu, putting my things in the back seat. Neither of us spoke. He started the car and quickly backed out of the garage into an open parking area. I felt I needed to say something, but didn't know what to say.

As I sat motionless, still stunned by what had transpired, Melanie's haunting words came back to me: "Bryce, you trust people too much. Please tell me you'll be careful." Trust or no trust, we never really know what's coming next. For all I knew, Rudy might be driving me to an isolated beach or park.

I suddenly blurted out, "How long have you been gay?" The words sounded flat, silly and stupid. I couldn't believe I asked that. It just came out.

"About four years, but I really don't want to talk about it."

He turned left onto a street that ran parallel to the ocean. Another long silent spell ensued. I tried to think of something else to say. Finally, I broke the uncomfortable silence with another question.

"What's the restaurant business like here?"

He hesitated before answering.

"It's okay, although robbers have hit my restaurant twice."

"Really?" I wanted to keep the conversation going. "What happened?"

"The first time a guy came in and flashed a knife, and then asked for all the money."

"What did you do?"

"I took the knife away from him and held him down until the police got there."

"That's pretty brave considering it's not your money."

Rudy geared down the Malibu engine to nearly a stop before glancing both ways at a four-way stop sign and easing on through the intersection. "Not really. I've got my black belt in karate."

A chill ran through me. I thought about what he would have done to me if I had given him an elbow to the stomach. I momentarily wondered if he really had his black belt. He looked strong and in good shape.

"What happened the second time?"

"A guy came in with a gun."

"What did you do then?"

"Huh," he grunted, "I gave him the money. I'm not stupid."

We rode the rest of the way in silence. He turned into the apartment's parking lot and stopped.

"Look," he said as he pulled out a pad and pen from his shirt pocket and began writing. "Here's my address and phone number. If you decide to stick around the area, come by and visit, or call me. Maybe I can help you find a job."

He pushed the piece of paper toward me with his left hand as he extended his right hand to shake. I took the paper and shook his hand.

"Thanks."

"Good luck," he added as I got out of the car and pulled my pack and guitar from the back seat. He backed up slowly while I waited for him to leave. I didn't want him to know my friends' apartment number. As he drove away, I waved, took in a deep breath and exhaled. With my heart still racing, I walked toward the sidewalk that led to my friends' apartment complex. I looked up at the twilight sky. "Thanks for getting me here safely," I said aloud.

Thanksgiving Holdup

"**D**amn," I said while staring at the closed Safeway store on the outskirts of Price, Utah. I couldn't stop thinking about one of those hoagies with turkey and cheese.

We saw the police car at the same time.

"A honker," Martin commented, "and it looks like he's heading our way."

The car turned into the parking lot and drove toward us. Two policemen were inside the car.

Martin and I had been hitchhiking together for two days. Martin was fairly tall, maybe six-foot-one, and thin. He had a tough and weathered appearance because of his bad complexion and wavy dark brown hair that hung to the top of his shoulders. He looked as if he had a bad case of chicken pox as a child and scratched them so hard it caused indentations and pocked scars. When he wasn't smiling, he looked mean. Although only 18 years old, Martin's pockmarks made him look five to ten years older. We met at sunrise the day before Thanksgiving along a Denver onramp to Interstate 70. As we stood there visiting, a pickup truck stopped and told us to throw our things in the back. We had been traveling together since then.

We spent our first night in a haystack on the west side of Rifle, Colorado. Fortunately, we both had good sleeping bags. The temperature plummeted to 10 degrees that evening. Although Martin originally planned to stop in Crescent Junction, Utah, to visit relatives for the holiday, he changed his mind when I told him I intended to visit the Mormon Temple in Salt Lake City.

"Would you mind if I tagged along with you to the temple?" he asked.

"That's fine with me."

117

After leaving my friends' apartment in southern California, I returned to Missouri and worked three weeks with a construction crew hired by my great uncle. The temporary job put a little more than $500 in my bank account, so I decided to hitchhike to Portland, Oregon, to pick up my wheels.

Surprisingly, Martin and I caught rides fairly fast, and that's unusual for two male hitchhikers. We were dropped off about 11 p.m. on a highway that ran behind a Safeway store in Price. The bright lights on the other side of the store made us think it might be opened.

As the police car pulled up beside us, the driver rolled down his window a few inches. "Pretty cold to be out on the road," he said.

I smiled and countered, "Yeah, do you know what the temperature is?"

"The last I heard it was three degrees." He paused slightly before continuing. "Do you boys have any identification?"

We both dug in our back pockets for our wallets. The policeman on the passenger's side got out of the car and walked to the front right fender and stood there. After we handed our licenses to the driver, he rolled up his window and spoke into his CB microphone. I walked around to the officer standing by the car, set my guitar down, and spoke to him in a friendly and joking manner.

"Do you do this to everyone passing through town?"

"No, it's just a routine check. You got nothing to worry about."

I loosened my pack and took it off. Although the cop smiled as he looked at me, his hands remained outside of his pockets, and he made sure he could see both of us. Martin walked around the squad car and joined me.

"It's really too cold for you to be out here," the officer said. "If I were you guys, I'd go over there," he motioned toward a hotel on the other side of the highway, "and get a room for the night."

"I'm a little short on funds," I said. "At least it won't be this cold in Portland."

"Is that where you're heading?"

"Yes."

Martin spoke up. "We hope to get to Salt Lake City tonight."

Before Martin finished his sentence, the other officer got out of the car. He walked to the front fender with his right hand resting on the gun in his holster. He stopped with his legs shoulder width apart. "I want both of you to get up against that wall and spread out!" he commanded in a deeper voice than when he greeted us. His left hand pointed toward the Safeway wall.

For a moment we did nothing. I think we were shocked by what he said. The other officer stepped away from us and put his hand on his gun. I looked at him incredulously.

"Now!" screamed the driver. "Move it!"

We both turned and walked toward the wall. I heard a snap, and then another. I later realized they were the snaps to their holsters. After taking several steps, I stopped and turned around to face them.

"Wait a minute, what's this all about? We've done nothing wrong."

The officer I had been talking to now held his gun in both hands. The gun perched next to his shoulder pointing toward the stars. He moved the gun to his chest and extended it forward, zeroing in on me. I experienced a moment of disbelief, and then shock and fear. Staring into the black hole at the end of the revolver, I realized that one man moving a thin metal trigger an eight of an inch with his index finger could alter my world dramatically.

For a split second, I imagined what it would be like to have a bullet rip through my skull. I thought of my parents, my brother and sister. They would know I had done nothing wrong, but in either case, I would be dead, and the policeman before me would walk free. I thought about Melanie. Would she even hear about my death? Then I thought about myself. Am I now going to find out what it's really all about? Is there life after death? Will I be able to remember this life when I'm dead? Will I meet friends and relatives already deceased?

"Get your hands in the air and get up against the wall!" the cop shouted.

I raised my hands as high as I could reach. "Take it easy, guys. We haven't done anything wrong."

I turned and leaned into the wall. I imagined the headlines above the one or two-paragraph story on the inside page of a Salt Lake City newspaper. "Vagrant Shot By Police," or "Suspected Thief Killed," or because I had a pocket knife, it might read, "Armed Transient Shot Dead."

If I saw a headline like that, then read the article based on the police report, I would probably say, "Let that be a warning to other out-of-state thieves that think they can come in here and rip us off." Articles can be so misleading. I laugh when I hear people say, "I'm just telling it like it is." Of course, that's the way it is, or was, according to that person's perception. This particular case was no different. I'm sure the police have their own version of that Thanksgiving night encounter.

Suddenly, I heard a car drive up and a car door slam. I turned my head to look, but saw nothing except the inside of my coat hood. I tried stretching my head out of the hood for a better view, but my neck was too short. My coat had a big hood with fur around the edge. Without pulling the hood off or turning around, I could see nothing behind me.

"Spread your legs out," I heard. I leaned my head forward and looked at Martin who stood five feet to my left. An officer kicked at Martin's ankles. "Spread your arms apart." Martin followed the officer's instructions. I heard a shuffling noise behind me. Keeping my hands held high, I slowly turned around. Before I reached a quarter of the way around, someone pushed me toward the wall with their hand in the middle of my back.

"Up against the wall and spread those arms out!" I did what he said. "Wider! And spread your legs," he commanded as if I were resisting.

He kicked my heels hard to make me spread my legs farther apart. I had on heavy leather hiking boots with two pairs of socks. His kicks didn't hurt, but they would have if I'd been wearing light boots or tennis shoes.

I felt his hands go into my coat pockets. He pulled out a bottle of brandy from my right coat pocket, looked at it, and then put it back. He reached around me and unzipped my coat. His hands touched my shoulders and slid down my chest. He stopped when he got to my flannel shirt pockets. He pulled out a harmonica from one pocket, glanced at it, and let it slide back into the pocket. He came down my chest to my waist, slid his hand along the belt to my rear, and then slipped his hand into my front left jean pocket. He felt the spare change and withdrew his hand. He reached into my right front pocket and pulled out my Swiss Army knife. He kept it. With one hand on my right thigh and the other hand on my right rear, he slid his hands down to my right boot. He reached inside the boot with a finger and circled around the edge. He moved to the left boot and did the same thing; then slid his hands up my left leg. When he got to my rear and thigh, he lightly slapped the back of his hand into my crotch. I flinched and grunted. Satisfied nothing was there that shouldn't be, he put one hand between my shoulder blades.

"Put your right hand behind your back," he commanded. As I did so, a cold metal handcuff touched my wrist. He squeezed the adjustable handcuff uncomfortably tight. "Now your left hand."

"Hey!" I blurted. "Not so hard."

He then slapped the cold metal on my left wrist and decided to show me how tight he could make it. He forced the metal deeper into my skin. My wrist throbbed beneath the handcuff.

"Let's go," he said.

He grabbed me by the back of my coat and swung me around. I felt vulnerable and helpless. I realized that if I tripped and fell, my head and face would crash into the pavement below me. Martin already sat in the back of a police car with both officers in the front seat. They were watching us. The officer took me to the passenger's side of his car and opened the front door. As he did so, the other cop car sped away.

"Get in," he said. As I bent down to get in the car, he put his hand on my head and pushed it down so I wouldn't bump my head on the door frame. He nearly pushed my head into the dash. After I scooted in, he slammed the door. Warm air blasting from the heater felt good. The cop climbed into the driver's seat next to me and pulled his door shut.

"Could you do me a favor?" I asked as pleasantly as I could.

"What?" he responded in a disgusted and authoritative tone.

"Could you please pull this hood off my head?"

He reached over and pulled the hood down. I looked at him as he put the car in gear, and we started to move.

"Now that I can see what's going on," I said, "do you mind telling me why I'm handcuffed and being taken to the police station?" I spoke in a calm and polite manner. The officer said nothing. "That is where we're going, isn't it?"

"Yes," he said as he looked to his left before pulling onto the street. "There's an APB out on your buddy."

An APB means an "all points bulletin." In other words, they wanted Martin for something.

"Really?" I took a second to think. "All I know is that he's a student from Denver. We met on the road. He seems like a nice guy to me. What did he do wrong?"

"He's not wanted for anything, just questioning."

"Oh."

I figured I'd find out more when we got to the station. My attention went back to the handcuffs. My wrists were aching, especially the left one. When we got to the police station, the officer came around to my door and helped me out of the car. He took me inside and escorted me through several sets of doors to a jail cell. Martin already stood in one. He opened the door to Martin's cell and gently pushed me in before shutting the door and walking away. Martin stared at me. I spun toward the entryway to see the officer walking through a set of swinging doors.

"Hey, I'm still..." The doors swung shut before he could hear the last word. "...handcuffed. Jesus, this is unreal." I turned and faced Martin.

"What did you do?" he asked.

"What do you mean what did I do?"

"They told me there's an APB out on you."

"That's what they told me about you," I said.

"Really?"

"Yeah, really. The cop told me you were wanted for questioning. Have you been involved in anything shady?"

"No, unless you call going to school a crime."

"They're just messing with us then."

The jail cell must have been bugged because as soon as we finished talking about the fact that we had done nothing wrong, the two officers that originally stopped us walked through the swinging doors. One carried a sheet of paper. The other officer opened the cell door and walked around behind me to take off my handcuffs. The officer carrying the paper spoke.

"I'm sorry for the inconvenience gentlemen, but we had a description that fit you, Mr. Yarborough."

The other officer had my right handcuff off. Before he unlocked the left handcuff, I said, "Oh yeah? Let me see his picture." I snatched the paper from the officer's hand and looked at it. Instead of a picture, it contained a blank white square. I looked at the name. He had a different first name, but my last name. They wanted him for robbery, assault with intent to kill and steeling a car. He lived in Atlanta, Georgia, stood five-foot-ten-inches tall, weighed 145 pounds and had brown eyes. Then I saw it, race—Negroid.

"It says..." I looked at the officer. They both laughed. "I can't believe this." I turned to Martin. "Let's get out of here."

I walked through the cell doors and then thought about my pocket knife. I turned to the officers.

"Where's my knife?"

"What knife?" asked the officer who had removed my handcuffs.

"The one you took from me."

"I didn't take a knife from you. Did you take a knife from him?" He looked at the other officer.

"I didn't take it."

I plopped down in a chair outside the jail cell. "Well, I'm not leaving until I get my knife back."

"Just a second," the other officer said, and he left the room. A minute later he returned.

"Is this it?"

Of course it was. He handed it to me and I slipped it in my pocket. When we got to the front office, I saw my backpack sitting on the floor. My heart leaped. I had forgotten about half a bag of pot hidden in the center of my aluminum mess kit at the bottom of a side pouch. Obviously, they had not found it. We picked up our gear and headed toward the door. The officer sitting at the front desk watched us.

"Where's the highway that goes to Salt Lake City?" I asked him.

He paused momentarily, and then spoke slowly.

"Go to the main road in front and turn left."

"Is that the road?"

"It turns into it."

If the cops had left us alone, we might have been halfway to Salt Lake City. Martin and I made it to Salt Lake City late that night. A power plant worker about 40 years old dropped us off several blocks from the Mormon Temple. According to the changing lights on a bank sign, we arrived at 1:43 a.m., the temperature two degrees. We tried opening an apartment complex door so we could sleep in the hall, but it was locked. I thought about waiting around until someone came out or went in, but then dropped the idea. We walked up a hill searching for a place to sleep when we spotted a house with no lights on and no curtains. Looking through the windows, we could see the rooms had no furniture. We tried lifting the windows and turning the door knobs, but they were locked. We walked around to the back yard where the lights of Salt Lake City stretched out below us.

"What do you think?" I said to Martin. "Do you want to camp here?"

"It's as good a place as any."

We spread our ponchos on the ground close to the back of the house and rolled out our sleeping bags. Within minutes after curling up in my sleeping bag and pulling the top of the bag over my head, I fell asleep.

When I popped my head out of my bag the next morning, the sun peaking over the mountains shot beams of light through the snow-covered trees and thick-bristled evergreens. Four inches of glistening snow covered the trees and ground around us. The thousands of twinkling sparkles glimmering off the snow's surface created an ethereal hue. In the distance, the snow-covered mountain range blazed with the sun's rays like the white glow of a welder's blowtorch.

The city still slept in silence beneath this pristine white comforter. No wind or breeze blew. For a moment, my ears rang from the silence, but then some snow fluttered down from an evergreen branch as two small birds flitted away from the tree and flew over me, their fluttering wings sputtering in the frigid air. One landed on the house gutter above us, the other in a hole beneath the gutter. They chirped at each other furiously as if they were racing to the hole and were now fighting about which one really got there first.

Martin twisted in his bag and gave a little cough. The snow had fallen off the top of Martin's bag, but the bottom of his bag remained buried. Martin laid on his side in a fetal position.

"Martin, wake up! Get a load of this!"

"What?" he mumbled.

"Just look."

He turned slightly to face me as he slowly pulled the sleeping bag away from his face to peek out.

"Shit!" He raised up on one elbow and looked around. Martin's stocking cap, pulled down to his eyebrows, made him tilt his head back to see. "Unreal!" he exclaimed as he pushed the cap to the middle of his forehead. Martin sat up and kicked the inside of his sleeping bag to knock the snow off it. He looked at the mountain range in the distance. "This is too much, and it's so quiet."

The distant sound of a snowplow's blade scraping pavement severed the stillness.

Martin looked at me and smiled. "How about breakfast in bed?"

I laughed. "Yeah, sure. Waiter?" I yelled, looking around as if I were in a restaurant.

"I'm serious." Martin leaned over and blew at the snow on his backpack. A small portion of the snow puffed out and settled back to the ground. He took his glove and dusted off the remaining snow. He reached in his pack and pulled out his one-burner stove and an aluminum egg carton holding six eggs. "It's about time I used these."

We ended up sipping apricot brandy while eating scrambled eggs and partially toasted bread.

123

"Look at us," I said, gazing toward the mountain range. "We're on top of the world."

Martin pushed his small aluminum frying pan into the snow. "We've come a long way in less than twelve hours. From a jail cell to the top of the world."

We each took several more hits of apricot brandy. I let out a huge belch.

"Mmm," I said, "nothing like a good belch after a great meal."

Martin tucked his chin slightly and let out a matching belch. "Agreed," he added.

We packed up our things and walked to the Mormon Temple visitor's center. Painted high above us on the domed ceiling stood Jesus with planets and stars behind him. It suggested, at least to me, that Jesus was the doorway to the Universe.

"Wow, that's heavy," Martin said as he stared at the ceiling. "What do you think?"

I stood with my head tilted back, gaping in awe. "Well," I said slowly, "whoever painted it must have been scared shitless."

"Yeah, that's a ways up there."

"And," I added, "if he fell forward, he would have disappeared into outer space."

We both laughed.

"Do you believe in God?" Martin asked, looking at me. He then looked back at the ceiling.

"Without a doubt," I replied, returning my gaze to the painting. "I don't believe this world is an accident. Besides, have you ever heard of Pascal's wager?"

"No," Martin said, still looking at the mural. "What's that?"

I paused momentarily as I thought back to my philosophy class at the university. "Well," I began, "if you don't believe in God, and there is a God, you've got problems. On the other hand, if you do believe in God, and there is no God, it's all the same. At least you covered your ass. That's not exactly how Pascal put it, but it's close enough to give you the idea."

"I never thought of it like that," he said, "but it makes sense." Martin looked up at the mural above us. "Do you believe Christ really existed?"

I looked up at the mural.

"Yes," I said. "There's been too much written about him."

I could see Martin look at me from my peripheral vision.

"Do you believe he was the son of God?"

I looked at him, remembering an experience I had at 17, a year younger than Martin.

I had been talking to a high school friend about God and Jesus when he invited me to hear an evangelist speak at the Shrine Mosque in Springfield, Missouri. Although I fail to recall the name of the speaker, when the evangelist asked for anyone who wanted to be saved to come to the stage, I went. My friend accompanied me. Literally hundreds came down from their seats. They took us to several large rooms and hooked us up with one of "God's" helpers. The person asked me to pray aloud what I felt and to ask for forgiveness. I had a tough time doing that. To the disappointment of my helper, I prayed to God for guidance and direction.

The emotional event, however, sparked me to begin reading the Bible. I figured I should read it like any other book and interpret it for myself.

"During my junior and senior years in high school," I told Martin, "I read the Bible from beginning to end, and then read the New Testament again. Christ had to have been plugged into spirit to be so wise. Like the time a group of people were about to stone Mary Magdalene for being a prostitute. He brought it to an abrupt end when he said, 'Let he who has never sinned throw the first stone.' That had to be divine wisdom."

"So you believe he was the son of God?"

"Yes, just like I believe we all are the sons and daughters of God."

"That's not what I mean," Martin replied.

"I know, but that's what I believe."

"So you think Jesus was the same as you and me?"

"Yes and no. He was a human being like you and me, and he was connected to spirit like you and me. His difference came in the power and strength of his spiritual connection. It was much stronger than the normal person's. But remember, he spent his whole life focused on spirit, and probably many lives before that."

"So you believe in reincarnation?"

"It makes sense, especially if our soul continues on forever."

Martin said nothing.

"Whether reincarnation is true or not," I continued, "I don't believe it matters. One thing is for sure. Christ was a wise and spiritual being. If everyone followed his teachings, this world would be a great place to live. I guess if I were to sum up what I got from reading about Christ, it would boil down to love. That was his main message. Love your neighbors, love your enemies, love everyone. I think he was saying God is love, and who can argue with that? Unless, of course, you're an atheist, but even an atheist must admit that love makes life worth living, or at least a lot more enjoyable."

We both looked up once more.

"It's too bad Jesus never wrote a book," I continued. "All we know about the man is what others claim he said and did in the Bible. Maybe he was too busy living his truth to write it down. One thing I do recall reading in the Bible is that Jesus said the kingdom of heaven is within us, and to find the truth, all we have to do is look within. He even said that if we do this, we could do greater things than he did."

125

"It's hard to know what to believe these days," Martin said.

We walked toward a glass window that showed pictures and artifacts recapping the Mormon's journey west.

I looked at Martin. "Just remember Pascal's wager."

By noon we left the Mormon Temple visitor's center. The sunshine and dry air put the temperature in the middle 40s. The once pure sparkling white blanket of snow now displayed wrinkles of gray. As a car zoomed past us, its tires sliced the slushy wet folds of soot, splashing it through the air onto the snow beside us like a child throwing dark paint onto a white canvas.

"You know," Martin said as we neared the on-ramp to Interstate 80, "I'm glad I met you. I've always wanted to try hitchhiking, and this is the first time I've ever done it. Thanks for letting me tag along."

"My pleasure," I said, putting out my hand. "Maybe we'll cross paths again some time."

"I hope so," he said, and we shook hands.

As I walked up the on-ramp to Interstate 80, Martin walked toward Interstate 15 about half a mile away. The third car going up the Interstate 80 on-ramp stopped to pick me up. When I pulled the door shut, I looked back toward Interstate 15. Martin stood waving to me. I rolled down the window and waved back. "All right!" he yelled.

Freeze Out

From Salt Lake City, I caught a ride to Boise, Idaho, where three prostitutes picked me up. All three of them sat in the front seat. They began comparing me to other men or clients by asking me a question to see if my response would be similar to that of the man they all knew. It turned into a rather strange head game, but an amusing one. After 10 minutes or so, the cutest one sitting on the passenger's side next to the door said she thought she had me pegged.

She turned and looked at me. "I can make you feel really good for $25," she said. She moved her tongue over her top lip, leaving it moist. "And I mean really good," she said seductively.

I saw the driver look at me in the rearview mirror. The girl in the middle glanced up at the rearview mirror, but she couldn't see me from her angle.

"I feel really good now," I said, "and it doesn't cost anything."

The other two girls cracked up laughing and teased the girl that propositioned me. From what I could gather, she expected me to try to bargain for a lower price. They had to stop in Ontario, Oregon, for business purposes—at least that's what they said. They took me to the last exit out of Ontario.

"If we see you again," the driver with glossy red lips said, "we'll pick you up and take you to Portland."

After picking up my car in Portland, I spent the next month traveling through Oregon and California before returning to Springfield, Missouri. Broke and in need of a job, I moved into a two-bedroom apartment with my sister and desperately searched for work. After filling out two to four job applications every weekday for three weeks, I became totally discouraged, so I decided to hitchhike to Columbia to visit some friends, and then head on to Kansas City to see my parents. Due to the potentially cold and wet weather, I left my guitar behind.

My friends in Columbia were intrigued with my travel stories. It was fun recounting them. When I got to Kansas City, my parents suggested I stay with them and search for work there. I told them I might do that if no jobs turned up in Springfield. During a cold, sunny mid-January day, my mother drove me to Interstate 70 just east of the Kansas City Royals' baseball stadium. Prepared for the climate, I wore long underwear, two pairs of socks (the first pair cotton and the second pair wool), blue jeans, a flannel shirt and sweater, leather ski mittens with a wool lining, a muffler, a stocking cap and a winter coat. Although my decision to hitchhike a new route to Springfield meant traveling 15 to 20 miles farther than the old route, I believed traffic would be heavier, which would increase my odds of making it to Springfield by 6 p.m. or sooner.

So much for logic, although it initially appeared to be a good decision. Within 10 minutes after my mom dropped me off, I caught a ride from an old man on his way home. I remember the old man's name because of a strange letter I received from him later. Richard seemed lonely and reminded me of my grandfather who had died several years before.

"Where are you going?" he asked.

"To Springfield to find a job." When I mentioned my travels to him, he got excited and kept asking questions about where I'd been and what happened. He wanted to stop for a beer and visit. I told him I needed to keep moving, but he insisted. What's 15 or 20 minutes, I thought. Besides, a beer would taste good. We took the Oak Grove exit and stopped at the first bar along the road. We drank a beer, then another, and another. An hour later, I was loaded. Richard motioned to the bartender.

"No more for me," I said as the bartender approached our table. "I need to get going. I want to make it to Springfield tonight."

"Just one more," Richard said.

"No thanks, I'm done. And I mean it." I gulped down the last swig and got up. "I'll be right back. I'm going to the john."

When I returned, Richard stood by the door. Once outside the bar, we found cloudy skies and a stronger north wind than when we entered. We continued driving east. When we came to the Odessa exit, about 10 or 12 miles from Oak Grove, Richard took it and said, "I'd like to buy you another beer. I know a good place."

"Richard, I appreciate the offer, but I don't really want another beer."

"Just one more beer. That's all. Besides, I need to use the bathroom."

Two beers later I got up from the table. The dials on the clock above the bar showed 3:25.

"I'm going to the john and then I've really got to go. I don't want to end up hitchhiking in the dark."

"Okay," Richard said. "I'll pay the bill, and we'll hit the road."

While I stood at the urinal, Richard came in. He entered the toilet stall.

"Do you think you have time to make it to Springfield before dark?" he asked as he urinated.

"No," I answered, knowing that by 5 or 5:15 the sun would set, "but if I can get a ride before it gets dark, I'll be fine."

This time, as we walked out of the bar, small yet numerous snowflakes whipped down at a north to south angle. Before the snow could accumulate on the highway, however, the speeding cars sent the flakes whirling into small funnels, causing the tiny tornadoes to disappear into the falling snow. Richard flipped on the radio. Within five minutes, a weather report said Missouri could expect blizzard conditions with temperatures dropping to 10 below zero. We were several minutes away from Highway 13 that led to Springfield.

"You know," Richard said as he put his hand on my knee, "I've really enjoyed our visit. It's rare to meet someone so adventurous as you. How old are you?"

He looked at me, and then looked back at the highway in front of him. I expected him to take his hand off my knee, but he didn't. I didn't give it much thought because some people are touchers. You know the kind—the hand on the shoulder, a light slap on the back, a hug.

"Twenty-two."

He rocked my leg back and forth.

"You've got a lot to look forward to. I'd give anything to be your age again. Just keep on living like you are. You're on the right track."

He gave my leg a gentle but firm squeeze and then returned his hand to the steering wheel. The squeeze made me question his motive. After a moment of silence, he spoke again.

"I was just thinking that if you want," he paused slightly, "you can stay at my house tonight and get an early start in the morning. That way you wouldn't risk traveling in the dark or getting stuck in this blizzard."

I considered his offer briefly. "Thanks, but I think I'll keep moving." I now had an uncomfortable feeling about Richard, but at the same time, what he said made sense. I regretted the beer stops. I looked at the cold blowing snow.

"It's no problem," he said. "I have plenty of room. You can sleep as late as you want. It's not a mansion or anything, but it's warm."

I hesitated another moment before responding. "I need to get to Springfield, but thanks. I appreciate the offer."

We turned onto the off ramp leading to Highway 13.

"Are you sure? I'd love to have you."

"Yeah, I'm sure."

"Okay, but will you do me a favor?"

We had reached the end of the ramp and Richard drove his car onto the shoulder.

"If I can."

He reached over to the glove compartment in front of me and leaned down, letting his arm rest on my leg and putting his head close to my crotch as he opened the glove box.

"I want to give you my address so you can drop me a letter or postcard to let me know you made it to Springfield. Will you do that?"

"Sure."

He slowly removed a small spiral notepad and pen from the glove box and pushed off my leg to sit back up. "I've really enjoyed our time together," he said as he wrote his name and address. "Here." He ripped the paper from the notepad and handed it to me. "Thanks so much for the stories." He held out his hand, and we shook.

"You're welcome. Thanks for the beer."

"It was my pleasure." He slowly let go of my hand.

I slipped the piece of paper in my pocket and pulled my zipper to the middle of my chest before wrapping my muffler around my neck and stuffing the ends inside my jacket. Then I zipped the coat up to my chin.

"I wish you the best."

"Thanks." I pulled my stocking cap down over my ears and pushed the door into the wind. A gust of cold air and snow hit me in the face. I pulled my muffler up over my nose and shut the front door. I opened the back door and grabbed my backpack. Richard watched me.

"So long," I said as I shut the back door. He waved his hand, and I heard a faint "Good luck" as his lips moved.

I slung the pack over one arm and walked along the shoulder of Highway 13 as the wind whipped snow into my back. The icy snowflakes pecked at my coat. I heard Richard's car pull out. I turned slightly and waved; then walked a short distance before I stopped along the shoulder and took off my pack. I danced around and flexed my muscles to stay warm. Keeping my back to the wind, I periodically glanced around to look for cars.

As soon as the two-door Chevy Impala turned onto Highway 13, I knew the driver planned to stop. There were two guys in the front seat with a girl sitting between them. One guy had hair down to his shoulders, and the other guy had a long ponytail. The girl had long brown hair parted in the middle. They stopped with their door next to me. The guy with shoulder length hair jumped out of the car and pushed the seat forward as the girl moved closer toward the driver.

"Jump in."

"Thanks for stopping." I tossed my pack in the back seat and climbed in after it. The driver looked at me through his rearview mirror and the girl turned and smiled. I could smell the stale smoke of marijuana in the car.

"You been waiting long?" the driver asked.

I looked at his reflection in the mirror.

"Not too long. Maybe 20 or 30 minutes." I had probably been there 10 minutes or less, but people giving rides feel better when you've been waiting longer. I usually exaggerated my waiting time by doubling or tripling it.

"That's a long time in this shit," said the other guy as he pulled the door shut. "You must be freezing."

"Yeah, I'm sure glad I wore long johns."

They laughed.

"My name's Eric," said the driver. "This is Elizabeth and that's Jason." Elizabeth said hi, and Jason reached back and shook my hand.

"Where you going?" Eric asked as he began pulling out onto the highway.

"Down to Springfield. How about you guys?"

"Warrensburg. We're in school there. Do you smoke?" He looked at me in the mirror.

"Not cigarettes."

He smiled at me in the mirror and looked over at Jason. "Fire another one up."

Jason slipped his fingers into his shirt pocket and pulled out a joint. Elizabeth struck a match and held it in front of him. He took a big hit and handed it back to me. He held the smoke in his lungs as he talked.

"Take a couple of hits before you pass it back." He sucked in a little more air and continued. "We're way ahead of you."

The others laughed, and Jason coughed out the smoke and chuckled.

"Smells good," I said as I took a medium-sized hit. The smoke went down smooth. I took several hits, and then reached forward to hand it to the driver. I could see the speedometer. We were up to 60 mph. I sucked in a little extra air to hold my hit longer.

"Take another one," Eric said. He had been watching me in the mirror.

"If you say so."

I blew out the smoke and took another hit; then held the joint between Eric and Elizabeth. Elizabeth took it and handed it to Eric.

"Hey," Jason said looking at me, "Want a swig of wine to wash it down?"

He reached down to the floor board in front of him and picked up a bottle of white wine. He removed the cork sticking out of it and held the half-full bottle in front of me.

"Thanks." Although still half crocked from the beer, I wanted something wet for my parched mouth. The dry German wine did little to quench my thirst, but it had a nice fruity flavor. I realized also how desperately I needed to piss. I looked at the snow accumulating on the ground. At least it wasn't sticking on the highway.

Eric grabbed rock singer Jethro Tull's tape *Aqualung* and pushed it into the tape player before cranking the volume up. There were two speakers below the rear window behind my head as well as a speaker in each door. I saw Jason say

131

something that made all three of them laugh, but I couldn't hear what he said. I leaned back and shut my eyes. My mind spun within the music.

Someone turned down the music as we entered Warrensburg. I leaned forward and looked around.

"This is our destination," Eric said.

I began bundling up again. It was now twilight, and the snowflakes were huge. Because of the wind, there were four to eight-inch drifts in some spots, while in other areas you could still see the grass or pavement. They dropped me off in front of a pizza parlor. I thanked them for the ride as Jason hopped out of the car and pulled the seat forward.

"God it's cold out here," he said.

I climbed out.

"Good luck," Eric yelled.

I bent down and looked at them. "Thanks for the ride and the buzz."

Jason reached out and shook my hand. "I hope you catch a ride straight through, brother."

"Me too. Thanks."

As Eric drove the car away from the curb, he beeped the horn.

I slipped my right arm through the pack strap and walked toward the pizza parlor—making new tracks in the snow as I went. After using the restroom and washing my hands, I put my mouth under the faucet for a drink. I looked in the mirror and saw water dripping from my three-week beard. I wiped the water off with the back of my hand and admired the fuzzy growth. Finally, I thought, I can grow a fairly decent beard. I had been wanting to grow a beard since my senior year in high school. It certainly wasn't a thick beard, but it was a beard nonetheless. My long hair stuck out from beneath my stocking cap. As I walked out of the john, the manager stood with his arms crossed watching me. He appeared upset. After starting toward the door, I changed direction and walked straight at the manager.

"Hi," I said, and smiled.

The manager was several inches taller than me and had a large gut. He looked like a beer drinker. At first he gave me a stern look, but then grinned. His brownish-blond hair, receding on top, covered his ears.

"How you doin'?"

"Fine," I said. "I hope it was okay to use your restroom. I was about to explode."

"Surrrrre," he drew out in a low southern drawl, "where ya goin'?"

"Springfield. Have you heard a weather report?"

I already knew the forecast from Richard's car radio, but wanted to make conversation.

"Supposed to get worse. They're callin' for ten to twelve inches of snow with blizzard conditions. It's eight degrees out there now, and they say the wind chill is twenty below. Are you hitchhikin' in this stuff?"

"Yeah. When I left Kansas City, it was twenty degrees and sunny."

"What time did you leave?"

"Around noon."

"Goin' kind of slow, ain't it?"

"Yeah." I looked outside. "And it usually goes slower at night."

"There won't be many cars out in this." His statement shot a pang of panic through me. "If it keeps snowin', we might even close up early. I've already sent two people home."

The only waitress working walked passed us and yelled to the cook in back she needed a medium pepperoni and mushroom pizza. She hung the ticket on a wheel and then looked at two tickets on the countertop. There were eight people in the restaurant at three different tables.

"I'd better get going before it gets any later. Thanks."

"Sure, any time," he said. "If you get cold and want to come in and warm up, feel free."

"Thanks, I might take you up on that."

The waitress looked at me. I smiled at her and she smiled back. I turned and walked out the door. I decided I would stay in front of the pizza parlor hitchhiking.

Eight or ten cars went by during the next hour, but no one stopped. The three college boys who had been watching me as they ate pizza, finished and left. I felt a sense of relief when five students entered the pizza parlor. It would take them at least an hour to eat. My toes started to hurt, so I went inside.

As I entered, the manager smiled. "No luck, huh?"

"Not yet. I thought I'd get something to drink. Do you guys have hot chocolate?"

"Sure. Have a seat and Sally will be right with you."

The manager disappeared behind the counter. I took off my boots so my feet would warm up faster. Sally finished taking the order from the five students and walked toward me.

"How are you?" she asked and smiled.

I smiled back. "Cold."

"I bet. I saw you standing out there. Where are you going?"

She probably already knew the answer to that question. More than likely she had asked the manager.

"Springfield."

She looked out the window. "That's a long way in a blizzard. Is hot chocolate all you want?"

She had heard me talking to the manager.

"That should do it. I'm really not that hungry."

Although she held a pen and ticket book in her hand, she wrote nothing down as she headed toward the kitchen.

Actually, I was starving, but wanted to save my money. I had some granola in my backpack. It's a great snack and it fills you up. Taking the bag of granola out of my pack, I put it between the window and me and laid my muffler over the top of it. The oats in the granola, which were stuck together in big chunks, made it easy to discreetly slip a few nuggets into my mouth. Sally returned with my hot chocolate immediately. The manager must have had it ready for her. She smiled as she put the cup in front of me. I smiled back, but neither of us said anything.

I sucked in the whip cream on top of the hot chocolate, getting some on my nose and mustache. It was too hot to drink. I rubbed my feet together and looked out the window. Snow swirled down from gusts of wind blowing over the roof. I looked at Sally as she headed to another table. I'd rather be in bed with her than hitchhiking in this shit, I thought. I wondered how I could get her to invite me over to her place. I dismissed the idea, but then thought about the possibility of sleeping on the manager's floor or couch. He seemed nice enough.

Slowly, I finished the cup. I sat there 10 minutes longer before putting on my boots. I went to the restroom to clean up and take a leak. When I came out of the restroom, the manager and waitress were standing by the cash register talking. I walked over to them and paid for my hot chocolate.

"You still going to try to make it to Springfield?" the manager asked me.

"Yeah. I really can't afford a hotel." I hoped for an offer from either of them, but they just looked at me. "Well, thanks."

"Your welcome," the waitress said. "I hope you get a ride."

"Me too. Take it easy."

"Good luck," the manager added as I pushed open the glass door. A gust of cold air whipped a flurry of snowflakes onto the floor.

I stood outside the pizza parlor for a long time. I watched the waitress leave. She waved as she drove out of the parking lot heading in the direction I wanted to go. I imagined what it would be like to sleep with her. In less than a half hour, the manager and a guy that must have been the cook also drove by me. I no longer had a place to get warm. There were now eight to 12-inch snowdrifts with three to four inches of snow covering most of the ground. I not only felt cold outwardly, but cold and alone inwardly. I thought about the waitress again. She probably had a boyfriend. I imagined the two of them snuggled together nude under a sheet covered by a comforter and thick wool blanket.

I began to feel sorry for myself. I had no job, no girlfriend and no hot leads for either. Instead, here I was in Warrensburg, Missouri, walking and jumping in place with my chin tucked into my muffler and a stocking cap nearly down to my nose. I saw some lights reflect off the snow in front of me. I turned around to see a car approaching. I put out my gloved hand and waved my thumb. It went by slowly.

A few minutes later another car headed toward me. The car started slowing down to stop. I could hardly believe my eyes. It stopped right beside me. I pulled open the back door of the 1963 or '64 Bonneville Pontiac and threw my pack onto the seat, then slammed the door and opened the front door.

"Thanks a lot for stopping," I said as I climbed in. "I appreciate it."

The old man had on a bright orange-billed cap—the kind hunters use—with the earflaps pulled down. He hadn't shaved for several days, and you could see his white whiskers as the light from the street lamp moved across his face. He wore a pair of black-rimmed glasses with bifocals.

"It's too damn cold to be out a hitchhikin'," he said.

"That's for sure, but I'm heading to Springfield."

"What fur?"

"I'm trying to find a job down there."

"Oh."

After a prolonged silence, I spoke.

"Where are you going?"

"What?"

I was fairly sure he heard me the first time, but I asked him again, this time louder.

"Ohhh," he paused slightly, "down the road a piece."

"How far?"

"Ohhh, it'll help you out a little bit."

I didn't push him for an answer. We rode together in silence for about 20 minutes before he began slowing down.

"I turn here."

I looked around. Besides the small country grocery store we passed about a hundred yards away, there were no other buildings in sight. The store had an old-time gas pump in front of it. It reminded me of a gas station and grocery store I had seen in the movie "Bonnie and Clyde." No lights were on inside the store.

"Well, thanks," I said hesitantly.

I opened the door and stepped out onto a patch of pavement that had remained clear of snow because of the wind. Except in a few spots, at least five inches of snow covered the ground. Some of the drifts were now 15 to 20 inches deep. I opened the back door and grabbed my pack.

"Take it easy," I said, while thinking this was a hell of a place to be.

"You betcha," he blurted out as I shut the door.

He drove east on the crossroad. As I watched his red tail lights disappear into the blowing and whirling snow, I pulled my muffler up over my nose and my stocking cap down to my eyebrows. Within minutes, I started jumping around to keep my blood circulating. Overall I felt okay as long as I kept my back to the wind. The falling snow was beautiful. It fell at a 45-degree angle, and just before it hit the ground, it blew across the top of the drifts.

Occasionally, the wind grabbed some of the flakes and whipped them into miniature white tornadoes that scooted across the road and faded into the veil of white. The drift in the ditch beside me, which must have been two feet tall, resembled a breaking ocean wave. For at least 30 minutes, I jumped around to keep warm. As far as I could tell, there wasn't a soul within a square mile from where I stood. I sang aloud, making up the words and tune as I went along.

Here you are in the middle of a blizzard
No one cares, too bad you ain't a wizard
But don't get down
A car could come around
the curve in the bend
and that could end
this crazy man's binge
of bad luck

I laughed at how everything rhymed. I wrote a fair amount of poetry while traveling on the road, and now the words came without my rhyming dictionary. While dancing around my backpack singing, I saw car lights shining a half a mile away, maybe farther.

"All right," I screamed. "My first car since I've been here. It only takes one. Come on baby," I yelled to the car and stooped low waving my thumb for fun. "How's this look to you? Huh?"

The car slowly approached.

"Or, maybe you prefer this?" I yelled. I stood on my tip toes and put my arms out to my sides with both thumbs extended, throwing my chest forward. I probably looked like a man on a cross or a scarecrow. The driver couldn't see me yet.

When the car was 50 yards away, I got ready. I held my thumb high and waved it. The car moved so slowly that I thought the driver was slowing down to stop.

"Yeah baby, that's it," I whispered.

Realizing he intended to keep going, I waved my right arm and thumb frantically, and then waved both arms to flag him down.

"You can't drive by mister," I yelled as he passed me. "I'm freezing out here. Give me a break." I continued to wave after he passed, hoping he might change his mind while looking in his rearview mirror.

"Thanks a lot," I hollered.

I jumped around and talked to myself. "Shake it off. You know it does no good to get pissed. He's cozy and warm, and you're still cold. All the screaming in the world won't change that. Think positive. A better ride is just around that curve. Come on baby, I'm ready."

I got out my granola and slowly untwisted the tie. My fingers were stiff, and with my gloves on, it made it difficult opening the bag. I poured the granola directly into my mouth. My mouth watered from the brown sugar, making me feel a little better. About 30 minutes later another car approached. I went through the same hitchhiking routine as before, but again no luck. The driver slowed down some when I waved, but chose to drive on. My heart sank.

"Well," I said aloud, speaking to myself, "if you had brought your good sleeping bag you could have dug a cave in that drift and gone to sleep."

God, I thought, what I would do for a warm bed and some hot chocolate. Or better yet, a beautiful, loving woman. To relieve my scratchy throat, I picked up some snow and stuffed it in my mouth. About 20 minutes after the second car went by, I felt a tingling, prickling sensation. It was similar to the feeling you get in your leg when it falls asleep. More curious about the sensation than scared, I kept jumping around to keep warm. Then the pain began. The tingling sensation turned into stinging pricks—like someone poking me with pine needles, and poking hard. I jumped even more vigorously.

"Jesus," I screamed, "this hurts!"

Then I felt a piercing stab at the base of my head, like someone was inside my neck or lower skull thrusting a knife through the skin. The burst of pain caused a reverberation throughout my body that sent a rippling and excruciating pulse through my brain and an uncontrollable shiver down my spine. My head jerked as I jumped. Then it hit me once more. This time, as the phantom dagger struck, I found myself 15 feet above my dancing body. There was a second of bewilderment before I returned to my body.

"God," I whispered, "what the hell was that."

Once again the horrendous and painful jab penetrated the base of my skull, and again it kicked my awareness some 20 feet into the air. It seemed like it took longer to return to my body than the first time. "I'm freezing to death," I said aloud when I came back to my body. I looked down the road at the store and gas pump. It was barely visible. A voice spoke inside my head.

"Go down there and break into that store," it said. "Call the police and tell them you broke in because you were freezing."

The sharp pain returned with an electrifying jolt. My consciousness rose to the bird's eye perspective. This is weird, I thought. That's you down there. But how can that be? As soon as I realized I was thinking while outside my body, I found myself back in it. This time, without delay, I picked up my backpack and walked toward the store. My body was numb. I felt nothing except heaviness, as if the snow beneath my feet was sucking me into the earth. Snowflakes danced before my eyes, mesmerizing me with their beauty.

I'm not going to make it, I thought. There was no malice or disappointment in my realization. In fact, the idea of death seemed like a relief, and even funny. My journey had ironically brought me back to my home state.

It seemed appropriate and fitting to die hitchhiking between the two cities I considered home.

Seconds later light skipped between the whirling snowflakes as two glowing balls rounded the curve and headed toward me. I set my pack down in the middle of the road and waited. I heard the rumbling blade of the Missouri state truck plowing the snow. I waved my arms, but the driver didn't seem to be slowing down. I remember thinking, God, he's going to hit me. I wasn't really scared or mad at the driver. It felt like watching a late-night movie and knowing you should go to bed, but not having the energy to get up. Instead, you keep on watching TV in a stupor.

The truck's engine roared as its pistons engaged into a higher gear. The headlights flipped to bright as the plow came to a halt in front of me. Snow piled in front of the blade covered the tips of my boots. The blade appeared close enough to touch. I heard the truck door slam, but it sounded far away.

"What the hell are you doing out here?" The masculine voice had an urgent yet concerned tone to it. I felt a hand on my shoulder. I turned and looked at the guy. I don't really remember what his face looked like, but he wore an insulated green jump suit.

"I'm freezing."

It felt like I said it as a joke, but he didn't take it jokingly. With one hand on my right shoulder and the other on my left forearm, he guided me toward the passenger's side of the truck.

"Get in the truck," he said as he opened the door. He gently pushed me forward as I stepped on the running board and climbed in. "I have some hot coffee that will warm you up."

"I don't drink coffee," I mumbled as he slammed the door.

Although I don't recall seeing him pick up my backpack, he must have. After he climbed into his seat, the backpack seemed to magically appear beside me. That became the beginning of a continued déjà vu experience. It felt like a dream or a vision I imagined before, where I sat in this exact truck, the snow coming down, and a backpack suddenly appeared beside me.

"Here, drink this."

His words were part of the dream, or whatever déjà vu is. Each sentence, even the words I spoke and every action that took place during my time in the truck, were like a memory replayed. When I talked, it sounded like someone else speaking a script I had written. The driver put the cup of coffee in my hands, and I took a sip. The hot coffee tasted horrible, but I kept sipping it. That too was part of the déjà vu, and it was necessary to keep drinking this horrible tasting medicine.

"How long have you been out here?"

I heard the question, but couldn't speak. A part of me wanted to answer, but another part of me said, "Just relax and let it go. Nothing really matters." I looked at him and smiled. I took another sip of coffee. The coffee seemed to help me. It couldn't have been the caffeine, because it had no time to take effect. More than likely it was the horrible taste in my mouth. The terribly sharp pain at the base of my head stopped. Although I stopped being knocked out of my body with pain, I felt like a part of me had left. The long pause became too much for the driver.

"Are you all right?"

He put his hand on my shoulder.

"I don't know. I left Kansas City around noon."

I meant my reply to be the answer for the first question, but realized it worked for both questions.

"I just heard the weather report, and they're calling for at least five more inches of snow with wind chills as low as 35 to 40 below. This ain't the kind of night to be out hiking around."

"Yeah, but look how beautiful it is," I mumbled.

I babbled about the way the snow fell and whirled into different shapes. I told him about the tingling sensations I had earlier, the pinpricking pain all over my body, and finally the out-of-body experience. It had a marked effect on him. I could sense his concern about my condition.

"I'm going to take you to a street light up the road a ways. I want you to stay there and not move. Someone is going to come along within a few minutes to give you a ride. Do you understand?"

"And you know something else?" I said. "I knew you were going to say that. Since I've been in this truck, and my backpack appeared out of nowhere, it's been one déjà vu experience after another."

The man put the truck in gear, and we began moving. The snowplow blade made a screeching, grinding sound as it pushed snow off to our right.

"How long have I been here?"

"What do you mean?"

"In this truck."

He looked at his watch.

"About 20 minutes, maybe a little longer."

I looked at the falling snow in front of the headlights. For me, sitting in his truck had lasted five minutes or less. I was baffled. Maybe he was joking. I recalled no long conversations with him. Had I said something besides what I remembered? I vaguely recollected talking about living on earth before, and how dying is okay—just the end of another dream. Or, had I said that? I wasn't sure. It seemed like my memory was playing tricks on me. Did I make up the conversation in my head, or did I really say it?

These thoughts were no longer part of the déjà vu. Something seemed wrong. I stared ahead of me without saying another word. The driver said nothing. I wondered if he had told me his name. I looked at him. No name came to mind. It doesn't really matter, I thought, looking at the road again. This feels good just sitting here, nice and warm. My body relaxed even more with that thought. I felt the tension release in my jaw, neck and shoulders. I saw a street lamp ahead. As I watched it come closer, I became fascinated with the snow dancing before my eyes. I heard the driver speak.

"Here's where I'm going to let you out."

My stomach lurched. Ugh, I thought, I don't want to go back out there.

"Listen to me." He paused and waited for me to look at him. The truck rolled to a stop. "Someone will be by in a few minutes. Don't leave this light pole. Stay right in front of it, do you hear me?"

I nodded as I wrapped my muffler around my face and pulled my stocking cap down over my ears and forehead. I opened the door and climbed down. He scooted over in the seat and handed me my pack.

"Now stay in front of the light, okay?"

"I will."

"Someone will be here in a few minutes."

"Thanks." I shut the door and stepped back as the truck slowly moved away, pushing snow to the right side of the highway. My whole body shook once as a chill shot through me. Car lights appeared in the distance within minutes. I experienced a moment of panic when I realized it was a cop.

An older woman, maybe 55 or 60, sat in the front seat next to the policeman. She wore a scarf over her head. She cracked her window when they stopped. "Get in."

I opened the back door and climbed in with my backpack.

"What are you doing out here on a night like this?" the cop asked.

"I'm trying to get to Springfield."

I shut the door and the car moved forward. The cop made a grunting sound. I interpreted his response to mean, "What a fool."

"There's not going to be much more traffic tonight. If you want, you can bunk in my jail cell. It's not the most comfortable bed, but it's a lot better than out here." He looked at me in the rearview mirror. After a brief pause, he continued. "Or, if you prefer to keep going, I can drop you off at an all-night gas station where Highway 13 and 7 meet in Clinton. That way you can go in and warm up if you get cold."

"That would be great. There should be more traffic coming down Highway 7."

We rode to Highway 7 in silence. It felt wonderful to be warm again. I half dozed off. It seemed like we arrived at the gas station fast.

"Now don't hesitate to go in and warm up if you get cold," the officer said. "It's dangerous to stay out in this weather for long."

"I will. Thanks for the ride. I really appreciate it."

"That's quite all right."

The cop car eased out onto the road heading east on Highway 7. I thought about going into the gas station, but then decided to try hitchhiking first. I could see two vehicles approaching in the distance.

It turned out to be a car followed by a pickup truck full of hay. The car went by, but the pickup truck stopped. Two huge guys were in the truck, and I mean gigantic. I would guess each of them weighed at least 250 pounds, probably more. Although I couldn't tell their actual height, their heads nearly touched the top of the truck. The door opened and the guy by the door scooted to the center of the seat.

"We can make room," he said, "but you'll have to put the pack in your lap."

"That's fine with me. Thanks for stopping."

The driver looked at me a few seconds and said half laughing, "What are you doing out here?"

"I left Kansas City this afternoon hoping to be in Springfield before dark. Now I hope I get there before daylight."

They both laughed.

"You're in luck," the driver said. "We're going right through Springfield."

"Eureka!" I said, my body relaxing into the seat. "Those words are music to my ears." Their names were Roger and Paul. I filled them in on what had happened to me and how a cop had dropped me off at the gas station.

"Shit," Roger said, "you're lucky. It sounds like you nearly froze to death."

Paul explained why they were on the road during a blizzard. He got a call from his father who lived near Branson, Missouri. Evidently Branson had about 14 or 15 inches of snow, and his dad desperately needed hay for his cattle. Roger came along to keep Paul company. Paul's truck had hay stacked higher than the cab with rope holding it down. Because of the road conditions and the oversized load, he drove 45 mph and sometimes slower.

My body melted into the corner of the truck seat. The warm cab and engine's vibration caused my muscles to relax. Just enjoy where you are, I thought. It sure beats jumping around on a desolate highway. I ended up dosing off before we made it to Springfield. We arrived after 4 a.m., and Paul dropped me off in front of my sister's apartment. She lived a few blocks from the freeway—Bypass 65—that went to Branson. I had to pound hard on my sister's door to wake her up. She was shocked to see me. She assumed I had decided to put off hitchhiking to Springfield until the weather improved.

It didn't really hit me until the next day that the snowplow driver saved my life. Although I intended to break into the country store, who knows if I would have made it that far. One thing I fail to understand to this day is why I had no frost bite. The only thing I can guess is that jumping around kept my blood circulating enough so my body temperature decreased uniformly.

Another bizarre thing happened as a result of that trip. I've only told a few people about this, probably because it involves one of my few regrets in life.

I mailed Richard (the old man that picked me up in Kansas City) a letter and told him about my experience. A week later I received a strange letter from him. "I knew you would have trouble," he wrote, "but if you had stayed at my place, I probably would have ended up raping you."

It was eerie seeing those words in print. I read it several times before throwing the letter away. My regret stems from an article I read several years later during one of my return trips to Missouri. I happened to be reading the *Springfield Leader and Press* when I noticed Richard's name on an inside page. The two-paragraph article said Richard had been killed in his own home when an 18-year-old man shot him with a 12-gauge shotgun. The article lacked the circumstances of the incident, but I knew what happened. I wondered if the kid had been raped before he shot the old man.

I didn't call the police and tell them about Richard. Granted, I no longer had Richard's letter to back up what I knew, but the call should have been made anyway. To this day, I don't know if the kid ever served any time for what I suspect was an act of self-protection or revenge. I hope the truth of the matter came out.

The Fat Man's Ring

Within two weeks after returning to Springfield, I found a job. I became the Drury College library custodian. Determined to pay off my school loan before the end of June, I lived a frugal life to say the least. I had no social life. I spent my time playing guitar, writing poetry and reading. I made my last loan payment the third week of June and promptly gave notice to my boss. By the first of July, I hit the road hitchhiking southwest in search of the Rainbow Tribe.

The next several months included a plethora of interesting experiences, yet none intense enough to be tagged a close call. After attending the Rainbow Tribe gathering in the Gila Wilderness of New Mexico, then visiting friends in California, I decided the time had come to head east.

I first ventured north to Michigan's Mackinac Island. I had read in a magazine how the island banned motorized vehicles except for a fire truck. The logic to my travel destinations evolved around what I read, heard and felt. From the island, I cut across Canada to upstate New York where a woman who owned a small country store raved about Lake Placid.

"You have to go," she said. "If you don't, you'll regret it the rest of your life."

The next day, two college dropouts on their way to apply for a job at the Lake Placid Club gave me a ride. After visiting with them for 15 minutes, they encouraged me to fill out an application too.

The club, nestled in the Adirondack Mountains next to Mirror Lake, originally had been built as a rehabilitation resort for New York City's alcoholic aristocrats: a place where they could rest, play golf and dry out. Now it was a fashionable setting used to wine and dine corporate executives and politicians. The resort desperately needed help. It was September, and their student

143

workers had returned to college. They were hiring wine stewards, waiters and busboys.

Besides being low on funds, I noticed the bridge of my guitar becoming unglued. Extra cash and a new guitar sounded like a smart move.

At the Lake Placid Club, I first inquired about their wine steward openings, but those positions had been filled. Although I had never waited tables, being a waiter sounded better than a busboy. I named several Kansas City restaurants as past employers. Despite my fairly long hair, they hired me on the spot. They also hired the two guys who brought me. We were told to check into one of the dormitory-style rooms on the resort's campus and to report to work at 6:30 a.m. the next day wearing black pants, socks and shoes, as well as a white shirt with a black bow tie. One of my new compadres loaned me money for clothes.

At breakfast the next morning, the manager teamed me up with a 50-year-old woman to wait on two tables of 10. Within 15 minutes, the woman said to me a bit disgusted: "You've never waited tables before, have you?"

When I admitted I hadn't, and asked for her help, she softened. "Waiting tables is eighty percent personality and twenty percent know-how. I can see you have the personality, but you need to know that twenty percent."

She proceeded to give me a crash course on table service and setup. Waiting tables turned out to be much more difficult than I imagined. By the end of three weeks, I had become a good waiter. In fact, when the club prepared to close from Thanksgiving to the first of the year, they laid off all wine stewards, busboys and waiters except me and one other waiter. They kept us on one extra week to serve management and other staff while they planned for reopening the first of the year.

The day before my last day, I saw a huge cockroach crawling across the kitchen floor. I had already served the club's president and his staff both diner and dessert, and they were drinking their second round of coffee. Feeling cantankerous and tired from partying the night before, I slightly smashed the cockroach with my shoe and put him on a silver dessert plate. He was still squirming.

"What are you doing?" asked the chef as I dribbled hot fudge syrup over the cockroach.

"I'm going to serve this to the president."

"Yeah, right," he said.

I took a polished silver cover and slipped it over the plate; then placed the plate in the middle of a tray. I felt my heart pounding. As I headed toward the door, I glanced back at the chef. He stood there with a steel wool pad in his hand, his mouth partially open. The assistant chef walked up beside him. I grabbed one of the tray stands beside the exit and leaned into the swinging door pushing it outward.

The club president sat at the head of the table for 12 with his back to me. I snapped open the tray stand and stoically placed the tray on it. Since dessert and coffee had already been served, my appearance attracted everyone's attention. When the president looked to see what was happening next to him, the table became silent.

I picked up the plate with both hands as if it were precious cargo and proceeded to the left side of the president to serve him, just as I had been taught by my mentor: serve from the left, clear plates from the right. I carefully and gently placed it in front of him.

"What have we here?" he asked, sounding pleased to be receiving something special.

"Monsieur, just for you," I said with the thickest French accent I could muster.

I left the cover on the plate, stepped away from him, grabbed the tray stand and swiftly walked toward the kitchen. Looking back, I could see everyone leaning forward to view the president's special delicacy. As I passed through the kitchen door, a roar of laughter came from the table. The chef and assistant chef were looking at me from behind the service line. The chef shook his head.

"I can't believe you did that!" he said and grinned. "You know you're history, don't you?"

"I'm history anyway," I said. "It's just one day sooner than scheduled."

I had never been fired from a job before, and I expected to be swiftly dismissed for my bold and crude display of irreverence. In all honesty, I wanted to leave the club when all my friends got laid off. They were now having fun partying and hiking. I planned to hang out with them until the snows hit, then hitchhike to Key West, Florida, to visit a college buddy who moved there.

After 10 minutes, although it felt a lot longer, the president pushed the kitchen's swinging door open and looked at me. "I've just got one question for you," he said. "Where did you find that cockroach?"

I pointed to the spot on the floor where I had stepped on the critter. The president nodded his head, turned and left. I cleaned off the table and returned the next morning for my last day of work; shocked I wasn't fired.

For the next several weeks, I did a lot of day hiking and bar-hopping with my friends. While temperatures dropped into the 20s at night, the days were a pleasant 40 to 50 degrees. One night, when I prepared to leave a bar, I couldn't find my winter coat. We hung our coats by the door, and either someone grabbed it by mistake or stole it. I took it as a sign to head south. Although several friends offered to give me their coats, and even buy me another one, I had made up my mind to leave. It felt right to push on toward the warm beaches of Florida.

The next day it started snowing, and snowed hard. I decided to travel once the snow stopped. By the third day of snow, however, it became debatable whether I could even make it to Interstate 87. When my roommate realized my adamant desire to leave despite the snow, he offered to take me to the interstate in his jeep. He and his girlfriend drove me through snow drifts and blizzard conditions to Witherbee next to I-87. We arrived late afternoon. Fortunately, Witherbee had less snow than Lake Placid. I purchased white mittens and a white stocking cap so I could be seen more easily. I planned to hitchhike day and night until I reached a friend's apartment in Knoxville, Tennessee. I wrote and told her I would be visiting on my way to Key West. I wore several layers of clothes covered by my North Face rain jacket, the gift from my California Tai Chi acquaintance.

Before I reached Albany, the snow turned to rain. I stood in the dark for an hour outside Albany trying to catch a ride. Although my new waterproof Army poncho covered my pack and much of my body, the northwest wind and gusts of air from passing trucks flipped up my poncho and allowed the rain to drench me. Fortunately, my new 12-string guitar stayed dry wrapped in a plastic bag inside its new hard-shell case. By 10 p.m., I got dropped off in Binghamton, New York. After standing in the wet and cold for three more hours, I ended up sleeping under an interstate bridge shivering the rest of the night.

At day break the rain stopped, but the sky remained covered with clouds. For some reason no one would stop. Maybe I looked too wet and miserable to pick up. I stayed under the bridge for fear it might start raining again. About 1 p.m., the low clouds dissipated, but higher clouds still blocked the sun. I chose to walk down the interstate. Minutes later a cop stopped and checked my identification. I told him where I had come from and where I was going. He felt sorry for me after hearing I hitchhiked all night in the rain. I withheld the part about sleeping under the bridge. No doubt there's a law against doing that. To my surprise, he let me stay on the interstate and even wished me luck on catching a ride.

Around midday an elderly man picked me up in his classic Studebaker. Despite its age, the car looked in great shape. The old man, seeing me wet and cold, flipped his heater switch to high. It got uncomfortably warm, but I didn't complain. I wanted all my clothes to dry out.

The man wore an old, light gray hat that had a crease in the center and a full rim running around it. If the hat rim had been pulled down in the front and back, he would have looked like a gangster wearing round wire-rimmed grandpa glasses. Although clean-shaven except for a gray mustache and short bushy sideburns, he most likely had a bald head, but he never gave me an opportunity to find out. He wore a red plaid flannel shirt and gray denim pants. The enthusiasm in his voice made him seem like a much younger man. The only aggravating thing about him was that he never drove faster than 55 mph. Every time a car passed us, I wondered if I would have been in that car had the old man not stopped. He enjoyed hearing my travel stories, and by the time we neared his turnoff, he was driving 45 mph. When I shook his hand, I realized I hadn't introduced myself. I told him my name and thanked him for the ride.

Although it remained cold outside—about 30 degrees—at least my clothes were dry. As dusk set in, a red Porsche stopped.

"Hi," I said to the driver. "Thanks for stopping." I noticed the car had no back seat. "Is there room for all my gear?"

"Sure," he said curtly. "We'll make room."

My backpack went behind us in the window, and my guitar sat between my legs resting against the smooth leather seat. I introduced myself and reached to shake his hand.

"I'm Pete," he said as we shook. "Glad to meet you. Where are you going?"

"Eventually to Key West, but first I want to stop and see a girlfriend in Knoxville, Tennessee."

Pete, clean shaven with thick black hair neatly feathered back over his ears, wore a gray pinstriped suit, white shirt and a grayish blue tie with red and gray stripes. An expensive gold watch encircled his left wrist, and a gold bracelet surrounded his right. I guessed him to be in his middle 30s. Looking at the car's posh interior, and the way Pete dressed, I felt lucky he stopped to give me a ride.

"Do you smoke pot?"

"No," Pete said, "I've never used any drugs. I've always wondered what it would be like though. Do you smoke?"

"Yeah. I've smoked since I was 17."

"Have you tried anything else?"

"About everything, I guess, but I've never stuck a needle in my arm. I've only snorted coke and heroine."

For the next 15 or 20 minutes, he asked me about the effects of the drugs and my experiences with them. It became apparent he thought he missed something by not trying them. At that time, I firmly believed drugs provided a beneficial mind-expanding experience. No doubt I told him that too. I found it hard to believe he'd never tried any drugs. Either he had lived a sheltered life, or he was lying. Pete took the Northeast Extension Pennsylvania Turnpike and drove fast.

"My exit is coming up. Where do you want me to let you out? It's against the law to hitchhike on the turnpike."

"I usually get rides before the cops come along. I think I'll take my chances on the turnpike."

I spent enough time standing beside on-ramps and in front of tollbooths to know that my odds for catching a ride were much better on the turnpike or freeway. Although I'd never been taken to jail for standing on an interstate or turnpike, a cop in Florida made me walk two miles to the next on-ramp in the blistering heat. He drove slowly behind me in his air-conditioned car. I carried my guitar and packed more than 60 pounds of gear. It took two weeks for my blisters to heal.

Pete slowed down. "Is this okay?"

"Perfect."

I thanked him for the ride, and he wished me luck. After I shut the door, he took off fast, his engine roared as he shifted gears. Standing in the dark with no street lamps made it difficult for drivers to see me. I held my hand up high with my white mitten thumb protruding straight up. I wondered what I looked like to the passing drivers. About 10 minutes later, a white Chevrolet slowed down and pulled onto the shoulder driving straight at me with the car's bright lights on.

Shit, I thought, a cop. The car slowed down and stopped about five feet in front of me. I left my gear beside the road and walked toward the driver's side of the car. The driver rolled down his window. I expected a voice to ask me if I had any identification.

"Do you want a ride or not?" the driver asked when I got next to him.

"Sure," I said excited, "I thought you were a cop."

I hustled back to my things and grabbed them quickly, and then opened the back door on the passenger's side of the car and tossed my gear onto the back seat.

"Thanks for stopping," I said while climbing into the front seat.

The guy was a giant. His bald head, the size of a basketball, nearly touched the car ceiling. He had three big rolls under his chin, a small nose and dark beady eyes that immediately gave me the creeps. He looked more like a rhinoceros without a horn than a human being. His stomach touched the steering wheel, and his huge fat hands—with fingernails bitten nearly to the cuticle—hung limply over the wheel at 10 and 2 o'clock. A large gold ring with a dark shiny stone circled his little finger on his right hand. He wore an open collared short-sleeved white shirt and dark blue pants that hung low on his waist. The pants looked as if they were about to split at the seams around his thighs. His arms and legs looked too short for his body.

"Why'd you think I was a cop?" he asked in a deep melodious voice as the car began slowly moving.

"Because you've got a white car, and you drove right up to me with your bright lights on. That's just what cops do."

"Oh." He glanced in the rearview mirror as his car moved faster. He made a slight turn of his head to look over his shoulder and check the blind spot. It was a sad effort, so I glanced back to make sure no cars were coming. As we eased over onto the right lane, he turned back to me—his penetrating eyes looking me up and down. I already felt uncomfortable in his presence, but now I felt sick to my stomach.

Shit, I thought to myself, what am I doing here? I looked out the window to my right and nonchalantly shifted my body as if getting more comfortable, which enabled me to move closer to the door. I looked at him. "Where are you going?"

"Oh, a little ways down the road." He adjusted himself in his seat while pulling his pants away from his crotch with his right hand. "How about you?" He looked at me like a rancher viewing a piece of livestock. "Where are you going?"

I looked him square in the eyes. "To see my girlfriend in Knoxville, Tennessee."

He looked back at the road and pursed his lips together. He spoke again without looking at me.

"How long have you been on the road?"

"I left upstate New York yesterday afternoon."

I hoped my comment about my girlfriend would end any ideas regarding a sexual encounter. Then, with his right hand, he reached into his shirt pocket and pulled out a large wad of bills and looked at me. I immediately turned away, but he knew I saw the money. The sinking, empty feeling in the pit of my stomach grew. I gazed out the window at the dots of light coming from houses in the distance. After a long silent pause he spoke again.

"I bet you don't have much money out here on the road, do you?"

It sounded more like a statement than a question, but I replied quickly.

"No, but I don't need much money hitchhiking." I kept looking out the side window.

Another long pause ensued.

"I'll give you twenty bucks for a head job."

I looked at him. "Sorry, I'm not into that." I looked back out the side window.

"Okay, thirty."

"No thanks," I said, not looking at him this time.

"Have you ever tried it?"

"No, and I have no desire to. I'm attracted to women."

"And what exactly do you do to your girlfriend?" he asked sarcastically, speaking very slowly. "Do you suck on her titties and lick her pussy lips?" He waited for a reply. "Huh? Is that what you do? Do you push your nose into her wet juices and stick your tongue up her cunt, swishing it around and lapping up her smelly secretions?"

I stared straight ahead, but I could see him looking at me through my peripheral vision. He waited for some kind of reaction to his words.

"And what does she do to you?" There was a slight pause. "Do you let her put your cock in her mouth?" Out of the corner of my eye I could see him put his right hand on his crotch. "Does she suck your penis head and squeeeeeeeze your balls until you fill her mouth with cum?"

I guess he hoped to arouse me. Instead, his words made me nauseous.

149

"I'll give you forty bucks for a head job and one hundred bucks if you let me fuck you."

"Hey," I said looking directly at him. He moved his hand back and forth over his crotch. "I'm straight, and I'm not interested in your money. It's nothing personal."

"Come on baby," he muttered.

I looked straight ahead once again.

"You can make forty bucks within a few minutes," he continued, "and I won't even need to stop the car."

He pushed back in his seat, and at first I thought he was making a move toward me. I turned sideways and pushed myself against the door. He supported the steering wheel with his stomach. I heard a zip and then saw the swollen penis in his right hand. He returned his left hand to the steering wheel and slowly caressed himself with his right. I felt the car slow down slightly. I couldn't help but momentarily stare at his penis, frozen from the bizarreness of it all.

"Go on," he urged. "Take me in your mouth and suck me dry."

I looked away. I felt queasy. I had little food in my stomach to throw up, but thought I might anyway. The car suddenly swerved to the right, causing the tires to squeal as we careened onto an off-ramp. "If you're not going to pay for your ride," he said disgustedly, "then you can get out here."

We were speeding down the off-ramp into darkness. The tollbooth stood at least half a mile from the end of the ramp. There were no cars anywhere in sight. I knew I could outrun this giant once outside his car, but what if he lunged for me and got a good hold before I could get away? Also, what about my gear? My heart shuddered as I searched the side of the car for the door handle while hugging the door with the side of my body.

As we neared the bottom of the ramp, he spoke again. "Look," he said, "you don't have to let me cum in your mouth. Just suck me off until I'm ready to cum. I'll let you know when. Then you can squeeze my balls until I'm done. You won't even get any on you. How about it? You'll be forty bucks richer too…"

The car slowed down rapidly. I wondered if he planned to stop before turning the corner, or stop after making the turn. About 10 yards from the corner, I found the door handle.

"Sorry. It's nothing personal."

He turned the corner sharply and slammed on the brakes, bringing the car to a screeching halt. I pushed my feet into the floorboard and put my right hand on the dash to keep from flying forward. At the same time, I firmly pushed my left hand down on the seat between us to keep me from sliding toward him. Once the car stopped, I quickly opened the door. The inside light came on, and from the corner of my eye I could see him still stroking his penis. I left the front door ajar while opening the back door. I pulled out my guitar and backpack at the same time. The backpack crashed to the ground beside the car.

"Thanks for the ride," I said out of habit before I realized it. The words sounded hollow and contrived.

"Yeah, right bud," he said as if itching for a fight. "A free ride. I bet you'd really like my cock up your fuckin' ass, wouldn't you?" His squinted black eyes focused on me. "I bet you'd like me to fill your ass with so much cum that it oozes out your mouth." He spoke slowly and in what I'm sure he considered a sexy, seductive voice. "Sounds appetizing, doesn't it?"

Both his hands massaged his penis as I shut the front door. The inside light went off. He raised his voice so I could hear him.

"I saw you eyeing my cock," he yelled. "You really want it. You know you do."

With the car in gear and his foot pushed firmly on the brake, I had no intentions of walking in front of the vehicle. It also was a gamble walking behind it, but I had to get away from there. Ready to drop my things if he popped the car in reverse, I swiftly walked behind the car and crossed the median. Once on the other side of the median and beside the on-ramp, I set my guitar down and slipped on my backpack. I pulled my mittens and stocking cap from my jacket pockets and put them on. I looked at the car. The windows looked black. I listened closely for a door to open. Even with the roar of passing cars and trucks on the turnpike, I felt confident I'd hear his car door open if he tried to get out. I quickly walked up the on-ramp, occasionally galloping a step or two. My backpack, which weighed 65 to 70 pounds, along with my new 12-string guitar and hard-shell case purchased in New York City, made it tough going. The adrenaline rush and the strenuous physical exertion caused my heart to pound hard. The farther I got up the on-ramp, the louder the sound of passing vehicles, which made it more difficult to listen for his car door opening. I glanced back to see if the inside car light came on.

I can out run him even with my gear, I thought, taking a few galloping steps and walking faster than before. Then a chill ran through my body. A creepy feeling prickled my skin. I wondered if a gun was being pointed at me. In my mind I imagined his big fat cheek resting against the stock of a gun and his beady dark eyes staring down the sights of the barrel. I even saw the gold ring on his pinkie hanging limply below his first finger poised and slowly squeezing the trigger.

"Shit," I mumbled, pulling the white stocking cap off my head and running up the on-ramp. I no longer looked back, knowing it didn't matter. A bullet would easily penetrate my backpack, leaving a big hole when it came out the front of me. I stooped over as low to the ground as possible without falling. Nearing the top of the turnpike, I frantically waved my extended thumb and arm at passing cars. The straps to my pack restricted me from taking in full breaths, making breathing difficult. I slowed down to a fast walk and looked back. The white car still sat at the bottom of the ramp.

I turned and glanced at the turnpike to see a car parked along the shoulder of the road about 75 yards away. Two people stood at the back of the car with the trunk lid raised. Although doubting they stopped for me, I started running for their car anyway. It turned out to be two tall African American men.

"I told ya I saw a hitchhiker," one guy said as I neared them. "Didn't I tell ya?"

"Hey man," I said, "thanks for stopping."

I literally threw my guitar in the trunk, and then swiftly shirked off my backpack and tossed it on top of my guitar case. The guy on my right had his hand on the trunk lid. I slammed the trunk shut leaving his hand suspended in mid air.

"Let's get out of here," I said with an urgent tone of panic. I quickly walked to the back door and opened it with such force that both guys, dumbfounded by my actions, moved quickly toward the front doors.

"What's the matter?" asked the guy on the driver's side.

"Once we're moving I'll tell you all about it," I said as I slammed the door behind me. Both guys jumped in and shut their doors. The driver put the car in gear and punched the accelerator. I turned and looked through the rear window. I could no longer see the white car. I took a deep breath and relaxed. The driver looked at me in the rearview mirror while his buddy sat sideways, more or less facing me.

"Are you okay?" the driver asked.

"Yeah," I said, letting out a sigh, "thanks to you guys. I just got out of a weirdo's car."

I introduced myself and shook their hands. Leroy drove and Earl sat in the passenger's seat. They were on their way to Birmingham, Alabama, and planned on driving all night. That meant they would pass right through Knoxville. I was relieved and elated. While I told them what just happened to me, we passed through a tollbooth and left the turnpike for Interstate 81. Before getting on the interstate, we stopped and picked up a six pack of Miller. Once on the freeway, Earl fired up a joint and passed it to me.

"This may help calm you down. Do you have a driver's license?"

I took a hit and passed the joint to Leroy, sucking in some extra air so I could answer Earl without losing any smoke. "Yeah. I can help drive if you want."

"That would be great."

After we finished the joint, Leroy stopped the car and let me take over. Earl stretched out in back while Leroy fell asleep in the front seat. Although I felt tired, the pot kept me awake. While pot relaxes and tires many people, it's a stimulant for me. After several hours of driving, however, it became a struggle to keep my eyes open. Earl raised up in the back seat to find me going 45 mph and nodding in and out. It's a wonder I hadn't crashed. Earl had me stop so he could drive. I climbed into the back seat. The next thing I knew someone pushed on my arm.

"Bryce, Bryce, wake up."

I raised my head in confusion, trying to recall where I was and what was going on.

"Where did you say you wanted to go?"

"Knoxville."

"This is Knoxville," Leroy bellowed with a big smile.

I sat up and saw that we were at a gas station. It was still dark outside, and an attendant stood beside the car pumping gas into it.

"What time is it?"

Leroy looked at his watch. "It's almost 4:30."

We were the only car at the station.

"Wow," I said still half asleep, "this is great."

I opened the back door and slowly climbed out—my legs and back stiff. Leroy opened the trunk, and I walked around to him. Earl got out and came back to me.

"Here." He handed me a piece of paper. "If you're ever in Alabama, stop in Birmingham and see us. We'll show you a good time."

"Thanks." He had written his address on the back of a bank envelope.

"Pay the man and let's go," Earl said.

Leroy handed the attendant a $20 bill. The guy had a moneychanger on his belt and gave Leroy several dollar bills and some change.

Earl looked at me. "Do you have any money you can throw in for gas?"

I pulled out my wallet, took out a $5 bill and handed it to Earl. "I know it's not much, but..."

"Thanks. Every bit helps."

He took the bill with his left hand and held out his right hand to shake. We shook and then did a finger-curl grip.

"Have a good one my man," Earl said, "and watch out for those crazy fat men." Leroy joined us in time to hear Earl's remark. We all laughed.

"Make the happening happen, brother," Leroy said as we shook hands and then locked fingers.

"You guys are cool. Thanks for everything."

"Let's make it happen, Leroy," Earl said and walked to the driver's door.

I waved gratefully as they drove away.

Regarding my short employment at the Lake Placid Club, I received a letter from the president after returning to Kansas City several months later. He offered me the position of dining room captain even though I hadn't applied. Several people who had worked there three years wanted the job. The position provided lodging in a fully furnished private cabin that included a fireplace. I'm sure I received the offer for two reasons.

First, after several waitresses dropped huge trays of food, I suggested to the captain that we have male runners deliver the food to all banquet stations and then let the other waiters and waitresses swiftly serve the food. After all, the chefs could only dish up a certain amount of food at a time. He used my suggestion.

Second, I once got upset while in the kitchen. Although it wasn't the first time I had gotten mad, it was the first I raised my voice and barked out several recommendations.

"We need more organization here!" I yelled. "Why aren't the tray stands near the door? And why don't we use one door as an exit and the other as an entrance? And why aren't those damn plate covers hanging above the serving line instead of below it? Not only will they stay warmer that way, but they're easier to grab."

As I quickly turned to head out the door, I nearly ran over the president. He must have been standing behind me the whole time. No wonder everyone quieted down and listened to me.

I doubt the cockroach incident endeared the president to me, but it certainly let him know my boldness. Anyway, I never had the opportunity to accept the position because I read the letter nearly 90 days after I should have started the job.

Florida Keys

I stood along Highway 1 for about 20 minutes when a white Chevy van stopped.

"Climb in," blurted the guy sitting in the front passenger's seat. His arm rested on the window ledge as his hand held the bar attached to the outside mirror. A green and black dragon tattoo with orange and red fire shooting from its mouth colored the middle of his forearm. The guy's brown, stringy hair hung down to an inch below his ears. He had a thick mustache and hadn't shaved for three or four days. A cigarette hung from his chapped and sunburned lips, and a layer of skin was peeling off his red forehead.

"All right," I said excited, and reached for the handle to the van's sliding door. Before I could open it, the door slid open.

"How's it going?" said a clean shaven kid with hair cut so short you could see his scalp. He wore a white tank top and baggy blue shorts. Although he appeared to be my height, he had more muscle and outweighed me by at least 40 pounds. He reached out to shake my hand.

"Great, now that I've got a ride," I said as we shook hands. The driver, whose hands clutched the steering wheel, sat looking at me. "Thanks for stopping," I said to him as the short-haired kid took the guitar out of my hand and put it in the back of the van.

"No problem."

The driver had a lower left tooth missing. His blond, sun-bleached, oily and unkempt hair looked the same length and untidy style as the front-seat passenger. He too had a mustache, although a bit thinner than his buddy's. He also needed a shave. He wore a soiled and wrinkled white t-shirt, and his arms and face looked sunburned and dirty.

155

"How long you been waitin' for a ride?" the driver asked in a rough, macho tone.

I pushed my backpack up against a mattress in the back of the van and climbed in as the kid slammed the sliding door shut.

"I don't have a watch, but I got here earlier this afternoon. Nobody's been nice enough to stop until you guys came along."

I had actually started hitchhiking around 3:30, and it couldn't have been much past four o'clock, but I wanted them to feel good about picking me up.

"Yeah, there's a bunch of god-dammed rednecks around here," the driver said. The van slowly moved forward as he looked out his window and eased back onto the highway. "Grab yourself a beer out of the cooler." He lifted his own beer bottle to his lips and took a long swig.

The kid sitting on the van floor next to me flipped open the cooler and pulled a Budweiser from the ice and handed it to me.

"Man, this is great!" Cold water dripped from the bottle onto my blue jeans. I quickly twisted the top off and took several big gulps. "Ahhh, that sure hits the spot," I yelled to be heard above the sound of the engine and wind blowing through the windows. "Thanks. By the way, my name's Bryce."

The driver looked at me. "I'm Jerry and this is George," he said loudly, motioning his head toward the passenger's seat.

George turned slightly and looked my way. He tipped his beer toward me and nodded.

"Good to meet you." I raised my beer in salute to both of them.

"What's your name again?" the driver asked as he lowered his head and looked at the kid sitting next to me.

"Tom."

"That's right, Tom," Jerry said straightening up. "He's a hitchhiker too."

"Hey Tom," I said, clinking my beer bottle against his and taking a sip.

Tom looked young, but he had to be somewhere between 18 and 24. The short haircut and hairless face made it hard to tell.

"You got any pot?" George barked at me.

"Sorry man, I don't," I lied. I had two joints a friend had given me just before he took me to the highway. I planned to smoke them with Karen, a former college friend now working in Miami. "I never carry a stash with me hitchhiking—you know, with the cops and all."

"Yeah, well that doesn't help us none," he said and looked out his open window.

"We ran out yesterday," Jerry added.

"Where you heading to?" Tom asked me. Jerry looked back at me as I answered.

"I'm going to see a girlfriend in Miami."

Jerry glanced around at me. "What part of Miami?"

"A place called Coco Beach," I hollered above the engine's roar. "Do you know where that is?"

"Yeah, we go right by there. That's the rich part of town. How do you know this babe?"

"We went to school together. She works for a television station."

"Which station?" George shouted, rolling his head to his left side to look at me. He appeared half crocked.

"I don't really know, but she's not on TV. She's a writer."

"Oh," George mumbled and rolled his head forward again.

"Do you live in Key West?" Jerry asked.

"No, I was just visiting friends. I'm on my way back to Missouri."

"So that's where you're from?"

"Yeah."

"How long you been on the road?"

I had to think for a few seconds. Jerry looked at me.

"I guess it's been about six or seven months now."

I considered my journey as actually starting in June when I quit my job in Springfield to attend the Rainbow Tribe gathering in New Mexico. I viewed my three-month stop in Lake Placid as still being on the road, even though I worked during that time. It was now the middle of December.

"That's a long time," Jerry said. "Where you been?"

I traced my travels beginning in New Mexico and continuing to California, back to Missouri, up to Wisconsin and Michigan, then across eastern Canada to New York, and finally south through New England to Key West. By the end of my brief synopsis, I had finished my first beer. Jerry told me to get another one.

"Here," George said, "give me your empty bottle."

I handed it to him, and he tossed it out the window. I raised the cooler top and took another beer. I told them about the Rainbow Tribe, and how the group met each year during the first week of July to help heal the Earth. The story enthralled them, especially when they heard that a lot of people at the gathering wore no clothes, did a lot of drugs, and that anyone could attend.

"Were there some good-looking cunts there?" George asked belligerently as he threw his empty beer bottle out the window.

"Yeah, a lot," I said, feeling uncomfortable about his attitude toward women, but keeping quiet because I needed a ride.

"We gotta go to the next one, Jerry." George laughed as he lifted the cooler top to take another beer. "I could use some raw pussy. Where's the next one going to be?"

"I don't really know. They talked about having it in Oregon, but weren't sure." My throat hurt from screaming above the roar of the van engine, so I stopped talking. After a few minutes, Jerry switched on the radio and turned it up loud.

"Yeaaaah," bellowed George as he sang along with Steve Miller. "Keep on rockin' me baby, keep on rockin' me baby, rock me, rock me, rock me..."

I placed my beer between my crossed legs and leaned back on my hands. Tom leaned toward me.

"These guys have been drinking all day." With the music and the roar of the engine, neither Jerry nor George could hear what Tom said. "I've been drinking as many beers as I can so there's less for them. Drink up."

George certainly looked smashed, but Jerry—the driver—appeared sober. Tom seemed sober too, but he had downed two beers since I climbed in the van and was close to finishing his third. I drank the remaining beer in my bottle.

"The beer tastes great," I shouted.

Jerry looked at me and saw my empty beer bottle. He held out his hand.

"Here, give me that." I put the bottle in his hand. Jerry smacked the bottle against George's arm. "Here man." George looked at him with squinted eyes. "Let her fly. See if you can get it to the water."

George took the bottle and flung it out the window toward the ocean.

"You didn't even come close," Jerry mocked.

"Ah, go fuck yourself," George said and looked straight ahead.

"Have another beer," Jerry said, looking at me in the rearview mirror.

"Are you sure?"

"Yeah I'm sure. What do you think it's for?" He looked back at the road.

I pulled the lid off the cooler and took another one. There were five beers left. I assumed they started with a case. As I started to put the lid back on, George pushed it away and reached for another beer.

"Oh, sorry, man." He stared at the bottle he had plucked from the cooler, and then his eyes shifted to me. His eyes looked cold and distant. He rolled his head, threw his bottle out the window and placed the new beer between his legs. The bottle he tossed out the window was half full. Jimmy Buffet's song *Margaritaville* came on the radio. George turned it up so loud that the speakers distorted.

"Are you in the service?" I asked Tom.

"No. My haircut makes me look like it, huh?"

"That's what I would have guessed."

"My hair was longer than yours a few days ago, but I decided to let my girlfriend cut it. She kept screwing up and had to cut it shorter and shorter. Finally, I got pissed and had a barber zap me." He sounded disappointed, but then added, "It'll grow out again."

Just as he finished his sentence, the van swayed a little and gravel churned beneath the wheels. We both looked up and stretched our necks to see where we were going. The van's two right wheels were off the highway and on the shoulder. Jerry jerked on the steering wheel, and we swayed back onto the road.

George, who had his head down and his hands on the beer between his legs, raised his head and looked around. Jerry acted as if nothing had happened.

I looked at Tom. Tom shifted his eyes to look at Jerry and George, and then looked at me and raised his eyebrows.

"One of us should be driving," he said, as Jimmy sang, "Wasting away again in Margaritaville..."

The sun, appearing as a luminous ball of fiery golden red, transformed into a shimmering orange dome as it dipped into the Gulf of Mexico. You could actually see it slowly sinking. I found myself viewing the scene through the van window as a painting on a wall, recalling what John, the bald-headed Tai Chi student from California, had said about "seeing" everything. Tom sat in my peripheral view. The white lines of cresting waves pulsed rhythmically onto the shoreline as the luminous sphere descended into the tranquil turquoise canvas. When the sun descended halfway below the horizon, my body swayed and gravel pummeled the bottom of the van. I put my hands on the floor to brace myself. Jerry steered the van back onto the highway. Tom grabbed the back of George's seat to keep from falling over.

"Everything's fine," Jerry bellowed and laughed. "Did I scare you guys?"

"You know," I said, "if you guys get tired and want someone else to drive, I have a driver's license. I'm a good driver."

Jerry laughed. He reached over and gave George a backhanded slap to his arm. "What do you think of that, George?" George, half asleep, flinched from the blow and looked at Jerry with wide eyes.

"The man's got a driver's license," Jerry said sarcastically as he waved his thumb toward me.

They both laughed now. Jerry turned and looked at me.

"We don't even have driver's licenses," he yelled, and they laughed again. Jerry pushed down on the gas pedal and the van lurched forward.

"Don't you think I can handle it?" Jerry bellowed as he looked at me again. He held his gaze on me far too long as the van continued to gain speed.

"Sure you can handle it. I just thought you might be getting tired—that's all. You guys have a mattress to crash on."

"If I get tirrrred," Jerry wailed, "I'll let you know."

I looked at Tom and raised my eyebrows and shrugged my arms as if to say, "I tried." I looked up to find George glaring at me with his eye lids half shut. He rolled his head back to a relatively forward position, but a little cockeyed to the right. The top of the sun disappeared into the Gulf. The orange luminous glow on the horizon faded into a green sky followed by a bluish turquoise, and then a soothing deep blue-violet. I heard the sound of a car horn. I sat up straight and looked out the front window in time to see our van swerve to the right as the car in the left lane swerved out of our way. The driver kept his horn blasting as he passed us. The van had obviously been over the centerline. George woke up with a start and put his hands on the dash.

"The mother fucker should stay on his side of the road," Jerry yelled. You could still hear the car horn in the distance. "Fuck you, asshole!" Jerry stuck his arm out the window and gave the car the finger.

"Maybe he didn't see you," I said. "Why don't you turn on your lights."

"Shut the fuck up. I'm driving."

He waited a few seconds, and then reached over and pulled the knob that turned the headlights on. George once again nodded off to sleep. Images of what might happen in a head-on collision flashed through my mind. My body would most likely be in one of two places: either all the way through the front windshield, or halfway through it. Tom turned around and put his back against George's seat. His new position would be the safest place if we crashed. Tom looked at me.

Jackson Browne now sang over the radio: "*...running on empty, running on, running blind...*"

"These guys are wasted," he said. Although I couldn't really hear him above the noise of the engine and blaring radio, I could easily read his lips.

"*Running into the sun but I'm running behind...*" continued Jackson Browne.

"Watch what you're doing, man," George blurted out, slurring his words as the van swerved again.

The van slowed down. I thought we were going to stop, but then the speed leveled off. Jerry said nothing. He had both hands on the steering wheel.

Tom shook his head back and forth. "This is crazy," he said softly as he leaned over to me. "We should get out."

Tom was right. It was only a matter of time before we crashed. Once again, the van went onto the shoulder causing gravel to smack the bottom of the floor. Instead of moving back toward the highway, however, the van kept going off the road until all four wheels were on gravel. Tom braced himself and looked at me. I raised up to see what was happening. We were moving into a large graveled area where fishermen could stop and fish. Jerry slammed on the brakes, causing the van to skid across gravel and stop with a jerk. George looked around, but said nothing. Jerry put the van in park, pushed the emergency brake down with his foot and switched the headlights off. He turned and put his hand on the engine cover and pushed himself up to climb back toward us.

"Move the cooler," he grumbled.

Tom pulled it out of his way.

"You drive, George," he said as he put his hand on George's shoulder for support, "and you," he continued while looking at Tom, "sit up front and watch him." Jerry stumbled past me and fell onto the mattress where he sprawled out face down. He adjusted his position once and passed out.

George, who looked as if he were in a daze, climbed into the driver's seat. I thought sure Tom would say something about getting out, but instead he climbed into the passenger's seat. Maybe with Tom helping out, I thought, we'll be all right. A pickup truck and a car were parked in the gravel turnout. Three dark figures sat on stools beside the water's edge, fishing poles rising into the twilight sky. They had no lantern, but two red glows, which I assumed were cigarettes, hung in front of their faces. George put the van in drive and started to move.

"Your lights," Tom said.

"I know," George mumbled as he squirmed in the seat and pulled the light switch.

"Your emergency brake's on."

"Oh yeah," George said, releasing it. We pulled out onto the highway with a jerk that made me brace myself to keep from falling over. George hugged the centerline with the van, but at least he stayed on the right side of the road. Tom appeared alert and ready to grab the wheel, yet he had to be high too. He'd put away at least five beers.

"Hey, watch out," I heard Tom say when the sound of a car horn blasted.

I sat up in time to see we had crossed the centerline by two or three feet into the path of an oncoming car. I braced myself with one hand on the back of Tom's seat and the other on George's seat. The car swerved off the road to miss us. Tom reached for the steering wheel just as George jerked the wheel causing the van to violently swerve back into our lane. The three cars behind the first car all went off the road onto the shoulder. George said nothing.

As we approached a bridge about a quarter of a mile away, George blurted out: "God dammit, I hate these bridges. They're too fuckin' narrow."

George eased up on the gas pedal. I raised up on my knees to look at the speedometer. We were going 40 mph. Two cars approached the bridge from the other side. George overcompensated by hugging the van to the right side of the road. It looked like we might hit the railing. Tom sat balanced on the edge of his seat with his hand resting on the engine cover ready to grab the wheel. I sat on my knees half crouched behind Tom's seat prepared for the worst.

"Shit," George mumbled.

"You're okay," Tom said. "Just keep the wheels straight."

We entered the bridge nearly touching the guard rail on our right. We were halfway across when the other two cars drove onto it. I wanted to tell George to move away from the guardrail, but I feared he might over react and put us in the path of the oncoming cars. Both cars sped by us, the drivers unaware of their luck.

Once the second car passed us, Tom spoke. "Move over toward the middle a little. You're really close to the guardrail over here."

"I hate these fuckin' bridges," George said as the van slowly moved closer to the centerline.

I took a deep breath and exhaled; then sat down behind Tom's seat and put my back against the vinyl. A thin line of light stretched across the horizon. The van's wheels hit gravel.

"What are you doing?" Tom asked.

I turned and raised up on my knees. Tom had his hand above the steering wheel. We were slowing down and pulling off into another turnout area. George hit the brake hard.

"I gotta piss," he said, "so get your fuckin' hand out of the way." He knocked Tom's hand back with his right hand.

"I gotta piss too," I piped in.

Once stopped, all three of us piled out of the van. Tom and I urinated near the right front wheel of the van.

"I'm not going any farther with this guy," Tom said with his voice lowered. "He's going to crash for sure."

"I know. One of us needs to be driving."

We were still pissing when George open the driver's door and climbed back in the van. Both the front passenger door and sliding door were open.

"Come on man," he said looking at us, "get the piss out and get the fuck back in here." He laughed at his own words.

"This is the end of the line for me," I said softly to Tom as I zipped up my pants. "I'm getting my things and spending the night here."

"God dammit," George yelled, "I knew I shouldn't have turned this fuckin' thing off." He slammed his open hand into the steering wheel. "Start you mother fucker!" He turned the key, but nothing happened. He tried it several times in a row—nothing.

"Fuck! Fuck! Fuck!" George yelled, now slamming both hands into the steering wheel.

"Has this happened before?" I asked.

"No, god dammit, but I knew I shouldn't have turned it off. I hate this fuckin' thing."

"Take it easy," Tom said. "We'll see if we can find some jumper cables. Just stay put. It'll work out."

"Come on," Tom said to me. "There's a truck up there. Let's see if he can help us."

When we were 30 or 40 yards away from the van, Tom spoke. "Can you believe what happened?"

"Someone's looking after us," I said, then paused momentarily. "You're not serious about trying to get the van started, are you?"

"We'll see if this guy's going to be fishing here for a while. If so, we'll let those guys sleep it off before going back with the jumpers."

It sounded like a good plan to me, but the fisherman had no jumper cables. I wanted to get my things and start hitchhiking.

"It's going to be hard catching a ride in the dark," Tom said as we turned to walk back to the van. "Hey, there's a light over there."

On the other side of the highway, we could see a light shining up from behind a side road that curved down and disappeared behind a rock embankment. We ran across the highway to beat an approaching car. As we walked down the side road, we saw a new van backed down to the water's edge with a trailer attached to it. A boat floated in the water several feet behind the trailer with two guys in it. Two other men were up to their knees in water beside the trailer. At first I thought they were launching the boat, but then realized they were trying to load it onto the trailer. A Coleman lantern sat beside the van, and one guy in the boat held a flashlight. No one noticed us approaching in the dark.

"Excuse me," I said. "Whose van is this?"

The guy in the water closest to us turned quickly and looked at me. He wore a swimsuit and a long-sleeved beige shirt that hung loosely about him. His dark hair hung down to the top of his shoulders.

"None of this stuff is mine," he said, holding his hands out and shrugging his shoulders. Everyone stopped what they were doing and turned toward us.

"What do you want?" asked a dark-bearded heavy set man standing in the boat. He had short hair and wore a dark baseball cap with white lettering on the front.

"We've got a van on the other side of the road that won't start," I said. "We were wondering if you had some jumper cables."

"No, we don't," he replied tersely. "Sorry we can't help you." He looked at the guy in the water next to the boat. "Have you got the line hooked in the ring?" The man in the water looked up at him. "Well?" the bearded man asked.

"Uh, oh yeah, it's hooked."

"Then start cranking the boat in," he commanded.

Tom and I turned and walked back toward the highway.

"That was weird," I whispered to Tom.

"Yeah. Something's going on."

"What do you mean?"

"They think we're cops."

"They what?"

"They think we're narcs. I've got short hair, you've got long hair, and they're doing something they're not suppose to be doing. Probably bringing in a load of pot. Did you hear what that guy said when you asked who owned the van? He was ready to deny knowing anything and everything. This place is swarming with drug runners. They bring it in here all the time from Columbia and Mexico. At least once a week they find bales of pot washed up on some beach."

When we got back to the van, we found George slumped limply over the steering wheel passed out. You could hear him breathing heavily. If someone looked in the van, they might think George was dead. I pushed the sliding door open wide so we could get our gear. Neither of them woke up. Once we had our things, we closed the doors as quietly as we could, walked about 100 yards away from the van, and set our stuff down. Tom pulled out a pair of jeans and slipped them on over his shorts.

"I thought I'd be in Miami by now," he said. He bent down and picked up a rock, then threw it as far as he could toward the water. "Where were you staying in the Keys?"

"With an old college buddy of mine. He's living with his girlfriend in a trailer not far from where you guys picked me up."

Tom and I stood beside the highway for at least an hour. It's amazing how much you can learn about someone within a short amount of time. Tom attended the University of Florida in Gainesville for two years before dropping out of school in May and moving to Key West with his girlfriend. He found work helping around the docks while his girlfriend waited tables. They dreamed of owning their own sailboat and sailing around the world. In the meantime, they hoped to find jobs aboard someone's yacht so they could travel.

"People need good deck hands," Tom said. "I started sailing with my uncle at five, so I know a lot about the sea. It's only a matter of time before someone hires us on as crew."

Tom planned to visit his mother in Miami for her birthday. Since Tom's departure from school, he and his father were not speaking to one another. Tom's dad worked as an international business consultant for a large firm in Miami.

"Dad won't be home. He's away on business, as usual. He'll call and wish mom a happy birthday."

"Does your mom know you're coming?"

"No. I'm going to stay at a friend's place tonight. I'll visit my mother tomorrow. She'll be surprised, especially when she sees my bald head." He smiled.

Why do fathers and sons have such a hard time getting along, I wondered. I had a few unpleasant memories about my dad, but then again, he was the one who disciplined us when we screwed up. He never put up with any bull, and when he made a decision, it was final. If my brother, sister or I wanted to spend the night at a friend's house, we always asked mom. If she said no, at least you might be able to change her mind. I told Tom about one of my more intense moments with my dad.

When I registered for the military at 18, I brought home CO (conscientious objector) papers. At that time, the Vietnam War still raged. I dropped the papers on the kitchen table and forgot them. Dad came to my room and stood at the door as I sat studying that evening.

"What are these?" he asked.

He had obviously read them.

"Dad, I don't believe in killing people."

"This is your country," he said. "If you want the freedom it offers you, then you must be willing to fight for it."

My dad spent four years in the Navy during World War II.

"But dad, it says in the Bible 'Thou shalt not kill.' It doesn't say 'Thou shalt not kill except for your country.' Besides, it's not like our country is being threatened. If the Chinese or Vietnamese come over here and attack us, I'll do what I have to do."

Dad took a few steps toward me and tossed the CO papers on my desk. "If you fill these out and send them in," he said, "plan on moving out."

"Did you fill them out?" Tom asked.

"No. I decided to wait until Uncle Sam sent me a draft notice. I figured I'd choose what to do at that point. As it turned out, my lottery number never got called."

Tom said nothing after the story. We stood there hitchhiking for a long time without a single car slowing down.

"You know," Tom said, "that battery may have charged up enough to start the van. What do you think?"

"Let's try it. Even if those guys wake up, they should be sober by now."

When we got to the van, George had moved back to the mattress with Jerry. We set our gear down outside the sliding door. As we opened the doors, Jerry mumbled something. Tom climbed in the driver's seat, and I got in on the passenger's side. I glanced into the back of the van. Jerry rose up on one arm and saw George asleep on the mattress beside him.

"What's going on?" he asked, sounding confused and bewildered.

"We stopped to take a piss," I said, "and George shut off the engine. We haven't been able to get it started since. It's been a while, so we thought maybe the battery has gained enough charge to kick it over."

"Well let me try starting it," Jerry said, standing up and stumbling to the front of the van.

Tom got out of the van and Jerry slipped into the seat. He pumped the gas pedal twice and turned the key. The engine almost kicked into gear. It sputtered once and then died.

"Shit! We gotta get this fuckin' van rolling. We have to work tomorrow."

Jerry got out of the van and lifted the hood to look at the battery. We were standing beside Jerry when a camper truck pulled onto the turnout and stopped 30 or 40 yards away.

"Maybe he's got jumper cables," Tom said. He walked toward the truck. I went with Tom while Jerry pulled and jerked on the battery cables. As we approached the truck, I saw the Michigan license plates.

"He's from up north," I said. "He'll have jumpers."

Sure enough he did. When we got back to the van, George stood with Jerry looking at the battery. Within a few minutes we had the van running.

"Thanks mister," Jerry said to the man with the cables. "I'm a little short on cash or I'd offer you a few bucks."

"That's all right," the man said. "Glad I could be of help."

Once we got back on the road, Jerry and George opened another beer and told us to grab one too. We did, which left one bottle in the cooler. We drove 15 or 20 minutes before we passed a tavern beside the road. Cars jammed the parking lot, so Jerry pulled into a construction site on the opposite side of the road, and then backed into a graveled area so we were facing forward.

"Run over there and grab us two sixes," Jerry said to George.

"Just keep the motor running," George replied as he climbed out of the van.

Within a few minutes, George returned with a sack. As soon as George shut the door, Jerry punched the gas. Instead of going forward, the van lunged backward. The arm of a huge crane shot through the back window showering glass onto the mattress. An eerie silence filled the van just after the crash. I checked my body for signs of glass.

"Shit!" George screamed. "What the hell are you doing?"

"God dammit!" Jerry yelled, looking back at the crane's arm sticking through the van window.

Sticking his head out the window and looking around, George said, "Let's get the hell out of here."

Surprisingly, the van hadn't stalled. Jerry threw the van into gear and punched it, spitting gravel behind us as we fishtailed out of the construction site onto the highway.

"What the fuck are we going to do?" George asked Jerry.

"Shit if I know."

For some reason, I thought they were referring to the crane they hit.

"I don't think you damaged the crane," I said.

"That's not the fuckin' problem," George sneered. "This is not our van."

"Whose is it?" Tom asked.

"Our boss's," Jerry replied, "and he doesn't know we took it to Key West."

I looked at the back of the van. In addition to the knocked out window, the top of the back door and part of the van's roof were caved in.

"We gotta think up a good story," George said as he put cans of Budweiser in the cooler.

"Fuck, shit!" Jerry yelled, "I can't believe I did that."

By the time we arrived in Miami, we had finished off the beer. We stopped at a Quick Stop for gas and more Budweiser. I called Karen and told her I was 10 or 15 minutes away from her apartment. She offered to come and get me, but I prided myself in making it to my destinations without intruding on my friends. Besides, Jerry insisted on taking me to her doorstep, and I feared what might happen if I snubbed him. Even though he had put away three or four beers since awakening from his last drinking spree, he appeared fairly sober.

We pulled up in front of Karen's apartment a little after 10:30. The building, with a white stucco exterior and large balconies surrounded by wrought-iron railings, looked luxurious. A long, white stucco carport covered a string of cars, including a Porsche and a Corvette. When we stopped, Jerry shut off the engine.

"Shit!" he yelled, slamming his hand into the steering wheel, "I forgot." He tried starting it, but there were only a few clicks and then silence. "God dammit! I can't believe this shit!"

Tom opened the van's side door and handed me my pack.

"Do you think your girlfriend has jumper cables?" Jerry asked me.

"Probably. She's from Chicago. I'll be right back."

With my pack and guitar, I walked down a short vine-covered walkway and climbed a stairway to Karen's apartment. Although somewhat embarrassed for her to see these drunk and disheveled characters, I also was concerned for her safety. With both George and Jerry tipsy again, I had no way of knowing how they would react when they saw her. I appreciated Tom's presence. Karen must have heard or seen me coming because she opened the door before I knocked.

"Bryce," Karen said, stepping into the hallway and hugging me awkwardly because of my pack and guitar. "It's good to see you."

No doubt she smelled beer on my breath.

"It's good to see you too. How have you been?"

"Great. Come on in. Let me help you with your things."

She took my guitar.

"There's a little problem outside," I said as I slipped my pack off and set it on the floor. "The guys that gave me a ride shut off their engine, and it won't start again. Do you have jumper cables?"

"Sure. Let me get my keys."

She put my guitar down and went to her bedroom before returning.

"These guys have had a few beers, and to put it mildly, are a bit crude."

Karen smiled at me as she slipped on a yellow Windbreaker. A sparkle flickered from her eyes. "I'll be fine, but thanks for the warning."

As we came down the apartment sidewalk to the carport, George gave out a whistle. Karen, a big-boned girl standing five-foot-nine-inches tall with long brown hair and strong facial features, firmly filled her tight-fitting jeans.

"Hey, hey, hey," Jerry said as we approached. He stood in front of the van with the hood up.

"This is Jerry, that's George and that's Tom. This is Karen, guys. Now be nice."

"Helloooooo," Jerry said, giving a little half bow.

"Glad to meet you," Karen said assuredly. "I'll get my car, and we'll get you going."

"She can get me goin' anytime," George said in a low voice as Karen walked to the garage. Karen heard the comment, but ignored it.

Fortunately, Karen owned neither the Porsche nor Corvette parked in the carport. She still had the Oldsmobile her parents gave her while in school. She handed one end of the cables to Jerry who attached them to the van's battery posts. Karen insisted on hooking the cables to her own battery. While they were starting the van, I whispered to Tom that Karen could take him wherever he needed to go. He thanked me, but said Jerry told him they would be driving right by his friend's house. As they pulled away from the curb, I thanked them again for the ride.

Jerry looked at me and shouted, "Have fun, man."

George, in the passenger's seat on the other side of the van, bellowed, "Go get her man," and gave out a hooting cry.

Jerry beeped the horn twice as the old white van, with its smashed back door, caved in roof and broken window, slowly sputtered down the street. The van certainly looked out of place amidst the neatly trimmed lawns, black iron gates and carefully placed palm trees. Just a couple of Florida's blue collar alcoholics cruising down a white collar boulevard after helping out a hitchhiker. They were dirty, wild, reckless, crude and generous.

The Knife

C ar headlights cut through the blowing snow as the Holiday Inn sign in Evansville, Indiana, glowed from across the highway. The cold, wind and snow reminded me of the frigid blizzard night in Missouri when I nearly froze to death. I decided to put my thumb down and seek shelter. I walked beneath the interstate bridge and crossed the hotel parking lot. A young man stood at the registration desk talking to a girl in a waitress uniform. He said something to the girl, and she turned to look at me.

"Hi," I said, slowly entering through the glass doors to keep my guitar from banging anything. "How much for a single room?"

"It's twenty-one fifty," the young man said.

"Do you have any cheaper rooms? I've only got fourteen bucks."

"No, I'm sorry. You might try the motel on the other side of the interstate." He walked around from the front desk and moved to the window. "I think you can see it from here. Yes, it's right there."

He pointed to the tip of a flashing blue neon sign.

"They've got cheaper rooms than us, but it's more than fourteen dollars."

I thanked him and walked out the door. The chilly wind made me quiver. I missed my winter coat that had been taken from the Lake Placid bar. Despite no winter coat, my layers of clothes were fairly warm. I wore long underwear, two pairs of socks, a flannel shirt, sweater, jacket, mittens and a stocking cap. I thought about Karen. Two days earlier she had taken me to a Florida highway. She tried to give me some money, but I refused it. A few more bucks would have gotten me a room.

I stepped over the curb of the Holiday Inn parking lot and walked under the interstate bridge. As a cold blast of wind and snow hit my face, I thought about how nice it would be to have someone to love—to really love with all my

169

heart. Nicolette, my friend in Knoxville, came to mind. Her pleasant, warm smile with her sparkling green eyes surrounded by soft white skin and thick curly locks of sandy brown hair always made me want to take her in my arms and pull her close.

For some reason, we never shared that intimacy. It seemed like every time one of us got in a romantic mood, ready to initiate that first kiss, the other person did or said something to break the spell. It felt sad in a way, but in another way it kept our friendship alive.

My friends thought my carefree life traveling the country and visiting single girls sounded great. Although never explicitly saying I made love to all the girls, it certainly became implied with remarks like, "Yeah, she and I had a great time," or "Boy, I wish I was with her right now."

My mind relived a feeling that had passed between Nicolette and me during my last stay with her. It happened one evening while we were visiting one of her neighbors. Just after we had entered their apartment and introductions had been made, Nicolette looked at me. A glow radiating from her face aroused feelings of warmth, compassion and love. Although our eyes locked together for but a brief moment, Nicolette's neighbor saw the "look" and said, "Wooo, somebody's in love."

We both smiled, embarrassed at being caught in such a personal exchange. It was the first evening we both felt in sync. We returned to her apartment after 1 a.m., and she put on a Dan Fogelberg album. Seconds after we sat on the couch, the phone rang. It was Nicolette's boyfriend. He screamed so loud that Nicolette held the phone away from her ear. He wanted to know where she'd been all night. She explained that she had been next door, and after a pause said, "That's fine," and hung up the phone. She looked at me. "He's on his way over here."

"Is he going to want to fight me?" I asked. "I'll leave if you think I should." "No," she said, "he won't start a fight, but he's drunk." She let out a sigh. "He has no reason to be upset or mad at me. I've done nothing wrong. Besides, it's not like we are married. He knew you were coming to visit me. I've been honest with him all the way."

I imagined how I would feel if my girlfriend were letting a guy spend a week with her. Most men would go nuts. Also, lovers often sense strong feelings between their mate and another person. Maybe he sensed it without even meeting me. Within 15 minutes, he knocked at the door. Nicolette introduced us. He appeared about my height with brown hair barely covering the top of his ears. He wore blue jeans and a red plaid flannel shirt with a light gray jacket. When we shook hands, he glanced at my eyes and then looked away. He looked emotionally distraught, weak and insecure. I felt sorry for him. After an uncomfortable moment of silence, he looked at Nicolette.

"Why isn't there any music playing?" he asked cynically.

"It just went off," I replied. "If there's a specific album you'd like to hear, I'll put it on."

I wasn't trying to be smart. The music had stopped playing moments before he arrived. He walked past me and went into the bedroom. Nicolette looked at me with sadness and compassion in her eyes, but I didn't know who it was meant for—maybe both of us. She followed her boyfriend into the bedroom and shut the door.

I recalled the night Melanie told me she had met someone else. I suspected something wrong months before she told me. I even dreamed that a friend of mine had an affair with her, and that she told me she was leaving me. I never mentioned the dream to Melanie, fearing it might come true. From the moment of the dream, suspicion and paranoia ripped through my thoughts daily like a constant headache slowly building into the equivalent torture of a migraine.

The weekend before Melanie told me about the other man, we had taken some LSD. I immediately felt something wrong as we started to get high. I confronted her, but she acted as if she didn't know what I was talking about. Because of the powerfully discordant feeling, I decided to take acid the following Friday as a way to more acutely tune into her feelings. I took the LSD an hour before Melanie normally came home from work. As soon as I got high on the acid, I felt the inharmonious feelings again. When Melanie failed to return home by 5:30, I called her office and got no answer. I called again at 6 and 6:30. When she walked into the apartment at 6:45, I sat in a chair scared and paranoid.

"Where have you been?" I tried not to sound mad.

"I had some things I had to finish up at work."

She sounded defensive to me. I knew she was lying, but I wanted to believe her.

"On a Friday night you had to work late?"

"Yes. I had to work late. And that's because it's a real job!" She emphasized "real job" as she quickly walked to the bedroom to change her clothes.

For weeks we'd been punching each other with verbal jabs. I'm sure most of it evolved from my fears, suspicions and insecurities. I followed her into the bedroom.

"I have to be responsible." This time she drew out the word "responsible." "There are things that won't get done if I don't do them."

She lifted her dress over her head and tossed it onto the bed.

"I called your office at 5:30 and nobody answered."

Wearing only a bra and panties, Melanie looked at me with fire in her eyes as she pulled her jeans to her hips.

"So you're checking up on me?" Her reply made me mad, but at the same time I felt guilty too. "That's a bunch of shit!" she screamed.

171

My whole body pulsated, my skin burned. I could feel sweat moving out my pores. The walls in the room were breathing. I knew the acid had altered my perceptions, but I also knew she was lying—I could feel it, and that really hurt.

"I called to see if you wanted to go out for pizza." I said it so calmly it surprised me. "I thought I'd walk to Pizza Inn and meet you there."

That would have been my excuse for calling if she'd been there. It seemed only natural to stick with it. She went to the dresser and took out a sweatshirt. She didn't look at me.

"I was in the dark room developing film."

She said it in a way that sent an apology for getting mad at me. It was a good answer, yet I wondered if she had been saving it for a moment like this. Maybe I'm just paranoid from the acid, I thought. I hoped. She pulled the sweatshirt on over her head.

"A pizza sounds good. Let's go."

At Pizza Inn we took a table near the window. A waitress served two huge pizzas to a large family near us. The girl who came to our table had a strange-looking hat on her head that said Pizza Inn. The hat fit a little cockeyed. Her nose seemed to be moving from cheek to cheek as she placed the silverware wrapped in napkins on our table. She said she'd give us a few minutes to decide what we wanted. I wasn't hungry at all. I rarely ate when high on acid. I told Melanie to choose whatever pizza she wanted. She ordered sausage and mushroom. After the waitress left our table, I looked at Melanie.

"How's it been going at work?"

"Fine. I'm learning a lot. Next Saturday there's an employee picnic. I have to shoot pictures for the newsletter."

"That sounds like fun. It will give me a chance to meet some of your coworkers."

"I really didn't think you'd want to go," she said quickly. "It's going to be boring." As she spoke, she looked at me, but never kept eye contact for more than a second or two. Instead, she looked around the room or out the window. "Besides," she added, "I'll be working. I won't have time to sit around and visit."

I wondered if there really was a picnic. It would be a four to seven-hour alibi on a Saturday. I now felt suspicious of everything she said.

"You put in a lot of overtime, don't you?"

"What do you mean?"

"Well, for the past month you've been staying late about every night." She looked at me a little longer before looking away.

"It hasn't been every night," she snapped. "I'm just trying to do a good job."

She paused for a moment. I could feel something happening. I had to remind myself to breathe.

"I have something I need to tell you."

My stomach churned. I felt empty and hollow inside. I looked into Melanie's eyes, but she looked away. Our waitress brought us two plates. She slid them in front of us. I said thanks softly as the waitress turned toward the kitchen. I waited, keeping my eyes on Melanie. She watched the waitress walk away; then glanced back at me. She looked down at her hands. Her hands were on top of the table—fingers intertwined. She rubbed her palms together, and then stopped and rubbed her thumbs back and forth over her forefingers. Although her eyes were directed at her hands, I could tell her mind was somewhere else. I couldn't stand the silence.

"Well?"

She looked at me momentarily before looking back down at her hands.

"I've met someone at work."

She said it softly and calmly, as if asking someone to pass the salt. I felt deflated and nauseous. My fears, harbored for months, were happening. Silence followed. Melanie kept her eyes on her hands.

"What do you mean?" I wanted her to look at me. She looked up from her hands and into my eyes. She said nothing and looked back at her hands.

"Are you in love with him?"

"I don't know."

"Do you still love me?"

She kept looking at her hands, her thumbs continuing to rub her forefingers.

"I don't know."

Again silence ensued.

"Have you slept with him?"

"No."

I felt a brief moment of relief.

"I want to, but he won't because I'm married."

The room began to spin. My heart plummeted into my already queasy stomach and disintegrated into its digestive juices. My muscles, bones and internal organs deflated like water balloons bursting and collapsing into wrinkles of rubbery heaps. Only a scarred, frayed and deranged consciousness remained. Although completely aware of the moment, I questioned its reality. The waitress brought our pizza, yet neither of us spoke.

"Enjoy your pizza," she said automatically and walked away.

Melanie quickly took a piece of pizza and put it on her plate. I slowly took a piece and put it on mine. I took a deep breath and exhaled. I looked at Melanie, but her eyes were on her pizza. She leaned over and took a bite. I looked over at the cash register. The girl who served our pizza stared at us. She must have felt something wrong. I looked down at the pizza on my plate, and then at Melanie. She had been looking at me, but quickly looked down when our eyes met. She took another bite and chewed slowly.

"I'm not very hungry," I said.

She put down her pizza.

"Neither am I."

I scooted out of the booth. "I need to get out of here." I got up and started for the door, my eyes tearing up.

"I'll pay for the pizza," I heard Melanie say. I walked around a large family standing near the cash register. The man handed the cashier some money. I pushed the door open and headed straight for the car. My breaths became short and erratic. Tears ran down my cheeks as I wiped my dribbling nose with the back of my hand. I walked to the car and leaned against the trunk. I looked away from the restaurant, not wanting anyone to see me. I brushed off my wet cheeks with the palm of my hand and took a deep breath. In my mind an inner voice kept saying, "What's the big shock? You knew this was coming."

The family came out of the restaurant and moved toward their car near the front door. I could hear them climbing into it. The fan belt whined when the car started. As they drove past me, I turned toward the restaurant to see Melanie exiting through the door.

"I'll walk home if you want," she said once she stood beside me.

"No, please get in the car." I got in and started the engine. She climbed in, and I backed out of the parking space, and then headed across the parking lot. "What do we do now?"

Melanie looked out the passenger window. "I just want to go home."

Neither of us said a word until I parked the car outside our apartment.

"I need to be alone for a while," Melanie said as we got out of the car. "I'm going for a walk."

As she walked away from the apartment, I followed her.

"Don't you think we should talk?"

She didn't say anything and kept walking. I went into the apartment, sat down in my reading chair and wailed. My whole body trembled. I never knew life could be so miserable.

A passing truck swirled a torrent of snow into my face, bringing me back to reality. I could plainly see the motel's neon sign. Maybe the clerk would accept $14. I had nothing to lose by asking. A car honked its horn to my left, causing me to flinch slightly. I turned to see a black, late-model Grand Prix stop beside me. The driver reached across the seat and rolled down the window. The window stuck after it came down an inch or two, so the driver quickly rolled it back up and then down again, but this time with more force, causing the window to come down five or six inches.

"Do you need a place to stay for the night?"

I bent down and looked into the car. The guy had short dark hair and a clean-shaven face. He looked about my age.

"Uhh, yes."

"Hop in. You can sleep on our couch." He reached over and unlocked the door.

"Thanks for the offer," I said, "but I think I should tell you I'm not gay."

He laughed. "Neither am I. I saw you out here in the cold and snow and thought you might need a place to crash. I'm in school here, and today was our last day of finals. My roommate and I are throwing a party tonight. I thought you might like to join us. Maybe play a little guitar."

I sensed no hostility or defensiveness from him.

"Sure, that sounds cool." I opened the door, pushed the bucket seat forward and tossed my things in the back seat.

"My name's Steve." He held out his hand.

"Bryce," I replied as we shook.

He asked me the usual questions: where was I from, where was I going and where had I been.

"You sure your roommate won't care if I crash on your couch?"

"I'm positive. Bobby will probably stay at his girlfriend's apartment anyway. Everything's cool. Will you play some music for us?"

"Sure, I love to play. I'm not the greatest guitar player, but it's fun."

"That's what it's all about. I don't know how many people will show up for the party, but it'll be a good time. I've got a case of beer in the trunk."

Steve, a junior studying to be an engineer, wore a nice pair of slacks, a pinstriped shirt with a gray collar, polished leather shoes and a new suede jacket. He dressed radically different from what I wore to school. My usual school clothes were blue jeans, a flannel shirt, sweater or sweatshirt, and tennis shoes.

Within five minutes, we arrived at a two-story apartment building. Steve got the beer out of the trunk, and I carried a sack of chips and dip along with my guitar and pack. We walked up a flight of steps and entered an apartment. Steve flipped on a light that hung over a wooden table in the dining room. All the curtains and shades were closed, and the apartment smelled stale and musty from beer and cigarette smoke. I pushed the door shut with my foot.

"You can put the sack on the table."

Steve pulled the Budweiser cans from their cardboard casing and stacked them in the refrigerator. The living room and dining room were actually connected in an L-shape, with the kitchen at the back of the dining room. The living room contained a long ugly brown plaid couch with a coffee table in front of it, two large lounge chairs, one green and the other brown, and a rocking chair. Nothing matched. A television, as well as a stereo receiver and turntable, sat on a two-by-ten board that ran across two stacks of bricks. A large selection of albums stood beneath the board between the bricks, and a three-foot tall speaker cabinet hugged each end of the two-by-ten.

"Make yourself at home. That's the couch you'll be sleeping on."

"Thanks." I leaned my pack against the wall behind the chair and slipped my guitar behind the couch. It kept my things out of the way, plus you couldn't see them unless you looked over the chair and couch. I heard a popping swish as Steve peeled back the top on a beer can. He took a sip of beer as he walked toward me carrying another beer.

"Here you go." He handed me a Budweiser.

"Thanks." I tapped the top of the beer can a couple of times and pulled the tab. "Cheers!" We clinked cans.

"I'm going to change into some jeans. Put on an album if you want." He reached down and turned on the stereo before disappearing into his bedroom, shutting the door behind him.

I dropped my beer top in the ashtray near the stereo. All the ashtrays had been emptied, but not washed or wiped out. I flipped through the albums: Leonard Skynard, Pink Floyd, James Taylor, Rod Stewart and more. I picked a Dave Mason album called *Headkeeper* and put it on, and then sat in the wooden rocking chair and rocked to the music.

"That's one of my favorite albums," Steve said when he returned to the room wearing blue jeans and a brown flannel shirt. "You like that chair?"

"Yeah, your body sort of molds to the wood and webbing."

"It was my grandmother's before she died. She told my mom she wanted me to have it." Steve took a deep breath and exhaled. "God it feels good to be done with finals." He sat down on the couch. "Do you get high?"

"You mean smoke?"

"Yeah."

"Sure, but I don't have any with me."

"No problem." He got up. "I've got a joint in my bedroom."

After Steve left the room, the front door opened and a short boyish-looking guy with a thin scraggly mustache and sandy blond hair covering his ears entered. Carrying two brown grocery sacks, he pushed the door shut with his back.

"Hello," I said, standing up.

"Hey," he replied setting the sacks on the table. "How's it going?"

"Good."

He walked toward me. "You a friend of Steve's?"

"Sort of."

He reached out his hand to shake.

"My name's Bobby."

"I'm Bryce."

Steve walked back into the room.

"Hey Bobby, you're just in time. Bryce and I were about to smoke a joint."

"I'm definitely ready."

"Where's Jenny?"

"She'll be here in about an hour. She wanted to take a shower and get cleaned up. How did your physics test go?"

"It was tough, but I think I did all right. How about you?"

"A German chocolate cakewalk." Bobby looked at me and smiled. "When it comes to English, I can bullshit my way through anything."

Bobby got himself a beer, and Steve fired up the joint. Steve told Bobby how he met me and that I had been on the road for two years.

"So you're just traveling around?" Bobby asked with enthusiasm.

Bobby stood a few inches shorter than me. All of his features were small, and his clear olive complexion looked as soft as a baby's face. When he wasn't speaking, he had a feminine look about him. If he shaved the long peach fuzz above his lip, one might mistake him for a girl. His voice had a smooth melodious tone, and mixed with his personality he came across confident, smart, shrewd and quite perceptive. He bubbled with energy as if he were about to do something he really enjoyed. As I told them travel stories, Bobby sat on the edge of his seat, his eyes sparkling and his mouth slightly open. Bobby and Steve both wanted to travel when they got out of school. A knock came at the door.

"The door's open," Bobby yelled, "come on in."

The door opened and in came a good looking long-haired brunette carrying a grocery sack.

"Hey babe," Bobby said and got up. She smiled.

"It smells like you guys have started without me."

"Hi Jenny," Steve said as Bobby walked toward her.

"Hello Steve. How'd your final go?"

"Good."

"What'd you bring?" Bobby asked as he took the sack out of her hands.

"Some chips and popcorn. I hope you guys have oil."

"We do." Bobby set the sack on the dining room table while Jenny slipped off her white down ski jacket and walked toward us.

"This is Bryce," Steve said. "He's just bumming around the country."

"Hi," Jenny said.

I stood up. Jenny had beautiful blue eyes and thick eyebrows that had been sparingly plucked. She wore a dash of makeup around her eyes to accent their natural beauty. Otherwise, she appeared to wear little or no cosmetics. She stood two inches shorter than Bobby, and her thick, long brown hair reminded me of Melanie's hair. Her slim and well-proportioned figure fit her natural and healthy aura of youthful vitality. She wore a black long-sleeved turtleneck sweater with no bra, and at times, her nipples hardened and protruded slightly from beneath the sweater. She had her sweater tucked into a pair of tight blue jeans that extended down to her brown leather hiking boots. Her wavy brown hair made her long, golden teardrop earrings stand out against her black sweater. A thin gold bracelet hung loosely around her left wrist, while a silver band with a small turquoise stone encircled her right ring finger. The way she moved and held herself, I assumed she came from a family of some means, but at the same time she appeared neither snobbish or stuck up. She had a confident and relaxed demeanor, similar to her boyfriend Bobby.

"It's nice to meet you," she added, looking straight into my eyes.

"It's nice to meet you too," I said softly.

Bobby stood behind Jenny and to her left. I could see him watching me as if judging my reaction to her. He exhibited no jealous or protective mannerisms, but instead held a smile that radiated admiration and trust. For being so young, the couple appeared quite mature.

"Bryce has been telling us some great travel stories," Bobby said as he moved toward the kitchen.

"Like what?" she asked, and turned her gaze to me.

"Oh, about different people he's met." Bobby opened the refrigerator door. "And the weird things that have happened to him."

"Tell her about the guy in L.A.," Steve said.

Bobby returned with a beer. "Yeah, that's a good one." He popped the top and handed it to Jenny.

"Thanks," she said in almost a whisper. She reached her arm around Bobby's waist, and they walked to the couch and sat together.

I told the story again, adding a few things I had forgotten to say earlier. Several more students arrived, and by 10 p.m. there must have been four or five couples and several single guys. Unfortunately, there were no single girls. On occasion a joint would be passed around, but for the most part everyone drank beer. Others brought beer too, so everyone had plenty.

When a Rod Stewart album finished playing, Steve went to the stereo and removed the album. "Hey Bryce, how about playing your guitar?"

"Good idea," Bobby said. They both looked at me.

"Sure." High from the pot and beer, I got out my guitar. While making a few tuning adjustments, I felt nervous and self-conscious. I decided to play a song called "The City." It had an upbeat rhythm, and my version of the song meant playing only two chords, which decreased my chances of error. Once I began playing, my inhibitions subsided and I zeroed in on the song. They clapped when I finished.

"Do you know 'House of the Rising Sun?'" one of the guys blurted out.

Although I had forgotten the man's name, he had come with a buddy of his. He looked out of place with the rest of the group. His stringy long brown hair hung down to his oil-stained blue jean jacket. His jeans looked like they had never been washed, and his leather work boots were scuffed and tattered. His hands, which appeared too large for his size, were callused and grease-stained with dirt beneath the fingernails. I guessed him to be six feet tall, but the soiled New York Yankee cap on his head made him look taller. He was husky, on the verge of being fat. His mischievous-looking brown eyes appeared to be floating at the back of his large deep eye sockets. When he looked at me, he seemed to be challenging me or daring me to try to stare him down. The long thin hairs sparsely spread across his face made me want to take a razor and cut them. A smirky grin was as close as he came to smiling, and his comments, which occasionally brought a laugh from someone, were usually a cut or a snide remark. He projected a presence of unpredictable physical power and explosiveness. Once when I looked at him and smiled, he just glared at me.

"I used to play it, but I'm not sure if I remember it." I picked the notes on my guitar.

"I know the words," he shouted, "keep playing." He began singing, "There is a house in New Orleans, they call the rising sun, and it's been the ruin of many a poor boy, and God I know I'm one..."

Actually, his singing sounded pretty good, and for the most part he stayed on key. When he didn't know the words, he used words from the previous verse. At the end of his third verse, I slowed the picking down to indicate the end.

"Keep playing," he demanded, "there's one more verse."

I kept the chords going and he repeated the beginning of the song and ended by standing up and bellowing with his arms spread out, "and God I know I'm one."

People clapped and someone said, "All right, Ricky."

Ricky looked down at me as if to say: "See, you're not the only hot shot that can do music around here." I looked into his eyes and smiled. This time I decided not to look away from his stare. He finally looked down at my belt.

"Is that a knife you've got there?" he asked and looked back into my eyes.

"Yeah."

"What do you have it for?" he asked in a mocking tone.

"It's a present from my brother."

My brother had given me the buck knife the Christmas before. He thought I might need it for protection on the road. Although I had never used it for self-defense, it came in handy cutting up apples and cheese as well as sharpening tent stakes and sticks to roast hot dogs and marshmallows.

"Let me see it," Ricky snapped, extending his hand.

I hesitated.

"What's the matter? You got a problem with showing us your knife?"

I noticed the pronoun change from "me" to "us."

"Why do you want to see it? It's just another knife."

"We just do. Come on."

Everyone seemed to be waiting for me to act. Ricky had his hand out. My arm felt like a lead weight as I reached toward my belt. I popped the snap holding the knife in its sheath and slipped it out. Ricky reached out and snatched it from my hand.

"Hey, this is a nice knife." He took a hold of the blade and pulled it out. The blade clicked as it locked into place. Ricky slowly grinned. "Well look at that, it even locks up tight." He pushed on the blade to demonstrate the knife's sturdiness. He held the blade in front of his eyes and slowly turned it.

"This looks like a helluva gut twister," he said in a cavalier manner. "Have you ever stabbed anyone with it?"

A sick sensation churned at the pit of my stomach. We were all drunk and stoned. A gloomy silence of anticipation and expectation filled the room.

"No," I said as calmly as I could, "but it comes in handy when I'm camping." I plucked a couple of chords on the guitar as if I no longer had interest in what he said or did.

"For what?" he asked. "Fighting off bears, maybe?"

He took a step back, and then thrust the knife forward, stabbing the air in front of him as if attacking something. My muscles tightened, ready to use my guitar for protection or as a weapon.

"Ya! Ya! Ya!" he screamed as he quickly jabbed the knife forward three more times. "Uhhhhhh," he groaned deeply as he pushed the knife forward a fourth time, but this time turning the knife slowly in a circle and then jerking it upward in short stabs as if he had stuck a bear and wanted to rip its guts out. Ricky's glossy eyes were wild and in a world of their own, his face a grimace with gritted teeth.

"That's enough," Bobby said calmly. "Give the knife back to Bryce."

Ricky, with a moist gleam in his eyes, turned slightly and looked at Bobby. Bobby sat with his arm around Jenny. I thought back to John.

"The ankles and knees are vulnerable spots," John told me one night as we sat beside a campfire. "A side kick to the knee joint will stop even the biggest man. Or, stomping on the ankle and foot with the side of your shoe can stop anyone."

By raising up and twisting sideways, I could deliver a hard kick to Ricky's right knee. The blow certainly would take him down, but would he be able to get up again? Even if on the ground, he still might hurt someone with the knife.

"No matter what the situation is," John continued, "a nonviolent solution is always best, even if you must lose face. Remember, our thoughts create the reality we experience. That being the case, your thoughts can provide the spark that ignites the smoldering coals, or become the gentle rain that extinguishes the fiery flames."

"But how do you do that?" I asked.

"Through your imagination and emotion. Picture the outcome you desire in complete detail and feel what it would be like."

I imagined Ricky smiling, lowering the knife and sitting down. I could hear the Moody Blues singing the song *Question of Balance* from an album I had seen in Steve's record collection. I also pictured people laughing and joking with each other as they had been doing minutes before.

"Ricky, please put the knife away," Jenny said. "You're scaring people." Jenny stood up. "Anyone else want another beer while I'm up?" Bobby moved to the edge of the couch, poised to protect Jenny.

Ricky stood still, keeping the knife in front of him. A triumphant sneer spread across his face. He pulled the knife close to his stomach as Jenny walked by him. The girl had nerve.

"I'll take one, Jenny," said the girl sitting in the rocking chair.

"How about another song?" Bobby said to me.

Bobby sat on the edge of his seat with his arms resting on his knees, focused and prepared to act. From the corner of my eye, I saw Ricky looking at me.

I looked at Bobby. "I noticed a Moody Blues album over there. Is that yours?"

"No, it's mine," Steve said, getting up. "I'll put it on." Steve walked past Ricky, ignoring him. Another guy got up and went to the bathroom.

"Yeah, it's a sturdy knife," Ricky said looking at me. His eyes sparkled, and he had a full grin on his face. He pressed the lever on the back of the knife handle and returned the blade into its stock with his palm.

I looked at Ricky. "Do you play guitar too?"

"No, but I think I might start," he said. "It doesn't look that hard."

"You ought to. You've got a good voice."

I made the compliment partly because it was true, and partly to ease the tension. Ricky looked pleased by the comment, but he seemed to know why it had been made. He extended his hand with the knife toward me, but when I tried to take it, he held it tightly. He had that same domineering sneer as when he first took it.

"I never take my knife out unless I plan on using it," he said, releasing his grip on the handle. It fell lightly into my hand.

Something besides the knife passed between us when he released his grip. Although he acted as if he performed this whole charade to teach me a lesson, at one point Ricky became totally lost in his power trip, as if something possessed him. By creating fear in the group, the terror seemed to feed his growing sense of power and control. When people began to ignore him, however, the spell broke.

Shortly after the Moody Blues album started playing, Ricky and his friend left the party.

A Gravel Lifeline

Something was wrong—I sensed it. She put her hands above my shoulders and slowly raised herself up. I felt the cool air flow over my chest as her warm skin left mine. Her long blonde hair fell down from around her face creating a tunnel to her glittering eyes and gentle smile. She lifted her hips off me and moved her legs to my side, pushing herself up to sit on her heels. She put her left hand on my shoulder.

"I've got to go," she said. She suddenly broke into uncontrollable laughter, causing her hand to shake my shoulder.

"Bryce," I heard a voice whisper, "we've got to get going."

I opened my eyes to see a hand move away from my shoulder. I pushed up on my elbows and looked down at the sleeping bag around me. A dim light on the horizon made the trees look like clay silhouettes.

"Shit!" I laid back down. "What time is it?"

Ron stood folding up his poncho. "Not so loud," he said in a whisper. "It's four-thirty, and we've gotta go. If you want a shower, you'd better hurry. I've already taken mine, and Doug's in there now."

Ron, Doug and I had been traveling together since noon the previous day. We met on the outskirts of Jasper, Alberta, in Canada.

I did not feel like hurrying anywhere. I wanted to return to the blonde in my dream. I took a deep breath and slowly climbed out of my sleeping bag. Canada's spring morning air felt cold. We arrived at the northern British Columbia campground a little after midnight. We planned to sneak into the $15-a-night site, sleep a few hours, use the showers and get out before anyone discovered us.

"Is there any hot water left?" I whispered to Ron as I pulled on my tennis shoes.

183

"I saw three stalls," Ron said softly, "so I'm sure there's plenty. But then again, Doug's been in there a long time."

I quickly pushed my down-feather sleeping bag back into its stuff sack and put the bag and my poncho in the back of Ron's Toyota truck. After grabbing the towel and shampoo from my backpack, I walked briskly toward the bath house. For the past week, cold mountain streams and a washcloth had been my only hygiene source.

I met Doug and Ron the day before. As I stood beside the highway beneath a warm Canadian sun just outside of Jasper, I saw Doug walking toward me in the distance. The closer he got, the more intriguing he appeared. He looked like a mountain man who had been living in the wild for years. Although he had a slim six-foot tall build, his hair and beard created the appearance of a much bigger man, as did his aluminum-framed backpack that rose above his head. His long curly brown hair and bushy beard, even at a hundred yards away, made him a curious sight. His hair hung down to his shoulder blades and cascaded over his chest. His long, thick and bushy beard matched the length of his hair in the front. He looked about 27 or 28 years old, and his wire-rimmed glasses gave him an intellectual touch.

"What's going on?" he asked when he got within talking distance.

"Not a lot. Where you heading?"

"Alaaaska, the last true frontier."

I laughed. "Me too. You ever been there before?"

"Nope. How about you?"

"First time for me too."

"Where are you from?"

"Missouri originally. You?"

"Born and raised in New York City, but I lived in Detroit before I hit the road."

"How long have you been on the road?"

"Going on three years now," Doug said.

"Wow, that's a long time. Where have you been?"

"I traveled Europe for a year, and now I've spent the last two years traveling the United States and Canada. How long have you been on the road?"

I glanced down the highway behind Doug to see if any cars were approaching. "Two years, but I stopped in upstate New York and Lake Tahoe, California, to work for a while."

"Where in upstate New York?"

"Lake Placid."

"That's a beautiful area. I've always loved the Adirondack Mountains. What were you doing up there?"

"I worked as a waiter at the Lake Placid Club."

"Oooo, that's a fancy place. Did you make good money?"

"Not bad, but they took a lot out of my check for room and board."

"So they put you up, eh? What were the living conditions like?"

I noticed his use of "eh." It's a common idiom in Canada, and his use of it meant he had been in Canada for a while.

"They were okay. Similar to a college dormitory. You had to share a room, but we got three meals a day."

"Was the food good?"

"I thought so, but everybody complained about it. Are you hungry? I've got some granola." I reached down and pulled out a sack from my backpack.

"I'm fine for now."

"Here, have a few bites." I opened the bag and pushed it toward him. "I'm going to have a few mouthfuls myself. It must be close to lunch time."

He reached in and took several large chunks of granola, and then looked up at the sun as he tossed a clump into his mouth.

"It's hard to tell time by looking at the sun, but I love these long days. It's like cramming two days into one."

"You got that right." I took a handful of granola and dropped some into my mouth. A car approached, and I held out my left thumb with my fingers still cupping a handful of granola. He turned around and held out his thumb too. The car slowed down and turned on the road leading to Jasper.

"False alarm." He turned toward me and threw the last chunk of granola into his mouth. "What's your name?"

"Bryce." I deposited the rest of the granola in my mouth, dusted off my hand on my jeans, and then shook his hand.

"I'm Doug. You been waiting here long?"

"Forty-five minutes or so."

"Help yourself." I pushed the open bag of granola toward him.

"Thanks, but that's enough for me. I'm going to walk up the road a ways. Maybe I'll see you in Alaska."

He walked backwards facing me as he talked.

"Maybe. Good luck."

"Same to you, and thanks for the granola."

He turned forward and walked north along the road. I took one more handful of granola and then pushed the bag back into my pack.

"Hey," Doug yelled, "when someone stops for you, see if you can get them to pick me up too."

"I'll try."

"Thanks." He raised his hand in a fist and shook it in the air. "Alaska, here we come!"

After Doug walked about a 100 yards, a car zoomed passed me without slowing down. I watched Doug turn and hold out his thumb. The car passed him too. Doug kept walking until he rounded a curve and disappeared from sight. About 20 minutes after the car passed, a Toyota truck with a small camper shell stopped.

I opened the passenger door. "Thanks for stopping."

"Glad to. After all, we're going the same direction, right? Toss your stuff in back. Just turn the handle and lift up."

The camper shell, no taller than the truck's cab, had a back door with a window in it that lifted up. Another camper window near the truck's cab made it possible to see into the camper from inside the truck. There were several huge duffel bags inside the camper shell, along with a toolbox, poncho and sleeping bag. As I set my things in back, Ron got out of the truck and walked to the rear of the camper. He left the engine running. I closed the hatch gently.

"I'm Bryce," I said, holding out my hand.

"Ron." He shook my hand firmly.

Ron looked strong and solid. He must have been six-foot-three and at least 200 pounds. He had short wavy black hair with a thick, neatly trimmed mustache. He hadn't shaved for a couple of days.

"Where are you going?"

"Fairbanks, Alaska," I said.

He smiled. "That's where I'm going."

Ron walked toward the truck door and I headed to the passenger's side.

"That's fantastic! Do you live up there?"

We climbed in the cab and pulled the doors shut.

"No," he glanced at his side mirror and pulled out onto the road, "but I'm going to be living there for the next two years. I'm in the army, and that's where they want me to go."

Thinking about Doug, I glanced into the back of the truck. If things were moved around, there would be room for him to lie down or recline against a sleeping bag or pack. I felt like I should at least say something. "There's another hitchhiker around this bend. He walked by me earlier. He's on his way to Alaska too."

"I think we've got room for him, if you don't mind sitting in the middle. We can put a pillow down for you to sit on."

The thought of sitting between two seats with no back support and a stick shift between my legs for 1,500 miles made me sorry I mentioned Doug.

"Well, yeah, I guess I could," I said hesitantly, looking through the back window into the truck bed covered by the camper, hoping Ron might suggest Doug ride in the back.

As we rounded the curve, there sat Doug on his backpack reading a book. He looked up and started to raise his arm until he saw us slowing down and pulling over. He stood up quickly and put the book in his backpack. Then he saw me and smiled. I rolled down my window as we pulled up beside him.

"All right!" he said as he bent over and looked in the window. "Do you have room for another rider?" He looked at Ron.

"You bet." Ron opened his door and got out. "Bring your pack back here."
I got out too.

"I can fix up a seat for, uh..." Ron looked at me.

"Bryce."

"Right, for Bryce." Ron opened the back window to the camper. "You can toss your pack in here after I get a pillow."

Ron climbed halfway into the camper and grabbed a pillow and small army tote bag. As he backed out of the camper he began talking.

"These are dirty clothes in the tote bag, but they'll be a good cushion beneath the pillow."

Doug pushed his pack into the bed of the truck, and then stuck out his hand to Ron.

"My name's Doug. I appreciate the ride."

"No problem." Ron stuck the pillow under his arm and shook Doug's hand.

"He's driving all the way to Fairbanks," I said to Doug.

"Really?"

"That's right. You guys have a clean shot. I don't plan on stopping much either."

"Sounds good to me."

My seat turned out to be better than I thought. My head nearly touched the ceiling, so neither Doug nor Ron could have sat there without bending forward. During our first pit stop, I got out my sleeping bag for better back support, which made my seat quite comfortable. Ron drove like a maniac. He kept his Toyota truck between 75 and 85 mph most of the time.

In 1978, the Alaskan Highway was gravel and dirt except for asphalt-testing sections about a mile long every 50 to 75 miles. Whether Ron slowed down for a curve or not, he always pushed down on the gas before the curve straightened out. Of course, that caused the truck to slide sideways in a slight fishtail, and invariably I'd have to put my hand on the dash to keep from leaning into either Doug or Ron. I felt vulnerable and unprotected sitting between the two seats. Although the Toyota had seat belts, neither Ron nor Doug wore them.

Once, in the middle of a curve, Ron accelerated so hard that the truck slid into the other lane and went right to the edge of the road. He never let up on the gas. We came out of the curve with Ron continuing to gain speed as the truck climbed a hill.

"Does my driving bother you guys?" Ron grinned.

We were both silent for a moment before Doug spoke first.

"You seem to know what you're doing."

Ron smiled and waited for a response from me.

"That last curve was a bit hairy."

Ron laughed. "I've driven stock cars for two years. It's in my blood to drive fast. You actually have more control accelerating on a curve."

187

I wondered about his logic on that one, but kept silent. After all, he was giving me a 1,500-mile lift. As we topped the hill, we all saw it at the same time, but Ron spoke first.

"My God," he exclaimed as his foot came off the gas pedal and the truck slowed down, "look at that!"

In the middle of a huge meadow not more than 100 yards from the road, glowed the end of a rainbow arching its spectrum of colors upward into the puffy white clouds above us.

"I thought you weren't suppose to be able to see the end of a rainbow," Doug said as Ron pressed on the brake.

"There's unmistakable proof you can," I said.

The car rolled to a halt and Ron opened his door. "Let's go. I've never been at the end of a rainbow."

We climbed out of the truck and started down the highway embankment. Once we reached the bottom, we stopped. This beautifully soft and gentle-looking meadow with the colorful rainbow in the center now showed us its depth and ruggedness. To make it to the rainbow, we'd have to traverse 100 yards of Canadian tundra—an open field with tufts of grass surrounded by 12 to 16 inches of water, possibly deeper in spots. We considered jumping to the grassy clumps leading to the rainbow, but staying on the clumps without slipping into the water would be a miracle.

"Shit," Ron said, "there's no way." He reached down and put his hand in the water. "It's not as cold as I thought it would be."

"We need an airboat," I said, "like they use in the Everglades."

We stood there in awe gawking at the rainbow.

Ron looked at us. "I'm glad you guys are with me. I don't think anyone's going to believe me when I tell them about this."

"Do you have a camera?" I asked.

"Yeah, but I'm out of film."

"I wonder what it looks like at the end," Doug said. "Do you think it would keep moving away the closer you got?"

"An old man in Tahoe told me that he and his family drove a car into the end of a rainbow," I said. "He claimed it resembled the rainbow you see around you when you take a shower on the beach."

We stood there several more minutes before returning to the truck. The end of the rainbow remained as we drove away. All of us kept glancing back at it. Ron got the truck back up to 80 mph. For the most part, we did little talking while driving except during the morning and evening when the chilly air caused us to roll up the windows. During the heat of the day, talking meant screaming above the sound of the engine and the air whipping through the cab. Occasionally, someone would yell and point at a rock structure, a strange cloud formation, a flock of birds or a herd of deer. We saw few cars on the highway, but there were a large number of trucks and RVs.

During one of our afternoon pit stops, which meant we stopped on the road and urinated, Doug asked Ron if he had a girlfriend.

"I did," he said, "but she refused to go to Alaska with me. To be honest, it felt like the relationship was over anyway. She was pretty much a recluse, and spent most of her time in our apartment."

Once we were back in the truck with the wind whipping through the cab, I thought back to the married student-housing apartment Melanie and I shared.

Because of our breakup and short departure notice, we lost our deposit. Despite that fact, with my name on the lease, I wanted the place to be left how we found it—clean. I drove by the apartment two days before everything had to be out and saw Melanie loading her things into a Chevy Nova Super Sport.

Rage suddenly swelled inside me as I thought of her boyfriend, whom I assumed was inside the apartment either packing or preparing to carry a box to the car. I parked my car on the opposite side of the building and headed toward the apartment. No matter how big her boyfriend, I wanted to fight. Even if he beat the hell out of me, I really didn't care.

While walking toward the apartment, a 12-year-old neighbor boy ran up to me. I often played with the apartment kids while taking a break from studying. Usually, we would throw around a football or Frisbee in the courtyard. Because John was older than the other kids, he and I would sometimes sit on the swings and talk. Although small for his age, John seemed much more mature than most 12-year-olds.

"Hi Bryce, how are you doing?" John asked as he stepped in front of me, slowing me down.

"Fine," I said rather curtly, stepping around him. He had to run to catch up with me. I figured he knew something was wrong. Probably everyone in the apartment complex knew Melanie and I were splitting up.

"Hey, how about tossing the football for a while?" John asked as he once again got in front of me.

I stopped this time and looked at him. "Have you talked to Melanie?"

"Yes," he answered, and then looked down.

He had never seen me upset. He appeared frightened. I put my hand on his shoulder.

"John, I consider you a friend. As I guess you know, I'm no longer living here, so we probably won't see much of each other anymore. I've got some things I need to do right now, but I appreciate your concern."

He looked at me, but said nothing. I smiled. "I feel better now. Thanks."

I held out my hand and John took it. We had never shaken hands before.

"Take it easy," I said, turning toward my old apartment. This time John stayed behind.

Once beside the apartment my heart pounded harder. I looked for Melanie's boyfriend. The apartment door was ajar. I walked in, but saw no one. I headed out the back stairway to see Melanie putting a box in the back of the blue Nova Super Sport. I walked down the steps toward her as she turned and saw me coming.

"Where's your boyfriend," I asked sarcastically when I got a few feet from her. I hadn't seen Melanie since moving out of the apartment two weeks earlier.

"He had a few things he had to do this morning," she said as she walked past me and up the steps toward the apartment.

Bounding up the steps two at a time, I caught up with her at the first landing.

"Are you guys having fun playing house?"

Melanie turned to me with tears running down her face. "I hate you," she screamed as she pounded on my chest with her fists.

The hits didn't really hurt, but her reaction surprised me. I grabbed her wrists to stop the hitting. She broke down and sobbed.

"You make everything seem so dirty," she said. "I can't help what I feel. I didn't know it would turn out like this."

I let go of her wrists. She put her hands to her face and sat down crying. My anger drained out of me. I sat beside her.

"Hey," I said softly, "I didn't know it was going to turn out like this either."

"Bryce, I'm so confused. Why's everything got to be so complicated?"

It felt strange. Up to that point I had been trying to get Melanie to sit down and talk about what was happening, but she refused. Now that we were together, and she seemed ready and willing to talk, I realized it didn't matter. She no longer loved me. What else was there to say? She avoided seeing me because she knew I would try to rekindle a fire that had been washed out by a flash flood. For her there were no more warm coals left, much less burning ones.

We didn't say a lot more. I offered to help load some of her things, but she refused my assistance. She wanted to know if I intended to take a large piece of carpeting I had put in the apartment. I ended up trading the carpeting for her typewriter. So much for court settlements.

After driving beneath the Canadian sun for several hours, we approached an RV more than halfway up a fairly steep hill. We were closing in on the RV fast. Ron could not know if an oncoming vehicle was on the other side of the hill, but he moved into the passing lane anyway. I could see the speedometer on 82 mph. My whole body tensed and constricted. Pushing on the dash with my hands helped steady my jangled nerves. I expected a truck or another RV to appear in front of us any second. The driver of the RV beside us must have thought we were crazy. Just as we cleared his bumper, we reached the crest of the hill. No vehicles in sight. I exhaled. I didn't realize until that moment that I had been holding my breath. Ron returned to the right lane.

I looked at Ron. "Are you tired of living?"

He laughed. "I figured our chances were pretty good. We've hardly seen any traffic for the past fifty miles."

"If you decide to do that again, stop and let me out first. I want to see Alaska."

Ron laughed again. Doug said nothing, but I think he agreed with me. It was near midnight that same day when we quietly slipped into the campground for a snooze and a shower.

As I entered the small bathhouse, Doug pulled a t-shirt over his head.

"I hope you left me some hot water."

"It's not hot anymore, but it's not cold. It's cold once you get out though."

Doug slipped on his sweatshirt and went out the door, quietly closing it. The water felt warm compared to the frigid air. I used shampoo for my hair and body. I got in and out of the shower fast; afraid the lukewarm water might turn cold any second. When I returned to the truck, Doug sat on a picnic table using a small flashlight to write in a notebook. Ron stood beside the camper shell eating an apple.

"Sorry I'm holding you up," I whispered. "I showered as fast as I could." I reached in the camper near the raised door and slipped my shampoo into my backpack.

"No problem," Ron said. "I figured you would be another five or 10 minutes. Was the water cold?"

"No, but it wasn't hot."

I spread my towel over the top of my pack to let it dry and grabbed my sleeping bag for back support. Ron lowered the camper door and closed it softly as he looked back over his shoulder at the campsite. Satisfied he had everything, he twisted the handle causing it to lock with a click. The click sounded loud compared to our whispering.

"Open the door quietly," Ron said as I neared the passenger's side of the truck, "and don't shut it until we're down the road a ways."

We climbed in, and Ron started the truck. He let it run a few seconds before putting it in gear and moving out of our campsite onto the driveway leading back to the main road. Ron and Doug held their doors ajar for about 100 yards, and then slammed them shut.

"We made it." Ron pulled out onto the Alaskan Highway. The fact that we quietly rolled in at midnight, slept a few hours, showered and departed without being detected created camaraderie. It reminded me of my teenage days when my friends and I would camp in the back yard and sneak around the neighborhood until the early hours of the morning.

During May in Canada and Alaska, the days get longer and the hours of dusk and dawn linger. That morning at the campground, what first appeared to be light cloud cover, turned out to be a storm. Within an hour of driving, we entered a steady downpour of rain that turned the gravel and dirt highway into a huge muddy path. Ron backed off to 70 mph. The first southbound truck that went by us covered Ron's pickup with mud. Ron quickly increased the windshield wipers' speed to high while squirting water on the windshield, but for a good five seconds we could see nothing but smeared mud. After that incident, Ron decreased our speed slightly as oncoming vehicles approached.

At that time, the Alaskan Highway had short patches of pavement and asphalt that usually ran for about a mile. Evidently, the government wanted to find the most suitable material for paving the road. On one slice of pavement, Ron shot up to 90 mph to pass a commercial bus. We had been following the bus at a distance, avoiding the mud it flung in all directions. The bus had been clipping right along though, traveling between 65 and 70 mph. As we passed the bus, the driver sped up. We hit the muddy gravel road going 80 mph with the bus on our tail.

"What's that guy doing?" Ron looked in his rearview mirror.

I turned around to see the bus less than two car lengths away, its windshield wipers rapidly flapping back and forth as if in a furious rage. Doug looked at the bus through the door's side mirror.

"I don't know," I said. "He must be pissed off you passed him."

"Well he's going a helluva lot faster now than when I was behind him." Ron glanced again in the mirror. "Shit, the son of a bitch is going to pass me."

Ron increased his speed slightly, but the bus kept gaining on us. Ron's eyes glanced ahead of us, and then looked at the speedometer before returning to the rearview mirror. We were starting to crest a hill. Ron had his Toyota truck going as fast as it could go considering the incline. None of us could see over the hill, which meant we could be moving toward a head-on collision. Ron slowed down. The speedometer read 75 mph when the bus pulled alongside us. Ron turned his windshield wipers to high just before the mud hit our window, but the wipers did no good. As mud smeared across the windshield with each passing blade, we could no longer see the bus or the road. The bus driver, sitting at a higher vantage point than us, could probably see without a problem.

"I hope no cars are coming," Ron said, now looking out his mud-splattered side window that allowed some visibility of the road. The speedometer had dropped to 65 mph. I turned and looked out the back window hoping to see if we were in the center of the road, but the filthy window looked like an opaque piece of quartz. I could see nothing. Doug had the best view from his side window.

"You're about twelve feet from the ditch," Doug said calmly as if he were an airplane copilot.

Ron steered the truck slowly toward Doug's side of the road, still looking out his own side window.

"About 10 feet now."

Ron held the steering wheel steady. I watched the speedometer and the front window. We were down to 55 mph. The windshield wipers rapidly flipped back and forth, but the mud still made it impossible to see. Ron held down the lever that shot water onto the flapping wipers. Finally, we caught glimpses of the bus between mud splatters pummeling the windshield. The bus moved farther and farther away from us.

"That fucking asshole!" Ron blurted. "We're lucky no trucks were coming." Ron picked up the mouthpiece to his CB for the first time since Doug and I had been in his truck. He flipped the CB on and held down the engage lever. "Do you have your ears on bus driver?"

No reply.

"In case you do, I thought you might like to know that your mother must have sucked a lot of donkey dicks to end up with a donkey-dick sucker like you."

He waited a few seconds for a reply, and then he hung up the mouthpiece and shut the CB off. The bus, now several hundred yards in front of us, kept moving at 70 mph. About 45 minutes later we came to one of the few gas station's along the highway. The bus pulled in and we followed. All of us watched the bus driver—dressed in a green jump suit—get off the bus first. He walked toward the gas station as his passengers filed out after him. A store and house were attached to the gas station.

Doug grabbed a windshield scrubber and cleaned the windows as Ron stuck the gas hose nozzle into the tank. I looked for another squeegee to help with the windows, but saw none. I walked to the gas station and entered.

The bus driver stood at the end of an aisle talking to one of the gas station attendants. The driver appeared to be about my height, but much stockier and bald on the top of his head with gray hair around his temples. He must have been about 45 to 50 years old. They both turned their heads and looked at me as I entered. I stared into the bus driver's eyes. You fucking asshole, I thought, as I continued to glare at him.

He stared back at me with a gleam in his eye and a smirky grin that seemed to say, "I guess I showed you." As I stared at him, his smirky grin disappeared, and his expression became what I imagined my facial expression to look like. I had gotten to him, and it delighted me. Still glaring at him, I spit some air in his direction as if getting rid of something that had been lodged between my teeth. I then looked down at the stack of candy on the rack in front of me.

The driver outweighed me by 40 or 50 pounds and could have probably kick my butt if it came to a fight. I looked back at him. He said something to the gas station attendant, and then turned his head toward me again. Our eyes locked together once more. I glared at him. The feelings must have been similar to western gunfighters squaring off for a duel. Without taking his eyes off me, he walked in my direction. He appeared ready for battle. My heart thumped against my chest and my senses heightened. I heard the gas station door opened behind me.

"Was that you that said something about my mother?" he asked between gritted teeth as he neared me.

So he had been listening to the CB. I started to say, "What if it was?" when a voice interrupted.

"That was me." Ron stepped to my side. "What are you going to do about it?"

The bus driver looked at Ron, but said nothing. There were a lot of people in the store, and most of them were watching us. I heard the door open again.

"What I said over the CB still stands," Ron said slowly.

After a brief moment of silence, the driver turned and walked away. Doug, who had entered the store in time to hear Ron's last words, walked up behind us.

"He's a weasel," Doug said loud enough for the driver and everyone else in the store to hear.

Although the driver's strut hesitated slightly, he never turned around—a wise decision on his part. In this desolate land, the driver had crossed three young hombres far from any law enforcement officer. We were angry and ready to unleash our rage on him.

Ron paid for the gas and picked up several candy and granola bars. Once we were back in the truck and moving down the road, Ron gave a granola bar to Doug and me. I'm not sure how long the bus remained at the gas station, but we never saw it again.

For most of the day the weather and road conditions remained horrible. Ron kept his speed at 70 mph. Then, just before sun set, the clouds broke away leaving a crisp freshness in the air. Sunrays reached down and touched the snow-peaked mountains like a magic wand, leaving a sparkling glitter of light radiating through the soothing blue ethers behind the large majestic expanse of stone, trees and snow. The tundra's shrubbery grasslands looked exceedingly green and lush. It felt magical—like one of those moments when you feel in tune with nature and say to yourself, "This is what life is all about." It's one of those instances when you're truly glad to be alive, and you thank whatever or whoever made it all possible.

When the sun disappeared below the horizon, hues of orange, green and turquoise illuminated the sky as distant cirrus clouds reflected a brush of pink on the horizon. The brightest stars were slow to peak through the dusk-like darkened sky, even though the Toyota's clock showed 10:20.

"What the hell is that?" Doug yelled as he turned sideways and looked out the window. His outburst startled Ron and me. Ron reacted immediately by taking his foot off the gas pedal. We both leaned forward, looking into a field of shadows beside the truck. I expected to see a UFO or a wild animal.

"Where?" I asked.

"Up there in the sky." Doug pointed. "Stop the truck!" Doug rolled down his window as Ron gently pumped the brakes.

"Wow," I said, now seeing what Doug saw, "what is it?"

It looked like a huge phosphorescent serpent weaving its way through the stars.

"You got me," Doug answered slowly in a tone of bewilderment.

Ron leaned forward as he slowed down the truck, but he couldn't see because Doug's head and mine blocked his view. Once we came to a stop, we piled out. Ron walked around the truck and stood beside Doug and me.

"Do you know what it is?" Doug asked Ron as we all stared at it. The light pulsated from the tail of this mile-long serpent to its head. It wove its way forward like a slow-moving sidewinder rattlesnake.

"I've never seen anything like it," Ron replied.

We stared at the object for several moments without saying a word. Suddenly, I blurted out, "It's got to be the northern lights. Have you ever seen them?"

"No," Doug replied.

"You must be right," Ron said, "but I never thought it would look like that."

"This is the second day in a row I've seen something I've never seen before," I said. "First the end of a rainbow, and now the aurora borealis."

"Yeah," Ron said, "that's the name I was trying to think of."

"Two good omens before we hit Alaska," I added. "I wonder what's going to happen when we get to the final frontier."

"Alaska, the final frontier," Doug said. "Let us boldly go where few men have gone before."

We all laughed. After viewing the radiant sky serpent for several minutes, we returned to the truck.

The road took a slight turn, and now the winding snake of light could be seen on the left side of the front window. The rain had not come this far north, so the gravel road remained dry. Ron kept the speedometer between 80 and 85. We were in a huge valley typical of the Alaskan Highway—flat and long. We could see the headlights of a vehicle approaching in the distance.

"You know," Ron said looking at the aurora borealis hovering above the hills and mountains on the horizon, "things like those lights make you realize there's more to this world than we know. It's like reality is not really real." He laughed at his statement. "Do you ever get that feeling?"

Ron glanced down at his speedometer and then looked back at the northern lights. The headlights from the approaching vehicle were probably a mile away.

195

"I mean," he continued, "it makes you wonder what's going on. What's really out there? At one time everyone thought the world was flat. We just didn't know the truth."

Just before he finished his sentence, we felt and heard gravel being kicked up from the truck's wheels. Ron tightened his grip on the steering wheel.

"Shit," Ron said as he let up on the gas. "We're stuck in a gravel ridge."

We were in the middle of the road and moving toward the opposite lane. The rapidly approaching vehicle, with its elevated headlights, had to be a semi truck. The 18-wheeler sent out two loud blasts from its horn.

"Get over," I said to Ron.

"I can't!" he cried.

The truck sped toward us, its horn blaring again, this time sending one long continuous blast. The semi truck moved to its right shoulder as far as it could without going off the road. We were still heading straight for the truck's headlight closest to the center lane. Gripping the steering wheel, Ron tried to turn the wheel to the right. His Toyota truck fishtailed slightly. If he continued turning, we'd be out of control going sideways.

"There's nothing I can do," Ron muttered as he held the steering wheel firm and stared intently as the truck closed in on us. His voice sounded like one of the pilots I heard on a news show just before the plane crashed, killing the crew and passengers. The pilot's voice had a calm resignation or detachment about it—like he had just lost a softball game in which sportsmanship meant more than winning.

I guess I should have ducked down below the dash, but I couldn't take my eyes off the truck. Everything went into slow motion. The same thing happened when I had a head-on collision in my dad's new Grand Prix Pontiac.

The car accident took place after returning home for the summer following my first year at the University of Missouri. It was the night of my sister's high school graduation. My parents were busy getting dressed when they realized they had no film for their camera. Dad handed me a five-dollar bill and asked me to run to the drugstore.

"Can I take your car?"

"Sure," he said, knowing that use of his car would serve as a reward for the errand.

Wearing a tank-top, cutoff jeans and no shoes, I grabbed the keys off the key hook hanging in the hallway and headed out the door. I backed the two-door, light yellow Pontiac with a white vinyl top out of the garage and glided past my faded turquoise Dodge Polara. The radio played an orchestrated version of the song *I Want To Hold Your Hand* by the Beatles. The car had a fantastic sound system. I flipped the dial to Rock 101 where rock singer Alice Cooper bellowed out the song *Eighteen*. I adjusted more bass into the song and cranked it up loud. Putting the car in drive, I punched the gas, causing the car to jump forward as the 454 engine snapped into gear. The power surprised me as the tires gave out a little squeal.

I slowed down at the top of the hill to turn right onto the road leading to the shopping center. The road descended sharply before coming to a steep incline. The house at the bottom of the hill had a car parked in the street about three or four feet away from the curb. I pushed down on the 454 engine to pick up some speed. The descent made my stomach rise like on a roller coaster. I pulled into the center of the road to avoid the parked car. When I got alongside the car, a Mustang came speeding over the hill in the center of the road, the driver looking down a side street.

I swerved to the right while lifting my foot off the gas pedal. At that moment, the driver looked forward and saw me. His mouth popped open as he yanked his car to his right. When he did so, I saw a clear road ahead, much like a football halfback sees a hole in the defensive line. Instead of hitting my brakes, I stomped on the gas pedal to get past him. As the Grand Prix kicked into passing gear, the driver of the Mustang slammed on his brakes, causing his car to flip sideways into my path. At that point, everything went into slow motion.

The back left side of his car smashed into the Grand Prix's front left fender. Debris slowly flew over the top of the car as the hood of the Grand Prix crinkled and buckled. The impact knocked the Mustang off to my left as I watched it disappear from view. I felt the pressure of my body push into the steering wheel as the Pontiac came to a grinding halt. I sat there in a daze for what seemed to be a long time, but what must have been a few seconds. I turned and looked through the back window.

The smashed and twisted Mustang sat sideways across the road, the driver stooped beside it with his hands on his head. He looked hurt. I tried getting out of the car, but I could only push open the door an inch or two. I leaned to one side as I kicked the door with both feet and pushed hard. The door opened several more inches, just wide enough to get my head through. I squeezed the rest of my thin body between the door and the frame. Once outside the car, I ran to the kid sitting in the road.

"Are you all right?"

"Yeah," he moaned, "but look at my car."

His statement caught me by surprise and made me mad. He sat worried about his old beat-up Mustang after he had just rammed my dad's beautiful new Grand Prix that probably cost 20 times the price of his Ford. Several kids had been playing in a yard at the top of the hill. Two of them came running toward us, one of them yelling, "Your car's on fire, your car's on fire." I turned to see dark, thick smoke mushrooming above the Grand Prix's charred vinyl top.

"Shit! I need to get my dad!"

I took off running barefoot toward home. It's funny, but at the time, it never really occurred to me that I could have been killed, mangled and disfigured, much less burned. It wasn't until talking to an engineering major at the university that I realized my good fortune.

"You're lucky you pushed on the gas instead of hitting your brakes," my friend said when I told him about the accident. "The momentum of your car forced you through his car, which kept you from being thrown through the windshield and ending up on the hood."

The Toyota had no chance for a similar outcome with the semi truck. Any collision at all would be disastrous for everyone, except maybe the trucker. Nonetheless, as the 18-wheeler's glaring lights and blasting horn barreled down upon us, I never considered dying or being flung through the Toyota windshield. Instead, I sat viewing the whole scene as if it were an exciting episode in a movie, wondering what would happen next.

The semi truck moved as close as it could to the shoulder without going off the road. Despite the maneuver, we remained on a collision course. Maybe the trucker figured out what had happened with the gravel on the road, or maybe he thought the Toyota driver had fallen asleep. I imagined him screaming, "What the hell are you doing!" as he kept a firm hand on the horn. I doubt he started hitting his brakes until he had blasted his horn a few times. I had no doubt his foot remained firmly on the brakes now.

"Move over!" I thought, leaning to my right and trying to alter the Toyota's path with my mind.

You know, like when you roll a bowling ball down the lane and it begins to curve a little off course toward the gutter? Sometimes you lean to one side while either thinking or even yelling, "This way! Come on, you can do it." It's as if we believe the bowling ball has a mind of its own and we are capable of swaying its choice of direction. It felt the same with the Toyota truck, although I stayed silent.

"I'm sorry," Ron said, as the collision appeared imminent.

Was he apologizing for our deaths, or possible worse? He gripped the wheel and punched the gas slightly. My body completely relaxed as I let go of any hope for an escape. This is it, I thought

Then, as if by a miracle, the Toyota truck moved slightly to the right literally seconds before impact. We passed each other inches apart, the 18-wheeler's horn blasting. The Toyota rocked after the semi passed us, which sent the Toyota into a fishtail. Ron quickly regained control and slowed down. He pulled off to the side of the road where we sat in silence for several seconds.

Ron let out a sigh. "Jesus!" he said shaking his head, "that was close!" He looked at us with a blank expression, and then grinned. "You guys look like you were almost hit by a truck."

His words broke the tension, and we burst into laughter, jubilant to be alive.

Doug opened his door. "I've got to get out for a second."

Ron and I got out too. The northern lights were still pulsating and moving through the sky.

"Boy, my heart's pounding," Doug said. "I thought sure it was over."

"We lucked out," Ron said. "The gravel rut we were caught in happened to turn back toward our side of the road."

I looked at the stars to the south. "Just think, a few inches made the difference between standing here or being out there somewhere."

"Somebody's looking out for us," Ron said. "Thanks for saving our asses," he yelled, looking to the sky.

Captain Cook's Bay

I opened my eyes and saw nothing but darkness. Lying on my left side, I felt my sleeping bag below me, but where was I? Palm tree fronds rustled in the wind as a breeze blew over my face. Ocean waves crashed on a shore nearby. Then it came back to me, my journey from Alaska to Hawaii.

After framing houses in Alaska for a month, I had a bundle of cash in my pocket. I went to the Anchorage airport and got in line to purchase my first plane ticket. The thought of flying both scared and excited me.

"What's your cheapest one-way flight to the 48 states," I asked the woman selling tickets.

"Ninety-five dollars to Seattle," she replied with no hesitation.

"What about to Portland, Oregon?"

"One way?"

"Yes."

"One hundred and thirty-five dollars."

"How about Kansas City, Missouri?"

She had to look that one up. "It's two hundred and five dollars."

Several people were now behind me.

"What about Hawaii?"

"Do you know where you want to go?" she asked, sounding a bit impatient as she glanced over my shoulder. The other clients could easily hear our conversation.

"When the price is right, I'm going."

She nodded her head and perused through the notebook in front of her.

"I can get you a one-way ticket from here to Portland, Oregon, with a layover in Portland for up to a year before you must fly on to Hawaii, for one hundred and sixty-five dollars."

"That's my ticket," I said, pulling out the cash in my pocket.

Hours later my buddy Hank picked me up from the Portland airport. After visiting a few days, I hitchhiked back to Missouri, visited family and friends, then hitchhiked to California and up the coast to Portland to catch a flight to Honolulu. After a few days on the island of Oahu, I took a commuter plane from Honolulu to a small airport on the dry side of Hawaii's Big Island.

From the modest terminal, I walked along the two-lane road leaving the airport. Looking across the desert of cactus with palm trees in the distance and the ocean behind them, a rush of emotion overwhelmed me. Although I had never been to the Middle East, it seemed as if the surroundings related to that area of the world from what I had seen in movies and magazine articles. I stopped walking and stared toward the ocean. In my peripheral vision stood three men dressed in robes and sandals with a shimmering aura around them. As I turned to look closer, the men dissolved. The experience felt familiar—like déjà vu.

A car zoomed past me and quickly shrank into the distance. I turned back toward the airport to see a light blue van approaching. I raised my thumb as the van slowed down. With no other vehicles near, the driver stopped in the middle of the road beside me. I opened the van's sliding door and tossed my things inside.

"Thanks for stopping."

"You're welcome," the driver said.

I shut the door and climbed in the passenger's seat. "I'm surprised there's not more traffic out here with the airport and all." We moved slowly down the road.

"The main airport is on the other side of the island in Hilo. They have a lot more traffic over there."

"My name's Bryce." I extended my hand.

"Joey," he said, as we shook.

Joey wore a typical Hawaiian shirt with blue and yellow hibiscus flowers on it, cutoff blue jeans and flip-flop sandals. He had a slight build, and although seated, I could tell he had to be at least six feet tall. His thick mustache nearly covered his mouth, and his wavy brown hair hung to his shoulders.

I looked around the van. "This is a nice van. Is it yours?"

"I got it a couple of months ago," he proudly exclaimed.

Plush sky-blue upholstery surrounded the seats with light oak trim on the doors and dash. The navy-blue carpet and the violet-velvet ceiling made the seats and oak trim stand out. It was immaculately clean.

"I guess you live on the island."

"I've been in Hawaii about three years."

"This place is unreal. Have you been to Maui and Kauai?"

He smiled before answering. "I've been there. I take it this is your first time to Hawaii?"

"Yeah, and I've never seen anything like it."

"Where are you going now?"

"I'm looking for a place to camp and hang out for a while. Do you know any good camping spots?"

"As a matter of fact I do. It's not a regular campsite, but it's a neat place. I stayed there when I first got here."

We drove past some cottages and resorts along the beach before Joey stopped at a convenience store beside the road.

"I'm going to get something to drink. Do you want anything?"

"No thanks." I wanted to conserve my money.

Joey returned quickly carrying a sack. He climbed in the van and handed it to me.

"Have a cold one." He started the van. "And open one for me."

As he backed the van out of our parking stall, I reached in the sack and pulled out a Heineken beer.

"There's an opener in the glove box."

I grabbed the opener, popped the cap off and handed it to Joey. Then I took a bottle for myself.

I raised my beer in salute. "Thanks."

"You're welcome. Have you got any pot?"

"Sure. I don't have a lot, but it's dynamite stuff, so it doesn't take much."

I put my beer in the plastic holder mounted on the engine cover. I dug down in my bag and pulled out my pipe and the small plastic film container holding the pot.

"Is that all the pot you've got?"

"Yeah, but there's plenty to get us loaded." I felt excited that things were going so well. "It's really good stuff. They call it Alaskan Thunderfuck."

Joey laughed. "I've heard of it, but save it for later. I've got some pot I can give you. Do you have something to put it in?"

"Wow, that would be great. If you could just fill this up," I held up my film container, "it would last me a long time."

"Don't you have something bigger than that?"

He glanced back at my backpack and saw the corner of a plastic fruit bag.

"How about that bag?"

"Sure," I said, turning the bag over and letting three apples fall into my pack.

"It's awfully big."

"It's perfect." He reached under his seat and pulled out a large black trash bag. "Hold your bag open."

Watching the road in front of him, he reached in the trash bag and grabbed a handful of pot, gave it a couple of shakes above his bag, and then transferred the pot mixed with buds to my container.

"Thanks a lot," I said enthusiastically. The pot's rich, heavy odor reeked with potency. "Wow, that smells great."

"Hold your sack down here again."

As I did so, he put another handful in my bag.

"That should hold you for a while."

"I can't smoke all of that." I looked at my bulging fruit bag.

Joey laughed at my reaction. "Then share it with others. That's what it's for. Now pack some of that pot in your pipe and fire it up. I think you'll find this Kona Gold to be as good as your Alaskan Thunderfuck."

As we drove down the road sipping beer and smoking pot, I told Joey about my travels. The pot made me feel as if someone else spoke through my vocal cords. When shifting my body in the seat, it felt like an invisible part of me took a while to catch up. It seemed as if I had two bodies that weren't quite in sync with one another. Everything around us appeared to be radiating extremely rich colors and hues. Puffy white clouds popped out of the blue sky like mushrooms, while the turquoise blue ocean came across calm and peaceful as its waves, curling onto the beach, brought a rhythmic and soothing tranquility. Along the shore stood tall sturdy coconut trees with long finger-like branches swaying gently in the ocean breeze. I found it hard to believe a place could be as beautiful as this. I feared waking up from the brilliance of the moment and having it fade into the distance like a colorful bird flying away. Joey turned down a road that descended into a lush jungle of ferns and palm trees.

"This is the bay I told you about. It's the place where I stayed three months when I first got here. In fact, I was a lot like you. I had a backpack, and that's it."

As we rounded one of the curves that wound down to the coastline, a peculiar white statue stood erect on a rock out in the bay.

"What's that white thing?"

"It's a statue of Captain James Cook, an English explorer and the first white man to make it to Hawaii, at least that's the story. Hawaiians killed him in this bay."

"When?"

"I don't know the exact date, but sometime in the 1700s."

According to information I read later, Captain Cook died February 14, 1779. Evidently, when he first sailed into the Kealakekua Bay several weeks before his death, the Hawaiians viewed him as a god. In fact, they thought he was the god Lono, which is the god of happiness, peace and bounty. Lono's symbol was a staff with white cloth attached to it. Cook's ships, the *Discovery* and *Resolution*, had huge masts with white cloth sails. And to top it off, legend foretold of Lono's return by sea. Combined with the fact that Hawaiians were celebrating the sacred season to Lono when Cook arrived, it's understandable why they deified these fair-skinned men in their mighty sea vessels.

Cook and his men were showered with gifts, supplies and women for 18 days. The *Discovery* and *Resolution* sailed from the bay February 4, but due to bad storms that damaged the ships and even broke a mast, the crew returned to the bay February 10. The Hawaiians were less receptive after realizing these gods could not overcome a storm. A few Hawaiians stole the *Discovery's* large cutter, the ship's chief lifeboat. In order to get the cutter back, Captain Cook decided to hold the chief hostage in exchange for the lifeboat. During a failed attempt to coax the chief to their ship, one of Cook's men shot and killed a Hawaiian. Several thousand Hawaiians retaliated. As a result, they stabbed and beat Captain Cook to death.

Joey parked his van in the small graveled parking lot that overlooked the bay. We were the only ones there, although we passed a small house and cottage that sat 100 yards or more from the parking area.

"You're going to like it here. I have great memories of this bay. It's like my second home. You never know, you might end up staying in Hawaii a long time."

The sun sank below the ocean's horizon. Orange, green, turquoise and blue layers of light fanned out across the sky above us.

"Shit," Joey said, looking at his watch, "I gotta get going."

A pang of disappointment shot through me. Joey and his van provided security. He held out his hand to shake.

"It's been fun. Maybe we'll see each other again."

"You never know," I said, shaking his hand.

The once inviting lush green jungle and soothing ocean waves swishing onto the shore now appeared ominous and foreboding. A wild wind whipped through the trees, displaying pockets of darkness above the shadowy rocky shoreline. I had expected to sleep on a soft sandy beach. Joey seemed to read my mind.

"If you walk up into the trees a ways, you'll find flat areas where you can camp. You won't have to worry about anyone bothering you. No one comes down here at night."

Drunk and stoned, I thanked Joey for his hospitality and climbed out of the van. The rocky shoreline made it difficult to walk. After hiking about 100 yards along the rocky beach, I staggered into the trees and plodded up the hillside. The jungle-thick terrain made it hard to see. Huffing and puffing from the ascent, I gave a push through a wall of ferns and literally fell into a small clearing. In front of me sat a small hut, or more precisely, a leaf canopy. There were no walls, just wooden poles holding up palm tree leaves woven between bamboo strips that sheltered a dirt floor. I decided to sleep beside the structure in case its owner returned in the night. Exhausted, I pulled out my poncho, spread it on the ground 20 feet from the canopy, and rolled out my sleeping bag. After flopping down on my back, I fell asleep within minutes.

I awoke in the middle of the night. As I lay on my left side in the fetal position, an eerie feeling swept over me. What aroused me? A twig snapped behind me. Fear caused my heart to pound. Someone must be returning to the shelter, I thought. Because of the pitch-blackness surrounding me, I knew anyone walking in the jungle would need a flashlight. I lay quietly, listening for any sounds and watching for a light. The ocean waves crashed on the rocky beach as the wind crossed the bay and swirled through the coconut tree fronds above me.

Suddenly, I felt and heard a thud as my chest pushed forward. Something had struck me in the back just below my right shoulder blade. Quickly sitting up, I got to my feet and spun around to face whatever or whoever hit me. I faltered in the darkness. I stooped to a crouched position, my fingertips touching the ground for balance.

As I sucked in a breath, my left lung filled rapidly while my right lung winced and gurgled. I gasped for another breath before it dawned on me what happened. Someone stabbed me in the back with a knife, and the blade had penetrated my right lung. I reached around to pull the knife out, but found nothing. It meant they shoved the knife in and pulled it out. It also meant they were still out there with a knife in their hand.

I went down on one knee and groped in front of me. My heart raced. I wanted to stand up, but the darkness made it impossible to orient myself. I could not see the ground or anything around me. I had no reference point to help maintain my balance. I looked up and saw the stars through the coconut trees. Out of terror, I began to hyperventilate. I heard and felt phlegm bubbling in my lungs.

Suddenly, despite the complete darkness, a Hawaiian man with long black hair, no shirt and a loincloth around his waist, stood in front of me. His right hand held a long thick-bladed knife that resembled a kitchen butcher knife. The smug look on his face caused the corners of his mouth to turn up slightly in a mocking grin. My breathing became even more erratic, and I started coughing. Still, I watched him closely. His eyes, drilling through mine, looked wild, angry and powerful.

His warrior-like stance in front of me, however, helped me regain my focus. I stood up prepared to fight. As I did, I naturally inhaled. This time, both lungs filled to capacity. Surprised, I exhaled quickly and took a deeper breath. Simultaneously, the man in front of me laughed, but no sound came from his mouth. Baffled, yet poised and ready for his attack, I looked into his dark eyes. I felt strong and fully alert. Adrenaline rushed through my body. The Hawaiian slowly lifted the knife in his hand until its tip pointed straight at me.

Then, just as quickly as he appeared, he was gone. Nothing but blackness remained.

I faltered and went down on one knee. I felt light headed and dizzy. I took in a deep breath. Both lungs felt normal. I reached over my shoulder with my left hand to feel the area where the blow had struck. I found no wound and nothing felt abnormal. With my heart still rapidly thumping, I sat down on my sleeping bag. I looked up through the palm leaves at the twinkling stars. I put my hand over my chest and felt my heart racing.

What the hell's going on, I thought. Maybe it's the pot and beer, or part of a bad dream, or both. Did I create the experience in my mind? Am I hallucinating? No, it felt too real.

As I lay on my sleeping bag thinking about what just happened, a strong gust of wind hit the fronds of the coconut trees surrounding me like a huge fist punching into a fluffy pillow. I heard a loud crack, and then the surrounding area shook as a huge tree crashed to the ground less than three feet from me, barely missing the leaf canopy. As quickly as the gust of wind hit, calmness followed. Only the sound of ocean waves pounding the shoreline remained.

That's no hallucination, I thought, sensing the huge tree beside me. Someone or something wants me out of here. It was too dark to wander around the jungle looking for a new campsite. I pulled my things farther away from the canopy and lay on my sleeping bag. I didn't sleep the rest of the night. At dawn, feeling drained and tired, I packed my things swiftly. Examining the huge, partially decayed tree trunk beside the canopy, I wondered how many campers had been killed from falling trees.

The experience that night stayed at the forefront of my consciousness during the following weeks. The image of the Hawaiian's eyes and his silent, triumphant laughter repeatedly played on the screen in my mind. Even now, as I write this, I can see him standing there with the knife in his hand and the smirky grin of conquest on his face.

A Hawaiian later told me about the uhane, or spirits, on the islands. He said the lapu, which is another name for ghosts, live between worlds and often haunt specific areas on the islands.

Nearly a week after the incident, I walked into a small museum on the Big Island that had a large painting on the wall. The local artist depicted Captain Cook's death in Kealakekua Bay. In the painting, Captain Cook faced his ships in the bay while a Hawaiian, dressed in a loin cloth, gripped a knife handle with the blade protruding from Cook's back just to the left of his right shoulder blade, the exact spot where I had been hit. A coincidence? A chill ran through me as goose bumps popped out on my neck, arms and legs.

The Cliff

Almost to the top of the sea cliff, I reached up to get a hold of what looked like a sturdy rock, but it pulled out and fell to my right, dropping a few small pebbles and dirt as it plunged through the space beneath me. Resisting the urge to watch it fall, I heard it hit the side of the cliff. The decision to concentrate on the rock wall in front of me kept me from looking down during the climb, and for good reason. I've always had a fear of heights, maybe not to the point of calling it a phobia, but close.

A rock I grabbed to the right of the hole where the last one had been felt solid. I pulled myself up and looked over the cliff's edge to find a 10-foot steep incline of lose dirt and sand. If I tried to climb the last few feet, I would be left clutching a handful of granules before sliding back over the edge and falling at least a hundred feet onto the rocks and crashing waves. It became apparent why so many stones had pulled loose during my ascent. What appeared from the bottom to be the shortest and easiest way out of the bay was actually a rain runoff gulch. Unless someone from the top threw me a rope, I couldn't get out.

The thought of going back down terrified me. Clinging to the lip of the precipice, my body trembled. Slowly maneuvering several feet to the left, I reached a large crevice where I wedged myself securely and turned around. Now I looked out over the bay as ocean waves pounded the rugged Maui shoreline below me. My whole body shook. I tried to control my muscles, but I couldn't. The stress, strain and lack of sleep during the previous two days were taking its toll. I had stayed up all night trying to talk a man out of killing himself. I wondered if Justin was dead yet, and if so, if it was my fate to join him.

"Does that feel better?" Cindy asked in a whisper as she massaged my neck and shoulders. We were inside my small pup tent, Cindy straddled over me as she sat on my butt with her lips close to my ear. A fire still crackled outside the tent. I could feel her breath on my neck as she spoke. I thought of the dream I had in Alaska only months earlier when Ron had awakened me.

"Much better," I said softly.

Cindy and I made love for the first time the night before. It was a beautiful experience, and although we met each other only five days earlier, we both knew there was something special about our connection. For three days preceding the relationship's consummation, we spent every waking moment together. The first night we met we went dancing. During the next several days, we talked incessantly, discussing our lives, dreams and subjects that take many couples months, maybe years to cover. From this intense communicative exchange about our mental, spiritual and physical lives, we even discovered that her last serious lover had been born seven days after me, and that her birthday came seven days after my ex-wife's birthday. That fact, combined with other magical and bizarre experiences, made us realize our meeting had to be more than chance.

"You know," she whispered in my ear, "I keep pinching myself to make sure this is real. I mean this place, this paradise, and you."

She reached down and pinched my butt.

"Hey," I whispered, laughing softly.

"I just wanted to make sure you're real. Did I hurt you? I'll make it better."

She moved down my body and kissed where she had pinched, her hand caressing the inside of my thigh as she slid her body over mine, kissing up my back. I turned sideways and reached my arm around her as our heads aligned, our lips touching. She gently pushed me onto my back and kissed down my neck as she climbed on top of me.

"We've got to be quiet," I whispered.

She raised herself up on her left elbow and put her right index finger to her lips like a teacher signaling a student to be quiet. She lifted her hips slightly and pushed down, closing her eyes and biting her lower lip with her upper teeth as I entered her. She sucked in a quick breath and held it. It was all I could do to keep from moaning. I inhaled slowly and slid my hands down her back. She raised her hips and swirled down on me, breathing in slowly when rising and exhaling as she came down.

Inside my head small speckles of light flashed and danced like sparks from a Fourth-of-July sparkler. I pulled her to me to keep her from moving. A moment later I exploded inside her. She drew some air into her mouth making a hissing type sound. She opened her eyes and then covered my mouth with her mouth. She raised her body and swirled down on me again, catching me by surprise and causing me to give out a slight groan.

210

She took her mouth off mine and looked at me, smiling, her hair dangling down to my neck.

"I think I'm in love with you," she whispered.

A small cough came from outside the pup tent. I first thought that Justin cleared his throat to let us know we were bothering him.

Cindy, I, and several other people staying at the Maui Youth Hostel met Justin along the road to the Seven Sacred Pools. He was stooped beside an old car changing a flat tire. Everyone who saw Justin stared at him. Justin looked exactly like the paintings used to portray Jesus. Justin's hair hung the same length with the same wave. His beard matched perfectly. His facial features appeared identical, and his six-foot-tall frame provided him a stature of authority while his soft clear blue eyes projected reverence, calm and peace. You had to wonder who this man might be.

Justin's voice, although gentle, exuded confidence and certitude. He knew about his appearance and the impression it had on people. He catered to the Jesus image by dressing in loose and flowing pullover shirts with either baggy pants or blue jeans, and sandals. His Hawaiian tan and no jewelry gave him a wholesome, natural look. He fit the profile of a modern-day Jesus.

Justin gave another small cough and then drew in a breath before we realized he was weeping. Within a few minutes, his soft whimpers turned to sobs.

"I've got to check what's wrong," I whispered to Cindy.

I slipped on a t-shirt and blue jeans, unzipped the screen net to the tent and pushed back the nylon door. Justin sat next to the campfire with his legs crossed and his face in his hands sobbing. His whole body shook with each sob.

"Justin, what's the matter?" I walked over to him and put my hand on his shoulder, then dropped to my knees beside him. I could feel the tension and strain of his body as he cried. He kept weeping without responding. "Look, it can't be that bad. What's wrong."

"I've lost her," he said between sobs. "She wrote me and said she could never see me again."

"Who?"

He removed his hands from his face and looked at me. His eyes and cheeks were wet as tears flowed down his face.

"The woman I love." Justin looked at the fire and sniffled.

"Hey, there are lots of women in the world," I said, trying to console him. I thought of Cindy less than 10 feet away.

"You don't understand. She's the one for me, and she knows that."

"Does she have the same feelings for you as you do for her?"

"She does," he snapped. "It's her parents that are stopping her."

"Why would they do that?"

211

Justin paused a moment as he gazed into the fire, and then shook his head side-to-side slightly as if he were answering an internal question or reflecting on a thought. Tears fell from his chin. "I did some stupid things when I was younger. I didn't hurt anyone," he quickly added, looking at me as if I had accused him of something. He looked back at the fire. "At least I didn't mean to if I did."

Holding his index finger over one nostril, he blew snot into the fire and repeated the action with the other nostril before wiping his nose with the back of his hand.

"What happened?"

"I robbed several places when I was 18. At first it was burglary: you know, I'd break into a store or house and take what I wanted. But the last two places I hit, I used a gun. I didn't shoot anyone, but I did shoot up one store a little. I had to," he said quickly as he looked at me. "The owner didn't take me seriously and started to walk toward me." Justin looked back at the fire. "I didn't want to shoot him, so I fired a few shots into the counter to let him know I meant business, that's all."

"And they caught you?"

"I spent three years in prison." Justin paused briefly. "I can't change what's already happened." His eyes filled with tears. "All I know is I love Sharon and don't want to live without her."

For the next hour or more I listened to all the things he and Sharon done, the hardships they had been through together, and the difficulties he had with her parents. At least while he talked he stopped crying.

"Justin, it's hard now because your breakup just happened." I thought about Melanie and what I had gone through during our divorce. "But believe me, in time you'll get over it. Some day you might even see it as a good thing."

He looked at me, his eyes watering again. "That's easy for you to say. You have Cindy."

His words reminded me of the times after my divorce when I saw couples outside theaters holding hands, or wrapped in each others arms slow dancing in bars, or playfully jostling each other while they walked in the park. Those pangs of loneliness lay only a memory away.

Justin's shoulders folded inward as he cried. "Sharon's in California somewhere, and she said she won't be writing anymore, and for me to stay away from her." He put his face in his hands and sobbed. "I don't want to live anymore," he said between wails. "It's just not worth it."

"You don't mean that, Justin."

"Yes I do. Death can't be worse than what I'm feeling right now."

I remembered my emotional state when Melanie left me. I was engulfed by loneliness, feelings of abandonment, and wondering if death would end the emotional pain.

"What do you think happens to you when you die?"

"I don't know, and I don't care." He gazed into the fire for a few moments. "I think death will be like sleep, and I prefer sleeping over this."

"Sure, as long as it's a pleasant dream. It's the nightmares that can be horrifying." I paused before going on. "If this place was a dream, how would you classify it? A nightmare or a beautiful dream."

Justin looked at me. "Hawaii is paradise, but what's paradise without someone to share it with?"

Justin turned his head and stared into the fire.

"I went through a lot of pain and suffering," I said, "when I broke up with my wife. I considered death many times, and it nearly happened after an overdose on downers, but an interesting thought came to me after I woke up two days later. I realized that if I had died or killed myself without facing up to the emotional trauma I was experiencing, that someday, somewhere, somehow I'd have to deal with those same emotions."

Justin kept his eyes on the fire.

"I even went for counseling right after the breakup. Although I don't think the therapy helped a lot, the counselor said one thing that made me think. He asked me how many woman had been in my life that I really knew, women that I shared more with than just sex. It made..."

"But I've tried it with lots of women. Sharon's the only one for me, and that's the way it is." He started crying again. "You don't understand."

We talked until daybreak, and still Justin believed suicide remained the best choice for ending his misery.

I finally said, "Listen Justin, if you really want to kill yourself, that's your business. It's your life. I don't think it's wise, and I think you'll miss a lot of opportunities here if you leave. I don't know where we go when we die, but I strongly suggest you think good thoughts on your way out of here."

I waited for Justin to say something, but he said nothing.

"How do you plan to do it?"

"I've got some "H" (heroin) back at my place."

My sympathy and patience were gone. "That sounds like a painless way to go. When are you going to do it?"

"Today." He stood up.

Although the sun remained below the horizon, it was light enough to see. I stood up with Justin. He picked up his blanket and wrapped it around his neck so it hung down to his waist on both sides of his body. We walked up the hill toward the road. We were camped about a mile from a bridge that towered at least 75 feet above a stream that flowed through Maui's Seven Sacred Pools. Just before we reached the road leading to the bridge, the sun peeked over the ocean's horizon and shot rays into the clouds turning them orange with slivers of pink. I stopped to look at them.

"That's nice," I said, staring at the sunrise. Justin stopped and turned toward me, then looked to the sky. I gazed in awe at the magnificent spectacle before I spoke again. "I wonder if death is as beautiful as that, or if heaven has places as beautiful as Hawaii. I wish you could come back to tell me."

We watched in silence as the sun rose above the lip of the world. Justin turned and walked up the hill. I followed him. Once we reached the road, we had a short walk to the bridge. A car stopped on the other side of the bridge and four people got out; a gray-haired gentleman, an older woman whom I assumed was his wife, and a younger couple, possibly the older couple's child with their spouse. We arrived at one end of the bridge as they began to cross from the other end. A four-inch wide, four-foot tall cement wall bordered each side of the bridge. Justin leaped up on the wall of the bridge as relaxed and calm as if he were a cat jumping on a fence in someone's backyard. His dexterity and agility surprised me. His blanket still hung loose around his shoulders. He casually strolled cross the bridge on the four-inch cement strip as if it were as wide as a sidewalk. If he fell to his right, he would smash into the rocks and shallow stream some 60 to 80-feet below. I thought about grabbing him and pulling him off, but feared it might cause him to fall.

A look of wonder appeared on the tourists' faces when they saw Justin walking on the edge of life and death in this Garden-of-Eden setting. The people could tell he had no fear of falling. Of course, this gave him an even greater angelic appearance. When the people were next to us, I said hello. They said hello, glancing at me and then looking up at Justin. Justin said nothing and kept walking. In my peripheral vision I could see their heads turn to watch us as we passed. When we reached the end of the bridge, Justin hopped off the wall as gracefully and lightly as he had jumped on it. I let out a silent sigh of relief.

"Good-bye, my friend." Justin held out his hand to shake. "I appreciate you listening."

"Remember," I said while shaking his hand, "picture in your mind the good times you've had here when you're on your way out."

"I'll try." He turned and walked down the road. I paused for several seconds, watching the sunlight and shadows dance off Justin's back as he slowly moved beneath the trees that formed a leafy canopy above the road. I turned and walked back across the bridge, lost in reverie about my all-night discussion with Justin. When I got about 25 or 30 yards past the bridge, someone behind me and slightly to my right yelled, "Hello."

I turned to see the old man we had passed on the bridge earlier. He stood along a path with the older woman several yards to his left.

"Who was that guy you were with?" he asked as he motioned his head toward the bridge.

"What?" I asked, turning and looking toward the bridge. Because of the curve in the road, we could no longer see Justin. "What guy?"

The man had a puzzled look his face. The older woman, whom I assumed was his wife, could easily hear our conversation. She walked over and stood beside the man. The younger man and woman had walked further up the path. They were both looking at us, but were too far away to hear our conversation.

"The guy walking on the bridge. I mean on the side of the bridge," he stammered. He motioned up and down with his hand to indicate the four-inch wide bridge wall.

"You saw a guy walking on that narrow wall?" I said with an incredulous tone.

"Yes. We all saw him."

He looked at the woman, and I looked at her too.

"Did you see him?"

"Yes." She kept her eyes on me.

"What did the guy look like?"

The woman looked at the man, and then looked back at me without responding, so I looked at the man.

"Like Jesus Christ," he blurted out.

I hesitated for a moment, looked at the woman, and then looked back at the man. "Did he say anything?"

"No," the man replied.

"Interesting." I paused as if in deep thought. "I didn't think anyone else could see him. I must go. Enjoy your stay in Hawaii."

I tilted my head down in salutation and turned around, which kept them from seeing me smile. The shenanigan must have been my way of releasing the foreboding thoughts and feelings that filled me. I took two steps before the man spoke.

"Wait a minute."

I continued for several more steps, stopped, released the smile, then turned and looked at them. The man had his mouth partially opened, but said nothing. Raising my hand as if taking an oath, I said, "Enjoy your life." Then I turned around and walked away.

I've often wondered what they said to the younger couple, or to their friends and family when they got home. Pranks like that cause rumors and bizarre stories, but who knows, maybe it inspired them in some way. When I got back to the campsite, Cindy sat around the small campfire with the other campers who had come with us from the youth hostel.

"How is he?" she asked as I approached.

"Still shook up."

Cindy had told the rest of the group what happened during the night.

"Could you guys hear him crying?" I asked.

"I thought I heard something," George said.

George, a Canadian merchant sailor taking some time off in Hawaii, had actually met Cindy before me, and they had a little fling. Then he disappeared on a drinking spree for four days. During his absence, I met Cindy. When he showed up again, Cindy and I were pretty tight. He appeared upset I had taken his place. The second day after he returned, he told a person sitting next to me that men wanting the same woman should "duel it out." Being much bigger than me, he obviously would win any type of physical fight.

"Are you referring to you, me, and Cindy?" I asked him point blank.

He looked at me and said nothing.

"As far as I'm concerned, it should be up to the woman to decide. If Cindy would rather be with you, that's okay by me."

George never brought the subject up again, and Cindy stayed with me. I had no fear of George as long as he remained sober.

"Justin said he was going to kill himself," I told them.

"You mean now, today?" Cindy asked.

"Yes." I chose to forego mentioning his acrobatic bridge walk.

"Someone should stick close to our campsite," George said, looking around the area. "People in that condition do funny things."

Cindy looked at George. "What do you mean?"

"I mean," George said sarcastically, "he might come back here and mess with our things. When people are in a desperate state, you can't trust them."

Cindy looked at me. "We can't let him do it. We've got to go after him."

"He'll get over it," George said.

"I think it's best to leave him alone at this point," I said. "We talked all night. He's had enough talk."

"Who wants to go spear fishing?" George asked, changing the subject. Nobody said anything. "Come on, I've got all the gear. We don't have to stay out there all day. Just long enough to get some fish for supper."

Still no one responded. I hoped someone would join him. Although I had never gone spear fishing, I knew the importance of the buddy system in such endeavors.

"Okay," George said somewhat disgusted, "I'll go by myself."

He picked up his fins, mask, and spear gun.

"Would that other pair of fins fit me?" I asked, figuring a swim might make me feel better.

"Sure. You just slip them on like a shoe."

Slipping off my right flip flop, I put my foot in the flipper and raised the fin up and down. It felt loose.

"See, it fits perfect," George said.

"I'll go, but I don't need any other gear. I'll just swim around while you fish." I put my flip flop back on and picked up the fins.

"Great," George said, holding his spear gun, mask and fins. "Let's do it."

"What about Justin?" Cindy asked.

"He'll cool off and be fine," George said.

Cindy looked at me.

"I hope he doesn't kill himself," I said, "but it's his life."

"Come on," George said, "the fish are waiting."

We turned and walked down the slope toward the bay.

"You guys get the skillet ready for a fish fry," George yelled back to the group.

"Do you really think you'll get something?" I asked George.

"Sure, this looks like a good bay for fishing."

I had no idea whether the bay looked good for fishing or not, but one thing I did know, it had no sandy beach. As we stood on top of a rock wall with waves crashing into it about five feet below us, George scanned the coastline.

"This looks like as good a place as any to get in."

"Really?" I questioned. "It looks like we'll be smashed into these rocks."

"I'll show you how to do it. Just do what I do, and you'll be fine."

George sat on the wall and pulled on his fins as a big wave crashed into the wall. He put the mask over his face and pickup up his spear gun. He let the next wave crash into the wall, and as the backwash headed out toward the sea, he hopped into the water and glided out into the bay vigorously flipping his fins. He made it look simple. He turned and looked at me as I sat down on the ledge to put on the fins.

"See? It's easy. Just slide into the water after the wave hits the rocks and swim out here."

After the next wave hit the wall, I slipped into the water and rapidly kicked with my fins. The backwash helped pull me away from the rocks as I swam over to George.

"That wasn't so hard, was it?"

"No, not really." I tried to sound calm.

The ocean, so big and powerful, made me feel small and insignificant. Once, while in Florida on spring break, I nearly drowned fighting an undercurrent pulling me out to sea. Luckily, I swam to a rock pier and climb out. Nonetheless, it left me badly skinned and bruised.

"Come on," George said, "let's swim out farther."

George moved out into the bay as I followed him. I kept my toes curled up inside my fins to keep them from falling off my feet. I had never been out in a bay like this. My mind envisioned sharks lurking on the cove's bottom. Fear caused me to have trouble breathing. I had to force each breath, just like breathing under water with a snorkel.

George swam out farther and disappeared below the surface. My feet were cramping, so I turned over on my back to float and rest. George came up for air and went back down. Floating on my back, I watched some high clouds pass over us. With the waves gently picking me up and letting me down, my breathing became more rhythmic. When George came up for the third time, he took off his mask and spit into it, then rubbed it around the inside of the glass. I swam over closer to him.

"Any luck?"

"No, not yet." He rinsed out his mask and slipped it back over his face. "It's deeper here than I thought it would be."

He swam toward shore, then took a deep breath and disappeared below the surface. I rolled over on my back again and relaxed. We were about 100 yards away from the rocky shoreline when I noticed the clouds getting thicker and darker above us. I raised up and looked out the bay's entrance. I blinked several times as shock and panic riveted through my body.

When George came to the surface, I screamed, "George! George!" and frantically swam toward him.

Although far away from me, he must have heard my voice because he looked. I pointed toward the mouth of the bay and the ocean beyond it.

He looked out to sea, and then took off his mask and looked again.

"Son of a bitch," I heard him say above the sound of the waves crashing behind us. He swam toward me.

"What are we going to do?"

"I don't know," he said, surveying the bay's coastline. "This rocky beach isn't a good place to go ashore." He turned and looked out to sea once more. A huge 30 to 40-foot wave approached the mouth of the bay. "We could swim out of the bay and go down the coastline until we find a sandy area. Do you think you could swim that far?"

It meant swimming at least a mile, probably farther. Not only were my feet cramping inside the fins, but also I felt exhausted from staying up all night.

"No, but if you feel that's the safest thing to do, you should do it. I'll have to go in here."

I scanned the shoreline's black rocks. They looked dark, rough and rugged.

"We stick together," George said. "We'll both go in here."

His words made me feel better, but I had no illusions about our predicament. My heart pounded.

As the first huge wave reached us, we went up on its crest and then plummeted down its back side. It felt like we were going to hit the bottom of the bay. My breath stopped as my solar plexus winced. The wave broke 45 to 50 yards behind us onto the shore.

"Shit!" I yelled. "That was unreal."

"Let's swim a little farther out," George said, swimming away from the shore. "If we get caught in the breaker, we're in trouble."

As we swam side-by-side he spoke again. "We'll ride out this first set of waves. Waves usually travel in groups of seven. Once this group passes, the next set should be smaller. At least I hope they are. That's when we'll work our way to shore."

The next wave seemed larger than the first one. Once again, my short shallow breaths came to a stop as we plummeted to the bottom of the swell. The bay's surrounding high cliffs echoed the thundering roar of the waves crashing onto the jagged shoreline.

"I want you to do everything I say when we start swimming in," George said. "When I yell 'swim,' that means swim as fast as you can toward shore. When I yell 'dive,' that means go under water and swim out to sea until the breaking wave passes over us. Have you got that?"

I nodded.

"Keep your eyes on me and do exactly what I do."

He seemed surprisingly calm. I looked at the shoreline in time to watch the third wave crash onto the rocks. The wave nearly reached the back of the bay, falling short of the cliff wall by what appeared to be a few feet. As the backwash of the wave returned toward the sea, thousands of rocks jostled and crackled as if they were marbles being shook in a huge hand.

We rode out the next several waves before George moved slowly toward shore. "Okay," he yelled, "after this next wave we swim toward shore as fast as we can go. You got it?"

"Yeah," I yelled.

As the wave passed us, we both took off swimming. George swam on his back facing the next wave closing in on us. I swam belly down as hard as I could, barely keeping up with him.

"Turn around and get ready to dive," he yelled.

When I turned around, the huge wave towering above us started to break.

"Dive!" George yelled, and he ducked under the water.

I went under too and swam down and out toward the sea. My whole body rocked and swayed toward shore and then back toward the sea as the wave passed above us. I shot to the top for air. George, already on the surface, was swimming toward the shore.

"Swim!" he screamed.

I swam as fast as I could, trying to catch up to him. When I got 10 to 12 feet from him, he yelled, "Turn around."

As I turned around he screamed, "Dive!"

I had no time to look at him. I slipped down and completed my turn under water, flapping the fins as hard as possible. This time I felt the water pushing on top of me. For a moment, I thought I was going to be swept toward the shore, but then the current switched directions. I tried to get to the top, but the undertow held me down. Struggling upward to catch a breath, I suddenly popped through the surface only seven or eight feet from George. He turned quickly and looked at me as I gasped for air and coughed.

"We'll stay here and go under the next wave," he said quickly. "But after this one, there's no more ducking waves, so swim your ass off toward shore."

The shoreline looked close, maybe 50 yards away, but now the large black rocks appeared more menacing than ever. The main thing, I thought, is not to get caught by the breaker. Several weeks earlier I had been tossed out of a breaker onto a sandy shore to have the wind knocked out of me and my chest scrapped raw. I tried not to think of what the rocks would do to my body.

"Here it comes," he said.

I turned to see a wall of white water rising above us. Feeling vulnerable and out of control, I watched George out of the corner of my eye. My instincts said dive, but instead, I waited for George's call. We rose up the inside of the curling wave as a tube of water formed above us.

"Dive!" George yelled, partially cutting off the end of the word as he ducked into the wall of water that now stood nearly perpendicular to the ocean floor.

As my body pierced the huge wall of water, the wave pulled at me like curling fingers wanting to wrap me securely in its grip and slam me onto the rocks below. For several moments, my body remained suspended within the wave's neutral zone—the point between the curl of the breaking wave and its back side. Survival instincts took over as my muscles snapped into gear to produce just enough propulsion to slip out of the finger-clawing currents curling into a monstrous fist. I popped to the surface to find George swimming after the wave breaking toward the shore in front of him. I swam with all my might as a flush of white water moved over the rocks in front of us like a swift flowing river. I fought to stay on top of the water to avoid smashing my feet into the rocks below. As the wave swept us forward, it appeared we were swiftly moving toward safety. George continued to furiously swim in the direction of shore. I more or less dog-paddled to keep my head above water.

The ocean around me came to a brief standstill before reversing its direction and dragging me back out to sea. I turned around to find another huge wave ready to break. Sucked helplessly forward by the undertow, I looked up at the powerful deluge of white water preparing to pound me into the rocks. During that horrifying moment, I could do nothing but watch. I surrendered to the wrath and mercy of the sea. My body relaxed and went limp. The struggle was futile. The sea had won.

Miraculously, the wave broke sooner than it should have, hurling thousands of pounds of water crashing onto the bay's rocky floor some 15 to 20 yards away from me. Within seconds, a wall of white water swallowed me in churning fury sending me tumbling forward into a roll. Both fins were torn off my feet like a mad parent yanking shoes off an obstinate child. My limp body curled and twisted with the wave. During my second or third somersault, my feet hit the rocky bottom as I rolled onto my back and then my butt. The rocks were round and smooth, making them less hazardous. Fortunately, no huge boulders lay in my path to stop my momentum by snagging an arm, leg, or worse—my head.

My lungs felt like they were collapsing. I had to have air. I pushed my feet hard into the rocks below. My face broke the surface as I gasped for a breath. Within a few seconds, I floated back toward the sea, my head barely above the water. I could hear another wave crashing behind me. I struggled to keep my nose and mouth above the water. A wall of white fury engulfed me again, pushing me closer to shore. This time my hands hit the rocks before my body rolled headfirst into a half-cockeyed somersault. I came to the surface as the water around me slowed to a stop. I could see George stooping in about a foot of water removing one of his fins.

Balancing myself in three to four feet of water, I tried to move closer to shore, but as the forceful undertow moved out, it took me with it. The next rush of white water washed over me, overtaking the undertow and twisting me between the two currents before pushing me forward. George moved out into the water to help me. He stood 10 to 15 feet in front of me as the backwash took me out again.

"Come on!" he yelled, holding his hand out toward me. "You can do it!"

Standing in about two feet of water rushing around his knees, George appeared to have a solid stance. As the next wave washed me closer to him, I struggled forward, pushing and clawing at the rocks. George leaned forward and I stretched out my arm to him. Our hands locked around each other's wrists when once again the water switched direction and rushed toward the bay.

"Hold on and push with your feet," George yelled. "We'll walk out of here when the next wave comes in."

George's strong grip and confident voice helped me dig in as the backwash pulled hard against my legs and sucked at my feet. The next wave finally overtook the backwash, causing us to stumble toward shore. George released his grip as we both hunched on all fours for balance and support amidst the rocks. This time, when the backwash headed out into the bay, small rocks and pebbles pummeled our feet and hands before settling onto the shore. The water disappeared into the cracks around the larger rocks like earthworms slithering into their holes. Once George reached the shore, he turned and sat on a huge boulder lodged at the base of the mammoth cliff wall surrounding the bay. Exhausted, I sat beside him.

"Are you okay?" he asked, massaging his right foot with both hands as it rested on his left thigh.

"I think so," I said in a daze, hardly believing we had made it. I looked down at my body, which felt sore all over. My legs and arms hurt the most from being smashed and bruised by rocks. I realized the burning sensation came from scraped skin being doused with salt water. "I hurt, but don't think anything's broken. How about you."

"If I hadn't crammed my big toe into a rock, I'd be fine."

He touched his swollen, blue toe. A wave came flowing up to the boulder, swishing over my feet and ankles. George looked at his gear to the right of the boulder, but the water failed to reach it.

"I'm sorry George, but I lost your fins. They came off when..."

"Don't worry about it. We're lucky to be alive. I'm surprised we made it." George laughed and shook his head. "You're lucky you didn't break any bones.

You were bouncing around out there like a bobber on a fishing line hooked to a shark."

We both laughed.

"Thanks for pulling me out. I'm not sure I would have made it."

"Yes you would have. The next wave would have brought you in."

Clouds now completely covered the sky, stopping any sunshine from filtering through. Another huge wave crashed onto the shore. I looked at George. "They look like they're growing."

"Yeah, we made it just in time."

I wondered if the waves would get big enough to crash into the wall behind us, leaving us no where to go. It appeared George thought the same thing, because we both looked at the cliff simultaneously.

"How are we going to get out of here?"

"I don't know," George replied. He turned his head and looked at the cliff to our left, then to our right. "I'm not much of a climber, but I don't think we have a choice."

On both sides of the bay the huge waves crashed against the rocks. We knew that if the storm got worse, the waves would be crashing on us unless we got out of there. We had to escape from the bay before the brunt of the storm hit. My climbing experience consisted of some uninstructed free climbing in Colorado and a few hours repelling on some Missouri River bluffs.

"That looks like the easiest place to climb." I pointed to an area about 75 yards away. "You wait here. I'll see if I can climb out. If I get out, then you can do it, but don't start climbing until I'm out."

"Okay," he said, still rubbing his foot. "Good luck."

"Can you climb with your foot?"

"Yeah, I'll be all right. I'll just go slow."

"What about your gear?"

"I'll figure something out. Go on. Check it out."

I walked along the rocky shoreline below the cliff. At one point, I had to walk through two feet of water before finally starting my climb. The first 20 feet went easy, but after that it became nearly straight up. It took at least 30 minutes before I pulled myself up and looked over the cliff's edge to find the 10-foot steep incline of lose dirt and sand. It horrified me to be so close to the top, but unable to advance forward. With nothing to grab onto, I had only one choice—to climb back down. With that thought, terror pulsed throughout my heart and mind.

Clinging to the lip of the precipice, my whole body started to shake. I tried to calm down, repeating to myself to stay focused on what's in front of me. I saw a large crevice a few feet to my left. I slowly edged over to it and wedged myself securely within it. I took several deep breaths, which helped me relax a little. I knew I needed to turn around. I carefully maneuvered a half-circle turn.

With my body still trembling, I looked out over the bay as ocean waves pounded the shoreline below me. Just relax, I kept saying to myself. I had purposely not looked down during my climb up, but to descend I would have no choice. After a moment of steadying myself, I finally got the nerve to look at the shoreline below me. George had started to climb the rocks. He looked up. I shook my head back and forth. I saw his mouth move, but only the sound of crashing waves came to my ears. He cupped his hands around his mouth and yelled.

"What's the matter?"

Afraid to scream for fear it might cause me to fall, I kept shaking my head back and forth. Still cupping his hands around his mouth, he yelled again.

"Can you go any higher?"

I shook my head back and forth.

"Are you stuck?" he screamed.

I nodded affirmatively. He backed down over the few rocks he had started to climb and walked along the coastline away from the area in which we had come ashore. I leaned my head back against the rock cliff and closed my eyes.

"God, don't let me fall," I said aloud.

Opening my eyes and looking out over the bay, I gasped in horror. I had seen this exact view during a dream three weeks earlier while on the island of Kauai.

In the dream, after viewing this scenic vista, I looked down at the waves crashing onto the shore. The waves and shoreline started to swirl and spin clockwise as nausea churned at the pit of my stomach. My grip loosened, and my body leaned forward as I plunged into the swirling vortex. The wind whisked past my face as the sensation of falling pulled my solar plexus to my throat. Moments before hitting the rocks below, my body tightened. Yet, unlike what I had heard about falling in dreams—that you awaken just before you hit—I slammed into the rocks. On impact, I experienced an intense pressure as if crushed by a road-repairing steamroller. A second later I felt light and free. I found myself floating, suspended in the air above my limp and broken body.

Wow, I'm dead, I thought. That's me down there.

Sirens screamed in the distance, but only when the ambulance arrived did I comprehend they had come for me. They put my smashed and lifeless body on a stretcher, covered me with a sheet and then placed me in the ambulance. I experienced no pain or sadness about my death. I felt more curiosity than anything else. Then the scene faded, and below me materialized a group of people. Because I first saw the top of their heads, it took me a second to recognize my mother, father, brother, sister, relatives and friends. Several people were crying, including my mother and sister.

"Steve," I yelled to my brother who stood with his arms crossed chatting with a cousin. He continued talking. "Hey! Up here!" I screamed. No one acknowledged my presence. I floated above the flowers to the casket and looked in. It felt strange seeing my face with its calm and peaceful expression. I'm really dead, I thought. So this is the next step.

Then I awoke with a start. A tremendous feeling of sadness filled me; not sadness about my death, but about missing people I loved.

The dream now became real with the exact same cliff, the exact same view, and the exact same fear. High above the crashing waves, my whole body trembled uncontrollably. I tried to stop the tremors, but the harder I tried, the more I shook. This is it, I thought. The dream's coming true. I closed my eyes and focused my attention inward toward the center of my head—the same as during meditation. "Have I completed what I'm suppose to do in this life?" I asked internally.

An image formed on the dark screen before my eyes. At first the picture looked like a sledgehammer, but then it clearly turned into a rubber-tipped dart from a dart gun. As children, we loved shooting darts and hearing their popping smack as they stuck to a mirror, window or wall. And, if we wanted them to stick even better, we licked a coat of saliva inside the concave tip.

The image grew until it reached the size of a toilet plunger. Now I saw and felt the huge suction cup extending out my back just above my waist, making me feel like a dart attached to the cliff wall. My body slowly relaxed. The trembling stopped. I opened my eyes and looked down at the waves crashing onto the shore. It appeared the same as in my dream, except without the spinning. I took a deep breath and sighed. A voice inside my head said, "You must go down. Go slowly. The suction cup will keep you centered and safe."

I started moving down the same way I had climbed up—making sure I had three good holds before advancing a step lower. After moving two, maybe three times, I heard George's voice above me.

"Bryce, are you there?"

I leaned back into the stony surface behind me and imagined the suction cup holding me tightly to the cliff. George was unable to see me from where he stood.

"Yes," I said with my head tilted back against the rocks.

"There's a ledge along the bottom of the cliff that leads around the bay to a path. If you follow that path, it takes you out of the bay. Do you think you can make it back down?"

"I don't know," I said as loud as I could without disturbing my hold.

"I'll go for help."

He spoke no more. I reached out my right foot and pushed on the rock that appeared to be my next hold. The rock came loose and tumbled down the side of the cliff, hitting a protrusion in the cliff and bouncing 10 or 15 feet out before splashing into the water below.

The slow descent, one foot and one handhold at a time, demanded my complete concentration. I have no idea how long it took to go down, but thank God it didn't start to rain. The cliff would have become a miniature waterfall. Reaching the bottom, I sat on a huge boulder exhausted. The waves breaking onto the shore seemed smaller. A streak of sunlight found its way through a crack in the clouds.

The path George talked about ran about two feet above the water level and blended into the cliff wall. It looked more like a water line on the rock wall instead of a ledge. Knowing it existed helped me to see it. I slowly made my way along the footpath. In several places, I had to stoop slightly to keep my head from hitting the cliff jutting out above me.

When I reached the other side of the bay, I started up the footpath leading to the top of the cliff. Although relatively easy to climb, the paths jagged rocks made it slow going barefoot. Once at the top of the cliff, I saw Cindy in the distance coming toward me. I waved my arms to her and she waved back. As she got closer, I could see she held my flip-flop sandals in her hand.

"You're okay," she said as we embraced. "George said you were stuck on the side of the cliff."

She leaned back and looked at me, dropping my flip flops to the ground as our lips came together. I wrapped my arms around her waist and pulled her to me as her arms moved over my shoulders and her fingers massaged the back of my neck and scalp. My mouth slid off her mouth, and I nestled my chin into the nape of her neck. She wore a pink swimsuit under a white t-shirt. I opened my eyes and surveyed the area around us, hoping to see a grassy spot large enough for both of us to lie down. I saw none. I slid my hands up the sides of her body and cupped them around the back of her neck, lightly massaging her hair and scalp. We looked into each other's eyes.

"God, you have no idea how good it feels to be with you."

"Yes I do," she said, and we kissed again

"By the way, where's George?"

"He said he was going to sleep. When he told me you were stuck, I went over to the spot where you guys got in the water. I could see you on the cliff. I yelled and waved. Did you see me?"

"No," I said, glad not to be clinging to the cliff waiting for help. "Thanks for bringing these." I picked up my flip flops and slipped them on, holding on to Cindy's arm for balance.

"You were really high up. Weren't you scared?"

"Terrified would be closer to the right word."

We kissed several more times, and as we walked back toward camp, I told Cindy about my dream and the cliff. Once back at our campsite, we found it deserted. Everyone had gone hiking or to the sacred pools, so Cindy and I climbed in my tent and made love. She then massaged my back until I fell asleep. I awoke with someone shaking and pulling my leg. I raised up and looked to the front of the tent.

"Wake up," George said belligerently, holding an opened bottle of wine in one hand as he gripped my leg with his other hand. "You and I have to drink this bottle of wine," he said loudly, slurring his words together. "We nearly died today."

"I need some sleep." I tried to turn over on my side.

"You can sleep after we finish this. It's not everyday you nearly die. Come on." He began dragging me out of the tent by my leg.

"Okay," I said, tired and aggravated. "Let go of my leg."

Even though George became obnoxious and belligerent at times, there was something about him I admired. Maybe it was his fearless and carefree happy-go-lucky nature.

We guzzled more than half the bottle before starting to reminisce about our experience and what the outcome could have been. We had struggled against the power of nature and miraculously survived relatively unscathed. Now we were dealing with the emotional side of the traumatic experience, and the wine served as the unifying link between us. Less than 15 minutes after we drained the bottle, George passed out.

I climbed back inside my tent and fell asleep. I awoke in the night to find Cindy sleeping beside me in her swimsuit. I put my hand on her back and softly massaged her warm skin. She let out a soft cooing sound. I moved close to her and kissed her cheek. She inhaled and released a whimper as the corners of her mouth turned up slightly to form a beautifully peaceful, tranquil and serene expression. I wanted to roll her over and take her into my arms, but instead I propped myself up on my elbows, put my head in my hands, and watched her sleep as she breathed softly.

"I'm in the Garden of Eden," I thought, "and Eve has changed her name to Cindy."

Less than a week later, Cindy and I were in Pauwela and spotted Justin.

"Justin!" I yelled. He turned and saw us, then immediately walked in our direction. As he gave Cindy a hug, I looked at him. "So you changed your mind."

"By the time I got back to my apartment," he said, "I felt better, thanks to you." He let go of Cindy and hugged me. "Besides, I'm not sure heaven can get any better than this place."

Harry's Bar and Grill

A fter returning from Hawaii, I spent several weeks with my brother and his family in Springfield, Missouri, before going to Kansas City and working for my great uncle building houses. I tried to start a rock band with some college buddies. We practiced during the evenings, but within a month it became apparent things were moving in the wrong direction. I realized that before joining forces with other musicians, I had to have it together myself. Once more the road became my teacher.

By early September, with money in my bank account, I took off for California. Two older men from Oklahoma, who had gotten drunk in a bar and decided to drive straight through to San Francisco, stopped and picked me up. They had me drive their old beat-up Oldsmobile for at least 500 miles while they slept.

After spending several nights in Golden Gate Park, I hitchhiked south to spend the fall camping in Big Sur's Andrew Molera Walk-In Campground.

A young man, his girlfriend and their dog dropped me off late Friday afternoon on the outskirts of Santa Cruz. With the sun steaming the city's streets, visions of cool ocean waves flowing over my tired and sweaty feet kept me walking through town toward the public beach. More than halfway through Santa Cruz, I saw a sign next to a bus stop bench that read, "Free Shuttle Service to the Beach." I put down my gear and got out my guitar. A man spoke from behind me.

"Hey, how's it going?"

I turned around to see a guy grinning and walking toward me. I immediately noticed his yellow, crooked teeth accented by his gold wire-rimmed granny glasses. His flat nose looked out of place compared to the rest of his face. He wore a light blue t-shirt, blue jeans and leather sandals with tire-tread bottoms. His wavy shoulder-length hair and short scraggly beard made his head look too big for his 5-foot 8-inch frame.

I smiled. "It's going good, but it'll be better when I get to the beach."

He put one hand on the back of the bench. "You just get into town?"

"Yeah, I got dropped off up the road a ways. I saw this sign and figured I might as well take advantage of it."

"First time here?"

"The first time I've stopped. I've passed through Santa Cruz before."

"Where are you from?"

"Missouri. How about you? Is this home?"

I pressed on the fifth fret of my E string and plucked it with a pick, and then adjusted my guitar strap.

He walked around to the front of the bench and sat beside me. "Yeah, I live here, but I grew up in a small community just outside of town. Have you played guitar long?"

I strummed an E seventh chord. The tuning sounded close enough. "I've played off-and-on since fourteen." Playing a blues-swing beat in E7, I hummed a few measures and then improvised words within a basic blues structure.

Here I am again waiting for a ride
I'm heading to the beach to spend another night
I hope to find a woman and give her all my love
And if I don't I'll fly away just like the morning dove.

The guy laughed and stuck out his hand. "My name's Walt."

"Bryce," I said as we shook.

"Is that something you wrote?"

"Just made it up."

"I play guitar too. Hey!" he added as if he'd just remembered something. "I know a couple of girls we can visit..." Walt paused and glanced behind him to see if anyone might overhear him. "...and I've got some stuff we can smoke if you feel like making a little party."

Although Walt looked and even acted a bit strange, he seemed like a safe enough guy just out to have a good time.

"Sure, why not. I got more time than money." I found myself using that expression more and more. I picked it up from my great uncle, although in his case he actually had more money than time.

Walt jumped up. "Great! I'll call a cab." He walked toward the phone booth behind us.

"Uhhh, wait a minute. I don't have much cash, and cabs are expensive."

He picked up the phone and dialed. "Don't worry, I can cover it."

Within a few minutes the cab arrived, and about 20 minutes later we stopped outside the city limits in front of an isolated house that sat back off the road. The cab fare cost $10. As the cabdriver drove away, I became a little paranoid walking up the gravel driveway. A yellow Volkswagen beetle sat beside the house.

"Who are these girls?"

"Carol and Janet. I've known them since high school."

"Do they live here alone?"

"Yeah, you'll like them."

Walt knocked on the door. A girl with long blonde haired wearing shorts and a t-shirt opened the door. Although her nose was a little large and she wore too much mascara, her great figure made up for what she lacked in facial beauty.

"Walt," the girl said somewhat hesitatingly. "Hi." Her reaction and reception indicated our visit an intrusion.

"Hi Janet!" He spoke as if she'd given us a hearty greeting. "How's it going?"

"Fine, just fine." She hadn't opened the screen door when another blonde girl walked up and stood beside Janet.

"Hello Carol. How are you?"

"Hi. I'm fine, thanks."

"This is a friend of mine, Bryce. He's a guitar player. I brought some hash and thought maybe you'd like to party a little."

"Sounds like fun," Janet said, "but I wish you had called. We've already got plans for tonight."

"What a bummer. We came all the way out here to party with you. Do you have time to smoke a bowl?"

Janet looked at Carol. "I guess, but just barely. Our dates will be here at seven, and we've got some things to do before then."

It had to be around 4:30 or 5 o'clock. Janet pushed open the door and let us in. We walked down the hall to a doorway covered by a tapestry. Janet held back the fabric, and we entered what appeared to be a bedroom turned into a small living room. A couch and several chairs surrounded a coffee table that sat on an eight-by-ten oriental rug. The room was thoroughly clean and everything neatly arranged. Janet turned on a fan in the corner as Walt flopped down on the couch. I set my guitar by the coffee table, and then took off my pack and leaned it against the end of the couch. Both girls sat on the edge of their chairs with the coffee table between us. Walt had a chunk of hashish the size of a half dollar wrapped in aluminum foil. He packed a pipe, handed it to Janet and held a match above the bowl. The pipe went around twice when Walt looked at me.

"Bryce, why don't you get out your guitar and play us a song?"

"Sure," I said, reaching for my guitar case.

"Listen," Carol said, looking at Walt and then at me, "we'd love to hear you play Bryce, but maybe some other time. We really have to get ready. I'm sorry. I wish you guys would have come earlier." She stood up.

"You never know when it's going to rain," Walt mumbled, "but when it does, you better take cover."

Although Walt made his statement without much expression, it sounded like a threat.

"What'd you say?" I asked Walt, who wrapped the foil back around his hashish and looked up at me, and then at Janet.

"What?" he asked.

"What'd you just say?"

Walt stood up and put the wrapped hashish in his pocket. "Nothing. We need to go so the girls can get ready for their dates." He picked up my guitar and walked to the tapestry, flipping it to one side as he passed through the doorway. Janet, who walked behind Walt, caught the drapery before it closed.

"Thanks for getting us high," she said to Walt's back as she held the cloth to one side for Carol and me. "It's really good hash."

Walt's comment and abrupt departure from the living room made me think he was pissed off, but by the time we reached the front door he smiled as if he'd had a great time.

"You girls have fun tonight," he said in a pleasant manner as we walked out on the porch. Walt sounded neither upset nor bitter.

"Thanks," Janet replied.

As we walked away from the house, Walt suggested we visit some other friends that lived nearby, but first he wanted to pick up a few steaks to grill at their trailer. We stopped at a grocery store and he bought two huge sirloins. We then walked about a mile to a trailer courtyard. Walt knocked on a trailer door. We could hear Fleetwood Mac playing on the stereo. Walt knocked a second time before a tanned barefoot brunette in short shorts with huge breasts covered by a skimpy white halter top answered the door. With her tousled hair, I thought maybe she'd fallen asleep listening to the stereo. She had a pretty face, but it was her voluptuous breasts that made her beautiful. Her firm nipples protruded outward beneath her halter top.

"Oh, hi," she said, about as enthusiastic to see Walt as the other two girls.

"Hi Jackie. Is John here?"

"No, he's playing at 'The Pub' tonight."

Walt told me later that 'The Pub' was a small bar on the other side of town where solo artists and small acoustical acts performed.

"Well that's good to hear. Has he been playing there long?"

"This is his second weekend."

"Far out. Hey, this is a friend of mine, Bryce. We picked up a couple of steaks hoping you guys might want to grill out."

A guy walked up behind Jackie. He wore a blue tank-top shirt. Walt looked at him and then at Jackie.

"Oh, I'm sorry. Are we interrupting something?"

Walt's insinuating tone and sarcasm made Jackie wince. She said nothing, but stared at Walt. The expressions on her face changed from embarrassment and shame to pleading for understanding, sympathy and secrecy.

"Here," Walt blurted, pushing the steaks to her stomach. She took them out of reaction to his sudden thrust. "You, John, and your friend here, can share these when John gets back. Tell him I dropped by, okay? I'll give him a call sometime soon. Bye."

Walt turned and headed down the trailer courtyard's gravel road. Jackie opened her mouth as if to say something, but stopped. Standing there holding the steaks, she looked at me as tears rolled down her cheeks. I shrugged my shoulders and turned to follow Walt, running a few steps to catch up with him.

"That fucking bitch. She fucks all of John's friends, and he has no idea what's going on."

I looked back at the trailer. The door was shut.

"I can't believe she fucks them in John's bed. Damn her." Walt headed across the paved road to a path cutting across a pasture. "Come on," he said, still sounding mad, "there's a pizza place on the other side of this field. You like pizza don't you?"

"Sure."

When we got to about the middle of the field, with me walking behind Walt, he said, "At least it doesn't snow here, but you've got the mountains if you like snow. I never understood why people would want to live in snow."

"What are you talking about?" I asked him. He didn't reply. "Walt!"

He stopped and looked at me, but said nothing.

"What are you talking about?" I repeated.

"What?"

"The snow and all. Why'd you bring that up?"

Walt looked bewildered. "I just asked you if you liked pizza. I didn't mention snow."

"I thought I heard you say it doesn't snow here."

Walt laughed. "That's true." He turned around and walked toward the strip mall in front of us. "Come on, I'm hungry, and beginning to smell pizza."

I wondered if Walt was messing with my head, or whether the hashish had gotten to him. At the pizza parlor, Walt ordered a pitcher of beer and a large pepperoni pizza. As we drank beer waiting for pizza, I discovered Walt attended one year of college before he dropped out. He was drafted and sent to Vietnam where he fought in the jungle for two years. He didn't want to talk about Vietnam, so I didn't press him.

During my junior and senior years in high school, I spent my summers working on a city garbage truck with a guy who fought four years in Vietnam (1964 to 1968).

"Whatever you do," he said one morning after I mentioned that on my next birthday I would have to register for the draft, "don't go to Vietnam."

When he told me he spent four years there, I hammered him with questions. He was wounded three times and sent back to the front line after each recovery. He showed me the scars on his chest, abdomen and legs. He said that out of his original platoon, seven survived. His stories had a profound impact on me.

"The gooks, after killing Americans," he said, "would cut off their pricks and stick them in the dead man's mouth. After we killed a gook, we'd cut out their eyes and put one in the center of their forehead. That always freaked them out."

When I brought up Lieutenant Kelly and the My Lai massacre, he grunted. "We did that to a lot of villages. We had orders to kill everything that moved, including animals and children. You didn't know who the hell your enemy was. Some kid might come up to you with explosives strapped around his body. It came down to kill and survive. You don't want to live through that. Whatever you do, just don't go over there. Move to Canada if you have to. Nothing is worth going through what I did."

At the end of that first week of stories, I decided not to go to Southeast Asia—draft, lottery or whatever. His stories also changed my perception of what seemed like a fun and happy-go-lucky guy. Knowing what he had been through and what he had done in Vietnam made it spooky to be around him. It's funny how little we know about people when we first meet them. We have no idea about their past and what they've experienced, and in many cases, that's probably for the best.

Walt and I had a second pitcher of beer with our pizza, and except for a small portion of the crust, we ate the whole thing. Walt insisted on visiting a bar he used to drink at years before. "I haven't been there since Nam. It's a great hometown bar. You'll like it."

Walt put down a tip for our waitress and we headed for the door. The clock above the pizza parlor's cash register showed 9:45. We walked five or six blocks to the tavern. Upon seeing it from a distance, I became leery. The long and narrow bar had a small house with an extension added on to the back of it. An old neon Busch sign hung above the screen door. Six or seven pickup trucks, along with a station wagon and several older cars, were sitting in the gravel parking lot. Walt carried my guitar as we walked through the short entrance hallway and pushed open the thick wooden door.

Inside the long L-shaped bar were three or four tables and chairs in the back. A low-hanging light above a pool table cast shadows on the ceiling. As we entered, a man stood bent over the table about to make a shot. His receding dark hair slicked back over his head made his long curly sideburns and thick mustache stand out. He had a pack of cigarettes tightly wrapped in his t-shirt sleeve just above the Harley Davidson motorcycle wings' tattoo on his left shoulder. A lit cigarette hung from his lips. Sighting a path for his cue ball, he took a moment to raise his eyes and look at us. In fact, everyone in the bar looked to see who joined them.

Seven men sat at the bar on stools, and not a single one had long hair. Two of the guys wore ball caps. No one smiled or greeted us, including the bartender. Instead, an eerie silence filled the room. One of the guys wearing a ball cap took a sip of beer out of his bottle and looked at me as if I had called him a fairy. Two women sat at a table for four in the corner. I assumed they were with the men at the pool table. Other than two bar stools at the far end of the bar and two stools close to the door, all the stools were taken.

"We can put your stuff here," Walt said, placing my guitar in a two-foot space between the cigarette machine and the jukebox. I set my pack next to it. We sat in the two empty bar stools closest to the door. The bartender, standing at the other end of the bar, also turned to look at us. After the few moments of silence upon our entry, the bartender talked to the two customers in front of him, but in a low tone as if telling them a secret. Then the bartender and his two customers quit talking, and all three looked at us. Walt nodded and raised his hand indicating we wanted something to drink. The bartender gave no acknowledgment, but instead looked back at his customers as they continued their conversation. For me, that clearly became a sign for us to leave. Walt reached in his pocket and pulled out several quarters.

"We need some music in here," he said loud enough for all the patrons to hear. He spun around on the stool, hopped off and walked to the juke box behind us. A country western song played as Walt pressed the buttons for more tunes. After Walt returned to his seat, a guy closer to our end of the bar yelled to the bartender for another drink. The bartender slowly walked toward us. He took the man's glass, dumped the ice out and added fresh ice, and then poured him a shot of Jack Daniel's.

"We could use a couple of beers," Walt said.

"Can't you see I'm busy?" the bartender snapped at us.

"I mean when you get a chance," Walt added nonchalantly, as if the bartender had spoken pleasantly.

The bartender put the drink in front of the man before he slowly and meticulously wiped the bar top in front of him. He asked the man next to the Jack Daniel's drinker if he needed another beer, and the man nodded. The bartender then picked up the guy's beer bottle, wiped beneath it, and got the man another beer. I felt compelled to leave more than ever, but Walt sat calmly and patiently waiting. Finally the bartender sauntered in our direction, rag in hand. He swiped his towel across the counter in front of us.

"Now," he said as if speaking to a couple of misbehaved kids, "what would you like?" Although he held a stern look on his face, I could see the victory sparkle in his eyes. If Walt saw it, he paid no attention.

"Do you still have Miller on draft?" Walt asked in an amiable tone, as if he and the bartender were buddies.

The bartender let out a sigh before replying, "Miller and Michelob." He stretched his arms out and put his hands on the bar as he leaned into it. His actions said, "Hurry up bud. I haven't got all night."

"Two Millers, please."

The bartender slowly walked to the spigot, picked up two glasses and filled them. "Buck fifty," he said as he sat them in front of us.

"Look, I didn't mean to rush you a few minutes ago." Walt spoke in a cordial tone without a hint of sarcasm. "I'd like to buy you a drink."

"I can't drink while I'm working," he replied curtly.

"I know, but I mean when you get off." Walt reached in his pocket. "As a matter of fact, I'd like to buy everybody in here a drink."

The bartender looked at Walt incredulously. "What?"

"I'd like to buy a drink for everyone in here. And be sure to take enough out of this to cover your drink for later." Walt tossed a fifty-dollar bill on the bar; then glanced around the room. "If that's not enough to cover it, just let me know."

For a few seconds, the bartender stared at Walt. He then walked to the far end of the bar. He talked to the two guys sitting there, and seconds later he nodded toward us. He poured them two shots of whisky and moved to the next customer. When the bartender got to a gray-haired gentleman sitting three customers away from us, the old man said, "Who's buying the drink?"

We could plainly hear the man. The bartender responded, "The guy at the end of the bar. The one on the right."

The old man looked at us. "Do I know you?"

The bar became quiet except for the song on the juke box, which now played the only song I recognized up to that point; *Desperado* by the Eagles. The words fit our situation. "Desperado, why don't you come to your senses..."

"Yeah," Walt said, taking a sip of his beer and licking his lips.

Everyone in the bar waited for Walt to continue. I wondered if Walt had decided to mess with this old man's head, or if he really knew him. Walt looked at the old man, but remained silent.

"Where do I know you from?"

Walt paused, took another sip of his beer and said, "Girl Scout camp."

Half the people in the bar laughed. One guy yelled to the old man, "Can't you find anyone your own age, Bill?" and another round of laughter broke out. I could see we were in definite trouble now. The two guys wearing baseball caps grinned, but I got the feeling they grinned because Walt's remark gave them the go-ahead to beat the hell out of us. The old man smiled and even appeared amused by Walt's statement, but during the laughter and the slap on his back by the guy next to him, he never took his eyes off of Walt.

"How do I know you?" the old man asked.

The bar grew silent again. The Eagles kept playing. "Desperado, you ain't getting no younger, your pain and your hunger, they're driving you home..."

"Don't you remember, Bill? You were playing banjo, and I played guitar at the Girl Scout camp up in..."

"Yes! Yes! Yes!" the old man screamed and hopped off his stool like a kid. He came bouncing down to the end of the bar and vigorously shook Walt's hand. "I didn't recognize you with all that hair, you old son of a bitch." The old man put his left hand on Walt's shoulder. "Where the hell have you been all these years?"

Everybody still watched us.

"They sent me over to Nam for a few years."

Those words completely changed the bar's atmosphere. The tension level dropped faster than air escaping from a runaway balloon. I let out a soft sigh of relief as the men in the bar engaged in conversation with one another again. The two men in ball caps said something to one another and then looked at us. Maybe it was my imagination, but I could have sworn I saw a glimmer of disappointment in their eyes, as if they were saying, "You were lucky this time you hippie freaks. We were about to kick your asses."

Walt introduced me to Bill, who then yelled to the bartender, "Jack, I want to buy these two guys a drink. Whatever they want—and make it a double."

Practically everybody in the bar started buying us drinks. Walt immediately changed to bourbon and coke. I stayed with beer. Within a few minutes, besides my original beer, I had five beers lined up in front of me. Everyone got smashed that night, including me. After last call at 1:30 a.m., Walt gave me a quarter and asked me to use the phone booth outside to hail a taxi. He wrote the cab company's phone number on a napkin. I stumbled outside and called. A woman answered the phone.

"Where are you calling from?" she asked.

I told her a phone booth outside Harry's Bar and Grill, and she asked me for the phone number. I had trouble reading the number in the center of the dial. She told me to hang up and wait a few minutes. Within 60 seconds the phone rang.

"A cab will be there in 10 to 15 minutes," she said.

I staggered back into the bar to find a fresh beer sitting next to my previous beer. Before I could finished it, a man entered the bar and asked who had called the cab. Walt, who now sat at the other end of the bar, motioned to the driver. I walked to my backpack, having to hold on to the jukebox and cigarette machine for balance. Walt picked up my guitar. There were several farewell greetings from people in the bar.

After shoving my gear in the back seat of the cab, I climbed in. Walt, who scooted into the front seat with the driver, had to be smashed, but he seemed to be functioning better than me. Walt told the driver an address. I had no idea where we were going, and frankly, I didn't really care. Several times I thought I might throw up. I felt the cab roll to a stop. The driver asked for $10. That seemed to be the going rate in Santa Cruz. I pushed open the door and climbed out. Walt helped me get out my gear. After the cabbie drove away, I realized we were standing in the middle of a shopping center parking lot.

"Where are we?"

"We're going there." Walt nodded to a place behind him.

I looked to see a massage parlor, but the lights surrounding it were off. "Are you sure it's open?"

"I'm sure. Come on."

Walt walked to the door and knocked hard, nearly to the point of pounding. At eyelevel there was a small window covered by wrought iron bars with a flower design on it. The small window opened and a woman looked out.

"Can I help you?"

"Yeah, how much for a massage?" Walt asked, slightly slurring his speech.

"Twenty dollars a half hour."

Walt smiled. "We'd like two massages."

The woman looked us over. I could tell she wondered if she should let us in. "Just the two of you?"

"That's it."

She paused before finally shutting the window and opening the door. We walked into a hallway entrance area. She closed the door and locked it. "This way," she said.

There were speakers in the hallway and Janis Joplin sang, "...Oh Lord won't you buy me a Mercedes Benz, my friends all drive Porches, I must make amends..." We followed the lady to a small room with a couch and several chairs. "Have a seat. Someone will be right with you."

After putting my gear down, Walt plopped on the couch, and I sat in a chair beside the couch. Within a few minutes, two girls came into the room wearing white blouses over short white dresses. They looked like they were ready to play tennis.

"Hi," said a cute sandy-brown haired girl as she sat in the chair beside me. "My name is Susan, and this is Debbie."

I smiled. "I'm Bryce and this is Walt." The alcohol made it difficult to talk.

Debbie sat on the couch next to Walt and crossed her long slinky legs. Susan sat on the edge of her chair leaning toward me. I had a good view down the front of her blouse. She wore no bra. She looked at Walt, and then back at me, catching me admiring her large breasts. She smiled.

"Are you guys from around here?"

"Walt is, but I'm from Missouri."

Susan leaned over the left side of her chair and put her face close to mine. I could smell the peppermint gum she chewed. "I've been there before. What part of Missouri?"

"All over," I replied, "but mainly Springfield, Columbia and Kansas City." I could hear Debbie asking Walt where he lived.

"I've been to Kansas City," Susan said, putting her hand on my leg and gently shaking it. "That's a great city. What's the name of the place down by the river?"

"The River Quay?"

"That's it. I had a lot of fun down there."

Although I could hear Walt and Debbie talking, it was all I could do to focus on Susan and keep a coherent conversation going. After a few minutes, Debbie turned to me and said, "Can you understand what he says?"

I looked at Walt who smiled at me.

"Well, yeah, most of the time."

"He doesn't make any sense to me."

I looked at Walt to see how he took her remark. He grinned as if she'd paid him a complement. "We've both had a lot to drink." I looked at Susan. "Do you understand what I'm saying?"

She smiled. "Yes. Come on." She took my hand and stood up. "I'll take you to your massage room."

As we walked toward the hallway, I looked back at Walt. He leaned back and took a deep breath, still grinning. Susan and I passed two rooms with closed doors before stopping at an open doorway. She waited for me to enter first. The room contained a padded table that reminded me of a doctor's table and an adjoining room with a partially opened door.

"There's the shower and restroom," Susan said pointing toward the adjoining room. "Go ahead and clean up. I'll be back in a few minutes. Put on the robe hanging on the other side of the door."

Not having taken a bath or shower for more than a week, I quickly slipped out of my clothes and stepped into the stall where I found soap, shampoo and conditioner. After a hot shower and cool rinse, I dried off and put on the white robe. I sat on the table waiting for Susan, feeling much more sober and self-conscious without my clothes. Janis Joplin now sang the song *Bobbie McGee*.

"Feeling better?" Susan asked as she entered the room.

"Much. It's amazing what a hot shower can do for you."

Susan laughed and moved in front of me so her hips and thighs were touching my knees and calves. She put her hands on the table, one on each side of my hips, and smiled, looking into my eyes. "Tell me something Bryce, are you associated with the police in any way?"

I laughed and shook my head. "No."

"It's fifteen dollars for a hand job, twenty for a blowjob, and thirty to go all the way, front or back."

She spoke as if she were a checkout lady at a grocery store. I had never been to a massage parlor before, and even though I suspected many parlors to be fronts for prostitution, her matter-of-fact proposition surprised me nonetheless.

"Uhh, I'm not the one paying for this. Walt's paying. Why don't we just go with the massage for now."

Susan smiled and stepped back. "Okay, but just a second. I'll be right back. Lay down and make yourself comfortable."

I didn't think about it then, but Walt had already committed us to a $20 half-hour massage, so I had two choices. Within a minute, Susan returned.

"I'm afraid your friend left," she said without smiling. "You'll have to get dressed and leave."

"Where did he go?"

"I don't know. I'll wait outside while you put your clothes on."

I remember thinking while getting dressed, "Well, at least I got a free shower." Then I wondered if Walt had taken my guitar and backpack. I dressed quickly and went to the waiting room. My pack and guitar were sitting next to the door. Susan sat in a chair. She got up and walked me to the door.

"Did you see which way Walt went?"

She opened the door. "No, sorry."

The shopping center parking lot was deserted. I walked to the end of the lot and crossed the street to a gravel driveway leading to a trailer park. Down the driveway some 20 yards were two large bushes that took up as much space as a school bus. I looked around, and seeing no one, pushed my guitar and pack under the bush and crawled in behind them. I rolled out my sleeping bag and fell asleep on top of it. The next morning, I opened my eyes to find two men stooped down looking under the bush at me.

"Good morning," I mumbled, wondering what they were doing.

"Just making sure you were all right," one guy said. They stood up and walked down the gravel road toward the trailers.

With a dry mouth and headache, I rolled over on my back and looked at the bushes above me. I thought about the bizarre day before and how Walt had strangely entered and exited my life. He appeared alone and lonely, and desperately seeking something or someone. I never saw Walt again.

Table Rock Dam

After hiking up from the lake and out of the woods, I crossed a small rocky ditch and climbed onto the blacktop road leading to southern Missouri's Table Rock Dam. Camping beside Table Rock Lake for a week helped me mentally prepare for what needed to be done. It was time to find a job. The thought of working a job for more than a month or two frightened me. A job in the city represented the height of mass hypnotism where people became hundreds of wheels spinning within one giant clock that slowly turns in a never-ending circle.

Standing half a mile or so from the dam, I began hitchhiking toward Springfield, Missouri, to visit my brother. A blue Camaro zoomed past me with a girl sitting close beside the driver. The hot sun beat down on my Kansas City Royals ball cap. I picked up my gear and began walking toward the dam. The sound of another car approaching came from behind. I held up my thumb without turning around to look at the car. The car sped by me as someone yelled out the window, "Get a horse!" I put my hand down as several teenagers looked out the back window of an old red Ford Galaxy.

"I'd like a horse!" I yelled. "It would sure beat walking in this heat!"

I watched the car cross the dam in front of me. The dam itself looked at least a mile long with no shade for a short reprieve from the sun's rays. Sweat ran down my chest and lower back beneath my white t-shirt. Upon reaching the dam, I heard another car. Once again I held out my thumb without looking back. A black and silver Bronco with four men in it sped by me, and suddenly its brake lights flashed as the Bronco skidded to a stop. Its reverse lights lit up as the Bronco backed toward me. The rear window above the tailgate had been lowered.

"Hurry and jump in," I heard someone yell.

"Come on, climb through the window before another car comes," another voice said as I galloped toward the vehicle.

I pushed my guitar through the window into the arms of a blond-haired kid in the back seat, and then shoved the pack in and climbed in through the window as the driver stepped on the gas. Another blond-haired guy in the back seat grabbed my arm to keep me from falling out onto the road. It wasn't until then that I realized the guys in the back seat were identical twins.

"Thanks," I said to the guy holding my arm as I pulled my legs into the Bronco. The twins laughed.

"Sure," one said. "It's hot out there, ain't it?"

"You got that right. Thanks for stopping," I said to the driver who looked at me through the rearview mirror.

"You're a might welcome," he said with a hick accent that incorporated a slight southern drawl. "Here, give that boy a drink." He looked in the mirror at the twins as he handed an opened bottle of Jack Daniel's to the guy sitting beside him.

"Yeah," the guy sitting next to him said. The front-seat passenger, with a thick black mustache and a receding hairline, looked quite a bit older than the other three. He held the bottle out to one of the twins. "He looks like he could use a nip or two. Yip, yip, yip, yip," he said flapping his arm like a duck. It reminded me of the movie *Easy Rider* where Jack Nicholson made a similar action and sound. Everyone laughed while one twin took the bottle and handed it to me. I turned the bottle up and took a mouthful, washing the liquor around my teeth and gums before letting it slowly ooze down my throat.

"Where you headin' to?" the driver asked me.

The whisky sent a fiery sensation down my esophagus and into my stomach. "That tastes good," I said, taking in a short breath and letting out a slight cough. "I'm going to Springfield to visit my brother."

"We can take you up the road a ways."

"I appreciate it," I replied, feeling a little uneasy, yet not knowing why. I turned the bottle up again and took a gulp, attributing my slight paranoia to the fact that the driver might be drunk.

The twins in the back seat looked and acted young. Both of them had hairless faces, and their playful and carefree manner—occasionally punching each other with an elbow and laughing—allowed me to relax a bit. The driver wore a red ball cap and had a thin scraggly beard. He looked about my age or a little older, but he was much bigger than me and on the verge of being fat. Later, when I saw him outside the Bronco, he appeared to be six feet tall and about 200 pounds.

I took a small sip from the bottle and handed it back to the twins. One twin raised the bottle and took a big swig. The driver turned the radio up loud as a female country singer sang a tune I had never heard.

"What's your name," yelled the driver above the radio.

"Bryce," I yelled back.

"I'm Jeff, and this is Jerry. The twins are Judd and Joel."

"Glad to meet you," I said, immediately noticing that all their names began with a 'J.'

"Give that whisky back to Bryce so he can catch up with us," Jeff hollered to the twins.

The twin at my side handed the bottle to me. The front-seat passenger looked at me as I lifted the bottle to my lips. I allowed several bubbles of air to rise through the bottle making it look like I actually drank—rather than sipped—the whisky. At the same time I swallowed saliva to create the illusion of guzzling it. Jerry punched the driver with his elbow.

"Look at that guy back there," he said softly. "He's drinkin' that stuff like it's water."

The driver looked at me in the rearview mirror, so I shut my eyes and let several more air bubbles rise through the liquor. They didn't think I could hear them talking, and to be honest, I'm not sure how I did. As I lowered the bottle, I could see the driver still watching me. Wiping my mouth and looking at the twins, I gave out an intentional cough and said, "Man, that stuff burns right down to your stomach." They laughed. "You know, either I'm seeing double, or there are two of you."

The twins roared as I took another drink. Jeff and Jerry were watching me. Once more, I let the air bubbles rise, swallowing saliva again to make my drinking appear realistic.

"He's gonna be smashed fast if he keeps drinkin' like that," Jerry whispered. "Maybe the city boy would like to squeal like a pig."

Lowering the bottle and wiping my mouth, I looked at the twins and laughed despite suddenly feeling nauseous. From my peripheral vision, I could see the driver still looking at me through the rearview mirror. Having seen the movie *Deliverance*, I knew they were talking about rape. Although I kept my eyes on the twins, my ears were focused toward the front seat. I handed the bottle to the twin next to me. He gave an elbow jab to the other twin, and they both giggled like a couple of junior high kids.

"Hey," Jerry said to me as he turned down the radio, "how would you like to rob a liquor store?"

"Oh sure, anytime." Then I laughed as the twins joined in with me.

"I mean it," he said. "We just robbed one about fifteen miles back. See?"

He held up a bunch of bills. From where I sat it looked like all one-dollar bills, but I couldn't be sure. There must have been 25 to 30 bills in his hand. A part of me wondered if they had really robbed a store because they seemed so indifferent about it.

"I don't know," I said casually. "I usually hold up banks and armored cars. I've never hit a liquor store before. Don't think I know how."

"We'll show you how," he said, and they all laughed.

It was Saturday, and I assumed they were making a liquor run with money people had pooled together. We all leaned to our left as we rounded a curve that went up a hill through the thick Ozark Mountain forest. Near the top of the hill, the driver pulled the steering wheel sharply to the left and the Bronco fishtailed into a liquor store's gravel parking area. We came to a sudden halt in front of the store as a large cloud of white dust floated over us. Jeff and Jerry got out. Jeff stood by the door as Jerry went inside. I wondered if they really intended to rob the store.

"Are you guys going on toward Springfield?" I asked the twins.

"Naw," one twin said as the other twin shook his head back and forth. "We're goin' back the way we came."

"Then I'll get out here," I said, and climbed out the back window.

One twin lifted my backpack to an upright position and shoved it to me as I pulled it through the tailgate window. The other twin pushed the guitar through the window, balancing it on the upright tailgate.

"I appreciate the ride."

I slipped on my pack before grabbing the guitar. I walked to the liquor store's porch steps to thank the driver for the ride. He stood watching his friend inside and hadn't noticed me getting out of the Bronco.

"Hey," I said, startling him as I walked up two porch steps. "I want to thank you for the ride."

"What the hell are you doin'?" he asked in a demanding voice.

"The twins told me you guys are heading back toward the dam, and I'm on my way to Springfield," I held out my hand to shake. "I want to thank you for the ride."

"Get back in that truck," he commanded. "We ain't done with you yet."

"But I'm heading the other way," I said, still smiling and holding out my hand.

He cocked his arm back and curled his hand into a fist. I stepped away from him as his fist rocketed toward my face. Turning my head quickly, I avoided the full brunt of the blow, but I still took a strong glancing punch to the side of my head that pushed my wire-rimmed glasses into my nose and face. Spinning with the force of his punch, I hopped down the porch steps and stumbled several feet before regaining my balance. I turned to see if he was coming after me, but he remained on the edge of the porch.

"Get back in that fuckin' truck!" he screamed.

"Hey, I'm going the other way," I said, looking at him while backpedaling toward the road, "and you just hit me in the face!"

"That ain't nothing as to what I'm gonna do to you if you don't get back in that fuckin' truck!" he yelled.

My breathing quickened with shallow breaths. I shook my head side-to-side and looked at the truck. The twins had bewildered expressions on their faces. I turned and walked as quickly as I could up the road away from the store and the dam.

"Did you hear me?" he screamed from the porch. I turned slightly and looked at him, quickening my pace. "I said get back in that fuckin' truck now! Do it! Right now, or I'm going to come out there and kick the shit out of your fuckin' ass!"

Raising my right hand and shrugging my shoulders, I yelled, "I'm going the other way."

"Don't raise your fuckin' hand to me," he shouted. "Just get your goddamn butt back in that truck!"

I turned and walked swiftly, almost galloping. My heavy leather hiking boots made it tough to walk fast.

"Hey," he shrieked again. "I'm talking to you, you fuckin' asshole! Turn your butt around!"

I turned toward him, but kept backpedaling away from the store. I held up my opened hand again and shook my head back and forth.

"Put your goddamn hand down and get your ass back here," he screamed at the top of his lungs. "You're pissing me off you mother fucker!"

I turned back around and moved as fast as I could. After walking about 75 yards, I heard the Bronco engine start. Crossing the road, I walked down a steep rocky embankment that would have been tough for any vehicle to go down, even a four-wheel drive Jeep. Hearing tires spitting gravel from the parking lot caused me to turn around and see a cloud of dust behind the Bronco speeding toward me. I quickly put my guitar on the ground, and then took off my pack and set it in front of me. Unzipping the top of my pack, I slid my hand inside and felt the leather sheath covering the head of my camping hatchet. The Bronco engine shifted into second gear. Popping the snap loose, I slid the sheath off the blade, and then covered the blade head so it appeared my hands were resting on my pack. The hatchet could be in my hand within a second. The Bronco engine went into third gear.

I made up my mind that if Jeff came down the incline and crossed the ditch to get me, I would pull out the hatchet at the last second and bury it deep into his skull. Adrenaline pulsated through me. I looked at the thick brush and trees behind me. How fast and far could I run through the woods wearing my heavy hiking boots? And, what about my gear? For some reason, I had to stand up to this asshole who punched me. For all I knew, the jerk might pull out a gun and shoot me from the road.

The Bronco downshifted into second gear to slow down, making the engine sound like a huge hissing mountain lion. Jeff now sat in the passenger's seat with Jerry driving. The Bronco stopped on the road some 20 yards from me. Because I had crossed the road, the driver was closest to me.

"Look," Jerry said through the window, "we picked up some liquor for a party we're having a few miles back. Would you like to join us?"

Jeff just glared at me with tightly pursed lips and squinted eyes. I kept my attention on the driver.

"Thanks for the offer, but my brother's expecting me in Springfield this afternoon." I wanted them to know I would be missed if not in Springfield within the next few hours.

"Are you sure you don't want to go?" he asked in a calm and pleasant voice. He sounded as if he were asking a friend instead of an acquaintance. "It's going to be a good party."

"I really have to get to Springfield."

"Suit yourself," he said, not sounding upset.

He pulled a U-turn in the middle of the road. Jeff, whose arm and elbow hung out the window, glared at me. Although he said nothing, he flipped me the bird as they drove off. The Bronco went past the liquor store and disappeared around the bend before I crossed the ditch and climbed the embankment.

Once on the highway, I walked rapidly up the road, occasionally glancing back toward the liquor store fearing the Bronco's return. The sound of a vehicle caused me to whirl around quickly. My heart raced. An old gray pickup truck rounded the curve and headed toward me.

"Please get me out of here," I said aloud, holding my thumb up high.

A young kid and his girlfriend were in the truck. The kid looked no older than 16. The truck moved slowly because of the incline. The kid pushed in the clutch and the truck came to a stop beside me.

"Thanks for stopping," I said, tossing my things in the back of the pickup and climbing in after them.

"There's room up here," the kid yelled from the cab. The girl moved over next to her boyfriend. My heart still pounded. "Too damn hot to be walking up this hill," the kid added as I scooted in and shut the door.

"I hear ya," I said, smiling and looking through the back window at the road behind us.

A strange revelation happened at that moment. I realized that my facial expressions presented a smiling and happy-go-lucky character, but my heart beat uncontrollably and fear pulsed through my veins. This kid and his girlfriend had no idea what I had just been through and how it had affected me. For all I knew, the kid, or his girlfriend, might be the brother or sister of the guy in the Bronco—the guy whose skull would have been split open by my hatchet had he walked that 20 yards across the ditch. I glanced back again. No sign of the Bronco.

I relaxed into the seat and closed my eyes. They were headed for Springfield. I'd be at my brother's house in an hour or two. It's amazing how fast circumstances can change.

I thought back to the time when my brother and I discussed whether or not we were capable of killing another person. My brother had no qualms about killing to protect his family and home. I, on the other hand, adamantly professed I could never kill anyone for any reason. Since then, far too much had happened to me while on the road to stick with that belief.

I'm certainly no killer, but freedom and survival are powerful, if not innate, motivators to remain alive.

Morocco's Rif Mountains

I glanced at Trevor and saw fear in his eyes. He stared at the Moroccans and then looked back at me. "We've got to do something," he said in a burst of panic. His tightly coiled body appeared ready to flee.

The five Moroccans behind us sounded like they were arguing amongst themselves. Two of the men had machetes, three others had knives. I felt just as scared as Trevor, but knew we would be cut down swiftly if we tried darting out of the hut into the night. I had been outside once to urinate. The moonless night created zero visibility. The only light available came from the glittering and exceedingly brilliant stars glowing above Morocco's Rif Mountains.

"Trevor," I said. He looked at me for a second, and then peered back at the Moroccans as if expecting them to pounce upon us at any moment. Besides being out-numbered, we had no weapons. For us to escape alive, it meant using our brains. "Trevor, look at me," I said in a suppressed but urgent voice.

When Trevor shifted his eyes back to me, I moved to my right to block his view of the Moroccans. I gazed directly into his eyes.

"There's only one way we're going to make it out of here." The statement got his attention. "I've been in similar situations before," I lied. Although I had confronted other drug dealers and had been in volatile settings, I had never been in a position where the drug dealers spoke little or no English. "We've both got to relax and mellow out," I said quickly. "Act as if you don't care about a thing, as if nothing really matters. It's our only chance to get out of here. It's pitch black outside, and besides, those dogs would tear us up. These guys know that. Do you understand what I'm saying?"

Trevor stared at me as if hypnotized. Between fear, paranoia and smoking hashish, we were both on the edge of losing it. Strangely enough, my voice sounded confident and calm, a direct contradiction to my feelings. Hearing my voice even made me calmer. Images of knives and machetes swinging, chopping and stabbing ran through my mind. It reaffirmed the unlikely chance of escaping alive. As for the drug dealers, it would be easy for them to dispose of our remains. Once dead, or near death, our bodies could be hacked to pieces and scattered over the mountain side for rats and wild animals to eat. Trevor took a deep breath and exhaled, his shoulders relaxing.

"Trevor?"

"Yes, I hear you," he said.

Trevor and I met two months earlier in Seville, Spain, where I had moved to learn Spanish and experience a foreign culture. After arriving in Spain, I realized that three months of self-taught Spanish through library books put my language skills at about a three-year-old's level, so I enrolled in a language school. The director of the school sent me to a Spanish family willing to take on a boarder. It turned out to be a great deal. The $7.25-a-day charge included three meals, laundry washed weekly, and a room with an adjacent bathroom and shower. After staying in pensions and huespedes ranging from $2.50 to $8 a day with no amenities, I was thrilled with the new arrangement.

The older couple who owned the flat spoke no English. They had a son serving in the military and a daughter who recently married and left home. I had been living with them for nearly a month when Trevor moved in as my roommate. A college junior visiting Seville for a semester to study Spanish, Trevor had enrolled in the same school I attended, and since he was an American, the director of the school recommended the same household to him. There were three single beds in the room. Since I claimed the bed closest to the window, Trevor took the one beside the wall, which left an empty bed as a boundary between us.

Trevor stood a couple of inches taller than me with sandy brown hair combed back over the top of his head. He looked strong and muscular, and from what I could gather, he had been a football star in high school. Although shy and modest, Trevor came across self-confident and friendly once you got to know him. I liked Trevor, and I enjoyed having someone to talk to in English. My Spanish conversations were limited to basic things like the weather, the location of Kansas City in the U.S., how long I planned to stay, what my family did for a living and other general topics. I reveled in our philosophical and metaphysical discussions, as well as exchanging comments about the beautiful señoritas we either met or saw around Seville.

During the next month and a half, Trevor and I became close friends. We walked through the streets of Seville exploring neighborhoods off the beaten track, stopping in small cafes or bars to drink a beer, or, as I was often inclined to do, order a cup of hot chocolate and spike it with a shot of cognac. In 1983, Spain served as an alcohol lover's paradise. A cervesa (beer) cost the same as a shot of cognac—a whopping 30 pesetas or approximately 25 cents.

One afternoon after class, Trevor and I sauntered into a small cantina and plopped down at the bar for a beer. We were discussing the pretty girls in our classes, and which ones we'd like to ask out, when two Americans entered. Both men looked liked typical tourists. One carried a black leather camera bag; the other held a folded-up tourist map of Seville. Each wore a new Spanish shirt, a pair of pleated American slacks, and shoes that resembled golfing shoes. The men appeared to be 45 to 50 years old.

The one carrying the map was average height with light brown hair and a deep receding hairline. He wore a pair of sporty gold-trimmed sunglasses that matched his gold watch band. He looked in fairly descent shape for his age. The other one had thick black hair speckled with gray, stood several inches taller than the first guy, and had a beer gut. Without his protruding belly, he would have looked in good shape. A more traditional dark-gray plastic frame surrounded his lightly tinted sunglasses. The two men sat at a table in the back of the bar next to two Spanish women drinking espresso. After the men had been seated for a few seconds, the sandy-brown haired American set his sunglasses on the table and got up. He walked to the bar and stood eight or 10 feet from us facing the bartender.

"Señor," he said, "how much is it for two cognacs?" When he said two, he held up two fingers.

"Ah, si," the bartender said, putting two shot glasses on the bar and picking up a bottle of cognac.

"No," the man said, "I want to know how much money for two cognacs?" He spoke slower as if that would make a difference.

"Si," the bartender replied, "dos cognacs." He lifted the bottle to fill the shot glasses.

"No," the man screamed, "I...want...to...know," he yelled, pausing after each word, "how...much...does...it...cost...for...two...cognacs?"

The confused bartender understood the word cognac and two fingers. Had the man rubbed his thumb and two fingers together, the bartender would have comprehended instantly.

"Señor," Trevor spoke up, "quanto dinero para dos cognacs?"

"Ahhhh," the bartender replied. He picked up a piece of chalk and wrote the price on the bar.

The man looked at the figure as if the numbers were a foreign language.

"That's sixty pesetas," Trevor said to the man. "It's about fifty cents."

"For both of them?" the man asked Trevor.

"Yes."

"Damn, that's cheap," he said, looking back at the bartender. "We'll take four cognacs." He now held up four fingers.

The bartender looked at Trevor, probably afraid of being shouted at if he tried to fill the shot glasses.

"Quiere quatro cognacs," Trevor said to the bartender.

"Bueno," the bartender replied, putting two more glasses on the bar and filling them.

The man pulled out a handful of peseta notes from his pocket.

"You pay when you're ready to leave," Trevor said.

"Really?"

Trevor nodded.

The man stuffed the money back in his pocket. I thought maybe the extra cognacs were for Trevor and me, but the man picked up two in each hand and returned to his table without even thanking Trevor. He set two cognacs on their table and then set a cognac in front of each woman at the table beside them.

"That's for you ladies," he said. "Enjoy it."

Trevor and I put our money on the bar and got up. As we were walking out the door, we heard the American that bought the drinks ask, "Are you ladies from around here?"

"Now I know where the term 'ugly American' comes from," Trevor said, once we were outside.

Our decision to go to North Africa came one Tuesday afternoon while eating lunch at our temporary home. The señora had television on when the station aired a 15-minute news special about Morocco. One Moroccan man sat in a town square charming cobras, while another man had scorpions and tarantulas walking on his face.

Trevor bit off a piece of his crusty roll. "I'd like to go down there sometime."

"Me too," I said. "Why don't we go?"

Trevor looked at me as he took a bite of fish and chewed for a second or two. "When?"

"Why not Friday? We're off next Monday and Tuesday, and if we skip classes Friday, that would give us five days down there."

Our school had a break similar to spring break in the United States, but shorter.

Trevor looked at me, still chewing, and smiled as he nodded his head and swallowed. "Okay, let's do it."

"Hablas en Español," the señora said, wondering what we were discussing. Neither she nor her husband liked it when we spoke English. I told her we had decided to go to Morocco for five days and that we'd be leaving Friday morning.

She looked at Trevor. "Si?"

Trevor nodded his head. "Si."

When we told other students and our teachers about our plans, they told us to be careful in Morocco. "It can be dangerous for Americans," Angela, a

Spanish classmate who liked Trevor, told us. "Watch out for thieves. They look for Americans."

Friday morning the señora had two large sack lunches ready for us. She put enough food in each bag for two meals. We caught the early train to Cadiz, and then rode a bus to Algeciras where we found a cheap hotel for the night. Late the next morning we boarded a ferry crossing the Strait of Gibraltar to the continent of Africa. Trevor took several pictures of the Rock of Gibraltar.

"When the British want to say something is far away," Trevor said, "they say, 'It's as far as from here to the Rock of Gibraltar.'"

The way Trevor imitated the British accent cracked me up. He began using the expression a lot, and every time it made me laugh.

The ferry ride to Ceuta, a Spanish city on the northern border of Africa governed by Spain's province of Cadiz, takes about three hours. After an hour out into the channel, Trevor and I went to the bar for an early afternoon beer. A couple of beers later, I headed to the restroom. As I washed my hands, a tall husky Arab wearing a three-piece gray pinstriped suit entered. He stood at least six-foot-two and appeared to be around 35 to 40 years old. He had black curly hair that covered the top of his ears and wore several gold rings on his fingers. He looked at me with his large dark eyes for several seconds, but said nothing. I shook my hands dry in the sink and wiped them on my jeans. Glancing in the mirror, I could see him still watching me as he stood in front of the urinal. I turned and walked out the door feeling a little uncomfortable.

Once we arrived in Ceuta, we passed through customs and walked out of the terminal onto the street. We had been told that prices in Ceuta and Morocco were a bargain, especially when shopping for electronic goods such as Walkman radios. Across the street from the terminal, a line of store windows exhibited all kinds of items ranging from electronic equipment like boom boxes and portable TVs to more personal possessions such as switchblades and machetes.

"Come on, let's check this stuff out," I said to Trevor. I hustled across the street to beat an approaching car. Trevor ran a few steps to catch up with me. We hadn't been there long when a man spoke from behind us.

"Hello."

I turned to see the tall Arab who had been in the restroom on the ferry.

"Remember me?" he said, with a heavy Arabic accent. "You see me on ship, yes?"

"Yes, I remember."

"What you do in Ceuta? You go to Morocco?"

"Yes, we thought we'd spend a few days traveling in Morocco."

"Where you go in Morocco?"

"We haven't really decided yet, but we'd like to see the real Morocco, not just the tourist areas."

"Go to Tetuan. No many tourists in Tetuan. Real Morocco. Come. I take you to Tetuan. My car here."

He turned and pointed to a small white car parked in front of the first store window where we had stopped. He took a few steps toward the car. I looked at Trevor. Something about the man made me uneasy. It might have been his three-piece suit, his size, his broken English, or all those put together. Whatever it was, I didn't trust him. Neither of us moved toward his car.

"What the matter? You no want see Tetuan?"

"I'm sure it's a great place," I said, "but we just got here. We thought we'd look around here for a while. We can catch a bus to Tetuan later."

"No take bus. Car faster." He pointed to the items in the store window. "Cheaper in Tetuan. Trust me. I help you. My name Abdul." He held out his hand in front of me and we shook. He then shook Trevor's hand. "You American, yes?"

"Yes," I said.

"First time to Africa?"

"Yes."

"You like Africa. Africa big, beautiful. Many things here. I help you see Morocco. Me tour guide. I show you license."

The huge Arab pulled out his wallet and began shuffling through some plastic cards.

"See?"

He showed us a card with his picture on it. It contained Arabic writing as well as "Turismo de Morocco," which is Spanish for tourism of Morocco. He pulled out a piece of paper from his wallet and opened it. There were five or six names and addresses listed on the paper, including a California and Ohio address.

"Me take Americans many places in Morocco. They have good time. See real Morocco. Come now. I take you to Tetuan." He turned again toward his car.

"Excuse me," I said. "We're students studying in Spain and we don't have much money. How much do you want to take us to Tetuan?"

He turned around. "You students?"

"Yes."

"What you study?"

"We're studying Spanish."

"My brother student too. I help you. No money. I must go to Tetuan. You can go. No problem for me. No cost money."

Something felt wrong, but if the guy planned to go to Tetuan anyway, it would make it easier for us. I looked at Trevor.

"What do you think? Should we go to Tetuan now?"

"Well, if he's going..." Trevor said when Abdul interrupted him.

"Yes, yes, come. No problem. Me go now. Come."

252

Abdul took a hold of my daypack and more or less pulled me in the direction of his car. Trevor and I both had daypacks over our shoulders. We came to Africa with only bare necessities since we planned to return to Spain in a few days. Abdul held on to my pack until we were all walking down the sidewalk toward his car. "You like Tetuan," he said. "No many tourists. Real Morocco."

Abdul walked quickly like an excited overgrown schoolboy. He opened the front passenger door for me and the back door for Trevor. He drove a small white compact foreign car. I don't recall the type of car, but the seats were nearly worn through to the stuffing, and the exterior white paint had lost its luster. He backed out quickly onto the street and threw the gear shift forward before speaking again.

"Before go to Tetuan, I pick up friend. He go to Tetuan too. Only take minute."

Abdul made a U-turn and we headed back toward the docks. He parked in a loading zone and briskly walked into the ship terminal.

I turned and looked at Trevor. "You think this guy's legitimate?"

"I don't know, but I'm not going to give him any money for the ride. He said he was going there anyway."

"Yeah, well, it will be faster than figuring out which bus to take."

Within five minutes, Abdul returned to the car with a small thin man wearing gray slacks and a long-sleeved white shirt with the cuffs rolled up past his elbows. He had short black wavy hair and a thin mustache. When he smiled, you could see he had several back teeth missing on the right side of his mouth. I got out of the car to let Abdul's friend sit in the front seat.

"This my friend, Amid."

"Glad to meet you." I reached out and we shook hands. "I'll sit in back."

As we climbed in the car, Abdul introduced Amid to Trevor.

"Now go to Tetuan," Abdul said, looking at us in the rearview mirror. Abdul spoke to Amid in Arabic as he drove away from the ship terminal. "Amid no speak English," Abdul added. As we turned left onto a street, Abdul looked in the mirror again. "Make one stop before go to Tetuan. No take long. House close."

I looked at Trevor. Abdul watched us in his mirror for a reaction.

"Amid need things from house," Abdul remarked. "No take long."

Once again, Abdul and Amid spoke in Arabic. After a few minutes, Abdul looked at us again in the rearview mirror.

"You speak Arabic?"

"No," I said, "only English, Spanish and French."

"Three language good. You speak Arabic?" He looked at Trevor.

"No, just English and Spanish."

"I speak Arabic, Spanish, French, and little English."

"Your English is good," I said.

"No, no good. I must know little English for business. I better in Spanish and French. Many Spanish and French visit Morocco."

"Can Amid speak Spanish?" Trevor asked. "We can all speak Spanish if you want."

Amid looked at Abdul when he heard his name.

"He speak Spanish," Abdul said, "but better if we speak English. I need practice English." Abdul said something to Amid in Arabic, and then looked at me in the mirror. "You want learn Arabic? I teach you Arabic."

"Sure," I said.

"To say hello, 'salam alekum.' Now you say."

Trevor and I repeated what he said.

"Salam alekum," Abdul repeated. "Say again."

We repeated it.

"Good," Abdul said, laughing with Amid.

"To say 'how are you,' 'la bess.' Now you say."

He taught us several more words before we parked in front of a small one-story white house. An old rusty car with two flat tires sat beside the curb. The neighborhood had dirt lawns and small white cracker-box houses in need of paint. A four or five-year-old girl wearing a soiled blue dress and old red tennis shoes sat on top of a weathered tricycle. Where there should have been bike pedals, two short rods protruded. She sat watching us as Abdul stopped the car and turned off the engine.

"You wait in car," Abdul said. "We come back, go to Tetuan."

Abdul and Amid got out of the car and walked toward the small house. The little girl spun her tricycle around and rode quickly across the dirt yard toward the back of the house. Trevor and I had eaten nothing since breakfast at the hotel. I took out a bag of roasted almonds from my daypack and pushed the opened sack toward Trevor. He took a handful.

"I guess we're getting to see a part of Ceuta that most tourists never see," Trevor said and tossed several almonds into his mouth.

I took a few almonds in my hand and popped one into my mouth. "You got that right." It took about 10 minutes before Abdul and Amid returned. Abdul carried a paper sack smaller than a grocery bag, but bigger than a lunch sack. He put it in the trunk.

"Now go," Abdul said while starting the car. "Make one more stop before Tetuan. No problem. House on way." He didn't bother looking at us in the rearview mirror. He turned to Amid and spoke Arabic.

Trevor looked at me and raised his eyebrows while shrugging his shoulders—my sentiments exactly.

This time we stopped in front of another run-down house. There were no glass windows on the house—just wooden shutters where the windows should have been. Plastic bags, beer bottles and candy wrappers lined the streets and were scattered across the dirt yards. Down the road from where we parked huddled a small group of kids. Two leaned against the fender of an old rusty car while three others stood in front of them. They were all smoking, and we could smell the unmistakable strong hashish odor. The fad in Seville was to roll a tobacco cigarette with hashish sprinkled over it. Obviously, it was the "in thing to do" in Ceuta too, but they were not passing several cigarettes among themselves. Instead, they each had their own rolled cigarette. I guessed they were 17 or 18. All of them had dark, medium-length hair except for one kid whose hair hung down to his shoulders. None of them had a beard or mustache. They wore blue jeans and various colored t-shirts with tennis shoes. Two of them had dark brown skin, while the others had a fair complexion equivalent to Trevor's and mine. They would talk among themselves for a few seconds, and then look in our direction.

"They're talking about us," Trevor said.

I glanced through the rear window to see if there were any kids behind us. A couple of small children played in a yard. After what seemed a long time, the teenagers started walking up the street toward us. Trevor discreetly rolled up his window leaving just a crack at the top. I thought about the commercial district and window displays we saw near the boat docks. Every storefront had a large selection of knives, switchblades and stilettos. The kids, who were now 25 feet from the car, broke into two groups. Three of them headed to my side of the car while the other two walked toward Trevor's side.

I glanced at the house and saw Abdul and Amid come through the doorway onto the front porch. Abdul carried another paper sack. "Here comes Abdul," I said, as the teens were nearly to our doors.

Abdul yelled something to them and the three heading toward me stopped and looked at him. The other two walked up to Trevor's window. Abdul increased his pace toward the car, but did not run.

"Americanos?" one kid asked Trevor through the one-inch crack at the top of the window.

"Si," Trevor replied.

"De donde en Estados Unidos?"

As Abdul reached the rear of the car, he spoke to the two young men in Spanish while opening the trunk and slipping the paper bag inside. He told them to get away from the car, adding that we were his customers and he our tour guide. Abdul was twice the size of the adolescents. Amid climbed in the front seat as Abdul slammed the trunk shut and walked to the driver's door. One boy told Abdul they just wanted to meet the Americans and say hello. Abdul opened his door.

"We are in a hurry," he said in Spanish. "We don't have time to talk. Adios."

He started the car, and we drove down the street. I looked back at the teenagers. The kid Abdul had been talking to yelled something and shook his fist.

"Must be careful," Abdul said. "Barrio malo," which means "bad neighborhood." "Now go Tetuan. Tetuan close. Twenty minutes. Bus take much longer."

As we drove to the Moroccan border, Amid kept turning and twisting in his seat while continually looking out the windows as if looking for someone. On occasion he would blurt out a rapid flow of syllables to Abdul, who in return would respond in a calm and relaxed manner. Something seemed wrong.

"What do you have in the paper sacks?" I asked Abdul.

"Bananas," he replied without hesitation, looking at me through the rearview mirror. After turning onto a major street, he spoke again. "Bananas hard to get in Morocco. Cost much money."

Within minutes we arrived at the border where six long lines of cars waited to cross into Morocco, and two lines of cars waited to enter Ceuta. No-man's land, or the area between the two border stations, appeared chaotic. There were donkey-drawn carts filled with bags of flour, wheat, and other kinds of grains and oats; hand-pulled carts carrying hats, pottery, woven baskets and rugs; and even a small group of goats with bells attached to their necks and a rope strung between them to keep them together. The men and women who tended the carts and animals wore long hooded robes, and all the women had veils covering their faces. It looked like two civilizations crashing together: the western world with business men in suits driving their cars, and the ancient Middle Eastern peasants with their animals and goods ready for market. It became apparent we would be waiting for a while before crossing the border. Abdul stopped his car in one of the lines and turned to us.

"Give me passports." He held out his hand. "I get stamped now. No wait so long."

Trevor and I looked at each other. At that point neither Trevor nor I had been outside of Spain. Neither of us knew if we should give him our passports or not. Without a passport, you're stranded in a foreign country until you get help from the American consulate. I looked at Abdul.

"What do you need the passports for?"

"To go Morocco, must stamp passport. More faster. I do now. Give me passport." I looked at Trevor. "No problem," Abdul said, becoming impatient. "I give back. It take five minute to get stamp. Give me passport now."

We took out our passports and handed them to Abdul. I felt stripped of my identity and vulnerable without it. Abdul got out of the car, but before walking to the border station to get our passports stamped, he opened the trunk and took both paper sacks with him. It couldn't have been much more than five minutes before he returned to the car, our passports in his hand and no sacks.

"See? No problem. We go now. Keep passport to show officer."

Abdul started the car, and we moved several car lengths forward to fill in the space created by Abdul's jaunt to the border station. After about 20 minutes, we were the next car in line to be checked by the border patrol. Just before the car ahead of us moved on through the border, Abdul turned around and slipped his hand into his upper left suit-coat pocket, pulling out a large group of bills held together by several rubber bands. He reached over the seat and slipped it into Trevor's daypack.

"You keep to cross border. No problem for American to have much money. Ask many questions if Moroccan have much money."

As Abdul turned back around, the car in front of us moved forward. Abdul put his car in gear, and we edged toward the custom officials. I looked at Trevor. He didn't know what to do. My palms turned sweaty. It became obvious that Abdul had a bigger agenda than being a tour guide. I could see a 10,000 Spanish peseta note on top of the stack. Ten thousand pesetas equaled about $70. The stack looked more than an inch thick. There could have been higher bills within the stack, but if they were all 10,000 peseta notes, Trevor had thousands of dollars in Spanish bills inside his pack. If they saw the money and asked Trevor how much he had, he wouldn't know. That would probably lead to a closer investigation by border officials. Trevor reached in his bag and put his hand on the stack. At first, I thought he might give it back to Abdul. Abdul had purposely waited until the last minute. Trevor pushed the bundle of bills to the bottom of his daypack and zipped it shut.

A border official spoke to Abdul. Although Abdul spoke back in Arabic, it became apparent he told the officer we were his American tourists and he planned to take us to Tetuan. The guard said a few words and Abdul turned to us.

"We get out. Must show stamp on passport."

Trevor shot me a worried look. Once we were out of the car, one guard examined our passports while the other guard climbed in the car and looked under the seat. He then checked beneath the dash, and even pulled the back seat forward and looked beneath it. After the guard examined our passports, he had Abdul open the trunk lid. The guard looked in the trunk for several seconds, and then shut the lid and said something to Abdul. Abdul gave a short reply and turned toward us.

"We go now."

We climbed in the car and passed through the border area; then pulled over and stopped amidst the Arab men and women in their robes standing next to their carts and animals. Abdul got out of the car and went back to the guard station. Two men in long dark robes near our car talked in loud voices even though they stood inches apart. It seemed like they were arguing, and I expected one of them to punch the other in the nose at any moment. Amid kept turning around and looking back at the border station. His nervous and worried look, in addition to the arguing men, made me even more anxious. Trevor's face appeared pasty and pale.

Abdul returned to the car within a minute carrying another paper sack. He put the sack in the trunk. As we drove away, Abdul kept his eyes focused on the rearview mirror. Amid turned around and looked. Abdul said something that made Amid face forward and sit motionless with his hands in his lap. When we finally rounded a curve and the border station had gone out of sight, Abdul smiled and spoke Arabic as he held out his hand to Amid. Amid slapped Abdul's hand and chattered while he laughed and bounced up and down in his seat. They were both ecstatic. Amid punched Abdul's arm and then slapped his own leg. He quickly turned around and said something to Trevor.

"He want money," Abdul translated as he looked in the rearview mirror.

Trevor unzipped his bag and handed Amid the money. Amid examined it as if he thought Trevor might have tried to take some. Satisfied it had not been tampered with, he smiled again and said something to Abdul, who then laughed. About 75 yards in front of us, a young man slowly walked across the road. Abdul said something to Amid, then he pushed on the accelerator. The man on the highway looked at us. He kept walking at the same pace. He still had time to make it across the road without rushing. Abdul swerved onto the shoulder heading straight for the man. The man hustled into the ditch and shook his fist at us. Abdul and Amid roared with laughter. I glanced at Trevor, wondering what our tour guides might do next in their jubilance. Trevor shook his head once, raised his eyebrows and shrugged his shoulders.

Abdul took us to Tetuan's town market and square. The crowded square held men and women wearing long robes. Hundreds of street stands were set up to sell teas, nuts, fruits, breads, vegetables, pottery, baskets, poultry, fish, meat, and about anything you might want or need. I was amazed at the huge sides of beef and pork hanging in the open air covered with flies. There were also live animals for sale, such as goats, chickens and sheep. The car rocked back and forth as we crept over the cobble-stoned street, bullying our way through the crowd as people begrudgingly moved to one side.

Abdul stopped in front of a two-story hotel a block off the square. We followed him into the hotel lobby where he spoke to the manager and checked us in. "You pay now," he said. "No much money. You go to room. I return soon, show you Tetuan."

A young girl guided us up the stairs to our second floor accommodation. Once in the room, we understood why it cost only $1.25 a piece. The small space, with its tiled floor, contained a wooden table with two rickety chairs, a roll of toilet paper, two twin beds that sunk nearly to the floor when you sat on them, and an old stained sink in the corner. The young girl, who spoke French, took us down the hall to the bathroom. The bathroom, which smelled like an outhouse, contained a six-inch diameter hole in the floor for both urine and feces. Painted shoe prints in front of the hole indicated where you were supposed to stand before squatting to take care of business. I saw no toilet paper, making a note to bring some with me.

We had been in our room maybe 15 minutes when someone knocked on the door. Trevor, sitting closest to the door, stood up and opened it.

"Me Ocman," said the man dressed in a long robe as he gave a slight bow from his waist. "Abdul busy. He send me to show you Tetuan. We go now?"

Ocman was a short, thin man probably 35 years old. He had cropped black hair and dark eyes. With decaying areas between all of his front teeth, his breath reeked so much it made me turn my head and cough. He said he studied English at a school in Tetuan, and since we were students too, he wanted us to visit his school. The school turned out to be a store where the owner and two salesmen pounced on us like tom cats on a mouse. The owner first had us sit on a couch and drink Moroccan tea, which is mint tea that tastes like mint-flavored syrup. There must have been at least four or five teaspoons of sugar in each cup. The owner clapped his hands and said something in Arabic, causing two salesmen to scurry around picking up clothes, jewelry, pottery, hand-woven baskets or woodcarvings. They presented them to us from various angles, much like a model turning to show all sides of a dress. The owner would explain where the object came from and how many hours a Moroccan had worked to make it. I finally told the owner that we were students and couldn't afford to buy anything.

He looked at Ocman and spoke Arabic. I assume the owner wanted to know why Ocman had brought us to him. It sounded like the owner was chewing out our guide. I heard Ocman mention Abdul's name, which caused a considerable change in the owner's manner. He looked at us and smiled.

"I understand," he said. "Students have little money, so me make you good deal. Student discount just for you." He clapped his hands and shouted a command. The two salesmen carried in a colorful and thick nine-by-twelve hand-woven Moroccan rug. It was beautiful. "This rug seven hundred dollar, but for you, friend of Abdul, only four hundred dollar."

Neither of us said anything. I started to tell him we weren't interested when he spoke again. "No, I make it three hundred fifty dollar for you. Very good price, yes?"

"Yes, that's a good price for such a fine rug." I reached over and combed the top of the rug with my hand. "In the United States this rug would be very expensive."

"Yes," he said, "much money in United States, but cheap if buy in Morocco."

"That's true," I continued, "but Trevor and I don't have $350. We're in school and just came to visit Morocco for a few days during school break."

"How much you pay for rug?" he asked, folding his arms across his chest.

A lump grew in my throat. "I'm sorry, but neither of us have enough money to buy it."

"Make me offer," he pressured. "What you pay for rug?"

"Look, I don't have the money. Any offer I could afford would be ridiculous. You would laugh."

"Make me laugh," he said without hesitation. "What you pay for rug? Make me laugh."

I looked at the rug, wondering what ludicrous offer to make so we could get out of there. "I can't buy it because..."

"Make me laugh," he interrupted. "How much you pay for rug?"

I looked at Trevor. "Well, I could only pay fifty dollars for it."

"Fifty dollar?" he said incredulously.

"See? It's ridiculous." I began feeling relieved. "You can't stay in business selling these beautiful rugs for fifty dollars, can you?"

After a brief moment of silence he said, "Okay, I sell you rug for fifty dollar."

My heart sank. "Uhhhh, look, that's nice of you, but I can't do that. It's not fair to you."

"I like you. I sell you rug for fifty dollar. You tell no one."

"I can't," I said, starting to stand up. He reached over and literally pushed me back into my seat by pressing his hand on my shoulder. His strength surprised me.

"Drink more tea," the merchant said in a demanding voice that now held tones of disgust. "You tell me you pay fifty dollar, now you say no. I no understand. You drink my tea. I give you best deal, same as brother, and you say no? What is problem. Rug not good enough for you?"

He had me. I didn't have the guts to say what I really felt such as, "Look, get the hell out of my face. I don't want your damn rug, and this tea tastes like lousy mint syrup." Instead, I searched for more excuses.

"It's a nice rug, but it's too big to carry around with me. Plus, I'd have to carry it on the plane when I return..."

"We mail rug," he said quickly, realizing the fight had ended and he was reeling me in. "Only ten dollar more. Look, I show you."

He briskly walked to a cabinet and took out a ledger. He opened it in front of me. "Many American buy rug here. I mail rug to them. No problem. Get rug in three weeks."

There were about 15 names in the ledger, most of them from states on the east or west coast. I felt trapped, obligated, and slightly ill. My bladder needed relieving, so I asked to use their restroom. The owner showed me to the bathroom and said, "We get rug ready for you."

At least the merchant had a regular toilet versus a hole in the ground. After urinating, I washed my hands and looked in the mirror. I thought about my cousin who had worked in Iran for two years while in the Peace Corps. She told me that the quickest way to get hurt or killed in an Arab country was to ridicule, degrade or dishonor someone's parents. "Arabs have a reverent respect for their mother and father," she said. The thought gave me an idea. I came back into the room where the two salesmen had the rug rolled and tied with string.

"What must I do to have the rug mailed to the U.S.?" I asked the owner.

"No problem," he said. "Write address here." He held the ledger out toward me.

"I want you to know that I'm not buying this rug for me," I said, taking the ledger and accepting the pen he held in his hand.

"What you mean?"

"I'm buying the rug for my mother and father." His eyes shifted to the salesmen, then to Ocman, and finally back to me. His smile faded.

"You no buy for you?" he asked as if he hadn't heard me correctly, or as if he was trying to decide if I lied.

"No, not for me. For my mother and father." I began writing in the ledger. "I'm putting their name and address in here. I'll write them and tell them to expect it in three weeks. That's how long it takes, right?"

The owner hesitated before speaking. "Maybe little longer. Mail not fast here."

"My parents' anniversary is June 22. Will they get it by then?" That was a full two months away.

He shrugged his shoulders and raised his hands. "I think so. Pay fifteen dollar mail go faster. Fifteen dollar better."

I think I could have backed out of the deal at that point, but the momentum of the experience caused me to accept the $15 mail cost. I handed the owner $65 worth of Spanish pesetas.

"Here," he said, handing me a black magic marker, "You sign rug, yes? You know you get same rug in mail."

I signed my initials on an inside bottom corner of the rug. I shook the owners hand, and we walked to the door. Ocman told us to wait for him outside.

"You'll be lucky to get the rug," Trevor said once we were on the front walkway.

"You're probably right," I said, and then told him about my cousin and the reverence Arabs give their parents.

Ocman joined us shortly and took us to another store. Trevor finally bought a couple of two-by-three-foot rugs for $5 so we could get out of the second store. Once again Ocman asked us to wait outside for him. When he joined us, we thanked him for his assistance and bid him farewell. He stood looking at us, as if he expected some money for his Tetuan tour. Trevor and I turned and walked the other way. We wandered through the narrow streets and watched people bargain with street venders. We saw far too many Arabs in hooded robes giving us what I call "the eye," which is more than a curious stare. It was as if they wanted to rob us, kill us, or both. On almost every corner there seemed to be a two-faced talkative guy who wanted to practice his

English. These characters ranged anywhere from eight or nine years old up to 40.

At about 9:30 p.m., I noticed two Arabs in long hooded robes following us. Sometimes they stood next to us as we looked at market goods; other times they watched us from the adjacent market stand or from the other side of the street. I told Trevor about the two men observing us. We decided to go back to the hotel. Earlier that afternoon, the hotel manager warned us that the streets filled with thieves after dark. He recommended we return before 10 o'clock.

As we entered the hotel, I glanced back and saw the men who had been following us cross the narrow street together and disappear into a shop. Inside the hotel lobby, we saw a young man at the front desk talking to the manager. He wore a green t-shirt, blue jeans and tennis shoes. He looked like an American.

When we passed the desk, I said, "Hey, how's it going?" I held out my hand to shake. He looked at me and smiled as we shook hands. "Where are you from?"

He looked at the manager, who said a few words to him in Arabic, and then looked back at me and smiled.

"Me speak little English," he said with a heavy Arabic accent.

"Oh, I'm sorry," I said, speaking slower. "Are you from Morocco?" He looked at the hotel manager. "De donde eres?" I said in Spanish. "Aqui? En Morocco?"

"Ah, si."

"I thought you were an American," I continued in Spanish. From the look on his face, he apparently took my comment as an insult. He looked at the hotel manager who laughed. They exchanged a few words in Arabic, and then the manager said something and laughed hard.

The young man smiled and looked back at me. "Me called Amad."

Amad stood no taller than five-foot-six-inches. His thick brown hair, stylishly cut, feathered back over three-quarters of his ears. With a clear and light complexion, radiant smile, and relatively clean and straight white teeth, Amad looked like an American or European. He came across as confident, smooth and easy going.

We exchanged the usual formalities about where we were from and how long we were going to be in Morocco. Amad usually began speaking in English, but then switched to Spanish when he failed to find the correct English translation for what he wanted to say. When Trevor or I spoke English slowly, he understood maybe 50 percent of what we said. He urged us to speak in English because he wanted to increase his English vocabulary. When we told Amad we wanted to see parts of Morocco beyond the normal tourist sites, he became excited and talked about his house in the mountains.

"Come to my house. No problema. Close. Only four hours on autobus." Amad said a few words to the manager who nodded his head and then opened a drawer. He took out a map and spread it on the desk in front of us. "House here!" He pointed to the heart of the Rif Mountains in northern Morocco. "Stay long as want. No problema. No worry, muy tranquilo. Mucho comida. You want go?"

I looked at Trevor. It sounded like a great experience to me. Before we said anything to each other, Amad spoke again.

"Go tomorrow. What time you want go?"

"What do you think?" I asked Trevor.

"I don't know. Do you want to go?"

"We don't have to decide now." I looked at Amad. "If we see you tomorrow, and it works out, it's possible we'll go," I said in Spanish.

"Bueno," Amad said. "Me go now. Hasta mañana." Amad said a few words to the hotel manager and then walked out the front door.

As we walked up the steps to our room, I asked Trevor what he thought.

"Sounds like it would be a neat trip," he said as we reached the top of the steps and turned to go down the hallway. "What do you think?"

"I'm for it, but I wasn't sure if you wanted to go." I watched Trevor unlock the door before we went in. "Hitchhiking in the states, I used to take side trips like this. I always had a great time, but you never know what might happen."

"We came down here to see a part of Morocco most tourists don't see," Trevor said. "I doubt if many tourists go into the mountains and stay at some farmhouse."

We both were extremely tired from the day's activities as well as culture shock. Within minutes after climbing in our beds, we were asleep. Because we had gone to bed so early, I awoke in the dark. I tried to go back to sleep, but couldn't. Sitting up in bed, I crossed my legs and put my back against the wall to meditate. I'd just reached a quiet and calm place within myself, when suddenly a man's voice blared over a loud speaker in a half-singing, half-chanting rhythm. Trevor shot straight up in bed.

"What the hell's going on?" he said looking at me, his voice expressing alarm and disgust. He thought the sound came from me.

I laughed. "I don't know, but it sounds pretty weird."

Trevor stared at me for several seconds. "What are you doing?"

"I woke up and couldn't get back to sleep, so I decided to meditate."

"Oh," Trevor said, laying back down on his bed.

We had discussed meditation several times. I usually meditated when Trevor either slept or left our room for school.

"How long is that guy going to scream like that?" Trevor asked.

"I don't know, but it is rather annoying."

"Annoying is not the word," Trevor said, rolling over and wrapping his pillow around his head. "Multiply annoying times obnoxious."

The chanting went on for what seemed like a long time, but probably not more than five or 10 minutes. We both fell back asleep and were awakened by the maid's knock on the door. We asked her about the loud speaker, and she told us the chant led the early morning prayer to Allah (or God) practiced by Muslims five times a day while they face Mecca, their spiritual center. It's a part of the Islam faith.

As we were coming down the steps to the lobby, daypacks hanging from our shoulders, we could see Amad standing at the front desk talking to the desk clerk. He saw us out of the corner of his eye and turned in our direction.

"Ah, bueno, you still here? Me just arrive. Me think you leave." Amad held out his hand and we shook. "Come, we drink tea. Me know good cafe." Amad said a few words to the clerk, who answered him in Arabic. "He say you pay already. We go now."

Amad put his hand on my back and guided me toward the hotel exit. I turned and glanced at the clerk as we were going out the door. He had a strange expression on his face. Although his mouth smiled, he eyes failed to match the smile.

Amad took us to an outdoor cafe that overlooked the town square. He ordered tea and a roll for each of us. When our order arrived, Amad stood up, said something to the waiter, and then looked at Trevor and me. "Me have friend want to go mi casa. Me get him now. Come back ten minute, comprende?"

"That's fine," I said, getting better at understanding his heavily accented and broken English mixed with Spanish.

"You stay, yes?" Amad looked at me, then at Trevor.

"We'll be here," I replied.

Amad walked briskly toward the main street leading out of the town square.

"What do you think?" I asked Trevor.

Trevor's eyebrows raised as he looked up at me while taking a sip of tea. "About what?"

"Do you still want to go?"

"Don't you?" Trevor asked.

"I don't know. After Abdul stopped to pick up his friend yesterday, we ended up being decoys for whatever deal they pulled off. This kind of smells like a repeat."

"We can just tell Amad we decided not to go," Trevor said, "if that's what you want to do."

I looked out across the cobblestone square and saw two women walking toward us wearing long robes, sandals, scarves and veils covering their faces. The square looked dirty. Actually, there wasn't a lot of trash lying around on the ground, but the dark gray stones and dark robes the men wore gave the square a fiendish ambiance amplified by the rancid odor of goat, cow and donkey feces randomly scattered amidst the stones. Something felt wrong, but I liked the idea of going to the mountains.

"Naahh, let's go," I said, as a fly circled around my head. "The mountain air will do us good." I swatted at the fly, sending him swirling away. "Everything will be cool."

Within 15 minutes Amad returned with his friend Fahim. Fahim was short too, maybe an inch taller than Amad. He had curly unkempt black hair that barely touched his shoulders. His smile revealed large gaps between his crooked teeth, and what teeth he had left were yellow with black decaying strips along their sides. Like Amad, he wore blue jeans, tennis shoes and a t-shirt. Unlike Amad, Fahim appeared closer to my expectations of what a native Moroccan should look like: dark hair, coal-black eyes and an olive brown complexion. When we shook hands, I noticed the extremely long and dirt-filled pointed fingernail on Fahim's right pinkie finger. While Amad looked 25 or 26 years old, Fahim could have passed for 20 or younger.

The waiter returned to the table and talked to Amad. I assumed the waiter asked him if we wanted anything else. Amad looked at me.

"You pay now. We take autobus."

I handed the waiter a dirham bill, and he gave me back several bills and some change. I tossed one of the bills on the table for a tip, equivalent to about a 40 cent tip.

"What you do?" Amad asked, pointing to the bill.

"Propina," I said, which is tip in Spanish.

"Too much." Amad picked up the bill and put it back in my hand. He took my other hand that held the change, picked out two coins, and laid them on the table.

"Bastante," he said, which means "enough" in Spanish.

As we left, the waiter walked by us and glared at Amad. Once we got to the station, about six or seven blocks from the café, Amad immediately went to the bus ticket window. He appeared to be arguing with the ticket clerk, but it seemed like most Arabs argued with each other during conversations. Arabs typically talk loud and stand close together, so close in fact, that their noses are nearly touching. This custom always made me nervous. Not only did it make me feel like they had invaded my space, but also their body odor, breath and rotting teeth made me want to gag. And it did no good to step back. When I stepped back, they would always step forward to get closer. Anyway, after a minute of what seemed to be yelling between Amad and the clerk, Amad turned to us.

"We pay driver on bus."

We climbed on the nearly full bus and walked to the back. Amad sat next to me, while Fahim and Trevor sat together across the aisle and one seat ahead of us. After 10 minutes or so, the driver's assistant got on the bus and counted the number of riders. Once he finished counting, he spoke to the passengers.

265

He appeared to be waiting for a reply, but no one spoke. After asking what sounded like another question and getting no response, he made a statement. This time passengers got out their tickets. Trevor looked at me. We both realized what must have happened. We were sitting in someone else's seats.

"Amad," I said, "we don't have tickets. I don't think we're suppose to be here." I started to get up.

"No," Amad said, pushing me back into my seat with his arm. "Ride autobus many years. No buy ticket. Pay when autobus go."

The driver's assistant walked down the aisle checking tickets. When he got to Fahim, Amad stood up and said something to the assistant. A shouting match ensued. Trevor looked at me. I could tell he felt the way I did, that we should get off. The driver started the engine and looked in his huge rearview mirror at Amad and his assistant.

"We can take the next bus," I said to Amad, who ignored me and kept pace in the yelling contest with the assistant. The assistant finally threw his arms up in disgust, walked to the front and slammed the door shut. The driver shifted into first gear, and we pulled away from the station. I looked out the window at two men, an old woman and young girl standing beside the bus. The windows were open, so they obviously overheard the argument between Amad and the driver's assistant. Both men in their long dark robes had beards. The older man had a black and gray-speckled beard, while the other man had a bushy dark brown beard. The lines on their foreheads stood out. When I looked at the women, the elderly woman immediately lowered her eyes, but the young girl looked at me a few seconds before looking down. I wanted to scream for the driver to stop so we could get off, but no words came from my mouth. The oldest man said something to me. I shrugged my shoulders while shaking my head and looked at Amad. Amad kept his eyes pointed forward, ignoring the people left behind.

As we turned onto the street beside the bus station, the driver flipped on the radio, sending Arabic music blaring out the eight-inch speaker mounted two feet above his head. The music, with a man's voice wailing melodic phrases that wavered between whole and half tones, reminded me of the sitar used in India. Both types of exotic music create an atmosphere of mystery and intrigue. My mind flashed back to Melanie and me getting high at a party with sitar musician Ravi Shankar playing in the background. The singing seemed to influence my thought patterns, leaving me feeling vulnerable and paranoid.

It took less than an hour to get to the foothills of the Rif Mountains. We passed through the beautiful and peaceful-looking mountain city of Chechaouen, with its steep incline of white stucco buildings laced with terraces overlooking the valley below. Once we crested the pass above Chechaouen, the driver drove like a maniac around the sharp and twisting curves. If the bus missed one of the curves, it would send us rolling end over end for hundreds and even thousands of feet into the cavernous rocky gorges.

At one point the driver stopped and everyone piled out in a mad rush. Amad told us to use the bathroom quickly and to get back to our seats, saying that once the driver returned, he would slam the door shut and leave behind anyone not on the bus. Many men disappeared behind rocks and bushes while the rest of the passengers used the toilets in a stone building. The toilets were similar to the hotel bathroom—a six-inch diameter hole in the ground—except in the mountain toilet there were no footprints painted on the floor. Within 10 minutes all passengers were back on the bus. After waiting 10 more minutes, I looked at Amad.

"Where's the driver?" I asked him.

"Ayi," Amad said pointing to a small white stucco adobe cubicle no bigger than 10 square feet. "Driver pray to Allah." Evidently, the cubicle served as a private chapel for drivers.

"That's probably a good idea," I said, "considering the way he's been driving."

Amad looked bewildered at my statement, so I explained to him in Spanish by saying, "That's probably necessary because he's driving very fast." Amad laughed.

For the next several hours, we rode along the twisting and winding curves through the beautiful Rif Mountains. Even though the sun shined brightly above us, the sky remained a deep rich blue like on a cold, cloudless winter's day in the Midwest. It felt good to be sitting by the window. Cool, fresh mountain air rushed in and created a menthol-type sensation in my nostrils. The Arabic music, combined with the air and elevated altitude, made me high. My vision was exceedingly clear, and colors appeared brilliant to the point of looking phosphorescent.

Amad had purchased a magazine before we left, so I glanced at the pictures while he read. One page showed a picture of a black man breaking through the shell of the world with his torso protruding from the heart of the United States. I asked Amad about the article. He said that in Morocco all races were equal and that the black man received the same privileges as everyone else. He asked me about discrimination in the United States. I told him the U.S. did have a racial problem, and added, "Hopefully, we'll see the day when people aren't judged by the color of their skin." A few pages later I noticed another photograph, a caricature sketch of a big man with a potbelly and a gold earring piercing through the bottom of his huge nose.

"Que es eso?" I asked pointing to the picture.

"You Jewish?" Amad asked, sitting up and moving to the edge of his seat, his eyes focused on me.

"No," I said calmly.

"You have Jew friends?" he asked quickly.

Of course I did, but Amad's contorted face indicated what impact my answer could make. "What's the matter, Amad?" I asked, avoiding his question and thinking about his statement moments before on racial equality in Morocco.

"Nada." He looked down at the magazine. "Jew make problemas. Hurt many people."

He quickly turned the page and read with pursed lips. I wanted to ask Amad if a Jew had personally hurt him, but I decided to drop the subject. About midafternoon or a little later, Amad screamed something to the driver. The driver looked in the mirror as he slowed the bus down.

"We go," Amad said.

There were no houses in sight, just mountains and the road. Before the bus came to a complete stop, Amad and Fahim got up and moved toward the door. Trevor and I followed them. Once off the bus, we stood on the mountain road as the driver drove away.

"Donde esta su casa?" Trevor asked Amad.

Amad watched the bus disappear around one of the curves. "Cinco kilometers, no mas. Venga."

We backtracked along the road about half a mile to a path leading down the mountain. The well-worn path was easy to hike. We walked approximately 30 minutes before seeing three people working in a field. At the same time, eight to 10 dogs ran toward us barking. Amad and Fahim waved to the workers who waved back, and then they both quickly picked up several rocks.

"Perros malo," Amad said.

Trevor and I decided to pick up rocks too. As the dogs got closer, Amad faked a throw at them, causing the leader of the pack to slow down. Then Amad let a rock fly, and the dogs scattered to avoid being struck as they came to a stop, barking and growling 30 to 40 feet from us. Amad and Fahim both hurled rocks at the dogs. The pack backed up. Trevor and I faked a few throws, but neither of us actually threw a rock. Personally, I wanted to keep my rocks in case I really needed them.

When the dogs dispersed, Amad ran toward them, slinging another rock and smacking one dog square on its left side. The dog yelped and ran. Amad laughed and yelled a victory cry as he picked up two more rocks and flung them as hard as he could toward the dogs. The dogs disappeared amid the brush and rocks. Amad and Fahim laughed and conversed in Arabic as we continued walking on the path.

In the distance we could see a large two-story structure made of clay bricks and a tin roof. It looked more like a barn than a house. Several smaller huts, some with grass roofs and others with tin, were attached to it. When we reached the house, we walked around to the back and entered one of the smaller huts.

The door to the hut, which was on the west side, faced a beautiful valley. The sun's rays shone onto the L-shaped entryway, but inside the hut it was dark. Amad struck a match and lit a candle on a small shelf built into the clay brick wall. The room, about 20 feet long, 15 feet wide and 8 feet high, had no windows. Near the top of the clay brick wall facing the west, however, were long rectangular slits the size of two bricks sitting side by side. The holes provided ventilation and a small amount of light. Each wall had several built-in shelves with candleholders and candles. A beautifully designed Moroccan rug covered the dirt floor. At the back of the room stood a rectangular wooden table that rose two feet above the floor. Around the table were pads to sit on. Otherwise, the room was bare. Amad lit several more candles.

"You wait," Amad said, and he disappeared through a door leading to the main part of the house. I asked Fahim if he had ever been here before. He said he had been to the mountain farm many times. Within a few minutes Amad returned.

"Come. Me give tour, then drink tea."

Amad said a few words to Fahim who then disappeared through the door leading to the main section of the house. We followed Amad back out into the bright sunlight and walked down a path that overlooked a huge valley surrounded by mountains. I sucked in a deep breath of the cool pristine breeze blowing up from the valley below us. Amad waved his arm above the expansive view as he spoke.

"Grow good kif. No problema. No paranoia. Mountain people good worker."

"Kif?" I said. "No comprende. What is it?"

"Si, kif, you know," Amad said in Spanish. "Marijuana. Make good hashish, good shit." (The 'i' in Spanish sounds like the long vowel 'e.' So the word 'kif' sounds like keef, Rif like reef, and shit like sheet.)

Up until that point we had no idea we were visiting a marijuana plantation and hashish factory. From the size of the valley and the numerous irrigation ditches, this was apparently a flourishing business. In the U.S., offering your guests and friends Moroccan pot or hashish indicated status and good drug connections, not to mention potent highs. I wondered if the Moroccan pot and hashish I had smoked in the U.S. during the 1970s came from this very valley.

"Plant first there," Amad said, pointing to a hill in the distance. "Later plant here. See water? Come from ground. Good for plants, yes?"

The irrigation ditches guiding the spring water through the fields created natural boundaries around large plots of land. It was an impressive sight, and Amad spoke with pride.

"Come, me show more." We walked back up the hillside to some rock and clay ovens built into the mountainside. "Cook mountain bread here. Mountain bread good. Berber bread. You know Berber people?"

Trevor and I shook our heads no.

"Berber people true Moroccan. Have own language. Tetuan no understand Berber people. Berber people here." Amad spread his arms to indicate the area around us.

I later discovered that the Berber people were the ancient and original inhabitants of Morocco consisting of a number of distinct clans or tribes scattered across northern Africa. The tribes are predominantly found along the southern coast of the Mediterranean, the northern Sahara and the Atlas Mountains. According to Amad, a mountain Berber tribe provided labor for the farm. I felt unconvinced that Amad owned and managed this establishment. He seemed an unlikely proprietor, although he called it his house and acted like the boss. After viewing the ovens, we returned to the hut to find four teacups, a bowl of sugar cubes and stirring sticks on the table.

"Come," Amad said as we continued through the adjoining doorway that led from the room to the main house. We walked down a flight of hard-packed dirt stairs carved into the mountainside. The house contoured to the landscape in such a way that the steps led out onto a flat area overlooking the valley, much like a patio. We walked around the side of the house and up a short incline before coming to larger hut the size of a three or four-car garage. As we entered the hut, a familiar rich odor filled my nostrils. Hashish bricks were stacked five feet high on one side of the room.

Amad turned to us. "No mucho hashish now. Sell many kilos."

Amad walked to a bin filled with dried marijuana buds. A roll of clear cellophane and a one-foot square screen with a wooden border sat on the table next to the bin. He picked up the cellophane roll and tore off a piece about a foot long.

"You hold." Amad put the cellophane strip in my hands and had me stretch it out above the bin. He picked up the screen and put a handful of buds on top of it. I could see an extremely fine fuzzy material on the buds. Amad smoothed the buds over the screen and then jostled it. Thousands of dust-like filaments fell through the screen and coated the cellophane. After a minute of shaking, he put the screen down and took the cellophane from my hands. Carefully pulling the corners up so the filaments fell together at the center, he twisted the cellophane, which compacted the filaments to create a small ball the size of a large grape. He vigorously rubbed the ball against his jeans. The friction and pressure created enough heat to tightly pack and melt the filaments together.

Amad smiled. "Come. We smoke."

Once outside the hut, Amad stopped and pointed to a grass-roof carport beside the hut. The single lane dirt driveway that led to the carport looked more like two walking paths through tall grass than a road. "Mercedes come here," Amad said. "Put hashish special places. Mercedes drive to boat, go to Europe. No problema."

It sounded too easy. There were, after all, custom inspections and drug-sniffing dogs that Trevor and I had seen when disembarking from the ferry in Ceuta.

Walking around the carport and another small building, we returned to the first hut we had entered. There were now several candles on the table to supplement the light from the candles on shelves attached to the wall. We sat on the cushioned pads surrounding the two-foot-high table. Amad unwrapped the cellophane and cut off a chunk of hash with a knife sitting on top of the table. The hashish crumbled into a partial powder. Amad scooped up the mixture with the knife's blade and dropped it in the bowl of a small pipe. He handed the pipe to me.

Trevor and I discussed drugs in depth late one evening in our room in Seville. Trevor said he experimented with smoking pot and hash in the States, but from what I gathered, he was an occasional weekend smoker. We both agreed it would be foolish to smoke or do any drugs in Europe. The risks were too great. But in this situation, a decision to not smoke could be misinterpreted. Besides being considered rude, we might appear suspicious as well as a potential threat to a thriving business. I stopped smoking pot nearly two years earlier after it started making me paranoid. I had no desire to smoke the hash, and I don't think Trevor did either.

Amad struck a wooden matchstick against the matchbox, but instead of holding it above the pipe, he handed the lit match to me. I took the match and held it over the bowl. Amad looked pleased as I slowly inhaled. I handed the pipe to Trevor. After blowing the smoke from my lungs, I bragged about how smooth the smoke went down compared to the hashish and reefer in America.

"Morocco have best shit in world," Amad said proudly.

As Amad struck another match and handed it to Trevor, Fahim entered carrying a container of tea. He filled our cups and sat down. After Fahim and Amad took a hit, Amad refilled the bowl and handed it to me again. I passed the pipe to Trevor and exhaled the smoke when a man walked into the room dressed in a long robe and sandals. His black curly hair covered his ears and came down to just above his shoulders. He had a thin, short beard. His eyebrows were as black as his hair, and his dark eyes sparkled in the candle light. From where we sat, he looked like a tall man. He had a stoic expression on his face and appeared to be assessing the room and its occupants. Although he looked young, maybe 25 or 26 years old, his movements, actions and demeanor were that of someone much older. Don't ask me why, but for some reason I stood up. At that moment he broke into a big smile and walked straight to me, giving me a hug with his head over my right shoulder, and then another hug with his head over my left shoulder. Feeling embarrassed, I looked at Amad.

"He Berber," Amad said, amused at my bewilderment. "You stand. Show respect. He greet you like Berber. He called Ohac."

I extended my hand to him and we shook. "Bryce," I said.

Amad spoke to Ohac, who then motioned for me to sit down. Ohac sat beside me and Fahim handed him the pipe. Amad clapped his hands twice and within seconds a barefoot boy, probably 11 or 12 years old, came through the doorway that led to the main house. He had short black hair and wore what looked like a long gray pullover shirt that hung to the top of his ankles. Unlike the wool-hooded burnoose or robe worn by many men in the mountains, the shirt, called a jalabiyah, appeared to be made of cotton. Amad said a few words to him and he disappeared.

Just after the boy left, two other men came through the door, pulling the hoods off their heads as they entered. Both carried machetes. Amad introduced them to us, but I forgot their names almost immediately. It's hard enough remembering American names, much less strange sounding Arabic or Berber names. They made no attempt to communicate with Trevor or me, but seemed very interested in talking to Amad. Amad pointed to the pads, and they joined us by sitting across from Trevor and me.

Ohac, the man who gave me a hug, tried to converse with us in Spanish, but his limited Spanish vocabulary made it difficult. In fact, he couldn't speak in sentences. Instead, he'd say a Spanish word or two and then speak Arabic, or possibly Berber, while trying to act out what he meant with his hands.

The young boy returned with more cups and tea, then brought in a kettle of food that he could barely carry. It smelled great and looked like beef stew. He set the kettle in the center of the table and left the room. He came back shortly with two round loaves of bread that were several inches thick and the size of a large pizza. It looked like dark whole wheat bread. He gave them to Amad, who set one loaf on the table in front of him, and then ripped off a piece of bread from the other loaf and handed it to Fahim, who sat on his right. Amad then ripped off another chunk of bread and handed it to me. After that, he tore off pieces of bread and tossed them over the table to everyone else. Once the others had their piece of bread, they broke off bite-sized chunks with their right hand and held it in the kettle of soupy stew until it soaked up the broth. With the soppy piece of bread, they scooped in some vegetables and meat with their fingers and threw it into their mouths. Trevor and I were observing this when Amad pulled off a piece of bread and held it up in his right hand.

"This hand," he said, waving his right hand toward the food. "Other hand do other business. Now eat."

Ever since this incident, I've always wiped my butt with my left hand.

The delicious stew contained several tangy spices that made my nose run. Once we finished the meal, Amad clapped his hands twice and the boy reappeared carrying two white hand towels; one wet, the other dry. He handed them to Amad, who wiped his hands with the wet towel and passed it to Fahim, who wiped his hands and passed the towel to me. After Amad dried his hands with the second towel, he gave it to Fahim. As the towels went around the circle, the boy cleared away the kettle and brought in a fresh pot of tea. Amad filled my cup and said several things to the boy who nodded and departed. Amad then packed the pipe with hashish. As the pipe circulated among us, the boy returned with a huge portable stereo and a large paper bag. Amad gave the stereo to Fahim, who removed its plastic back and took batteries from the sack and shoved them into the empty slots.

Amad looked at Trevor and me. "You like music, yes?"

"Sure," I said.

He smiled. "Play America music for you." Amad slipped a tape in and turned it on. Eric Clapton and the group Cream from the early 1970s began playing. "You like?"

"Cream," I said, "they're good. I like Eric Clapton's guitar work."

Amad was delighted I knew the group. He turned the music up loud and kept filling the pipe with more hashish. After the pipe had gone around the circle at least three times, Amad set the pipe down. We were all sitting on floor cushions. No one tried to speak over the sound of the music. I kept getting a strange eerie feeling from the two Berber men who had been talking with Amad. Their gaze made me feel as if they were looking right through me. Once, when I caught one of them staring at me, our eyes locked. I smiled, but he displayed no change in his facial expression—just a cold stare. They both had smiled once, but that was when Amad had said something to them when they first arrived.

Amad switched tapes and the song *Rider's On The Storm* by the rock group The Doors came blasting through the speakers. Amad acted as if it were a miracle when Trevor named the group. Amad, in contrast to the two Berber men, always had a pleasant and congenial look about him. He appeared on a perpetual high, whether smoking hashish or not. Amad turned the music down and clapped for the boy. The boy must have been seated right outside the door because he always appeared within a few seconds after Amad's claps. Amad said something to him, and then turned the music back up. About a song later, the boy returned carrying two clear plastic bags with three kilos of hashish in each bag. He put them on the table in front of us. Amad took out a long white sheet of paper he got from beneath the table and spread it out in front of him. He took the bricks of hashish out of their bags and laid them side-by-side on the paper. He reached over, popped out the tape, and put in a Jimmy Hendrix cassette. He started the tape, and then turned the volume down and looked at me.

"Best hashish in Morocco," he said and smiled. "How many kilo you buy?"

I looked at Trevor, and then back at Amad. His question caught me off guard. "Huh, we didn't really come here to buy hashish."

A slight pause ensued before he spoke again in English, but this time slower. "I say, how m-a-n-y k-i-l-o you buy?"

I looked at Trevor again. The two expressionless Berber men sitting next to him seemed to be glaring at me. I turned toward Amad.

"Amad, we did not come here to buy hashish," I said, also speaking slowly and distinctly.

Amad spoke Arabic to Fahim and the Berber men.

I looked at Trevor. "Do you think he believes we came here to buy hash?"

"He never said anything about buying hash in Tetuan," Trevor said.

Amad turned back to me and smiled, this time speaking in Spanish. "I don't think you understand. I asked you how many kilos of hashish do you want to buy?"

I looked at Amad. "In Tetuan you said nothing about buying hashish," I replied in Spanish. "We don't have money to buy hashish."

Amad's face turned solemn. He spoke to the Berber men again, but briefly this time, then turned back to me.

"Okay," he said with a serious look, "you buy two kilo, maybe three, no more, yes? For you good price. You friend. Only $300 for kilo. Sell same kilo $500 to German. You American. Good deal for you, yes?"

Neither Trevor nor I wanted to buy any hash, and even if we did, we lacked the funds. We brought enough money to stay a couple of nights in Morocco and purchase a few items like a Walkman stereo set. We had about $200 worth of Spanish pesetas and another $50 to $75 in Moroccan currency.

"Amad, your hashish is really good," I said, hoping to appeal to his sense of pride. "If we had more money, we'd buy some."

His dark glazed eyes were focused and intense. The room seemed to shrink. A suffocating shroud of stale hashish smoke surrounded me. Amad's normally pleasant and congenial appearance switched to a menacing glare. A completely changed man sat in front of me. Jimmy Hendrix played in the background. As he sang, "Hey Joe, where you going with that gun in your hand," I looked around the room. It became a dungeon, a place of torture and death. Two machetes leaned against the wall beside their owners. I felt sick to my stomach.

Amad spoke Arabic to the men and then gestured by throwing his hands up into the air above him. He turned his head and looked directly into my eyes. For several seconds he just stared. "What you think this is?" Amad spoke through gritted teeth as he slammed his fist hard onto the tabletop and screamed, "Hotel? This business! We make business here! Not tourist shop! We look like shopkeeper?" He held out his hands to indicate the other people present.

"Amad, you didn't mention buying hashish at the hotel," I repeated in Spanish. "We don't have enough money to buy hashish."

"How much money you have?" he snapped, still gritting his teeth.

"Not enough," I said in English.

"Cuanto dinero?" he repeated slowly with more force.

"No mucho. No bastante para uno kilo," I said.

Amad slapped his hand down hard on the table. "Put money on table."

I looked at Trevor.

"Now!" he screamed, raising his hand and slamming his fist on the table. "All money on table now!"

I leaned forward and took out my wallet. Trevor did the same. I took out the peseta and dirham notes and tossed them on the tabletop, then started to put my wallet back in my pocket.

"On table!" Amad demanded. I reluctantly set my wallet beside the money. Trevor pulled his money out of his wallet and placed both on the table. Amad pointed to my jean pockets. "Put on table." I looked at him. He leaned forward and put his face inches from mine. "Immediamente, entiende señor?"

He slowly spoke the words in a threatening tone. The sentence literally means, 'Immediately, do you understand sir?' I took it how he meant it, which was, 'Immediately, buster. You said you didn't understand me before, but there's no misunderstanding me now, right?'

I removed the spare change and Swiss Army knife from my pockets and placed them on the table as Amad flipped through my wallet. Trevor emptied his pockets too, which consisted of several Moroccan coins and a few dirham notes.

Fahim picked up my Swiss Army knife. "Ah, que bueno. Gift for me?"

I felt in no position to contest his request, and he knew it. "Si, for you," I said, as the churning in my stomach grew. He opened the different blades and admired the knife.

"Empty!" Amad commanded, touching my jean pocket.

"I just did."

"Me want see."

I turned my pockets inside out. Amad reached over and raised my shirt to expose my bare belly. Many Americans and foreigners wore money belts around their waists. I actually had a money belt, but not the traditional kind that wraps around the waist beneath a shirt. My leather belt had a zipper on the inside that allowed just enough room for a row of bills. My dad bought it in Italy and gave it to me for my trip to Europe. I had six fifty-dollar bills folded up inside the belt in case of an emergency, and hashish did not meet that criteria.

"Where money?" he asked.

I pointed to the table. "It's all there!"

"Si?" he said. Amad seemed to sense I was holding out.

"Si," I said, resorting to Spanish so I would not be misunderstood. "En Seville, yo tengo mas dinero, pero aqui, no mas."

I wondered what I would do if Amad or Fahim liked my belt and said, "A gift for me?" As soon as I thought the question, the solution popped into my mind. I'd say my father gave it to me, which was true, and that it had sentimental value.

Amad turned his head and looked at Trevor. He then pointed to Trevor's pockets. Trevor got up on his knees and turned his pockets inside out. Amad motioned with his hand for Trevor to raise his shirt. Trevor had no money belt either. With my wallet still in his hand, Amad looked at our daypacks leaning against the wall on the other side of the room. He nodded toward them. "Put on table." Amad's attention went back to my wallet. He pulled things out of my wallet's clear plastic holders and pitched them on the table; such as business cards people had given me, my social security card, and my only remaining photograph of Melanie, which had been tucked behind the social security card.

Although I had burned all her photographs while living in Columbia, I found this picture in a drawer at my parent's house. It had been taken the summer we got married. She wore a blue-halter top and white shorts that accentuated her tanned legs. Her beautiful smile reminded me how much joy and love we had shared. For a split second, I wondered where she was and if she was happy.

In my peripheral vision, I saw Fahim move, and turned in time to see him put my Swiss Army knife in his pocket and begin rifling through Trevor's wallet. Amad talked to Fahim as Trevor and I went to our packs.

I spoke to Trevor, swiftly running my sentences together. If Trevor and I conversed slowly in English, Amad understand a fair amount of what we said. If Trevor and I talked rapidly, however, leaving no pauses or breaks between sentences, Amad understood little if anything.

"We have to play it cool and relax and however we feel we must act as if nothing matters and we are having a great time even if they have all our money and belongings because to get out of here alive we must use our brains because you can see we are outnumbered and they have machetes, knives and who knows what else so just stick with me and go along with whatever I say or do..."

Out of the corner of my eye, I could see Amad speaking to Fahim and trying to eavesdrop on what we were saying.

"Bring backpack now!" Amad demanded, looking directly at us.

We picked up our packs and walked back to the center of the room.

"What you say?" Amad asked.

"What?" I responded.

"There," he point to where we had been standing. "What you say?"

"We were just saying how we wish we had more money to buy some hashish," I said slowly. "Su hashish esta muy muy bueno," I added.

"Ah si," Amad said, smiling for the first time since the shakedown began. From the look on his face, I knew he was trying to decide if I lied or not. "Put packs on table," he added in a lighter tone of voice.

We set our packs on the table. Seeing the photograph of Melanie, my baby niece and 4-year-old nephew strewn haphazardly across the table made me feel desecrated and vulnerable. I wondered if I would ever see any of them again.

We put our packs on the table and sat down. I leaned back on my hands and smiled, creating the impression of being high, happy and laid back. I had done enough drugs that I knew how my facial expressions and appearance should be. Although feeling far from high, acting the part made me more relaxed.

"Quisiera fumar mas hashish," I said, which means, "I would like to smoke more hashish."

"Si?" Amad said as he pulled my daypack across the table closer to him. He smiled and added, "You like hashish, si?"

"Claro," I exaggerated, "me gusta su hashish mucho. Esta muy bueno."

My words pleased Amad. He said a few words to the two Berber men in the corner. One of them filled the pipe and fired it up; then handed the pipe to me. My intentions were to keep everyone high. I knew my fear would keep me straight no matter how much I smoked.

As I inhaled slowly, Amad took things out of my pack and put them on the table. Fahim must have been afraid Amad would beat him to something, so he laid down Trevor's wallet and rummaged through Trevor's pack. Within a second or two, Fahim removed a Kodak camera and held it in his hand.

"Ah, a gift for me?" he asked, looking at Trevor.

"Si," Trevor reluctantly replied.

Amad found my harmonica in one of my side pouches and blew through it. "Me like," he said. "Gift for me?"

"Sure," I said, "that's for you." I handed Amad the pipe. "Here's another gift for you." I picked up the small two-by-three-foot Moroccan rug that Amad had already removed from my pack and placed on the table. Trevor had given me one of the small rugs he purchased to get us out of a Tetuan store. I handed the rug to Amad.

He glanced at it. "Ah, bueno Moroccan rug." He handed it back to me. "You keep. Good souvenir."

Fahim, finding nothing else he wanted in Trevor's pack, returned his attention to Trevor's wallet. He slipped out a Visa credit card from behind Trevor's driver's license and looked at it. The card belonged to Trevor's father. Fahim talked to Amad as they both examined it.

Amad took the card from Fahim and looked at Trevor. "You get money at bank with card?"

I was unsure if Amad knew how to use a credit card, but if he did and had asked Trevor in order to test Trevor's honesty, Trevor's answer became risky. If you get caught lying in Morocco, it's considered detestable and grounds for a payoff, a fight or worse. The fact that Amad associated the card with a bank meant he or Fahim knew something about it. Also, if Trevor said we could get money from the bank, we might be in even greater danger. I looked into Amad's eyes.

"You can get $50 from each country with the card," I said quickly, before Trevor had a chance to reply. I said it fast enough so that only Trevor understood. Although $50 may not sound like a lot of money to an American, for a Moroccan in 1983 it came to a considerable amount, especially when you consider hotel rooms were available for $1.25 a night and a hearty meal for less than a dollar.

Amad looked at me. Then Trevor spoke in Spanish.

"With that card you can get $50 from each country."

"Ah si," Amad said. He paused briefly, and then looked at me and said, "Tomorrow, you stay," then he looked at Trevor, "and you go with Fahim to bank for fifty dollar."

Amad's plan to hold me hostage for a $50 ransom was totally unacceptable. Besides, I wouldn't blame Trevor if he didn't return. Who would want to go back to a place where you might be hacked to death with machetes?

"No," I said in English, "we cannot do that." I spoke in Spanish to make sure I made my point. "We are students from Seville, and we're on break. If we're not back in school the day after tomorrow, they will call our hotel in Tetuan."

Amad needed to know that we would be missed, and that people knew where we had been staying. Amad was aware that the hotel clerk knew we were going to Amad's home. I hoped Amad would make the connection that we could be traced to his farm. Actually, nobody had any idea where we were in Morocco—not a smart move on our part. Another idea came to me.

"This is powerful hashish, but as you see," I pointed to the money on the table, "we don't have enough money to buy even one kilo. I would like to buy some. I have more money in Spain, and when school is out next month, I want to return and get some hashish. I can't buy much. I only have one thousand dollars." I picked up one of the kilo bricks of hash and smelled it.

Amad's eyes sparkled, but before he could say anything, Trevor spoke. "I'd like to buy some too, maybe two thousand dollars worth. What about sending it through the mail? I have friends in Minneapolis who would love this. If we send you money, can you mail the hashish to us?"

"Ah si," Amad said, now thoroughly excited. "No problema. We mail many kilo."

I could have hugged Trevor at that moment. Amad's congenial, pleasant and warm radiant smile returned to his face.

"When you come again," he said, "we make good deal for you. You friend. We make good deal."

To help make Amad believe we were serious, I asked, "But tell me Amad, how do we get the hashish across the border? We don't want to get arrested by the police."

"No problema. Put hashish in bag and swallow, or put here." Amad pointed to his butt. Amad picked up the butcher knife sitting on the table and cut off a big chunk of hashish from one of the bricks. He picked up the chunk of hashish in one hand and our money in the other.

"We do business." Amad held out the hashish to me. "Money for hashish, si? Business amigos, si?"

"Bueno," I said, accepting the hashish.

Amad leaned back slightly and pushed our money into his jean pocket as he spoke to Fahim, Ohac and the two Berber men. For $250 cash, my Swiss army knife and Trevor's camera, Amad should have kept the chunk of hashish and given us the rest of the brick. My thoughts, however, were already pondering ways to get rid of the hash. I had seen *Midnight Express*. The movie's message was clear: don't try to smuggle drugs out of a foreign country unless you're willing to pay the price, which might include prison, torture, rape and/or death.

Although our new circumstances had taken a lot of pressure off Trevor and me, we were still a long way from the border. Amad clapped his hands, and the boy appeared. After a few words, the boy left. Amad said he had told the boy to prepare our sleeping quarters. We smoked several more rounds of hashish before Amad and Fahim bid the Berber men goodnight and led us to the guest bedroom, located in another hut attached to the main house. The dirt-floor room, maybe 12 square feet in size, contained a small table, a stool and two beds that were long wooden slabs elevated 24 inches above the floor. A thick wool blanket covered the bed's thin foam cushion.

Amad and Fahim were both smiling and cheerful. The boy brought in another pot of tea and four cups. Fahim spoke to the boy who then poured our tea. Amad asked us what our fathers did in America. Trevor told Amad that his dad managed a tavern, and I told him my dad sold insurance. Amad appeared unimpressed by our answers. He asked me if my dad owned the insurance company. When I said no, he made a grunting sound and took a drink of tea. Amad seemed to be assessing the value of his American catch. I wondered how many other tourists had been through this sham. After finishing our tea, Amad stood up and said we'd be catching the 7 a.m. bus. He told us the thick wool blankets on the bed should be enough to keep us warm for the night, and they departed.

Despite the positive turn in our situation, I remained paranoid and scared.

"What do you think?" Trevor asked.

I put a finger to my lips indicating silence. "I don't know," I said, giving Trevor a wink. "How many kilos do you think you'll buy when we come back?" I spoke slow and clear while taking out a note pad and pen from my daypack. Trevor played along.

"I can afford about $2,000, but once we get back to the States, I'll want more than that."

I wrote on the note pad and showed Trevor. "Keep cool. It's working out."

He nodded. "It's great hashish," he continued. "It will sell fast in the United States."

Our conversation went on like that for several minutes before we climbed under the wool blankets with our clothes on. After blowing out the candle, I thought I heard someone creeping away, but it could have been my imagination. The darkness made the room feel twice as cool. Trevor fell asleep quickly. I envied his deep, slow and rhythmic breathing. Although we were out of immediate danger, my mind kept replaying the shakedown, especially the part where Amad slammed his fist onto the table and screamed, "What you think this is? Hotel?" How could a person, who initially seemed so vibrant, positive and joyful, turn into such a ruthless, raving maniac intent upon one goal—to get us for every cent we had. And worse, how had he deceived us so easily?

I longed for the moment when we would be back on the bus returning to Tetuan. After 10 or 15 minutes, I heard something scurry across the room. Too dark to see anything, I remained motionless and listened. Then I heard more scurrying sounds around the room. It had to be mice or rats. Suddenly, they were everywhere: on the grass roof and rafters above me as well as under my bed. Pulling the thick wool blanket over my head and tucking in the corners around me, I curled into a fetal position and tightly shut my eyes. Somehow I managed to fall asleep.

The next morning, awakening to the sound of a dog barking in the distance, I lifted the wool blanket off my head to find sunlight shining through the cracks in the walls, around the doorway and between spaces in the roof. Trevor remained sound asleep. Pushing the blanket back, I sat up in bed and put my feet on the dirt floor, still wearing my tennis shoes. I quietly got up and opened the squeaky front door to find a magnificent view of the mountains and valley below. A long thin line of smoke hovered above the valley. The fresh mountain air smelled great, and the sun, barely peeking over the mountain ridge, filled me with a renewed confidence about our situation.

I walked a few feet past the path beside our hut and urinated, facing the valley. A twig crackled behind me. I turned to see a young woman walking up the path carrying two baskets that hung from a wooden pole balanced across her shoulders. She wore a long robe, sandals and scarf over her head with no veil. She concentrated on the ground beneath her as she walked. She looked up a split second after I turned toward her. She was young and beautiful, maybe 16 or 17 years old, and for a moment our eyes met in surprise and embarrassment. I quickly turned my back to her as she continued on her way, passing within several feet of me.

A sick feeling enveloped me. Just when things seemed to be going so well, I had inadvertently exposed myself to an unveiled young woman. Never mind that I was following the dictates of mother nature. This was Morocco, and in the mountains of Morocco no telling what the punishment could be for such an act. I returned to the room once again filled with anxiety and fear.

As I walked through the door, the loud squeak from the door hinge caused Trevor to raise up slightly and look at me. He dropped his head back onto the foam pad.

"Out for a morning stroll?" he asked.

"You might say that," I replied, deciding not to mention what had just happened. No point both of us feeling scared. "What time is it?"

"Shit!" Trevor said, looking at his watch and sitting up. "We can forget the seven o'clock bus. It's after eight."

The previous night's fear and paranoia flooded back into me. "I don't know about you," I said, "but I want to get out of here."

Trevor flipped his tattered wool blanket back and spun around, dangling his stocking feet above the tops of his tennis shoes. "I don't know," he said slowly and facetiously, "I think we should stick around here a few more days."

"Yeah, right."

Trevor laughed as he bent down and lifted the tongue of his tennis shoe to slip it on.

"I'd check your shoes for scorpions if I were you."

Trevor quickly jerked his foot away from his shoe. "Do you really think there are scorpions around here?"

"I'm not sure about scorpions, but I heard rats running around this room last night."

Trevor turned his tennis shoes upside down and shook them. "Get off it," he said, half laughing.

"I'm serious. They were all over the place. I even..."

"Buenas dias," Amad said, walking through the doorway. "You sleep good, yes?" Fahim followed behind him.

"Yes," Trevor said, "we slept good."

"Are there rats around here?" I asked.

Amad looked at me. "What you say?"

The young boy came into the room carrying a tray holding a pot of tea, cups and what appeared to be cinnamon wafers. He placed the tray on the table and left.

"Hay muchas ratas aquí?" Trevor asked before I could ask again.

"Ah, si," Amad replied. "You see ratas?"

"No," I spoke up, "but I heard them last night."

Amad spoke to Fahim, and they both laughed. Amad picked up the tea pot and poured tea into the cups. "Ratas like las montañas," he said.

"It's too late to catch the 7 a.m. bus," Trevor said in Spanish as he looked at his watch. "What time does the next bus arrive?"

"Si, un poco tarde," Amad said. "Eat, drink now. Autobus come at nine. No problema."

Amad picked up his cup of tea and one of the crusty cinnamon wafers the size of a pancake. The rest of us did the same. The wafers were good. They were similar to piecrust baked with cinnamon, sugar and butter on top. As I took my second bite, a man yelled from outside the hut. Then came a more forceful yell. Amad and Fahim put their teacups down and walked toward the door. As they pushed the door open, we could see seven or eight men dressed in long robes standing together. Tightness seized my chest. I knew why they were there. The girl must have told them she saw me urinating beside the path. Amad and one of the men shouted at each other.

Within a few minutes, Ohac, the Berber tribe member whom I had stood up for when we first arrived, entered through the door. He appeared anxious and tried to speak in Spanish. He kept saying, "dinero" and "autobus." We finally realized he wanted to know if we had enough money for the bus. I told him that Amad had all of our money, but he didn't understand. So I shook my head no and shrugged my shoulders. "No dinero," I said. "Nada."

Ohac then handed me several dirham notes for our bus fare back to Tetuan. I asked him if that meant we should leave now. I tried to use sign language, but Ohac looked bewildered.

"I think we need to go," I said to Trevor, picking up my daypack sitting on the floor beside my bed.

"Do you know what's going on?" Trevor asked as he picked up his pack.

"Maybe. When I went outside this morning..."

Amad entered swiftly through the door. "We go now," he said abruptly. "Come." Amad and Fahim walked through the door leading to the main house. Trevor, Ohac and I followed. We walked down a long hallway and exited through a door close to the path that led back up the mountain to the road. Once outside, I looked for men wearing robes, but saw no one. I kept glancing back until we were well on our way up the path. While walking, I told Trevor what happened earlier while urinating. Once I saw the mountain road in the distance, a heavy burden lifted from my shoulders. It actually looked like we were going to make it out.

We reached the road by 8:50. It wasn't until then I realized that neither Amad nor Fahim had confiscated our watches, or rather asked for them as a gift. I resisted the urge to glance at my watch again. At 9:05, however, there was still no bus. I thought maybe it had already gone by, but Amad said the buses were always late. Ohac said something to Amad, who in turn told us that Ohac would be returning to the house. Ohac probably came along to keep us from getting into any more trouble. He gave Trevor and me a little cheek-to-cheek hug before disappearing along the path leading down the mountain.

While waiting on the gravel mountain road, Amad and Fahim played around as if they were boxing one another. Their coordination and moves indicated they knew little about fighting. Then Fahim gave out a yell and pointed to a mountain curve in the distance. We could see the white bus slowly winding its way toward us. I took in a deep breath and exhaled. Things were looking much better. From the time Fahim saw the bus, it took the bus six or seven minutes before it rounded the last curve and headed toward us. Amad waved his arms as the bus approached, but the bus went right by us without slowing down. It was jammed full. Amad screamed and yelled as he shook his fist at the driver. I took in a gasp of the dusty air as nausea once again churned at the pit of my stomach. It would be two hours before the next bus with no guarantee it would have vacant seats.

We sat down beside the road as Amad cursed in Arabic, or at least it sounded like he cursed. We picked up rocks and threw them at bushes and boulders below us. It became a game to see who could hit a designated object first. After waiting 30 minutes, a taxi came toward us, but heading in the opposite direction we wanted to go. Amad jumped up and waved his arms at the driver. All the mountain taxis we had seen the day before carried at least five people, and sometimes six or seven. But in this taxi sat one woman in the back seat. Amad talked to the driver for several minutes before he came over to us.

"Ohac gave money for autobus, yes?"

"What?" I asked, knowing he referred to the bus money Ohac had given me, but not wanting to give up our only ticket out of here.

"Dinero Ohac gave for autobus. You have?"

"Yes," I said reluctantly, "but he gave us just enough for the bus."

Amad held out his hand. "Give me now."

I reached in my pocket and slowly pulled out the bills. Amad took it and returned to the taxi. He handed the driver the money. The driver then sped away and Amad came back to us.

"Driver my friend. He come back twenty minute. Go Tetuan." He looked at Trevor. "In Tetuan, you go bank. Pay driver fifty dollar."

"Fifty dollars?" I said. "The bus charges one dollar."

"Taxi better," Amad said. "We make business. Mucho rapido. No many people. Discrito, si? Autobus four hour. Taxi two. Esta mejor, si? Taxi take you border. Bueno, si? We go house now. You want go?"

Neither Trevor nor I cared to return to Amad's mountain home. "We'll stay here," I said without hesitation.

"Bueno. Taxi come twenty minute."

"Are you coming back?" I asked.

"Si. We go taxi too. Rapido, entiende?"

"Si," I said. "Hasta luego."

"No, hasta pronto," Amad said as he and Fahim headed down the mountain trail.

"Those fucking assholes," Trevor said. "They're getting us for every dime they can. I'd like to punch out that little twerp Amad."

"You and me both," I said. "There's no way they can get down there and back up here in twenty minutes. It will take them at least forty-five."

"If the cab returns before they do," Trevor said, "they're out of luck. I'm the one with the credit card."

We watched Amad and Fahim disappear around some high bushes. "You know," I said, "we could get our money back if we wanted to."

"How?"

"It's obvious they know nothing about fighting. We could take them down, tie them up and leave them in the bushes somewhere."

Trevor looked at me incredulously. "Are you serious?"

I grinned.

"You are!"

"What's the matter," I said, "don't you think we can handle them?"

"Huh," Trevor grunted, "don't make me laugh. I could squash them both. No problema." he added, mimicking Amad. "But you know, they probably have knives."

"Yeah, like my Swiss Army knife. I figure we could have them on the ground before they had a chance to pull one on us."

"I get Amad," Trevor said hotly.

"That's who I want. Let's flip for it." I reached in my pocket before I remembered there were no coins there.

"Forget flipping," Trevor said adamantly, "that little bastard's mine."

The determined gleam in Trevor's eye and grin on his face settled the matter.

"Okay, I'll nail Fahim, but I want to stuff that chunk of hashish in Amad's mouth to shut him up."

Trevor laughed. "Good idea."

"Also, it's important we take them down at the same time," I said. "We don't want one of them getting away and going for help."

"Amad won't be going anywhere when I get done with him. You just take care of Fahim."

"I'm not talking about killing these guys."

Trevor grinned. "That would be going easy on them."

Trevor laughed and held up his hand for a high five. I slapped it with mine, and we both laughed. It felt great to be in control again. As we excitedly planned our attack, however, I thought about the results if we got caught.

I had heard a rumor about Morocco circulating among travelers. Supposedly, an American and his wife were driving through a small town when a child dashed out in front of them. The man tried to avoid the little girl, but hit and killed her. He ran to a house to call for help, and when he returned, he found his wife hanging by her neck from a tree. I knew that if the Berbers at Amad's home caught us, we'd be hung, or worse. They already wanted me for accidentally exposing myself to a young girl.

"You know," I finally said, "there's little chance we'd get caught out here if we pay these guys back, but if for some reason we do get caught, we're dead.

First of all, if the police get involved, it's not likely they'll understand English. Even if they do, who are they going to believe? Americans, or their own people? And no telling what story Amad would use to defend himself, or how much money he'd pay to bribe them."

As we discussed the possible ramifications of our retaliation plan, we decided the risks were too great. After all, money and material possessions are not worth dying for, or having our hands cut off. Nonetheless, just thinking about roughing up Amad and Fahim did us some good. When they returned some 45 minutes later, I couldn't help but notice all the prime opportunities we had to carry out our plan. During one of those moments, I looked at Trevor and we both smiled. Amad noticed the look between us and asked if something was wrong. Even though I said no, he had a skeptical expression on his face.

While we sat there waiting for the taxi, a bus went by with plenty of vacant seats. Trevor and I both wanted to take it, but Amad said no, saying the taxi would be much faster and less conspicuous. The taxi arrived 20 minutes after the bus passed us. Trevor and I sat in the back seat, while the three of them sat in the front seat. After sitting in the cab for 30 minutes or so, I thought of a plan to get our money back.

"How long have you been driving a taxi," I said slowly. The driver looked at me in the rearview mirror when he heard the word taxi.

Amad said something to the driver, who then shook his head. "No speak English," Amad said.

I asked the driver the same question in Spanish, and he told me seven years. I asked him if he liked it, then asked a few other trivial questions before ending the conversation. When Amad and Fahim began talking, I turned to Trevor and once again spoke swiftly with no punctuation.

"I've got an idea on how we can get some if not all of our bucks back when we get to Tetuan," I said in a fast monotone voice, "but for it to work you must back me up on everything I say as if it were true." Amad cocked his head sideways to hear me better. "I can see you-know-who is trying to hear me but I know he won't understand as long as I keep talking like this and let you know that my plan will work only if you agree with me on everything without hesitation and if you do that I'm pretty sure we can get most if not all of our cash back but I don't think we can discuss it anymore without drawing too much suspicion."

By running all the sentences together, I knew Amad would not understand. When I stopped talking, Amad turned and looked at me, then smiled. "What you speak?"

I looked at Amad and smiled back. "I was telling Trevor that we need to remember how to get back here, so when we return in May we can find your house."

Amad grinned. "Bueno. I make map. No problema. When return, take taxi. Mucho mejor. We make business. Discrito, si?"

"Si," I said, "muy bueno."

"You have paper?" he asked.

I got out my notepad and pen from my daypack and held it in front of him.

"You write," he said and dictated the directions and approximate number of kilometers. As we drove along the road, Amad pointed out landmarks: a farmhouse, a stone wall and an unusual tree.

It turned out to be a major mistake not divulging more details of my plan to Trevor. I intended to have the teller at the bank refuse to give us the $50 by telling her (or him) to shake their head no and push the card back to us. I would then tell Amad that we had used the card earlier to get $25, because sometimes that allowed you to get $50 at a different time, providing a total of $75 versus the normal $50. I knew that Amad's devious mind would fall for such logic. With no money, Trevor and I would have the problem of paying the cabdriver, so I would ask Amad for our money back. Without doubt he'd refuse or balk at my request, at which time I planned to act like an Arab and begin screaming in Amad's face, "What's the matter, don't you trust your business partners?" I felt fairly confident I could get Amad to hand over the money, or at least some of it.

If Amad continued to say no, however, I would put more pressure on him until he either handed me the money or we broke out into a fight. The public setting would certainly be in my favor. The last thing a drug dealer wants is a scene attracting attention, or worse yet, the police. Once Amad handed me the money, I planned to take $60 off the top and give the rest to Trevor for safekeeping. Of the $60, $25 would go to the driver for getting us to Tetuan, with a promise to give him $25 more once we got to the border. Ten dollars would go to Amad for food and lodging. I kept seeing Amad's evil look and hearing his threatening tone of voice when he had screamed, "What you think this is? Hotel?"

Although fairly confident Amad would turn over some of the money, the last thing I wanted was a chunk of hashish in my pack if a fight ensued. So, while returning my notepad to my pack, which now contained directions to Amad's home, I set the hashish on the floor and pushed it under the front seat with my foot. Strangely enough, minutes later a man dressed in a brown uniform standing on the road beside his car motioned our taxi driver to stop.

Amad said something to the driver, who got out of the taxi and walked back to the man in uniform. They stood behind the taxi and talked briefly before leaning against the trunk to continue their conversation. When they moved away from the back of the car, the taxi shook slightly. I glanced around just in time to see the taxi driver give the man some money. The driver got back in the taxi and off we went. Amad said the officer checked vehicles to make sure they had no problems.

A few more miles down the road we drove up behind the bus that had passed us while waiting for the taxi. "Mira," Amad said, "autobus much slower." Amad said something to the driver, who then zoomed passed the bus.

When we arrived in Tetuan, Amad had the driver park the taxi several blocks from a bank. It became apparent that Amad had pulled similar scams on other tourists. His actions were too smooth and calculated. Either he suspected we were up to something, or other victims had given him the slip. Once the taxi stopped, Amad jumped out of the car and blocked my door. My heart fell. My plan revolved around going into the bank with Trevor.

Amad looked at Trevor. "You and Fahim go to bank," he said. "We wait here."

I guess I should have insisted on going with Trevor, or tried to do something, but before I could think of anything, Fahim and Trevor were walking away from the taxi. If Trevor had known the plan, my presence at the bank would have made no difference. I pulled the door handle to get out of the taxi.

"What you do?" Amad asked.

"I want to stretch my legs," I said, pushing the door open. Amad held on to the door, creating some resistance, but not enough to stop me from opening it. Once out of the car, I stretched and did some knee bends. I wanted to be ready for whatever happened when Trevor and Fahim came back. They returned within 15 minutes. I told Trevor to pay the driver half the money now and that we'd pay him the rest when we got to the border. As Trevor handed the driver $25, he explained in Spanish what we were doing.

"No," Amad said, "pay now."

Amad used his demanding voice as if we were still at his home in the mountains.

"No, Amad," I said. "We pay twenty-five dollars now and the rest at the border."

Amad stepped closer to me. We stared into each other's eyes. I stood my ground.

"You say you pay fifty dollar. Now you no pay?" he said raising his voice.

"We said we'd pay when we got to the border," Trevor said, stepping to my side. "And this is not the border."

I cocked my head slightly to keep an eye on Fahim. If he reached for a weapon in his pocket, I would level him with a right hook and give him a foot to the groin. I knew Trevor would gladly take care of Amad. The cabdriver could see a fight in the making. He had $25 in his hand, and if a fight broke out, he knew he wouldn't see the other $25. He spoke to Amad in Arabic. Once the driver finished talking, a smile spread across Amad's face.

"He say okay," Amad said. "You pay twenty-five dollar at border, yes?"

"Si," I said.

Amad gave me a cheek-to-cheek hug. I wanted to haul off and punch the twerp. As he gave Trevor the same farewell greeting, Fahim stepped up and gave me a hug too.

"I like," Fahim said in Spanish as he touched the red bandanna around my neck.

"Si?" I replied, knowing he wanted it as another gift. "I like it too."

I opened the taxi door and climbed in. Trevor got in behind me.

"Hasta Mayo, si?" Amad said through the window.

"Si," I replied, "pero possiblé Junio."

As the cab began moving, Trevor added softly, "I'd say more like never."

I looked at the driver. "How far is it to Ceuta?" I asked slowly, still wondering if he knew any English.

He looked at me and shook his head back and forth, and then said in Spanish, "I'm sorry, but I don't understand English."

"No English at all?" I asked in Spanish.

"Nada."

I then asked him my original question in Spanish. He said 20 minutes. I turned around to Trevor. "I think we can talk freely." I explained to Trevor my original plan for getting our money back, then added, "I don't think we should give the driver the twenty-five dollars. What do you think?"

"No way. They've got enough of our money."

I reached under the seat and pulled out the chunk of hashish. "This should be payment enough. After all, it cost us more than two hundred and fifty dollars, so he's getting a great deal!"

I held the hashish out in front of the driver. He looked at the hashish and then looked at me. "This is for you," I said in Spanish.

"For me?" he asked.

"Si, for you. It's a little gift. Go ahead, it's yours." I held it out to him. He looked at Trevor. He obviously wanted it, but he wasn't sure why we were giving it to him.

"Propina," I said, which means tip.

"Ah," he replied, promptly taking the hashish from my hand. "Mucho gracias." He smelled the hashish. "Huele bueno," he said. He pulled the car's ashtray out of its holder, stuffed the hashish in the hole, and then pushed the ashtray back in, leaving the ashtray sticking out several inches.

Once we reached the border, Trevor got out and walked toward the customs' office. The driver knew Trevor had his money. He jumped out of the car and yelled at Trevor, who just kept walking. I started to follow Trevor, but the driver grabbed me by the arm and demanded his money in Spanish.

"We paid you in Tetuan," I said in English, and turned to walk toward the border. Trevor now stood beside the customs' office watching us. The cabdriver grabbed my arm again and spun me around, yelling both Spanish and

Arabic words in my face. A second later a voice behind me spoke with a thick Arabic accent, "Is there problem here?"

I turned around to see a tall Arab with thick black eyebrows, dark curly short hair and a well-trimmed black mustache. He wore a light yellow sport shirt and nice gray slacks. The cabdriver spoke to him in Arabic.

The Arab looked at me. "He say you owe money for taxi."

"We paid him in Tetuan," I said.

The Arab spoke to the cabdriver again, and then turned back to me. "He say you pay half in Tetuan."

"We paid him enough money in Tetuan."

"How much you pay?"

"Twenty-five dollars."

"Twenty-five dollar?"

"Yes," I said.

"That not what he say."

"I tell you what, you tell him that I said we paid him twenty-five dollars, and we'll both look him in the eye and see what he does."

The Arab smiled and nodded. He liked the idea. He spoke to the driver. The driver, saying nothing, first looked at me, then looked at the Arab, and then looked down.

The English-speaking Arab with his heavy accent said, "You go now. I take care this."

I turned and walked toward Trevor. The border station attendant stamped our passports and waved us through without examining our bags. We could have been carrying six or seven kilos for all they knew.

In Ceuta, we hopped on a bus heading to the ferry terminal. When I reached into my backpack to retrieve my bottled water, my hand brushed my wallet. Even though it contained no cash, it still held Melanie's photo. My breakup with her initiated my trek into the unknown, and so much had happened in my life since then. While taking a long drink, I wondered about her present life and whether she was married with children.

"The first Arab I see in America I'm going to kick his ass," Trevor said with gritted teeth.

Water shot out my mouth and nose to splatter the bus seat in front of me. Fortunately, no one sat in front of us or they would have been sprayed.

"What's so funny?" Trevor asked while partially laughing, astonished at my outburst and amused at the reaction his statement had on me.

"You can't do that," I said, wiping my nose and mouth between coughing and laughing.

"Why not?"

"Because the guy might be a decent person."

Trevor looked out the window. "Yeah, you're right. It wouldn't be cool, but God I'd like to see that shithead Amad in Minneapolis."

"Maybe we should invite him over for a visit," I said. "We can have him stuff a few kilos up his butt, and then call customs and have his ass busted."

We cracked up laughing. One thing was for certain, we saw a part of Morocco few tourists see, and it thoroughly captivated us. Ironically enough, Tetuan means "open your eyes."

Epilogue

L ooking back at the time on the road, I am grateful for my marriage at age 21 and divorce at 22 because it sent me on a journey I longed to embark upon, yet lacked the courage and fortitude to begin. It took despair, emotional chaos and desperation mixed with poor choices to help me realize the crossroads I faced. Failure to follow my desire to travel could have resulted in either a fatal drug overdose or similar demise.

Despite looking forward to a life beyond my divorce and academia, I also wondered where I might actually end up. While there were instances of doubt and fear regarding my adventures, each time they arose I thought about the pain and rejection of losing my dearest friend and lover, my former wife.

Those thoughts, coupled with my aspirations to be a writer and gain the experiences Ray Bradbury spoke about when he said you had to "be a kind of hysterical, emotional, vibrant creature who lives at the top of his lungs for a lifetime" kept the excitement of my quest alive.

When money ran out during my travels, I stopped and worked temporary jobs along the way. The repetitive questions that lingered in my mind and repeatedly pushed me back to the road were: What is life really all about? Why am I here? Do I have a greater purpose?

My journeys gave me much time to ponder those questions. I spent countless days standing beside highways thumbing rides. I trekked into the backcountry of California, Colorado, New Mexico, Arizona, Nevada, Montana, Wyoming, New York, Alaska, Hawaii and numerous Canadian provinces for days, weeks and months. I spent large amounts of time alone.

During the first few years on the road, I often raised my arms to the sky and asked the powers that be to let me die if my mission had been completed. At that time, I felt my purpose might be as simple as handing someone a glass of water, giving a person a handful of granola, or playing a song for several people around a campfire.

Many times I wondered whether I should remain on the road or settle down and start a family. Invariably, something influenced me to continue my vagabond lifestyle.

For instance, subsequent to being on the road for three years, I decided to leave Fairbanks, Alaska, and hitchhike home to establish some roots. Upon arriving at the Alaska-Canada border, I was thwarted by Canadian officials. I already knew about the $300 requirement to cross into Canada, so when the customs' officer asked how much money I had, I confidently said $325.

"I need to see it," he said.

I acted disgusted while reaching into my pocket and pulling out a ten, two fives and five ones.

"Here's twenty-five. I've got the rest hidden in my pack. Is it really necessary to dig it out?"

"Yes."

"It's not that easy to get to."

"Take your time," he said. "I'll wait."

I unzipped my pack and rummaged through my clothes, hoping to convince him the money existed without actually showing it. When I finally glanced up at him, he smiled.

"You don't have it, do you?"

"Look, twenty-five bucks will buy me enough peanut butter and granola to make it to Mexico and back."

"I'm sorry," he said. "I'm unable to authorize your entry into Canada."

"What am I supposed to do?"

He grinned. "Stay in the United States."

"You know," I said, "I can easily hike around this station and get back on the road a mile or two into Canada."

His smile faded. "True," he said in a stern voice. "And there's a good chance you'd get away with it if you hike far enough. But if we catch you, I will see that you receive the maximum fine and prison sentence allowed by law."

I could tell he meant it, and because of my less-than-perfect record in Canada, I decided to hitchhike to Fairbanks, pick up some basic provisions, and head to Denali (McKinley) National Park to contemplate my predicament.

Upon arriving at the park, I discovered that a bus left each morning for a 55-mile backcountry tour toward Mt. McKinley on a dirt and gravel road. Hikers and mountain climbers could get off the bus anywhere along the road to explore the wilderness.

I rode to the end of the trail and hiked toward the base of Mt. McKinley. I spent approximately three weeks camped near a stream beneath the grandeur of North America's tallest mountain at 20,320 feet. The natives of the area call it

Denali, which means "The Great One." Other than seeing too many grizzly bears and being attacked by hordes of mosquitoes, I camped in solitude.

During Alaska's long daylight summer hours, I went on hikes, gathered berries to eat, played my guitar, and sat beside my tent contemplating the past several years living on the road. I pondered whether I should go home, begin a career and find a woman to love. It seemed like the practical thing to do despite my mixed emotions. First, however, I had to earn enough money to get out of Alaska.

Hiking back to the dirt road to catch the bus out of the park, I climbed up the steps to find a near-empty vehicle. An old man and his wife sat toward the front of the bus, and a young girl sat across the aisle several seats behind them. The old man cocked his head sideways with his lips slightly puckered up and looked at me.

"How long have you been out here?" he asked.

"I've kind of lost track of time," I replied, but somewhere around three weeks."

"What in the world were you doing?"

"Playing my guitar and taking in nature."

The old man asked more questions, and during our three-hour trip to the park entrance, I recounted numerous travel stories.

"My God," he finally said, "I'd love to do what you are doing, but look at me. I'm too damn old to put on a backpack and take off into the woods. Sure, I'm retired and have the time, but my body's not up to it. You're doing the right thing. See the world while you're young and strong."

His words made sense. At 25 years old and three years behind me touring the 48 states, Canada and Alaska, I still had places I wanted to see—lots of them.

So, what did I gain from living on the road for more than a decade? I discovered my life's purpose. A purpose that allowed me to be free, to live as I desired, and to travel my chosen path at my own pace.

This discovery, at least in part, came from one ride I caught between Santa Barbara and Los Angeles, California. It surprised me when I saw the new two-door white Cadillac with gold trim pull over. Most of my rides came from poor people driving old cars. I opened the passenger door and peered in at the driver. He stared at me with a somewhat curious and unsmiling face.

"Hi," I said, grinning. "Thanks for stopping."

"Put your things in back," he said matter-of-factly, pulling the passenger's bucket seat forward to allow room for my gear.

The driver wore a light yellow Polo shirt, impeccably pressed tan slacks, and polished brown leather shoes surrounding yellow and brown socks. A large gold ring encircled his right little finger and a huge diamond ring bejeweled his left ring finger. An opulent gold and diamond-studded watch adorned his tanned wrist and a thin gold chain hung loosely around his neck. He had a receding hairline with brown hair feathered back over his ears.

"Where are you going," he asked as I pulled the door shut.

"To visit friends in Los Angeles."

He glanced over his shoulder as we moved back onto Highway 101.

"Do you live around here?" I asked.

"I have a home in Santa Barbara and one in Los Angeles. How about you?"

"I guess you could say the road's my home."

He asked where I originally came from and what I had been doing. I eagerly tossed out a few of my travel stories and told them with enthusiasm. While my tales usually excited my listeners, each story seemed to aggravate him more and more.

He finally said, "What if everybody did what you're doing?"

"What do you mean?"

"I mean gallivanting around the country without a care and not working, basically being a bum. What kind of world would this be if everyone lived like you?"

I looked at him and said without hesitating, "If everyone did what I'm doing, this world would be a great place to live."

I felt no defensiveness, anger or frustration with my reply. Instead, I was amused by his question. He glared at me for a second before turning his gaze back to the road.

"Huh," he grunted, shaking his head back and forth. "How do you figure that?"

"Because I'm doing exactly what I want to do. I doubt most people can honestly say that. I believe if everyone did what they truly wanted to do, this world would be fantastic. We'd have a lot of happy people, and that makes life more fun. And, if people did what they wanted to do, I suspect very few would choose hitchhiking around the country."

The man gripped the Cadillac's steering wheel tighter. I had no idea what he did for a living, but he appeared unhappy. I could see he was living a materially wealthy life, yet sensed it was an unfulfilled existence. I also could tell he resented me. I had no material possessions of value, yet I was enjoying my life.

All of us seek happiness through whatever means we believe provides it, and rightly so because it is a desire at the core of our being. My life purpose is to live in joy, and I believe that's everyone's purpose. I realize that everything we do is done for one reason and one reason only: we believe the action will, in some way, make us feel good.

The key, however, is enjoying the activity or process along the way, because if we don't, we miss life's meaning. The way to joy and happiness is not through struggle and hardship, but found in the thrill and exuberance of living each moment. It's recognizing that our life is about right now, and that this eternal now is the only thing that's truly real. The past and the future are but memories, dreams, fears or desires.

When things became overwhelming for me while living on the road, I grounded myself by focusing on what was good about the moment and what could bring me joy. Sometimes, other people helped me regain that focus.

For example, after being on the Big Island in Hawaii a short time, I found a beautiful isolated beach with five or six-foot waves crashing onto the shore. I had never seen waves that tall, but being a good swimmer, I decided to try body surfing. After battling the waves for 15 to 20 minutes, one wave picked me up and slammed me into the sandy shoreline, scraping my stomach raw. The salt water tripled the pain.

Crawling my way onto the beach, I stared in disbelief at my towel and blanket. My backpack and guitar were gone. I frantically scanned the area for the culprit who took my belongings. Seeing no one on the beach, I spotted a small truck parked on a hill about 200 yards away. I ran up the hill to find a young Hawaiian sitting on the hood of his truck looking at the mountains in the distance and smoking a joint.

"Hi," I said, glancing in the back of his truck and cab looking for my backpack and guitar.

"Hey bra," he replied, smiling at me.

"Have you seen anyone on the beach or on this road up here?"

"No, not really," he responded, still holding smoke in his lungs. "Did you lose someone?"

"No. Someone stole my backpack and guitar. They got my passport, my driver's license and all my money. I've lost everything."

One eyebrow rose slightly as he exhaled a puff of smoke. "You didn't lose everything." He sucked in another hit off his joint and held it out to me. As I accepted it, he spoke again. "You're still alive."

I put the joint to my lips, perplexed on how to interpret his statement. I took a drag and handed it back to him as he exhaled.

"This time last year I nearly lost everything," he said.

The man drove stockcars, and the previous year he slammed into another car and a wall that, according to his account, should have killed him. He experienced a long stay in the hospital and months of rehabilitation. He told me that in less than 24 hours he would compete in his first stockcar race since the accident.

After he bid me farewell, I returned to what the thief or thieves left me, which included a thin blanket spread out on the sand, my towel, a book called *The Light of the Soul* by Alice Bailey, my tennis shoes, green Army pants, socks and white t-shirt. It was apparent the robber or robbers rummaged through my pant pockets before running off with my backpack and guitar.

The Hawaiian was right. I was alive. I had not drowned in the ocean, and although two years of journaling and songwriting were gone, all of the other items could be replaced. I relaxed and allowed myself to become totally immersed in the present moment. I was safe, I was warm, and I was standing alone on a beautiful and isolated island beach.

Despite losing my identification and worldly possessions, I never felt more connected to the world, and to God—or whatever you want to call the creator of life. At that moment, I realized what a powerfully fresh new beginning life held for me, and I understood how true that was for every breathing moment we exist, for every night as we fall asleep, and for every morning when we awaken.

What initially appeared as a catastrophic occurrence turned out to be one of the most illuminating experiences that could have happened to me. I had been stripped of everything except that which I truly am—my unique essence encased within my body. As I experienced this identity awakening, I realized the power and importance of the present moment. I understood that the here and now truly is all I ever have, and it remains with me wherever I go.

Today, I value more than ever this eternal now and the thrill of living in its powerful force. My purpose rests within my choice to focus my conscious attention on its never-ending presence and the realization that joy is a choice I can make in each new moment.

Thank you for joining me on this journey. May your life be filled with peace and happiness. I bid you farewell with a poem I wrote.

This Golden Moment

Cosmic thought explodes into love
to form a blaze of light
expanding outward
at fantastic speeds,
turning blackness to white...

And while the dazzling brilliance expands,
pushing through endless space,
God unfolds a loving plan
to form a special place
upon an arm of swirling stars,
a speck of dust to be
the spawning ground
for seeds of love,
known as you and me.

Here together
we share this time
to nurture and perceive
the ever-changing ceaseless flame
of love's unfolding dream
that captures life
here and now,
within
this golden moment.

This Golden Moment is part of a collection of poems written and recited by Bryce Yarborough on a 57-minute CD entitled, *Believe In Life: A poetic journey*. It contains 46 poems enhanced by music, ocean waves and other natural sounds to create a relaxed, contemplative and meditative poetic journey.

About the Author

For more than a decade, Bryce Yarborough traveled throughout the United States, Canada, Europe, Mexico, Central America and South America. He spent weeks and months camping and hiking alone in wilderness areas. To support his travels, he worked odd jobs such as waiting tables in New York and California, framing houses in Alaska, trimming coconut trees in Hawaii, picking grapes in France and working as a street musician.

After returning to the University of Missouri and graduating from the School of Journalism, Yarborough worked several years as a newspaper reporter in Colorado before boarding a cruise ship as its newspaper editor. Just short of a year at sea, he left the cruise ship to travel in Mexico and Central America. He then returned to Kansas City, Missouri, where he began a rock band. He also worked as a travel copywriter and a public relations professional.

Yarborough lives in Stanley, Kansas, with his wife and two cats. He is presently working on two novels, a collection of books about his travels, a book on the nature of reality, and a second volume of poems.

His first volume of poems, *Believe In Life: A Poetic Journey*, is available on a 57-minute CD that provides the listener a relaxed, contemplative voyage through words, musical accompaniment and sound effects.

Yarborough also is available for speaking engagements. For a complete list of his literary works, visit www.bryceyarborough.com.

Printed in the United States
19552LVS00005BA/237